How the Special Needs Brain Learns

Third Edition

How the Special Needs Brain Learns

Third Edition

David A. Sousa

A SAGE Publishing Company

FOR INFORMATION:

Corwin

A SAGE Company

2455 Teller Road

Thousand Oaks, California 91320

(800) 233-9936

www.corwin.com

SAGE Publications Ltd.

1 Oliver's Yard

55 City Road

London EC1Y 1SP

United Kingdom

SAGE Publications India Pvt. Ltd.

B 1/I 1 Mohan Cooperative Industrial Area

Mathura Road, New Delhi 110 044

India

SAGE Publications Asia-Pacific Pte. Ltd.

3 Church Street

#10-04 Samsung Hub

Singapore 049483

Senior Acquisitions Editor: Jessica Allan

Senior Associate Editor: Kimberly Greenberg

Editorial Assistant: Katie Crilley

Production Editor: Amy Schroller

Copy Editor: Kimberly Hill

Typesetter: C&M Digitals (P) Ltd.

Proofreader: Dennis W. Webb

Cover Designer: Gail Buschman

Marketing Manager: Jill Margulies

Library of Congress Cataloging-in-Publication Data

Names: Sousa, David A.

Title: How the special needs brain learns / David A. Sousa.

Description: Third edition. | Thousand Oaks, California : Corwin, 2016. | Includes bibliographical references and index.

Identifiers: LCCN 2015042655 | ISBN 978-1-5063-2702-0 (pbk. : alk. paper)

Subjects: LCSH: Learning disabled children—Education. | Learning. | Cognition in children.

Classification: LCC LC4704.5.S68 2016 | DDC 371.9—dc23 LC record available at http://lccn.loc.gov/2015042655

This book is printed on acid-free paper.

16 17 18 19 20 10 9 8 7 6 5 4 3 2

Contents

List of Strategies to Consider

Preface to the Third Edition

Welcome to the third edition! Since the publication of the first edition, there have been major developments in our understanding of how the human brain develops and functions. Brain imaging studies now number more than 3,000 a year. Technologies, such as transcranial magnetic stimulation, are gathering more information about cerebral processes. Researchers in genetics have found new links to physical, psychological, and learning disorders. Investigations into mirror neurons may explain why certain learning problems arise and yield clues as to how they can be treated. All the chapters in this third edition have undergone major revisions to include these developments and the findings of new studies. In addition, I have

- Updated the terminology of disorders to align with the newest edition of the *Diagnostic and Statistical Manual of Mental Disorders*, 5th Edition (DSM-5)
- Updated and added nearly 400 citations and references
- Updated the section on resources
- Added video links that further explain certain topics
- Added a section on memory systems
- Included numerous forms of **assistive technology** for students with learning difficulties
- Added a section on sleep difficulties
- Added a section on future trends in special education
- Added a section on the effects of poverty

Researchers and clinicians have made considerable progress in recent years understanding the genetic and environmental triggers that result in learning problems in children and adolescents. Nonetheless, arriving at a specific diagnosis can be tricky. Teachers and parents often cannot tell the difference between a normally rambunctious child and one who may have a developmental disorder. My hope is that the information here will provide educators and parents with some of the strategies they need to help their students and children lead happy and successful lives.

David A. Sousa

Publisher's Acknowledgments

Corwin gratefully acknowledges the contributions of the following individuals:

Dr. Carolyn A. Bishop
Director of Elementary Education
    Associate Professor
Biola University
La Mirada, CA

Dr. Nancy G. Burton
Associate Professor of Education-
    SPED
Concord University
Athens, WV

Sharon Carter
Associate Professor
Davidson County Community
    College
Thomasville, NC

Francine Del Vecchio, EdD
Associate Professor
Division of Education
Caldwell University
Caldwell, NJ

Dr. Jennifer C. Etheridge
Director of Special Projects
    Adjunct Professor of Educational
    Leadership

Fairfield County School District
    Winthrop University
Rock Hill, SC

Gina Garner, PhD
Assistant Professor of Education
Learning Disabilities Program
    Coordinator
Aquinas College
Grand Rapids, MI

Joanne Healy
Assistant Professor of Special
    Education
University of Alaska Fairbanks
Fairbanks, AK

Beverly Kling, EdD
Professor
Kean University
Union, NJ

Theresa Knipstein Meyer
Faculty
Milken Educator Award recipient
Butler University, College of
    Education
Indianapolis, IN

About the Author

David A. Sousa, EdD, is an international consultant in educational neuroscience. He has made presentations to more than 200,000 educators at national conventions of educational organizations and has conducted workshops on brain research and science education in hundreds of school districts and colleges and universities across the United States, Canada, Europe, Australia, New Zealand, and Asia.

Dr. Sousa has a bachelor of science degree in chemistry from Bridgewater State University in Massachusetts, a master of arts in teaching degree in science from Harvard University, and a doctorate from Rutgers University. His teaching experience covers all levels. He has taught senior high school science, served as a K–12 director of science, supervisor of instruction, and district superintendent in New Jersey schools. He was an adjunct professor of education at Seton Hall University for ten years and a visiting lecturer at Rutgers University. He is past president of the National Staff Development Council (now Learning Forward).

Dr. Sousa has edited science books and published numerous books and articles in leading educational journals on staff development, science education, and brain research. He has received awards from professional associations and school districts for his commitment and contributions to research, staff development, and science education. He received the Distinguished Alumni Award and an honorary doctorate in education from Bridgewater State University and an honorary doctorate in humane letters from Gratz College in Philadelphia.

He has been interviewed on the NBC *Today* show, by other television programs, and by National Public Radio about his work with schools using brain research.

He makes his home in south Florida.

Treat people as if they were what they ought to be and you help them to become what they are capable of being.

—*Johann Wolfgang von Goethe*

Introduction

Teachers and students get up every school-day morning hoping to succeed. That hope is not always realized because many factors exist that affect the degree of success or failure in a teaching and learning situation. Some of these factors are well beyond the control of the teacher and the school staff. What teachers *do* control, of course, are the decisions they make about how to present the lesson so that student learning is most likely to occur. In making these decisions, teachers draw on their knowledge base and experience to design activities, ask questions, and respond to the efforts of their students.

Educators are finding themselves searching for new strategies and techniques to meet the needs of an ethnically, culturally, and socially diverse student population. Some tried-and-true strategies do not seem to be as successful as they were in the past, and more students seem to be having difficulty acquiring just the basic skills of reading, writing, and computation. The number of public school students being diagnosed with specific learning disabilities is growing. In 2012–2013, 13 percent of the total public school population was classified as having specific learning disabilities and speech or language impairments, compared to 8.3 percent 10 years earlier (National Center for Education Statistics, 2014).

This situation is generating frustration in different parts of the educational community. As a result, educators are searching for new approaches, parents are seeking alternative schooling formats (charter schools and vouchers), and state legislators are demanding accountability through higher standards and standardized testing. Added to this mix are the requirements of the federal Every Student Succeeds Act and the Individuals with Disabilities Education Improvement Act's focus on response to intervention. All these activities are in full swing, but stakeholders are debating whether these efforts are resulting in more effective services to students with special needs.

Meanwhile, more students diagnosed with learning disabilities are being included in general education classrooms, and teachers continue to search for new ways to help these struggling students achieve. As more students with learning difficulties enter general education classes, their teachers are finding that they need help adjusting to the added responsibility of meeting the varied needs of these students. Consequently, special education teachers will need to collaborate more

> General and special education teachers will need to collaborate more than ever on ways to differentiate instruction.

1

than ever with their general education colleagues on ways to differentiate instruction in the inclusive classroom.

WHO ARE SPECIAL NEEDS STUDENTS?

For the purposes of this book, the term *special needs* refers to students who are:

- Diagnosed and classified as having specific learning problems, including speech, reading, writing, mathematics, and emotional and behavioral disorders
- Enrolled in supplemental instruction programs for basic skills, such as those receiving federal funding under Title I of the Elementary and Secondary Education Act
- Not classified for special education or assigned to Title I programs, but still struggling with problems affecting their learning

The term, as used here, does not refer to students with learning problems resulting primarily from hearing, visual, or physical handicaps.

CAN BRAIN RESEARCH HELP?

Teachers may face significant challenges when meeting the needs of children who have learning problems. Trying to figure out what is happening in the brains of these children can be frustrating and exhausting. Until recently, science could tell us little about the causes of learning disorders and even less about ways to address them successfully.

The nature of the difficulties facing students with learning problems varies from maintaining focus, acquiring language, learning to read and write, and solving mathematical problems to remembering important information. Thanks to the development of imaging and other technologies, neuroscientists can now look inside the live brain and gain new knowledge about its structure and functions. Some of this research is already revealing clues to help guide the decisions and practices of educators working with students who have special needs.

Because of the efforts of scientists over the years to cure brain disorders, we know more about troubled brains than we do about healthy ones. Early ventures into the brain involved extensive risks that were justified by the potential for curing or improving the patient's condition. But now, essentially risk-free imaging technologies (such as functional magnetic resonance imaging or fMRI) are giving us greater knowledge about how the normal brain works. It all started in just one project a decade ago, when scientists compiled a database of brain scans of about 500 children without apparent health problems aged 7 days to 18 years. That information helped researchers study different stages of brain growth and expanded our understanding of what normal brain development is (Evans, 2006). Today, that database has thousands of scans.

Students with learning problems comprise such a heterogeneous group that no one strategy, technique, or intervention can address all their needs. Today, more than ever, neuroscientists, psychologists, computer experts, and educators are working together in a common crusade to improve our understanding of the learning process. Comparing the functions of brains without deficits to the functions of brains with deficits is revealing some remarkable new insights about learning and behavioral disorders. Some of the findings are challenging long-held beliefs about the cause, progress, and treatment of specific learning disorders. Educators in both general and special education should be aware of this research so that they can decide what implications the findings have for their practice.

> Comparing the functions of brains without deficits to the functions of brains with deficits is revealing some remarkable new insights about learning and behavioral disorders.

UNDERSTANDING THE EFFECTS OF POVERTY

Studies have shown for decades that children growing up in severe poverty do not perform as well academically as their peers. Explanations for this achievement gap have centered on environmental and social issues, although some researchers suspected that the gap was associated in part with delays in brain growth and development. Now we have evidence that living in severe poverty can indeed affect the brain, especially in those cerebral areas responsible for cognitive processing, language development, and memory. A six-year study by researchers at the University of Wisconsin-Madison showed that children living in severe poverty had significantly smaller volumes in their brains' frontal and temporal lobes, and the hippocampus (Luby, 2015).

The frontal lobe is responsible for directing attention, controlling emotions, planning, and performing complex cognitive processing, while the temporal lobe provides for language comprehension and auditory processing. The hippocampus is critical for converting information into long-term memory. Children in poverty are often under severe stress from crowded housing, exposure to violence, and poor nutrition. Furthermore, they receive less nurturing and stimulation from their parents. Despite these dire conditions and their negative effects on brain growth and development, it is possible that brain plasticity can compensate for cognitive deficits when these children are placed in a more nourishing and stimulating environment.

WHAT IS IN THIS BOOK?

This book provides research information about common learning disabilities to prospective and current teachers and administrators so that they may consider alternative instructional approaches. It will help answer such questions as:

- How different are the brains of today's students?
- What kinds of strategies are particularly effective for students with learning disabilities?
- What progress is research making in discovering the causes of different learning disorders?

- Will brain research help us make more accurate diagnoses of learning problems?
- Can schools inadvertently promote ADHD-like behavior in students?
- Can students with native language problems learn another language?
- How does the brain learn to read?
- Can young brains with developmental reading problems be "rewired" to improve reading?
- How can we address the emotional needs of students in the classroom?
- What more do we know about autism spectrum disorder (ASD)?
- What kinds of assistive technologies are available for students with learning difficulties?
- What are some important current and future trends in special education?

Authors must decide on the sequence that the content of a book follows. My decision here was to start with a look at basic brain structures and functions (Chapter 1) and then move on to explaining some problems that can arise during brain development (Chapter 2). Because attention is a critical component of nearly all learning, that seemed to be the next logical topic (Chapter 3). Then I turned to examining learning difficulties in the basic skill areas of speech, reading, writing, and mathematics (Chapters 4 to 7). Thereafter follows a discussion of emotional and behavioral problems (Chapter 8) and autism spectrum disorder (Chapter 9). I conclude with an effort to tie this information together into a review of effective ways to serve students with learning disabilities, as well as a look to future trends in special education (Chapter 10).

Practical applications of the research can be found in the chapter sections called "Strategies to Consider," which suggest how educators might translate the research into school and classroom practice so that students with learning difficulties can be more successful. Obviously, some of the strategies would be appropriate for all learners. However, the suggestions have been written specifically to address the special needs of students with learning difficulties.

Some of the information and suggestions found here came from advocacy organizations, including the National Institute of Mental Health, the National Information Center for Children and Youth With Disabilities, and the Learning Disability Association of America (see the "Resources" section). I have sought out original medical research reports whenever possible, and these are included in the "References" section of the book. A few of the strategies are derived or adapted from the fourth edition of my book, *How the Brain Learns*, also published by Corwin.

Most chapters have a section on *Assistive Technologies* that remove barriers to learning for students with specific learning difficulties. It is important for school personnel to do a thorough assessment of a student's needs and the tasks that a student is expected to accomplish in order to select the appropriate technology and software. To be of value, there should be a reasonable expectation that the selected assistive technology will improve student learning. A good database of assistive technologies can be found at www.techmatrix.org.

This book is not intended to be a comprehensive text describing all the types of barriers that can affect learning. Rather, it focuses on the common difficulties and disorders that any teacher is likely to encounter in the general or special education classroom. On a broader scale, the updates on research and some of the suggested strategies may benefit all who work to educate children.

> As we gain a greater understanding of the human brain, we may discover that some students designated as "learning disabled" may be merely "schooling disabled."

As we gain a greater understanding of the human brain, we may discover that some students designated as "learning disabled" may be merely "schooling disabled." Sometimes these students are struggling to learn in an environment that is designed inadvertently to frustrate their efforts. Just changing our instructional approach may be enough to move these students to the ranks of successful learners. My hope is that this book will encourage all school professionals to learn more about how the brain learns so that they can work together for the benefit of all students.

A NOTE ABOUT EFFECT SIZE

In several sections throughout the book, you will see references to the *effect size* of a particular intervention. Effect size is a statistical measure of the strength of an intervention and is commonly used in educational studies, especially in meta-analyses. It is a quantitative attempt to measure how much of an impact a particular intervention had on the experimental group compared to the group that did not have the intervention (control group). The scale for these types of studies runs in values from 0 to 2.0, although the full scale is from −3.0 to 3.0. Educational researchers generally see effect sizes of 0.2 to 0.4 as small, 0.5 to 0.7 as medium, and 0.8 and higher as large. Effect sizes are another indicator that educators can use to guide them in selecting interventions for students with learning difficulties.

A WORD OF CAUTION

Several chapters contain lists of symptoms that are used to help identify specific disorders. The symptoms are included only for informational purposes, and they should not be used as a basis for diagnosis or treatment. Any individual who exhibits persistent learning problems should be referred to qualified clinical personnel for assessment.

1

The Brain and Learning

If we teach today's students as we taught yesterday's, we rob them of tomorrow.

—John Dewey, Philosopher, Educator (1859–1952)

The human brain is an amazing structure. At birth, it is equipped with more than 100 billion nerve cells designed to collect information and learn the skills necessary to keep its owner alive. Although comparatively slow in its growth and development compared to the brains of other mammals, it can learn complex skills, master any of nearly 7,000 languages, store memories for a lifetime, and marvel at the glory of a radiant sunset. Early in life, the brain's cells grow and connect with each other—at the rate of thousands per second—to store information and skills gathered from its environment. The brain's ability to continually reorganize and reconnect its neural pathways because of input from the environment is called neuroplasticity. Most of the connections result in the development of neural networks that will help the individual successfully face life's challenges. But sometimes, certain connections go awry, setting the stage instead for problems.

 The brain's executive system matures more slowly than the emotional system, so adolescents often resort to high-risk behavior.

To understand the complexity of human brain growth and development, let's review some basic information about its structure. For our purposes, we will first look at major parts of the outside of the brain (Figure 1.1): the frontal, temporal, occipital, and parietal lobes; the motor cortex; and the cerebellum.

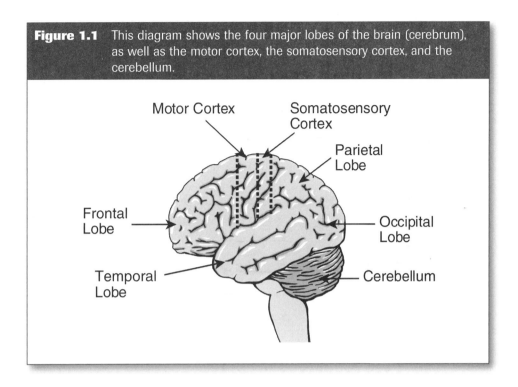

Figure 1.1   This diagram shows the four major lobes of the brain (cerebrum), as well as the motor cortex, the somatosensory cortex, and the cerebellum.

SOME EXTERIOR PARTS OF THE BRAIN

Lobes of the Brain

Although the minor wrinkles are unique in each brain, several major wrinkles and folds are common to all brains. These folds form a set of four lobes in each hemisphere. Each lobe tends to specialize for certain functions but can be called on to assist other lobes during complex tasks.

Frontal Lobe. At the front of the brain is the **frontal lobe**, containing almost 50 percent of the volume of the cerebral hemispheres. Lying just behind the forehead is a portion of the frontal lobe called the *prefrontal cortex*. The frontal lobe deals with planning and thinking. It comprises the rational and executive control center of the brain, monitoring higher order thinking, directing problem solving, and regulating the excesses of the emotional system. Because emotions drive attention, the efficiency of this area is linked to the limbic centers.

The frontal lobe also contains our self-will area—what some might call our personality. Trauma to the frontal lobe can cause dramatic—and sometimes permanent—behavior and personality changes. (One wonders why we allow 10-year-olds to play football and soccer, where the risk of trauma to the developing frontal lobe is so high.)

Because most of the working memory is located here, it is the area where focus occurs. The frontal lobe matures slowly. Brain imaging studies of adolescents and postadolescents reveal that the frontal lobe continues to mature into early adulthood. During this time, used neural pathways are being strengthened while unused neurons are being pruned.

In Figure 1.2, the lighter areas on the brain images show the increasing maturation of the frontal lobe over the span of 15 years between the ages of 5 and 20 (Giedd, 2015). Thus the capability of the frontal lobe to control the excesses of the emotional system is not fully operational during adolescence and is not likely to be fully mature until about the age of 24 (Dennis et al., 2013; Giedd, 2015). Full maturation occurs about a year earlier in females than in males. In other words, the last part of the brain to grow up is the part capable of making rational decisions, understanding the consequences of one's actions, and putting the brakes on emotional impulses. Consequently, this slow development of the frontal lobe is one important reason why adolescents are more likely than mature adults to submit to their emotions and resort to high-risk behavior.

Temporal Lobe. Above the ears rests the *temporal lobe*, which deals with sound, music, face and object recognition, and some parts of long-term memory. It also houses the speech centers, although this is usually on the left side only.

Occipital Lobe. At the back of the brain is the *occipital lobe*, which is used almost exclusively for visual processing.

Parietal Lobe. Near the top is the *parietal lobe*, which deals mainly with spatial orientation, calculation, and certain types of recognition.

Motor Cortex and Somatosensory Cortex

Between the parietal and frontal lobes are two bands across the top of the brain from ear to ear. The band closer to the front is the **motor cortex.** This strip controls body movement and, as we will learn later, works with the cerebellum to coordinate the learning of motor skills. Just behind the

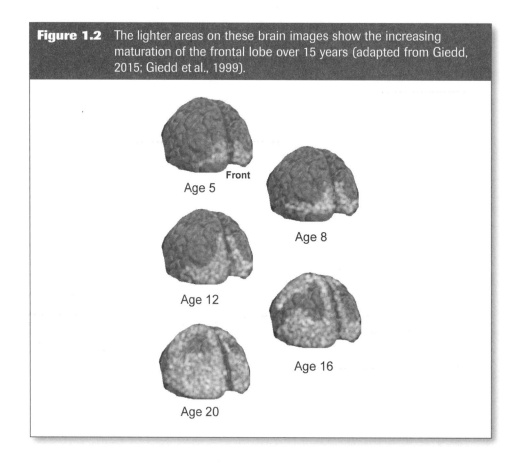

Figure 1.2   The lighter areas on these brain images show the increasing maturation of the frontal lobe over 15 years (adapted from Giedd, 2015; Giedd et al., 1999).

Front
Age 5

Age 8

Age 12

Age 16

Age 20

motor cortex, at the beginning of the parietal lobe, is the *somatosensory cortex*, which processes touch signals received from various parts of the body.

Cerebellum

The *cerebellum* (Latin for "little brain") is a two-hemisphere structure located just below the rear part of the cerebrum, right behind the brainstem. Representing about 11 percent of the brain's weight, it is a deeply folded and highly organized structure containing more neurons than all the rest of the brain put together. The surface area of the entire cerebellum is about the same as that of one of the cerebral hemispheres.

This area coordinates movement. Because the cerebellum monitors impulses from nerve endings in the muscles, it is important in the performance and timing of complex motor tasks, such as playing the piano or basketball. It modifies and coordinates commands to swing a golf club, smooth a dancer's footsteps, and allow a hand to bring a cup to the lips without spilling its contents. The cerebellum may also store the memory of automated movements, such as touch-typing, hitting a baseball, and tying a shoelace. Through such automation, performance can be improved as the sequences of movements can be made with greater speed, greater accuracy, and less effort. The cerebellum also is known to be involved in the mental rehearsal of motor tasks, which also can improve performance and make it more skilled. A person whose cerebellum is damaged slows down and simplifies movement and would have difficulty with finely tuned motion, such as catching a ball or completing a handshake.

Recent studies indicate that the role of the cerebellum has been underestimated. Researchers now believe that it also acts as a support structure in cognitive processing by coordinating and fine-tuning our thoughts, emotions, senses (especially touch), and memories. Because the cerebellum is connected to regions of the brain that perform mental and sensory tasks, it can perform these skills automatically, without conscious attention to detail. This allows the conscious part of the brain the freedom to attend to other mental activities, thus enlarging its cognitive scope. Such enlargement of human capabilities is attributable in no small part to the cerebellum and its contribution to the automation of numerous mental activities.

SOME INTERIOR PARTS OF THE BRAIN

Brainstem

The brainstem is the oldest and deepest area of the brain. It is often referred to as the reptilian brain because it resembles the entire brain of a reptile. Of the 12 body nerves that go to the brain, 11 end in the brainstem (the olfactory nerve—for smell—goes directly to the limbic system, an evolutionary artifact). Here is where vital body functions, such as heartbeat, respiration, swallowing, sleep and wakefulness, body temperature, and digestion, are monitored and controlled. The brainstem also houses the reticular activating system (RAS), responsible for the brain's alertness.

Limbic System

Located above the brainstem and below the cerebrum lies a collection of structures commonly referred to as the *limbic* (Greek for "border") system and sometimes called the old mammalian brain. Most of the structures in the limbic system are duplicated in each hemisphere of the brain. These structures carry out a number of different functions, including the generation of emotions and processing emotional memories. Its placement between the cerebrum and the brainstem permits the interplay of emotion and reason.

Four parts of the limbic system are important to learning and memory. They are:

The Thalamus. All incoming sensory information (except smell) goes first to the *thalamus* (Greek for "inner chamber"). From here information is directed to other parts of the brain for additional processing. The cerebrum and cerebellum also send signals to the thalamus, thus involving it in many cognitive activities.

The Hypothalamus. Nestled just below the thalamus is a pearl-sized structure called the hypothalamus. While the thalamus monitors information coming in from the outside, the hypothalamus monitors the internal systems to maintain the normal state of the body (called *homeostasis*). By controlling the release of a variety of hormones, it moderates numerous body functions, including sleep, food intake, and liquid intake. If body systems slip out of balance, it is difficult for the individual to concentrate on cognitive processing of curriculum material.

The Hippocampus. Located near the base of the **limbic area** is the *hippocampus* (the Greek word for "seahorse," because of its shape). It plays a major role in consolidating learning and in converting information from working memory via electrical signals to the long-term storage regions, a process that may take days to months. It constantly checks information relayed to working memory and compares it to stored experiences. This process is essential for the creation of meaning.

Its role was first revealed by patients whose hippocampus was damaged by lesions or removed because of disease. These patients could remember everything that happened before the surgery but not afterward. If they were introduced to you today, you would be a stranger to them tomorrow. Because they can remember information for only a few minutes, they can read the same article repeatedly and believe on each occasion that it is the first time they have read it. Brain scans have confirmed the role of the hippocampus in permanent memory storage. Alzheimer's disease progressively destroys neurons in the hippocampus, resulting in memory loss.

The Amygdala. Close to the tip of the hippocampus is the *amygdala* (Greek for "almond"). This structure plays an important role in emotions, especially fear and anxiety. It regulates the individual's interactions with the environment than can affect survival, such as whether to attack, escape, mate, or eat.

Because of its proximity to the hippocampus and its activity on brain scans, researchers believe that the amygdala encodes an emotional message, if one is present, whenever the hippocampus tags a memory for long-term storage. It seems that only the emotional component of a memory is stored in the amygdala while other cognitive components of that memory (names and dates) are stored elsewhere. The emotional component is recalled whenever the memory is recalled. This explains why people recalling a strong emotional memory will often experience those emotions again. The interactions between the amygdala and the hippocampus ensure that we remember for a long time those events that are important and emotional.

Teachers plan and present their lessons with the intention that their students will permanently remember what was taught. Thus it is worth noting that the two structures in the brain mainly responsible for long-term remembering are located in the *emotional* area of the brain. Tying emotions to new learning can be a powerful memory device.

Cerebrum

A soft jellylike mass resembling a huge walnut, the **cerebrum** is the largest area, representing nearly 80 percent of the brain by weight. Its surface is pale gray, wrinkled, and marked by furrows called fissures. One large fissure runs from front to back and divides the cerebrum into two halves, called the *cerebral hemispheres*. For some still unexplained reason, the nerves from the left side of the body cross over to the right hemisphere, and those from the right side of the body cross to the left hemisphere. The two hemispheres are connected by a thick cable of more than 250 million nerve fibers called the *corpus callosum* (Latin for "large body"). The hemispheres use this bridge to communicate with each other and coordinate activities.

The hemispheres are covered by a thin but tough laminated *cortex* (meaning "tree bark"), rich in cells, that is about one-tenth of an inch (2.5 mm) thick and, because of its folds, has a surface area of about two square feet (0.19 m²). That is about the size of a large dinner napkin. The cortex is composed of six layers of cells meshed in about 10,000 miles (16,100 km)

Figure 1.3 A cross section of the human brain.

of connecting fibers per cubic inch (16.4 cm^3)! Here is where most of the action takes place. Thinking, memory, speech, and muscular movement are controlled by areas in the cerebrum. The cortex layer is often referred to as the brain's gray matter.

The neurons in the thin cortex form columns whose branches extend down through the cortical layer into a dense web below known as the white matter. Here, neurons connect with each other to form vast arrays of neural networks that carry out specific functions.

Brain Cells

The control functions and other activities of the brain are carried out by signals traveling along brain cells. The brain is composed of a trillion cells of at least two known types: nerve cells and their support cells. Nerve cells are called **neurons** and represent about one-tenth of the total number of cells—roughly 100 billion in the mature brain. Most of the cells are support cells, called *glial* (Greek for "glue") **cells,** that hold the neurons together and act as filters to keep harmful substances out of the neurons.

Neurons are the functioning core for the brain and the entire nervous system. They come in different sizes, but it takes about 30,000 brain neurons to fit on the head of a pin. Unlike other cells, the neuron (Figure 1.4) can have tens of thousands of branches or *dendrites* (from the Greek word for "tree") emerging from its center. The dendrites receive electrical impulses from other neurons and transmit them along a long fiber, called the *axon* (Greek for "axis"). Each neuron has only one axon. A layer called the *myelin* (related to the Greek word for "marrow") *sheath* surrounds each axon. The sheath insulates the axon from the other cells and increases the speed of impulse transmission. The impulse travels along the neurons through an electrochemical process and can move the entire length of a six-foot (183 cm) adult in two-tenths of a second. A neuron can transmit between 250 and 2,500 impulses per second.

Video: To see how nerve impulses travel across the synapse, go to:

https://www.youtube.com/watch?v=c5cab4hgmoE

Neurons have no direct contact with each other. Between each dendrite and axon is a small gap of about a millionth of an inch called a *synapse* (from the Greek meaning "to join together"). A typical neuron collects signals from others through the dendrites. The neuron sends out spikes of electrical activity (impulses) through the axon to the synapse, where the activity releases chemicals stored in sacs (called *synaptic vesicles*) at the end of the axon.

The chemicals, called **neurotransmitters,** either excite or inhibit the neighboring neuron. More than 100 neurotransmitters have been discovered so far, but only about 10 or so do most of the work. Some of the more common neurotransmitters are acetylcholine, epinephrine, serotonin, and **dopamine.**

Mirror Neurons

Scientists using scanning technology discovered clusters of neurons in the premotor cortex (the area in front of the motor cortex that plans movements) firing just before a person carries out a planned movement.

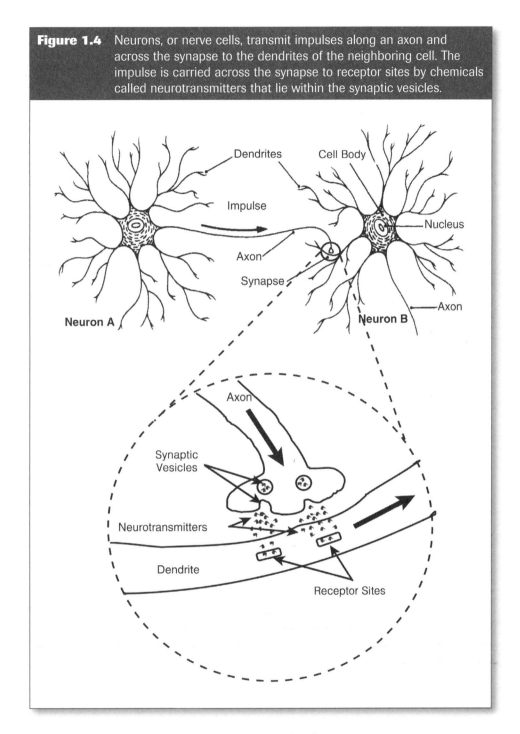

Figure 1.4 Neurons, or nerve cells, transmit impulses along an axon and across the synapse to the dendrites of the neighboring cell. The impulse is carried across the synapse to receptor sites by chemicals called neurotransmitters that lie within the synaptic vesicles.

Curiously, these neurons also fired when a person saw someone else perform the movement. For example, the firing pattern of these neurons that preceded the subject grasping a cup of coffee, was identical to the pattern when the subject saw someone else do that. Thus, similar brain areas process both the *production* and *perception* of movement. Neuroscientists believe these mirror neurons may help an individual decode the intentions and predict the behavior of others. If you see someone reach for a ball even though his hand is out of sight, your mirror neurons tell you that he is going to pick up the ball even before he does it (Fadiga, Craighero, & Olivier, 2005; Iacoboni et al., 2005).

Studies also show that structures in the limbic system that activate during one's own pain also activate during empathy for pain. Mirror neurons allow us to re-create the experience of others within ourselves and to understand others' emotions and empathize. Seeing the look of disgust or joy on other people's faces causes mirror neurons to trigger similar emotions in us. We start to feel their actions and sensations as though we were doing them (Corradini & Antonietti, 2013; Lamm & Majdandžić, 2015).

Mirror neurons probably explain the mimicry we see in young children when they imitate our smile and many of our other movements. We all experience this phenomenon when we attempt to stifle a yawn after seeing someone else yawning. Neuroscientists believe that mirror neurons may explain a lot about mental behaviors that have remained a mystery. For instance, there is experimental evidence that children with autism spectrum disorders may have a deficit in their mirror-neuron system. That would explain why they have difficulty inferring the intentions and mental state of others (Oberman et al., 2005). However, the evidence is far from conclusive, and some researchers question the mirror neuron-autism connection (Hamilton, 2013). See Chapter 9 for a discussion of these findings and their implications. Researchers also suspect that mirror neurons play a role in our ability to develop articulate speech.

LEARNING AND RETENTION

Learning occurs when the synapses make physical and chemical changes so that the influence of one neuron on another also changes. For instance, a set of neurons "learns" to fire together. Repeated firings make successive firings easier and, eventually, automatic under certain conditions. Thus, a memory is formed.

For all practical purposes, the capacity of the brain to store information is unlimited. That is, with about 100 billion neurons, each with thousands of dendrites, the number of potential neural pathways is incomprehensible. The brain will hardly run out of space to store all that an individual learns in a lifetime. Learning is the process by which we *acquire* new knowledge and skills; memory is the process by which we *retain* knowledge and skills for the future.

Investigations into the neural mechanisms required for different types of learning are revealing more about the interactions between learning new information, memory, and changes in brain structure. Just as muscles improve with exercise, the brain seems to improve with use. Learning allows brain cells to increase their size, their branches, and their ability to form more complex networks.

The brain goes through physical and chemical changes when it stores new information as the result of learning. Storing gives rise to new neural pathways and strengthens existing pathways. Hence every time we learn something, our long-term storage areas undergo anatomical changes that, together with our unique genetic makeup, constitute the expression of our individuality.

Learning and retention also occur in different ways. Learning involves the brain, the nervous system, and the environment, and the process by which their interplay acquires information and skills. Sometimes, we need information for just a short period of time, such as the telephone number for a pizza delivery, and then the information decays after just a few seconds. Thus learning does not always involve or require long-term retention.

A Look at Memory Systems

A good portion of the teaching done in schools centers on delivering facts and information for building concepts that explain a body of knowledge. We teach numbers, arithmetic operations, ratios, and theorems to explain mathematics. We teach about atoms, momentum, gravity, and cells to explain science. We talk about countries and famous leaders and discuss their trials and battles to explain history. Students may hold on to this information in working memory just long enough to take a test, after which the knowledge readily decays and is lost. Retention, however, requires that the learner not only give conscious attention during learning but also build conceptual frameworks that have sense and meaning for eventual consolidation into long-term storage networks.

> Learning is the process by which we acquire knowledge; memory is the process by which we retain it.

Figure 1.5 illustrates the basic components of the human memory systems. Incoming information makes a brief stop at **immediate memory**, a place where information is held for only seconds. This memory is helpful when you need to carry information just long enough to carry out a simple task, such as remembering that phone number for a pizza delivery we mentioned earlier. If we want to actually take time to process and manipulate new information, we move it into **working memory**. Anything that you are thinking about right at this moment is in your working memory. In addition to processing verbal information, a cerebral region called visual working memory processes visual information, including both new and already retained images. Working memory has a limited capacity; that is, it can process only a small number of items at one time. Some students have learning difficulties either because their working memory capacity is lower than average or it does not hold information long

Figure 1.5 The diagram shows the basic components of memory, consisting of two temporary memories (immediate and working) and one permanent memory (long-term).

enough for the student to use it successfully. This can cause serious problems when learning to read, as we will discuss in Chapter 5.

At some point after processing information (and skills) in working memory, the memory systems have an important decision to make: either to tag the new learning for eventual storage into long-term memory or to discard it from the system to be forgotten. As we shall learn in the ensuing paragraphs, how the memory systems make this choice depends on a few important factors. A key point here is that *how* the teacher presents new learning can make the difference between whether the learner remembers it or not. Knowledge of how the brain learns and remembers is a powerful tool for success in the teaching learning process.

Implications for Students With Learning Difficulties

Because students with learning difficulties can have problems focusing for very long, they are even more likely to perceive learning facts as a temporary effort just to please the teacher or to pass a test. It becomes increasingly important, then, for teachers of these students to emphasize *why* they need to learn certain material. Meaning (or relevancy) becomes the key to focus, learning, and retention.

Retention is the process whereby long-term memory preserves a learning in such a way that the memory can be located, identified, and retrieved accurately in the future. This is an inexact process influenced by many factors, including the degree of student focus, the length and type of rehearsal that occurred, the critical attributes that may have been identified, the student's learning style, the impact of any learning difficulties, and, of course, the inescapable influence of prior learning.

Rehearsal

The brain's decision to retain a learning seems to be based primarily on two criteria: *sense* and *meaning*. Sense refers to whether the student understands the learning: "Does this fit my perception of how the world works?" Meaning, on the other hand, refers to relevancy. Although the student may understand the learning, the more important question may be, "So what? What's this got to do with me?" Attaching sense and meaning to new learning can occur only if the learner has adequate time to process and reprocess it. This continuing reprocessing is called *rehearsal* and is a critical component in the transference of information from working memory to long-term storage.

Two major factors should be considered in evaluating rehearsal: the amount of time devoted to it, which determines whether there is both initial and secondary rehearsal, and the type of rehearsal carried out, which can be rote or elaborative.

Learning is likely to be remembered if it makes sense and has meaning for the learner.

Time for Initial and Secondary Rehearsal

Time is a critical component of rehearsal. Initial rehearsal occurs when the information first enters working memory. If the learner cannot attach sense or meaning and if there is no time for further processing, the new information is likely to be lost. Providing sufficient time to go beyond initial processing to secondary rehearsal allows the learner to review the information, to make sense of it, to elaborate on the details, and to assign value and relevance, thus increasing significantly the chance of long-term storage.

Scanning studies of the brain indicate that the frontal lobe is very much involved during the rehearsal process and, ultimately, in long-term memory formation. This makes sense because working memory is also located in the frontal lobe. Several studies using scans of humans showed that, during longer and frequent rehearsals, the amount of activity in the frontal lobe determined whether items were stored or forgotten (Buckner, Kelley, & Petersen, 1999; Fegen, Buchsbaum, & D'Esposito, 2015; Philips, Kopec, & Carew, 2013).

Students carry out initial and secondary rehearsal at different rates of speed and in different ways, depending on the type of information in the new learning and on their learning styles, including any learning difficulties. As the learning task changes, learners automatically shift to different patterns of rehearsal.

Rote and Elaborative Rehearsal

Rote Rehearsal. Rote rehearsal is used when learners need to remember and store information exactly as it is entered into working memory. It is a simple strategy necessary for learning information or a skill in a specific form or sequence. We employ rote rehearsal to remember a poem, the lyrics and melody of a song, multiplication tables, telephone numbers, and steps in a procedure. This rehearsal usually involves direct instruction. However, students with learning difficulties often perceive rote rehearsal as intensely boring, forcing the teacher to find creative and interesting ways to accomplish the rehearsal while keeping students on task.

Elaborative Rehearsal. Elaborative rehearsal is used when it is unnecessary to store information exactly as learned and when it is important to associate new learnings with prior learnings to detect relationships. In this complex thinking process, learners review the information several times to make connections to previous learnings and assign meaning. Students use rote rehearsal to memorize a poem but elaborative rehearsal to interpret its message. When students get very little time for, or training in, elaborative rehearsal, they resort more frequently to rote rehearsal. Consequently, they fail to make the associations or discover the relationships that only elaborative rehearsal can provide. Also, they continue to believe that the value of learning is merely the recalling of information as learned rather than the generating of new ideas, concepts, and solutions.

Students with learning difficulties need more time and guidance than others to rehearse the new learning in order to determine sense and recognize meaning. They need help with both types of rehearsal, including a rationale for each. When deciding how to use rehearsal in a lesson, teachers should consider the time available and the type of rehearsal appropriate for the specific learning objective. Keep in mind that rehearsal only contributes to, but does not guarantee, information transfer into long-term storage. However, there is almost no long-term retention *without* rehearsal.

Learning Motor Skills

Scanning studies show that a person uses the frontal lobe, motor cortex, and cerebellum while learning a new physical skill. Learning a motor skill involves following a set of procedures and can be eventually carried out largely without conscious attention. In fact, too much conscious attention directed to a motor skill while performing it can diminish the quality of its execution.

When first learning the skill, attention and awareness are obviously required. The frontal lobe is engaged because working memory is needed, and the motor cortex of the cerebrum (located across the top of the brain) interacts with the cerebellum to control muscle movement. As practice continues, the activated areas of the motor cortex become larger as nearby neurons are recruited into the new skill network. However, the memory of the skill is not established (i.e., stored) until after practice stops (Boutin, Panzer, & Blandin, 2013). It takes about 4–12 hours for this consolidation to take place in the cerebellum, and most of it occurs during deep sleep. Once the skill is mastered, brain activity shifts to the cerebellum, which organizes and coordinates the movements and the timing to perform the task. Procedural memory is the mechanism, and the brain no longer needs to use its higher order processes as the performance of the skill becomes automatic (Borragán, Urbain, Schmitz, Mary, & Peigneux, 2015; Tzvi, Münte, & Krämer, 2014).

Continued practice of the skill changes the brain structurally, and the younger the learner is, the easier it is for these changes to occur. Most music and sports prodigies began practicing their skills very early in life. Because their brains were most sensitive to the structural changes needed to acquire the skills, they can perform them masterfully. These skills become so much a part of the individual that they are difficult to change later in life (Schack & Mechsner, 2006).

Learning Difficulties and Motor Skills

Children with low motor ability will have difficulty learning motor skills. But it is a mistake to assume that low motor ability also means low perceptual or intellectual ability. Research studies indicate that individuals with low motor ability often have problems interpreting visual scenes involving movement, but that this limitation does not affect their intellectual or perceptual abilities (Bonifacci, 2004). One promising technique for helping individuals with low motor ability involves the stimulation of the motor cortex (see Figure 1.1) with a strong magnetic field. The procedure, called repetitive transcranial magnetic stimulation, appears to facilitate the learning of sequential motor skills (Kaminski et al., 2013; Stagg et al., 2011).

Individuals with developmental dyslexia often have problems learning motor skills. Researchers suspect that people with this disorder may suffer from an implicit motor learning deficit that not only affects their reading but also impairs their ability to acquire motor skills easily and accurately (Nicolson & Fawcett, 2008; Stoodley, Harrison, & Stein, 2006).

Children with attention deficits may have difficulty focusing sufficiently to acquire some specific motor skills. Often, what little focus they have is directed internally. Studies show that getting students to focus externally (i.e., on objects outside the body) enhances the acquisition and accuracy of motor skills. In these studies, the researchers suggested that the external focus of attention improves the efficiency of body movement and reduces the noise signals in the motor system that hamper the movement control and make it less reliable (Zachry, Wulf, Mercer, & Bezodis, 2005). Studies also show that students who are on medication for their attention difficulties can improve their motor skills (Kaiser, Schoemaker, Albaret, & Geuze, 2015).

HOW DIFFERENT ARE THE BRAINS OF TODAY'S STUDENTS?

Teachers remark more than ever that students of today are different in the way they learn. They seem to have shorter attention spans and become bored more easily than ever before. Why is that? Is something happening in the environment of learners that alters the way they approach the learning process? Does this mean that more students will have learning problems?

The Search for Novelty

Part of our success as a species can be attributed to the brain's persistent interest in novelty—that is, changes occurring in the environment. The brain is constantly scanning its environment for stimuli. When an unexpected stimulus arises—such as a loud noise from an empty room—a rush of adrenaline closes down all unnecessary activity and focuses the brain's attention so it can spring into action. It needs to determine quickly whether the unexpected stimulus is a threat and, if so, what to do about it. Conversely, an environment that contains mainly predictable or repeated stimuli (such as some classrooms?) lowers the brain's interest in the outside world and tempts it to turn within for novel sensations.

Recent and profound changes in our culture, such as the pervasive use of technology, have enhanced the brain's interest in novelty. Let's compare the environment that a child grew up in, say 20 years ago, compared to the environment that encompasses the developing brain today.

The Environment of the Past

The home environment for many children several decades ago was quite different from that of today. For example,

- The home was quieter.
- Parents and children did a lot of talking and reading.
- The family unit was more stable and ate together, and the dinner hour was an opportunity for parents to discuss their children's activities as well as reaffirm their love and support.
- If the home had a television, it was in a common area and controlled by adults. What children watched could be carefully monitored.
- School was an interesting place because it had television, films, field trips, and guest speakers. There were few other distractions, so school was an important influence in a child's life and the primary source of information.

- The neighborhood was also an important part of growing up. Children played together, developing their motor skills and learning the social skills needed to interact successfully with other children in the neighborhood.

The Environment of Today

In recent years, children have been growing up in a very different environment.

- Family units are not as stable as they once were. Single-parent families are more common, and children have fewer opportunities to talk with the adults who care for them. Their dietary habits are changing as home cooking is becoming a lost art.
- They are surrounded by media: cell phones, multiple televisions, movies, computers, video games, e-mail, and the Internet. According to the Pew Research Center, 92 percent of teens report going online daily, and 24 percent go online almost constantly (Pew Research Center, 2015). Many 10- to 18-year-olds can now watch television, play video games, and use other technology in their own bedrooms, leading to sleep deprivation. The average 6- to 12-year old needs about 10.5 hours of sleep but is getting 7.5 hours, and the average teenager needs 8.5 hours but is getting 6.5 hours (National Sleep Foundation, 2014). This accumulated sleep deprivation leads to irritability, hyperactivity, and lack of focus. Furthermore, with no adult present, what kind of moral compass is evolving in the impressionable preadolescent mind as a result of watching programs containing violence and sex on television and the Internet? See more about sleep later in this chapter.
- They get information from many different sources besides school, but they often do not know how to evaluate the reliability and veracity of these sources.
- The multimedia environment divides their attention. Even newscasts are different. In the past, only the reporter's face was on the screen. Now, the TV screen is loaded with information set in the corners and scrolling across the bottom. Children have become accustomed to these information-rich and rapidly changing messages. They try to pay attention to several things at once, but they do not go into any one thing in depth.
- They spend much more time indoors with their technology, thereby missing outdoor opportunities to develop gross motor skills and socialization skills necessary to communicate and interact personally with others. One unintended consequence of spending so much time indoors is the rapid rise in the number of overweight children and adolescents, now more than 17 percent of 2- to 19-year-olds, according to the National Institute of Child Health and Human Development.
- Because of neuroplasticity, young brains have responded to the technology by rewiring some functions and reorganizing neural networks to accommodate the large amount of stimulation occurring in the environment. By acclimating itself to these changes, brains respond

more than ever to the unique and different—what is called *novelty*. There is a dark side to this increased novelty-seeking behavior. Some adolescents who perceive little novelty in their environment may turn to mind-altering drugs, such as ecstasy and amphetamines, for stimulation. This drug dependence can further enhance the brain's demand for novelty to the point that it becomes unbalanced and resorts to extremely risky behavior.

- Their diet contains increasing amounts of substances that can affect brain and body functions. Caffeine is a strong brain stimulant, considered safe for most adults in small quantities. But caffeine is found in many of the foods and drinks that teens consume daily. Too much caffeine causes insomnia, anxiety, irritability, headaches, and nausea. Some teens can also develop allergies to aspartame (an artificial sugar found in children's vitamins and many "lite" foods) and other food additives. Possible symptoms of these allergic reactions include hyperactivity, difficulty concentrating, and headaches (Nigg, Lewis, Edinger, & Falk, 2012). Some children considered learning disabled may be merely displaying the symptoms of serious allergic reactions to their diet. Many states now limit or prohibit the sale of foods high in caffeine and sugar in public schools and encourage the sale of fresh fruit and other nutritious items.

- Their social behavior is changing dramatically. Instead of face-to-face socializing with their peers, they now do it face-to-screen, greatly minimizing the human connection and missing the nonverbal communication cues that help them understand a person's true intent. This impersonal interaction increases the risk that students will text someone something inappropriate and hurtful that they would never say to that person's face.

- No matter where they are, their attention turns immediately to a buzzing phone, leading to an addiction of "being in the know" right now, and giving them no tolerance for delayed gratification.

When we add the changes in family lifestyles, the narcissistic values of hip-hop, as well as the temptations of alcohol and drugs, we can realize how very different the environment of today's child is from that of just 20 years ago.

Have Schools Changed to Deal With This Different Brain?

Many educators are recognizing the characteristics of the new brain, but they do not always agree on what to do about it. Granted, teaching methodologies are changing, new technologies are being used, and teachers are even introducing pop music and culture to supplement traditional classroom materials. But schools and teaching are not changing fast enough. In high schools, lecturing continues to be the main method of instruction, and the interactive whiteboard is often the most advanced technology used. Many students remark that school is a dull, nonengaging environment that is much less

The brains of today's students are attracted more than ever to the unique and different—what is called novelty.

interesting than what is available outside of school. They have a difficult time focusing for extended periods and are easily distracted. Because they see little novelty and relevancy in what they are learning, they keep asking the eternal question, "Why do we need to know this?" Some teachers interpret this attitude as alienation from school while other teachers see it as a sign of a learning difficulty. In both instances, they are likely to refer the student for counseling and diagnosis. Consequently, it is possible that more children are being referred for special education evaluation not because they have true learning difficulties but because an inflexible (though well-meaning) school environment has not adapted to their changing brains.

Rather than ignoring the changing brain and culture, we should recognize that we must adjust schools to accommodate these changes. As we gain a more scientifically based understanding about today's novel brain and how it learns, we must rethink what we do in classrooms and schools. Maybe then more children will stay in the educational mainstream rather than be sidelined for labeling.

Some students, of course, do develop learning difficulties that need to be accurately diagnosed and addressed. The following chapters will discuss several types of learning difficulties, review recent research about them, and suggest ways of helping students who demonstrate them. Is it possible that some children are referred for special education evaluation not because they have true learning difficulties but because a school has not adapted to their changing brains?

DIFFICULTIES WITH SLEEP

In recent years, researchers have given more attention to the increasing number of students who are having problems with adequate sleep and the effect that sleep loss is having on their ability to learn. The American Academy of Pediatrics recommends that children 6–13 years of age should get 9–11 hours of sleep per night, while those from 14 to 17 years should get 8–10 hours (Moon, 2013). When a student is not getting enough sleep, there are three possible causes: (1) engaging distractions in the bedroom are robbing the student of sleep time, (2) the student actually has a sleep-related disorder, such a sleep apnea, or (3) the loss of sleep is a side effect of some other medical condition, such as **attention-deficit hyperactivity disorder (ADHD)**.

Sleep Deprivation

Of the three potential causes, studies show that distractions in the bedroom are the major cause of preadolescent and adolescent sleep loss. We mentioned earlier about the large percentage of students who are not getting enough sleep and who are arriving at school sleep-deprived. The effects of sleep deprivation are worrisome to say the least. The immediate and obvious signs include sleepiness, yawning, grogginess, and irritability. Chronic sleep deprivation is serious and often leads to weight gain and memory loss as well as to problems with muscle coordination and balance. Even temporary sleep loss can affect decision-making abilities, leading to a decline in general alertness (Killgore, 2010). Learning new information becomes tedious as attention drifts.

Effects on Memory

Sleep has a big impact on memory. The encoding of new learning into long-term memory occurs during sleep, specifically during the rapid eye movement (REM) cycles. Most individuals who get about eight hours of sleep will have five REM cycles. However, with just five to six hours of sleep, there are only three REM cycles. In other words, two of those valuable times, when the retention of new learning should be occurring, are eliminated when sleep time is reduced. Furthermore, REM time is also when new learning can be consolidated and linked to what the student already has stored in long-term memory. This is a slow process that needs all REM cycles to complete (Cipolli, Mazzetti, & Plazzi, 2013). Persistent sleep loss in students with learning difficulties means that they have another obstacle to overcome in order to remember what they have learned during their school day.

Sleep loss can affect teenagers' perception of their quality of life. A study of nearly 3,500 adolescents revealed that those who were sleep deprived had increasing difficulty falling asleep, felt they had a lower quality of life than before the sleep loss, and had more health complaints (mainly headaches) than adolescents who were not sleep deprived (Paiva, Gaspar, & Matos, 2015). Sleep loss also has an impact on our emotional brain, making it easier for us to get angry, confused, or anxious (Short & Louca, 2015). Eventually, consistent sleep loss can degrade the body's immune system, leaving one susceptible to systemic inflammation and various infections (Irwin, Olmstead, & Carroll, in press). Contrary to popular belief, stimulants such as caffeine are unable to override the body's acute need for sleep.

Some of the negative effects of sleep deprivation can be misread by educators as signs of a disorder. For example, students whose sleep loss makes them particularly vulnerable to irritation and inattentiveness may be considered as possibly having an attention disorder, such as ADHD. In these instances, educators should first investigate whether the student is sleep deprived before looking for a more serious condition. The good news is that sleep deprivation in many teenagers can be eliminated by removing the distractions that they have in their bedrooms. Surveys indicate that about 75 percent of children have at least one electronic device in their bedrooms, with 51 percent having two or more devices (National Sleep Foundation, 2014). Instead of sleeping, these devices allow students to spend time surfing the Internet or sending messages through social media (Wolfe et al., 2014). This practice is known as *vamping*. The message is clear: Make certain that all students, including those with learning difficulties, get adequate sleep.

Sleep Disorders

There are some causes of sleep loss that are neurobiological and genetic and are independent of the voluntary sleep deprivation scenario we just discussed. These disorders include breathing-related conditions, such as sleep apnea and sleep-related hypoventilation (abnormally slow breathing); an irregular sleep-wake cycle; rapid eye movement sleep behavior disorder; and restless legs syndrome. These conditions should be treated by medical specialists.

Some sleeping difficulties are the result of a coexisting condition (medical or mental). For example, students with emotional and behavioral disorders, attention-deficit hyperactivity disorder, and anxiety disorders often have difficulty sleeping. Successful treatment of the underlying condition often results in improved sleep patterns.

2

When Learning Difficulties Arise

✳ *Real education should consist of drawing the goodness and the best out of our own students.*

—Cesar Chavez, Labor Leader (1927–1993)

Neuron development starts in the embryo shortly after conception and proceeds at an astonishing rate. Between 50,000 and 100,000 new brain cells are generated *each second* from the 5th to the 20th week of life. Genetic instructions govern the rate of growth and direct the migration of neurons to different levels, forming the six layers of the fetus's cerebral cortex. In the first four months of gestation, about 200 billion neurons are formed, but about half will die off during the fetus's fifth month because they fail to connect with any areas of the growing embryo. This purposeful destruction of neurons (called **apoptosis**) is genetically programmed to ensure that only those neurons that have made connections are preserved and to prevent the brain from being overcrowded with unconnected cells. Sometimes apoptosis gets out of control, and connections that might otherwise have imparted certain intuitive skills—such as photographic memory—may be pruned as well. Defective apoptosis may also explain both the amazing abilities and deficits of autistic savants and the impaired intelligence associated with Down syndrome. Any drugs or alcohol that the mother takes during this time can interfere with the growing brain cells, increasing the risk of fetal addiction and mental defects. Neuron growth in the fetus can also be damaged if the mother is under continual stress, because of high levels of the hormone cortisol in the bloodstream.

Neurons in a child's brain make many more connections than do those in an adult's brain. The 20 hours of sleep that most infants require daily preserve the energy necessary for such rapid brain development.

A newborn's brain makes connections at an incredible pace as the child absorbs its environment. The richer the environment, the greater the number of interconnections that are made; consequently, learning can take place faster and with greater meaning.

As the child approaches puberty, the pace slackens, and two other processes begin: Connections the brain finds useful become permanent; those not useful are eliminated (by a second round of apoptosis) as the brain selectively strengthens and prunes connections based on experience. This process continues throughout our lives, but it appears to be most intense between the ages of 3 and 12 years. Thus at an early age experiences are already shaping the brain and designing the unique neural architecture that will influence how it handles future experiences in school, work, and other places.

RESEARCH EXAMINES LEARNING DIFFICULTIES

Possible Causes of Learning Difficulties

Neuroscientists once believed that all learning difficulties were caused by a single neurological problem. By contrast, recent research has shown that learning difficulties do not stem from a single cause but from problems in bringing together information from different regions of the brain. These difficulties can arise during the fetal development of the child.

> Some children may exhibit behavior that looks like a learning disability but may simply be a delay in maturation.

During pregnancy, the development of the brain is vulnerable to all kinds of disruptions. If the disruption occurs later in the pregnancy, errors may occur in the makeup of brain cells, their location, or the connections they make with neighboring cells. Some researchers believe that these errors may show up later as learning disorders.

Experiments with animals and imaging scans of the human brain have shown that other factors can disrupt brain development as well. Table 2.1 shows some of the factors currently under investigation and their potential impact on the development of the young brain. Problems in brain development that occur before, during, or after the birth of a child may eventually lead to learning difficulties.

Genetic Links

There is considerable evidence that genes play a role in developmental learning disabilities, especially since parents often display the same or similar learning difficulties as their children. In some cases, scientists have been able to link a specific gene to a specific common learning difficulty. But the general consensus among researchers currently is that most genes associated with common learning disabilities, such as language impairment, reading problems, and mathematics disability, are *generalist* genes, not specific ones (Chow, Ho, Wong, Waye, & Bishop, 2013; Haworth et al., 2009; Plomin & Kovas, 2005). The term *generalist* means three things:

1. Genes that affect learning disabilities are largely the same genes responsible for normal variations in learning abilities.

Table 2.1   Some Factors That Affect Brain Development

Genetic Links	Because learning difficulties tend to run in families, a genetic link is likely. However, the parent's learning difficulty often takes a slightly different form in the child. This may indicate that inheriting a specific learning difficulty involves several genes. Even though a child inherits a subtle brain dysfunction that can lead to a learning difficulty, the dysfunction may not become evident. Some learning difficulties may stem from the family environment. Parents with an expressive language disorder, for example, may talk less to their children, or their language may be atypical. Hence the child lacks a good model for acquiring language and, consequently, may seem learning disabled.
Tobacco, Alcohol, and Other Drug Use	The mother's use of cigarettes, alcohol, or other drugs may damage the unborn child. Mothers who smoke during pregnancy often bear smaller babies who tend to be at risk for problems, including learning disorders. Alcohol can distort neural growth, which often leads to hyperactivity and intellectual impairment. Even small amounts of alcohol during pregnancy can affect the frontal lobe and lead later to problems with attention, learning, and memory. Drugs such as cocaine (especially crack) seem to affect the development of the receptor cells that transmit incoming information from our senses. This receptor damage may cause children to have difficulty understanding speech sounds or letters, a common problem found in the offspring of crack-addicted mothers.
Problems During Pregnancy or Delivery	Sometimes the mother's immune system attacks the fetus, causing newly formed brain cells to settle in the wrong part of the brain. This migration may disturb the formation of neural networks needed for language and cognitive thought. During delivery, the umbilical cord may become twisted and temporarily cut off oxygen to the brain, which can damage or kill neurons and lead to learning disorders.
Toxins in the Child's Environment	Environmental toxins may disrupt brain cell growth and development in the early years. Lead and cadmium are getting particular research attention. Lead and mercury are still found in the environment, and both can cause learning difficulties and behavior problems.
Stress in the Child's Environment	Prolonged and inappropriate stress in the environment can harm the brain at any age. Corticosteroids, such as cortisol, released into the bloodstream during stress can damage the hippocampus and thus interfere with the coding of new information into memory. These chemicals also damage neurons in other brain areas, thereby increasing the risk of stroke, seizure, and infections.

2. Genes affecting any one aspect of a learning disability affect other aspects of that disability.

3. Genes affecting one learning disability are also likely to affect other learning disabilities.

Inheriting a genetic tendency for a learning problem does not necessarily mean that the trait will appear. We recognize now the <u>powerful influence of the environment in determining whether certain genetic traits arise and affect one's behavior and learning.</u> For example, a child born with the genetic components for expressive language problems and who lives in a household where there is little interactive conversation is apt to display the symptoms of this disorder. Conversely, if the parents frequently encourage the child to participate in family discussions, then there is a smaller likelihood that the expressive language problem will emerge.

Tobacco, Alcohol, and Other Drug Use

Tobacco. It has been known for some time that mothers who smoke during pregnancy often bear children of lower than average birth weight, making these newborns more susceptible to infection, mental retardation,

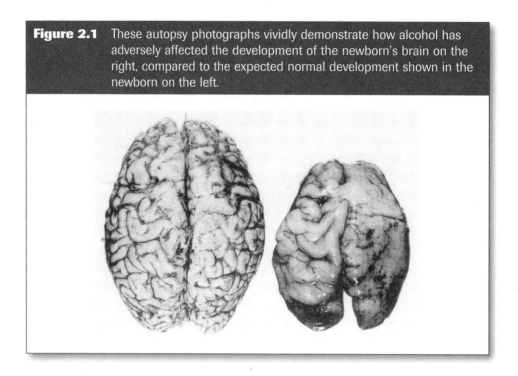

Figure 2.1 These autopsy photographs vividly demonstrate how alcohol has adversely affected the development of the newborn's brain on the right, compared to the expected normal development shown in the newborn on the left.

and cerebral palsy. Studies have also found that the nicotine in tobacco smoke affects the development of the fetal brainstem, which can lead to the death of the fetus before birth (Lavezzi, Ottaviani, & Matturri, 2005; Zhou et al., 2014). Fetal kidney development may also be affected (Kooijman et al., 2015). Nicotine also affects the development of the fetal lungs and heart. After birth, these babies are more at risk for sleep apnea, labored breathing, and irregular heart rate (Hafström, Milerad, Sandberg, & Sundell, 2005).

There is evidence that some young children exposed to second-hand smoke in their environment are at a greater risk of developing attention-deficit hyperactivity disorder and psychomotor development disorders (Pagani, 2014; Santos & Costa, 2015).

Alcohol. Most medical professionals agree that there are no known safe times and no safe amount of alcohol to drink during pregnancy. When a pregnant woman drinks alcohol, so does her unborn baby. Alcohol passes easily and quickly through the placenta to the fetus. In the unborn baby's immature body, alcohol is broken down much more slowly than in an adult's body. As a result, the alcohol level of the baby's blood can be higher, and can remain elevated longer, than in the mother's blood. This sometimes causes the baby to suffer lifelong damage. Brain damage from alcohol runs a gamut from mild to severe. The mild forms are called Fetal Alcohol Effects, and severe damage is called Fetal Alcohol Syndrome. Fetal alcohol exposure can result in impairments in behavior, verbal learning, visual-spatial skills, attention, reaction times, and executive control functions, such as problem solving and abstract thinking (NIAAA, 2015).

Excessive drinking of alcoholic beverages during pregnancy can cause extreme and often fatal damage to the developing fetal brain. The autopsy photographs in Figure 2.1 show the dramatic difference in brain shape and size between the brain of a newborn whose mother drank alcohol excessively during pregnancy, compared to the normally developed newborn brain on the left. Apparently, the alcohol interrupts the normal growth of neurons and signals them to commit suicide, that form of cell death known as apoptosis that we discussed earlier. The cell death results in a smaller brain size (Olney, 2014).

Marijuana. Drug abuse during pregnancy can also lead to problems for the developing fetus. Studies suggest that use of marijuana during pregnancy slows fetal growth and slightly decreases the length of pregnancy. After delivery, some babies who were regularly exposed to marijuana in the womb appear to undergo withdrawal-like symptoms, including excessive crying and trembling.

There have been a limited number of studies following marijuana-exposed babies through childhood. Some did not find any increased risk of learning or behavioral problems. However, others found that children who are exposed to marijuana before birth are more likely to have subtle problems that affect their ability to pay attention and to solve visual problems. Exposed children do not appear to have a decrease in IQ (Huizink, 2014). One study with more than 600 participants did find that marijuana-exposed children were much more likely to suffer depression by the age of 10 (Gray, Day, Leech, & Richardson, 2005).

Cocaine. The cocaine molecule is small enough to pass through the placental barrier into the fetal bloodstream. Its use during pregnancy can lead to a variety of physical problems for the baby after birth. Cocaine-exposed babies tend to have smaller heads, which generally reflect smaller brains. They may score lower than unexposed babies on tests given at birth to assess the newborn's physical condition and overall responsiveness. They may not do as well as unexposed babies on measures of motor ability, reflexes, attention, and mood control, and they appear less likely to respond to a human face or voice. As newborns, some are jittery and irritable, and they may startle and cry at the gentlest touch or sound. Generally, these behavioral disturbances are temporary and resolve over the first few months of life (Lester & Lagasse, 2010).

Studies suggest that most children who are exposed to cocaine before birth have normal intelligence, although their IQ levels may have been lowered somewhat by the exposure (Gautam, Warner, Kan, & Sowell, 2015). Furthermore, researchers have found that some of the attention and learning difficulties that cocaine-exposed children demonstrate in early childhood can be improved when these children are placed in a nurturing and enriched environment (Ackerman, Riggins, & Black, 2010; Cone-Wesson, 2005; Lewis et al., 2004; Miller-Loncar et al., 2005). This is encouraging news for parents and early childhood educators, in light of earlier predictions that many of these children would be permanently brain damaged. Language problems may persist, however. Apparently, cocaine interferes with the development of brain cells that transmit information from the senses. This receptor damage may cause children to have difficulty hearing and discriminating speech sounds, a common problem found in the offspring of crack-addicted mothers.

Follow-up studies suggest that most adolescents who were exposed to cocaine before birth seem to function normally. However, some adolescents may have subtle impairments in the ability to control emotions, focus attention, and process language that could put them at risk for behavioral and learning problems (Betancourt et al., 2011; Lebel et al., 2013; Richardson,

Some of the attention and learning difficulties that cocaine-exposed children demonstrate in early childhood can be improved in a nurturing and enriched environment.

Goldschmidt, Larkby, & Day, 2015). Researchers continue to follow cocaine-exposed children through their teen years to clarify their long-term outlook.

Problems During Pregnancy or Delivery

Problems during pregnancy can result in brain damage that affects learning. Sometimes the mother's immune system attacks the fetus, causing newly formed brain cells to settle in the wrong part of the brain. This migration may disturb the formation of neural networks needed for language and cognitive thought. Blows to the stomach area can decrease the oxygen and blood supply to the fetus, causing the death of brain cells. During delivery, the umbilical cord may become twisted and temporarily cut off oxygen to the brain, which can damage or kill neurons and lead to learning disorders. Being under continual stress during pregnancy can cause premature birth and low birth weight. The child is at greater risk for attention-deficit hyperactivity disorder as well as long-term effects on behavioral and emotional development (Glover, 2015). Babies born prematurely (at or before seven months of gestation) can exhibit abnormal brain growth and injury to the white matter. Strategic areas of the brain, such as those responsible for language, emotion, and behavior, remain smaller than normal even years later. The brains of premature boys are more severely affected than the brains of premature girls (Larroque et al., 2008).

Toxins in the Child's Environment

Children are particularly susceptible to environmental toxins because, pound for pound, they drink more water, eat more food, and breathe more air than adults. Thus children have substantially heavier exposure than adults to the toxins lurking in water, food, and air. Furthermore, their hand-to-mouth behavior and their preference for playing close to the ground only add to the risk of exposure.

Lead. The effect of lead on children's health is one of those most clearly understood in the environmental field. Despite the removal of lead from gasoline and paint, nearly half a million children a year in the United State exhibit signs of lead poisoning, mostly poor minority children in urban settings. For children, the primary route for lead is oral ingestion via food, water, soil, and dust. Once absorbed, lead follows the distribution of calcium in the body. Children are especially sensitive to the toxic effects of lead because, compared with adults, more is absorbed through the gastrointestinal tract, a greater proportion of circulating lead reaches the brain (especially under 5 years of age), and the developing nervous system is especially vulnerable to damage. Follow-up studies of children who had high blood levels of lead show that they have lower IQ levels, more frequent behavior problems, and score lower on elementary grade level cognitive tests than children who were not exposed (Magzamen et al., 2013; Sun et al., 2015).

Mercury. Mercury, like lead, is toxic to the developing brain. Mercury occurs in the earth's crust, and natural sources, such as volcano emissions, contribute significantly to atmospheric levels. Industrial sources of mercury emissions have declined dramatically in the past two decades. However, current main sources include waste incineration, chlorine manufacturing, and the burning of coal. Methylmercury, the more toxic form, is produced by microorganisms acting on mercury in deposits in the sea and the soil. Since mercury accumulates through the food chain, the highest levels of methylmercury occur in predatory fish, which in turn are a major source of human exposure. Increased levels of mercury and mercury compounds have been shown to cause excessive mood swings, weaken muscles, and impair cognitive performance in children and adolescents (Environmental Protection Agency, 2014).

Stress in the Child's Environment

Stress causes the body to release cortisol, a corticosteroid that arouses the brain to consider what action to take. Stress can have positive effects by encouraging individuals to raise their level of performance. But persistent stress from living in poverty or with abusive parents or siblings has negative consequences. Continued and undesired stress can cause high amounts of cortisol to remain in the body for prolonged periods, thereby damaging cells in multiple organs. In the child's brain, persistent stress can impair the hippocampus, the structure responsible for permanent memory storage and recall. Corticosteroids also damage neurons in other brain areas, thereby increasing the risk of stroke, seizure, and infections (Glover, 2015). However, not all children exposed to constant stress develop stress-related symptoms. Some children demonstrate resiliency, the ability to thrive and excel, even when exposed to severe stress (Little & Akin-Little, 2015).

Of course, not all learning difficulties are technically learning disabilities. For example, many children are just slower in developing certain skills. Therefore, some children may exhibit behavior that *looks like* a learning disability but may simply be a delay in maturation.

Learning disabilities are characterized by a significant difference between a child's achievement and that individual's overall intelligence. Students with learning disabilities often exhibit a wide variety of traits, including problems with spoken and written language, reading, arithmetic, reasoning ability, and organization skills. These may be accompanied with inattention, hyperactivity, impulsivity, motor disorders, perceptual impairment, and a low tolerance for frustration. Because each of these traits can run the gamut from mild to severe, it is necessary to assess each student's disabilities carefully to determine the best approach for effective teaching.

Gender Differences

Nearly two-thirds of students diagnosed with a learning disability are boys, and three times as many boys are diagnosed with dyslexia or reading problems (Cortiella & Horowitz, 2014). Are these gender differences accurate, and what accounts for them? No one knows for sure, but research is shedding light on a few possible explanations. Early studies showed that boys were referred more often than girls for a reading disability because they were more likely than girls to express frustration associated with their reading problems and to display disruptive behavior (Shaywitz, 2003; Wheldall & Limbrick, 2010). This is referred to as **ascertainment bias.** Some of these referred boys did not display reading problems when assessed with objective criteria. Furthermore, many girls with learning difficulties are neither identified nor treated.

Although ascertainment bias explains some of the magnitude of gender differences in reading difficulties, it does not explain all. This leads researchers to believe that boys do have a genuine vulnerability to reading problems more than girls, but by a narrower margin than previously thought (Quinn & Wagner, 2013). The causes of this vulnerability remain elusive. Some researchers contend that an unknown factor (maybe testosterone) present during the last trimester of pregnancy slows the formation of the brain's cortex, especially in the left hemisphere where much of reading is processed. Because girls are not influenced by this mysterious factor, their brains mature normally and are therefore better able to handle the stresses of pregnancy and birth.

Another and more likely possibility is that certain brain deficits affecting learning result from genetic mutations on the X chromosome. Females have two X chromosomes, so they are protected if the healthy chromosome can prevent the unwanted effects of the mutated one. Males, on the other hand, possess only one X chromosome, so they suffer the full consequences of any mutations on that chromosome. The best we can say at the moment is that gender differences do exist, that they are less pronounced than previously believed, that their causes are still not fully understood, and that the research continues.

What Forms of Instruction Are Most Effective?

An analysis of more than 30 years of research indicates that the following interventions are most effective with students who have learning difficulties:

- The most effective form of teaching was one that combined direct instruction (e.g., teacher-directed lecture, discussion, and learning from textbooks) with teaching students the strategies of learning (e.g., memorization techniques, study skills). Using technology, such as computers and presentation media, can make these practice sessions more interesting and interactive.
- The component that had the greatest effect on student achievement was *control of task difficulty*, in which, for example, the teacher provided the necessary assistance or sequenced the tasks from easy to difficult. Working in small groups (five or less) and using structured questioning were also highly effective. Students also made fewer errors when teachers systematically modeled how to solve problems. See suggestions on forming these groups in "**Strategies to Consider.**"
- When groups of students with learning difficulties were exposed to strategy instruction (i.e., understanding how to learn), their achievement was greater than that of groups exposed solely to direct instruction.

Misconceptions About Learning Difficulties

Table 2.2 deals with some common misconceptions about the causes and implications of learning difficulties.

Table 2.2 Misconceptions About Learning Difficulties

Misconception	Explanation
Learning difficulties are common and therefore easy to diagnose.	Learning difficulties are often hidden and thus difficult to diagnose. Brain imaging and genetic testing continue to show promise in the diagnosis of some learning difficulties. Until these methods become more accurate and feasible, diagnosis of a learning disability needs to result from extensive observation and testing by a clinical team.
Children with learning difficulties are identified in kindergarten or first grade.	Learning difficulties can be identified in kindergarten or first grade but may go unrecognized in the early years, and some are not identified until third grade. Some bright children learn how to mask their difficulties. Furthermore, some kinds of learning difficulties do not surface until middle school, high school, or later.
Children outgrow their learning difficulties.	Most learning difficulties last throughout life, and an increasing number can be remediated. Many adults have devised strategies to cope successfully with their difficulties and lead productive lives.
Learning difficulties are caused by poor parenting.	No definitive association exists between the child-rearing skills of parents and the presence or absence of *permanent* learning disabilities in their children, as these generally have biological causes. However, home discipline, persistent stress, bullying, high-risk health behaviors such as smoking and alcohol use, the degree of parental interaction, and other factors may affect a child's self-image and enthusiasm for success in school. Physical abuse *can* cause permanent changes in the brain that lead to learning difficulties.
Accommodations provided to students with learning difficulties, particularly during testing, gives them an unfair advantage over students without difficulties.	Accommodations do not favor these students. Rather, accommodations allow access to the information that gives students with a learning difficulty the means to demonstrate their knowledge, skills, and abilities. Without modifications, common forms of instruction and testing often inadvertently reflect a student's difficulty rather than the subject at hand. For example, a student who has a writing difficulty would be greatly impaired during a written essay exam, even though the student was skilled in the art and mechanics of composing an essay. The use of a word processor or other assistive technology allows this student to be assessed on knowledge rather than on the limitations that the writing difficulties imposed.
Medication, diet, or other treatments can cure learning difficulties.	No quick fix exists to *cure* learning difficulties. Even medication given to ADHD children mediates the symptoms but does not cure the difficulty. Because most learning difficulties are considered lifelong, the support and understanding of, and attention to, the child's needs are basic to long-term treatment. However, certain interventions for children with dyslexia have been successful.
Students with learning difficulties don't try hard enough in school.	Ironically, brain scans show that many students with learning difficulties are working harder at certain tasks than other students, but the result is less successful. Merely trying harder does not correct their problem. Students with learning difficulties often give up trying at school because of their fear of failure or lack of adequate support.
Learning difficulties affect everything the child does at school.	Some learning difficulties are very specific. Thus a student's weakness may affect performance in one classroom setting but not in another, or only at a particular grade level.
Children with learning difficulties are just "slow."	This is one of the most harmful misconceptions. Most learning difficulties are independent of cognitive ability. Children at all intellectual levels—including the gifted—can have learning problems. They have the cognitive capacity and mechanisms to learn but often interpret, organize, and retrieve learnings in unique ways.

Gifted Children With Learning Difficulties

The notion that a gifted child can have learning difficulties strikes some people as bizarre, something like an oxymoron. Consequently, many children who are gifted in some ways and deficient in others (G/LD students) go undetected and unserved by their schools. They tend to fall through the cracks because the system is not designed to deal with such widely different conditions occurring in the same student. Interviews with these students revealed that they perceive their overall school experiences failed to assist them in learning their potential or addressing their weaknesses (Willard-Holt, Weber, Morrison, & Horgan, 2013). Despite more than 30 years of research on these twice-exceptional students, it is only in recent years that educators have even begun to accept that high abilities and learning problems can exist together in the same person. But interest is increasing, and educators are looking to the research to help them identify these students and find ways to meet their needs.

About two to five percent of all students are likely to be gifted and also have learning disabilities. Researchers continue to search for measurement activities that will accurately identify children with both talents and learning difficulties. This process has been particularly difficult because there is no standard definition of what constitutes giftedness when coupled with a learning difficulty and vice versa (Lovett & Sparks, 2013). Nonetheless, as school districts pay more attention to twice-exceptional students, programs are emerging that address their needs. These include interventions in the general education classroom, partial pullout programs, and self-contained programs. A few useful models that have emerged for screening and helping G/LD students use the Response to Intervention paradigm (Crepeau-Hobson & Bianco, 2013; McCallum et al., 2013).

> Many children who are gifted in some ways and deficient in others go undetected and unserved by their schools.

RESPONSE TO INTERVENTION

Identifying and helping students with learning difficulties have never been easy tasks. The number of students identified as having learning disabilities has increased more than 200 percent since the category was first established in 1977.

In recent years, one method of determining whether students have learning difficulties is assessing if their responses to the methods, strategies, curriculum, and interventions they encounter lead to increased learning and appropriate progress. This concept forms the basis of the approach known as **response to intervention**, and it was addressed in the Individuals with Disabilities Education Improvement Act of 2004 (IDEA, 2004).

Key Elements of Response to Intervention

A key element of a response to intervention (RTI) approach is to provide early intervention when students first experience academic difficulties, with the goal of improving the achievement of all students, including those who may have learning disabilities. In addition to the preventive and reme-dial services this approach provides at-risk students, it contributes data useful for accurately identifying learning disabilities. Thus a student exhib-iting significantly low achievement and insufficient RTI may be viewed as being at risk for learning disability and possibly in need of special educa-tion services. The assumption behind this model, referred to as a dual discrepancy, is that when provided with quality instruction and remedial services, a student without disabilities will make satisfactory progress.

A Problem-Solving Approach Using Data

Another key element of RTI is that it uses a systematic problem-solving process involving the following steps:

- Identifying and analyzing the problem, including collection of base-line data
- Generating possible scientific, research-based strategies or interventions
- Implementing an intervention plan
- Monitoring student progress to determine the student's response to these interventions
- Using the RTI data to review and revise plans as needed

The data used in the RTI process should include the following (NASP, 2015; NCLD, 2015):

- High-quality, research-based instruction and behavioral supports in general education
- Scientific, research-based interventions focused specifically on indi-vidual student difficulties and delivered with appropriate intensity
- Use of a collaborative approach by school staff for development, implementation, and monitoring of the intervention process
- Data-based documentation reflecting continuous monitoring of stu-dent performance and progress during interventions
- Documentation of parent involvement throughout the process
- Documentation that the time lines described in the federal regula-tions are followed unless extended by mutual written agreement of the child's parents and a team of qualified professionals as described in these regulations
- Systematic assessment and documentation that the interventions used were implemented with fidelity

The Individuals with Disabilities Education Act addresses the use of RTI in two respects. First, it allows for the use of RTI data as part of an evalua-tion for special education to assist in the identification and determination of eligibility of students with learning disabilities, as an alternative to use of the ability-achievement discrepancy criterion. It should be noted that the new DSM-5 abandons the ability-achievement discrepancy as a criterion for diagnosing specific learning disabilities. Second, it creates the option of using up to 15 percent of funds for early intervention services for students who have not been identified as needing special education services but who need additional academic and behavioral support to succeed in a general education environment.

Multiple-Tiered Model

Although there is no universal RTI model, it is generally viewed as having three tiers, consisting of the following (NASP, 2015; NCLD, 2015):

Tier 1. High-quality <u>instructional and behavioral supports are provided for all students in general education.</u>

80-85%.

- School personnel conduct universal screening of literacy skills, academics, and behavior.
- Teachers implement a variety of research-supported teaching strategies and approaches.
- Ongoing, curriculum-based assessment and continuous progress monitoring are used to guide high-quality instruction.
- Students receive differentiated instruction based on data from ongoing assessments.

Tier 2. Students whose performance and rate of progress lag behind those of peers in their classroom, school, or district <u>receive more specialized prevention or remediation within general education.</u>

15%.

- Curriculum-based measures are used to identify which students continue to need assistance, and with what specific kinds of skills.
- Collaborative problem solving is used to design and implement instructional support for students that may consist of a standard protocol or more individualized strategies and interventions.
- Identified students receive more intensive scientific, research-based instruction targeted to their individual needs.
- Student progress is monitored frequently to determine intervention effectiveness and needed modifications.
- Systematic assessment is conducted to determine the fidelity or integrity with which instruction and interventions are implemented.
- Parents are informed and included in the planning and monitoring of their child's progress in the Tier 2 specialized interventions.
- General education teachers receive support (e.g., training, consultation, direct services for students), as needed, from other qualified educators in implementing interventions and monitoring student progress.

Tier 3. Comprehensive evaluation is conducted by a multidisciplinary team to <u>determine eligibility for special education</u> and related services.

5%.

- Parents are informed of their due process rights, and consent is obtained for the comprehensive evaluation needed to determine whether the student has a disability and is eligible for special education and related services.
- Evaluation consists of multiple sources of assessment data, which may include data from standardized and norm-referenced measures, observations made by parents, students, and teachers, and data collected in Tiers 1 and 2.

- Intensive, systematic, specialized instruction is provided, and additional RTI data are collected, as needed, in accordance with special education time lines and other mandates.
- Procedural safeguards on evaluations and eligibility apply, as required by the IDEA 2004 mandates.

Variations on this basic framework may occur. For example, Tier 2 might consist of two hierarchical steps, or subtiers (e.g., a teacher first collaborates with a single colleague, then works on problem solving with a multidisciplinary team, creating in effect a four-tiered model). Another possibility is that more than one type of intervention might be provided within Tier 2 (e.g., both a standard protocol and individualized planning, based on the student's apparent needs).

> *Video:* To see an explanation of RTI, go to:
>
> https://www.youtube.com/watch?v=nkK1bT8IsOM

Potential Benefits of RTI

Proponents of RTI cite the following potential benefits:

- Earlier identification of students with learning disabilities using a problem-solving approach rather than an ability-achievement discrepancy formula, thus minimizing the "wait to fail" approach
- Reduction in the number of students referred for special education
- Reduction in the overidentification of minority students
- Data that have the maximum relevancy to instruction
- Focus on student outcomes with increased accountability
- Promotion of shared responsibility and collaboration

How Successful Is RTI?

After a decade of implementation, educational journals are filled with articles reporting the success of RTI in identifying and improving the achievement of students with learning difficulties in a variety of learning situations and environments. Not surprisingly, the largest portion of these interventions was in reading, followed by mathematics. Numerous studies show successful implementation of RTI in preschool and primary grades literacy (e.g., Carta et al., 2014; Denton, 2012; O'Connor, Bocian, Sanchez, & Beach, 2014), as a predictor of third grade reading skills (e.g., Beach & O'Connor, 2015), in middle school (e.g., Graves, Brandon, Duesbery, McIntosh, & Pyle, 2011) and high school reading (e.g., Vaughn & Fletcher, 2012).

Researchers who have reviewed these studies report that the most successful programs had similar supporting factors for their sustainability (Hughes & Dexter, 2015). These were:

- Adequate meeting time to coordinate efforts
- Involvement of all school personnel
- Administrative support for the process at all levels in the school district
- Willingness of teachers to accept the process and adjust their instruction
- Ongoing and extensive professional development regarding the process

General education teachers reported that they initially had little understanding of how to implement the interventions. However, they also stated that working collaboratively with special education teachers within professional learning communities greatly improved their efficacy and gave them greater incentive to help all students, including those with learning difficulties (Printy & Williams, 2015). These findings are further evidence of the importance of ongoing professional development that focuses on the effective implementation of response to intervention.

HELPING STUDENTS BECOME STRATEGIC LEARNERS

What actually makes learning difficult for students with learning difficulties has been the subject of research for many years. Examining the challenges of these students yields clues about the way they interact with their environment and possible interventions that may help them be more successful.

What Is Learning?

Learning is an active process of acquiring and retaining knowledge so it can be applied in future situations. The ability to recall and apply new learning involves a complex interaction between the learner and the material being learned. Learning is likely to occur when a student has opportunities to practice the new information, receive feedback from the teacher, and apply the knowledge or skill in familiar and unfamiliar situations with less and less assistance from others.

Students bring to each new learning task a varied background of their own ideas, beliefs, opinions, attitudes, motivation, skills, and prior knowledge. They also bring the strategies and techniques they have learned in order to make learning more efficient. All these aspects contribute directly to students' ability to learn and to remember and use what has been learned.

Teachers can facilitate a lifetime of successful learning by equipping students with a repertoire of strategies and tools for learning. These might include ways to organize oneself and new material; techniques to use while reading, writing, and studying mathematics or other subjects; and systematic steps to follow when working through a learning task or reflecting on one's own learning.

Learning Difficulties of Students

There can be numerous reasons why students have learning difficulties. It may be because they (Silver, 2008)

- Are often overwhelmed, disorganized, and frustrated in new learning situations
- Have difficulty following directions, either oral or written
- Have trouble with the visual or auditory perception of information

- Have problems performing school tasks, such as writing compositions, taking notes, doing written homework, taking paper-and-pencil tests, or interacting with technology
- Have a history of academic problems and may believe that they cannot learn, that school tasks are just too difficult and not worth the effort, or that, if they do succeed at a task, it must have been due to luck rather than effort
- Do not readily believe that there is a connection between what they do, the effort they make, and the likelihood of academic success. These negative beliefs about their ability to learn and the nature of learning itself are signs of a fixed mindset that can lower self-esteem and have far-reaching academic consequences.

Coping With the Difficulties

Acquiring the necessary knowledge, skills, and strategies for functioning independently in our society is as important to students with learning disabilities as it is to their peers without disabilities. Perhaps one of the most fundamental skills for everyone to learn is *how to learn*. Students can become effective, lifelong learners when they master certain techniques and strategies to assist learning and when they know which techniques are useful in different kinds of learning situations.

We all use various methods and strategies to help us remember new information or skills. Yet some of us are more conscious of our own learning processes than others. For instance, many students know little about the learning process, their own strengths and weaknesses in a learning situation, and what strategies and techniques they naturally tend to use when learning something new.

Hence students with learning difficulties need to become strategic learners and not haphazardly use whatever strategies or techniques they have developed on their own. To be able to decide which strategies to use, for example, students need to observe how others think or act when using various strategies. Learning skills develop when students receive opportunities to discuss, reflect on, and practice personal strategies with classroom materials and appropriate skills. Through feedback, teachers help students refine new strategies and monitor their choices. Over time, teachers can diminish active guidance as students assume more responsibility for their own strategic learning.

> Students with learning disabilities need to know what strategies are useful in a learning situation and be able to use them effectively.

What Are Learning Strategies?

Learning strategies are efficient, effective, and organized steps or procedures used when learning, remembering, or performing. These tools and techniques help us understand and retain new material or skills, to integrate this new information with what we already know in a way that makes sense, and to recall the information or skill later. When we are trying to learn new information or perform a task, our strategies include both cognitive and behavioral aspects.

Strategies can be simple or complex. Simple learning strategies are cognitive activities usually associated with less challenging learning tasks. Some examples of simple strategies and the rationale for using them are the following:

- Taking notes: Assuming the learning difficulty is not related to writing problems, adding the kinesthetic act of writing increases attention and the likelihood that the student will retain the new information. This is particularly advantageous in this era of keyboarding because recent studies have shown that students who take notes by writing them on paper remember, integrate, and apply their new learning better than students who take notes on laptops (Mueller & Oppenheimer, 2014).
- Making a chart or outline: Many students with learning difficulties need visual schemes to help them organize their thoughts.
- Asking the teacher questions: This clarifies any misconceptions that the students may have and forces the students to rehearse the information in their heads in order to compose the question.
- Asking ourselves questions: Helps students detect any gaps they have in their learning and decide what other information they need to fill those gaps.
- Using resource books or the Internet: Expands the number of resources where students can get information not found in the text.
- Rereading what we don't understand: This strategy gives students another opportunity to comprehend what they are reading.
- Asking someone to check our work: Peer feedback is a valuable and nonthreatening tool to verify the accuracy and completeness of the assignment.
- Developing a **mnemonic** device: Memory tricks such as mnemonic devices are very helpful for remembering isolated facts. See "Strategies to Consider" at the end of this chapter.

Complex strategies help us accomplish tasks involving multiple steps or higher order thinking, such as analysis or answering "What if . . . ?" questions. Here are some examples of complex strategies and their rationale:

- Planning, writing, and revising an essay: These steps allow the students to organize their thoughts, decide on the central theme, and select the correct vocabulary to express their ideas.
- Identifying sources of information: Students need to recognize the importance of finding credible sources to support their arguments and of citing them to avoid plagiarism.
- Stating main ideas and supporting our position: The main theme should be clear to the reader, and the facts should support the writer's views.
- Distinguishing fact from opinion: Understanding the difference between facts and opinion is a critical skill in this day of high-pressure advertising, publicity, and news commentary.
- Searching for and correcting errors in our work: Students are less likely to repeat errors that they discover on their own.

- Keeping track of our progress: Timetables help students track the progress of their work, keep them on task, and increase the chances that their work will be submitted on time.
- Being aware of our thought processes: Reflecting on our thought processes (metacognition) helps us determine which approaches work best for solving specific problems.
- Evaluating the validity of sources: With so much information available on the Internet, students need to be able to judge the validity of what they find and the credibility of the sources.

Some of the suggestions in the research literature for strategy interventions designed to make learners more aware of what they are doing are found at the end of this chapter in "Strategies to Consider."

Types of Learning Strategies

Learning strategies can be categorized as either cognitive or metacognitive.

Cognitive Strategies. These help a person process and manipulate information to perform tasks such as taking notes, asking questions, or filling out a chart. They tend to be task specific; that is, certain cognitive strategies are useful when learning or performing certain tasks.

Metacognitive Strategies. These are more executive-type functions and are used when planning, monitoring, and evaluating learning or strategy performance. They are often referred to as self-regulatory strategies, helping students become aware of learning as a process and of what actions will facilitate that process. For example, taking the time to plan before writing assists students in writing a good composition. The ability to evaluate one's work, the effectiveness of learning, or even the use of a strategy is also metacognitive, demonstrating that a learner is aware of and thinking about how learning occurs. Students who use metacognitive strategies frequently tend to become self-regulated learners. They set goals for learning, coach themselves in positive ways, and use self-instruction to guide themselves through learning problems. Further, they monitor their comprehension or progress and reward themselves for success. Just as students can be taught cognitive, task-specific strategies, so can they be taught self-regulatory, metacognitive ones. In fact, the most effective interventions combine the use of cognitive and metacognitive strategies.

> Learning and retention are more likely to occur when students can observe, engage in, discuss, reflect on, and practice the new learning.

Research About the Effectiveness of Learning Strategies

Research into strategies of learning has been going on for more than 30 years, long before the availability of brain-scanning technologies. Since the 1970s, researchers at the University of Kansas have investigated the benefits of strategy instruction, especially for individuals with learning disabilities. Their work produced one of the most well-researched and well-articulated models for teaching students to use learning strategies. Known as the Strategies Integration Model, or SIM, this method outlines a series of steps so that educators can effectively teach any number of strategies or strategic approaches. See the model at the end of this chapter in "Strategies to Consider."

Recent cognitive research supports the notion that <u>learning and retention are more likely to occur when students can observe, engage in, discuss, reflect on, and practice the new learning</u>. When teachers help students use learning strategies and to generalize their strategic knowledge to other academic and nonacademic situations, they are promoting student independence in the process of learning.

For students who have learning difficulties, learning-strategy instruction holds great educational promise for the following reasons:

- Instruction helps students learn how to learn and become more effective in the successful performance of academic, social, or job-related tasks. Students can better deal with immediate academic demands as well as cope with similar tasks in different settings under different conditions throughout life. The strategies are particularly powerful in the face of new learning situations.
- Instruction makes students aware of how strategies work, why they work, when they work, and where they can be used. To assist students, teachers will need to

  o talk about strategies explicitly,
  o name and describe each strategy,
  o model how each strategy is used by thinking aloud while performing tasks relevant to students,
  o provide students with multiple opportunities to use the strategies with a variety of materials, and
  o provide feedback and guidance while students refine and internalize the use of each strategy.

Ultimately, responsibility for strategy use needs to shift from teachers to students. This promotes independent learners with the cognitive flexibility necessary to address the many learning challenges they will encounter in their lives. Although no single technique or intervention can address all the varied needs of students with learning difficulties, studies confirm that <u>teaching the strategies of learning will help these students become better equipped to face current and future learning tasks</u> (e.g., Baker, Chard, Ketterlin-Geller, Apichatabutra, & Doabler, 2009; Klassen & Lynch, 2007). By learning how to learn, they can become independent, lifelong learners—one of the primary goals of education.

> Learning strategies help students become better equipped to face current and future learning tasks.

How Important Is Self-Esteem?

Self-esteem is a subjective and often emotional evaluation of one's own worth. <u>Students with learning difficulties often have negative feelings about learning and about themselves.</u> Because of past experiences, these students believe they cannot learn or that the work is simply too difficult or that they do not have the intellectual capacity to accomplish the task. As a result, they may believe they cannot achieve success in learning through their own efforts and attribute too much of their situation to genetic limitations or other factors beyond their control (Nelson & Harwood, 2011). Teachers should address this issue when presenting information on the strategies of learning. Teachers can convince students to attribute success in learning to their own efforts and to the use of appropriate learning strategies. For learning strategies to be successful, students need to not only have a positive self-image but recognize the connection between their efforts and success.

Research in this area has been inconclusive, yielding both positive and negative findings. Low self-esteem can certainly diminish one's academic performance, but high self-esteem does not guarantee improved academic performance. Ironically, trying to improve self-esteem can actually cause academic performance to decline. In one study of college students with poor grades, students whose self-esteem was boosted got poorer grades than those in the control group (Forsyth, Kerr, Burnette, & Baumeister, 2007). Given this surprise result, the researchers suggested that simply telling people to think they are great in the absence of personal achievement may lead to overconfidence, or it may foster a sense of being too competent to work hard.

Used with caution, school-based interventions designed to boost the self-esteem of students with learning disabilities can be effective if tied to improved achievement. Researchers found that interventions using both skill development and self-enhancement succeeded in raising self-esteem because these focused on the value of intrinsic effort. Interventions using group counseling techniques were effective with students at all grade levels. Academic interventions were particularly helpful for middle school students. A major component of many of the successful academic interventions was an emphasis on students working together with their classmates and receiving specific and constructive feedback from classmates on their academic progress (El-Daw & Hammoud, 2015; Zuffianò et al., 2013). See this chapter's "Strategies to Consider" for suggestions on how to build student self-esteem.

Important Cautions About Self-Esteem

Although research studies show that raising self-esteem in students with learning disabilities is promising, some important cautions are in order. Many people assume that high self-esteem generally leads to positive outcomes and that low self-esteem often results in undesirable behaviors. But this is not always the case. In fact, the research on how self-esteem correlates with positive outcomes is mixed. Contrary to popular belief, bullies do not typically suffer from low self-esteem nor do those prone to drug and alcohol abuse. Raising self-esteem does not automatically translate into improved academic achievement. In fact, attempts to boost self-esteem in struggling students may backfire if the focus is primarily on making them feel good about themselves. However, motivation and achievement do improve when self-esteem interventions center on instilling a sense of personal responsibility for academic performance (Baumeister, Campbell, Krueger, & Vohs, 2005). See Chapter 10 for suggestions on how to motivate students with learning difficulties.

Strategies to Consider

GUIDELINES FOR WORKING WITH STUDENTS WHO HAVE SPECIAL NEEDS

Teachers should consider these guidelines to help students with special needs succeed. The following general strategies are appropriate for all grade levels and subject areas.

- **Capitalize on the student's strengths.** This is more likely to give the student a feeling of success and lessen any feelings of inadequacy that flow from the learning difficulty.
- **Provide high structure and clear expectations.** These students do better in an organized environment and need to know what is expected of them. Take nothing for granted, and make sure the student is aware of acceptable and unacceptable types of behavior.
- **Use short sentences and simple vocabulary.** These students often have difficulty processing complex sentence structures and usually have a limited vocabulary. Behavior problems can arise when the student is unclear about what the teacher said.
- **Allow flexibility in classroom procedures.** For example, permit students with written language difficulties to use voice recorders for note taking and test taking.
- **Make use of self-correcting materials that provide immediate feedback without embarrassment.** Because many of these students have a short attention span, activities that give immediate feedback are desirable. Students can assess their own progress quickly and without knowing each other's results.
- **Use computers for drill and practice and for teaching word processing.** Computers are patient devices, and many programs provide varied opportunities to practice and usually give a running score of the student's progress. Word processing programs can often convince students to try creative writing despite any problems with written language.
- **Provide positive reinforcement of appropriate social skills.** Appropriate social behavior at school is likely to be repeated if it is positively reinforced. Look for opportunities to "catch the student being good."
- **Recognize that students with learning difficulties can greatly benefit from the gift of time to grow and mature.** These students often progress slowly, but many progress nonetheless. Patience with them can be rewarding for both teachers and students.

Strategies to Consider

STRATEGIES FOR
INVOLVEMENT AND RETENTION OF LEARNING

Students with attention difficulties need help to maximize their engagement and to improve their retention of learning. The following strategies are appropriate for all students, especially those who have learning problems.

- **Get their attention.** Use humor, unexpected introductions, and various other attention grabbers to stimulate student interest in the lesson.
- **Make it relevant.** Relevancy (or meaning) is one of the major factors affecting retention. Students are not likely to retain what they perceive as irrelevant. Keep in mind that it is *their* perception of relevancy that matters, not *yours.*
- **Model, model, model.** Show students how to do it. Use models, simulations, and examples for simple as well as complex concepts. Ask them to develop original models. Models that cannot be shown in the classroom are often available on the Internet.
- **Use teams.** Students with learning problems are particularly successful when working in teams. The opportunity to discuss what they are learning keeps them actively engaged and helps them practice interpersonal skills, rehearse new learnings, and find meaning.
- **Set goals.** Success is a key factor in maintaining involvement. Set clear and realistic goals with the students (e.g., "Let's try to solve three problems this time").
- **Find out what they already know.** Take the time to assess in advance what students already know about the topic you are about to teach. Building on this prior knowledge is an effective way of helping students establish relevancy.
- **Use visuals.** We live in a visually oriented culture, and students are acclimated to continuous visual stimuli from their digital devices. Graphs, pictures, diagrams, and visual organizers are very effective learning and retention devices.
- **Go for the big picture.** The brain is a pattern seeker. Use your own or computer-generated graphics to put together the big picture, showing how concepts are connected. Discuss the patterns that emerge, and link them to what students have already learned.
- **Think and talk aloud.** When teachers think aloud, they model the steps in cognitive processing and reveal what information or skills can be used to approach and solve a problem. Talking aloud is an excellent memory enhancer, especially when students discuss open-ended questions, such as "What might have happened if . . . ?" or "What would you have done instead?"
- **Suggest mnemonic devices.** All memory tricks are valuable. Teach mnemonic devices to help students remember factual information

or steps in a procedure. Examples are acronyms (e.g., ROY G BIV for colors of the spectrum, HOMES for the Great Lakes), keywords or phrases (e.g., "Please excuse my dear Aunt Sally" for the order of solving arithmetic operations: parenthesis, exponents, multiplication, division, addition, and subtraction) and rhymes (e.g., "Divorced, beheaded, died; divorced, beheaded, survived" for the fate of King Henry VIII's six wives, in chronological order).

Use a variety of practice formats. Practice is the key to retention but can be perceived as boring when the teacher uses only one practice format. Try small dry-erase boards, computer programs, or simulations to keep practice interesting and varied. And, if students can correctly solve five problems, do we need to give them 20?

Explain the value of note taking. Writing is not only a good memory tool but also helps students organize their thoughts and focus on what is important. As mentioned earlier, students remember more of what they write than what they type. Gradually decrease the amount of information you give in an outline so that students need to provide more input.

- **Use closure strategies regularly.** Closure strategies, such as journal writing and group processing ("Tell your partner two things you learned today"), enhance retention of learning because it causes the brain to reprocess the new learning to find sense and meaning.

Strategies to Consider

TEACHING STUDENTS TO USE LEARNING STRATEGIES

Much has been learned through research regarding effective learning-strategy instruction. A well-articulated instructional approach, originally known as the Strategies Integration Model (SIM), that emerged from research conducted at the University of Kansas continues to be an effective intervention (Ellis, Deshler, Lenz, Schumaker, & Clark, 1991). Now called the Strategic Instruction Model™ (SIM), it is based on cognitive behavior modification and is one of the field's most comprehensive tools for providing strategy instruction. It can be used to teach virtually any strategic intervention (e.g., Boudah, 2014; Datchuk & Kubina, 2013; Deshler, 2015; Kennedy, Deshler, & Lloyd, 2015).

Selecting the Strategy. First, the teacher selects a strategy that is clearly linked to the tasks students need to perform at the place they need to perform them. When the strategy is matched to student needs, they perceive relevancy and tend to be motivated to learn and use the strategy. After selecting the strategy or approach to teach, the six steps of the SIM guide the actual instruction.

Step 1—Determine prior knowledge and generate interest in learning the strategy. It is important to give a pretest to determine how much students already know about using the strategy. This information provides a starting point for instruction. Younger students, for example, may have no understanding of how they learn; older students may have already encountered their learning weaknesses. Motivate students by letting them know that gains in learning can occur when the strategy is used effectively. Studies show it is important to tell students directly that learning this strategy using effort and persistence will help them achieve whatever skill is being addressed.

Use a pretest that centers on the materials and tasks that students actually encounter in class. Following the pretest, the class should discuss the results by asking questions such as

- How did we do?
- Were we able to perform the task successfully?
- What types of errors did we make? Why?
- What did we do, or think about, to help ourselves while taking the pretest?
- What difficulties did we have? How did we address those difficulties?

If students did not perform particularly well, then discuss a strategy or technique that will help them perform that task more successfully in the future.

According to the SIM model, it is important to obtain a commitment from students to learning the strategy. To accomplish this, teachers can discuss the value of the strategy and the fact that they are committed to helping the students. Teachers should point out the likelihood that success may not be immediate, but that success will come if the student perseveres and practices the strategy.

Student-teacher collaboration in use of the strategy is especially important with elementary school students. Teachers need to discuss and practice strategies with these young students frequently. The commitments can be verbal or in writing, but the idea here is to get the students involved and to make them aware that their participation in learning and in using the strategy is vital to their eventual success.

Step 2—Describe the strategy. In this step, teachers clearly define the strategy, give examples, discuss the benefits of learning the strategy, and ask students to determine various ways the strategy can be used. The teacher should also identify real-life assignments in specific classes in which students can apply the strategy and ask students if they can think of other work for which the strategy might be useful. Students should also be told the various stages involved in learning the strategy, so they know what to expect.

After this overview, the students are ready to delve more deeply into hearing about and using the strategy. Instruction becomes more specific so that each step of the strategy is described in detail and presented in such a way that students can easily remember it. Acronyms can help students remember the various steps involved. An example is the COPS strategy, which helps students detect common writing errors (Shannon & Polloway, 1993). Displaying a poster or chart about the strategy and its steps will also help memory and retention. During this phase, the class discusses how this new approach to a specific task differs from what students are currently using. For closure, conclude with a review of what has been learned.

Step 3—Model the strategy. Modeling the strategy is an essential component of strategy instruction. In this step, teachers overtly use the strategy to help students perform a relevant classroom or authentic task, talking aloud as they work so that students can observe how a person thinks and what a person does while using the strategy. For example, you could model

- Deciding which strategy to use to perform the task at hand
- Working through the task using that strategy
- Monitoring performance (i.e., Is the strategy being applied correctly, and is it helping the learner effectively complete the work?)
- Revising one's strategic approach
- Making positive self-statements

The self-talk that the teacher provides as a model can become a powerful guide for students as responsibility for using the strategy transfers to them.

ACRONYMS HELP STUDENTS REMEMBER THE STEPS IN USING A STRATEGY

COPS is the acronym for a strategic approach that helps students detect and correct common writing errors. Each letter stands for an aspect of writing that students need to check for accuracy.

C   Capitalization of appropriate letters

O   Overall appearance of paper

P   Punctuation used correctly

S   Spelling accuracy

④ **Step 4—Practice the strategy.** Practice leads to retention of learning. The more students and teachers collaborate to use the strategy, the more likely the strategy will become part of the students' strategic repertoire. Initial guided practice is designed to check for understanding and first applications.

Students should be encouraged to think aloud as they work through their practice tasks, explaining the problems they are having, the decisions they are making, or the physical actions they are taking. These student "think-alouds" should increasingly reveal the specific strategy being used to help them complete the task successfully. Initially, the think-alouds should be part of teacher-directed instruction. Later, the students benefit greatly from practicing in small groups, where they listen and help each other understand the task, why the strategy might be useful in completing the task, and how to apply the strategy to the task. Eventually, the practice sessions become self-mediated as students work independently to complete tasks while using the strategy.

As practice continues, the level of difficulty of the materials being used should gradually increase. In the beginning, students practice using the strategy with materials that are at or slightly below their comfort level, so they do not become frustrated by overly difficult content. The materials must be well matched to the strategy so that students can readily understand the strategy's value. As students become more proficient in using the strategy, teachers introduce materials that are more difficult.

⑤ **Step 5—Provide feedback.** The feedback that teachers give students on their use of the strategy is a critical component of the SIM model. It helps students learn how to use a strategy effectively and how to change what they are doing when a particular approach is unsuccessful. It is also important for students to reflect on their approach to and completion of the task and to self-correct when necessary. What aspects of the task did they complete well? What aspects were hard? Did any problems arise, and what did they do to solve the problems? What might they do differently the next time they have to complete a similar task?

⑥ **Step 6—Promote application to other tasks (generalization).** The value of using learning strategies increases greatly when students are able to apply the strategy in new situations. It may not become obvious to many students that the strategy they have been learning and practicing may be ideal for helping them complete a learning task in a different classroom or learning situation. This is particularly true of students with learning disabilities. Thus merely exposing the students to strategy training is not sufficient for both strategy learning and strategy utilization to occur. Guided and consistent practice in generalizing how the strategies can transfer to various settings and tasks is vital for students with learning disabilities, as are repeated reminders that strategies of learning can be used in new situations.

Therefore, teachers need to discuss with students what **transfer** is all about (Sousa, 2011) and how and when students might use the strategy in other settings. An important part of this discussion will be getting students to review the actual work that they have in other classes and discussing with students how the strategy might be useful in completing that work. Actually going through the steps of the strategy with specific work assignments can be very effective.

Students can generate their own examples of contexts in which to apply the strategy. For example, they could use the COPS strategy discussed in Step 2 for homework assignments, job applications, friendly letters, English papers, written problems in mathematics, and spelling practice. Additionally, teachers within a school may wish to coordinate among themselves to promote student use of strategies across settings so that the strategies being taught in one classroom are mentioned and supported by other teachers as well. All these approaches will promote student generalization of the strategy.

Content Enhancement Routines

In recent years, the SIM has expanded to include content enhancement routines that help teachers think deeply about their course content and to teach in ways that engage all students. All the routines promote direct, explicit instruction because it helps students who are struggling while at the same time facilitating problem-solving and critical-thinking skills for those students who are doing well. The routines cover the following four areas (SIM, 2015):

- Planning: To help teachers organize their content and present it so students can also understand the organization
- Exploring: To help teachers and students explore related topics
- Concepts: To help teachers present complex topics in a way that students gain a deep understanding and develop a shared vocabulary when talking about important information
- Performance: To help students complete their work in the classroom

Strategies to Consider

TECHNIQUES FOR BUILDING SELF-ESTEEM

The main purpose for building self-esteem in students with learning difficulties is to help them accept responsibility for their academic performance and to realize that their achievement is mainly the result of the effort they invest in a learning task. Praise for work accomplished successfully must be genuine; insincere praise can do more harm than good. The following strategies can be used to help students build their self-esteem:

- Use students' names when addressing them.
- Have conversations with *every* student.
- Have student work occasionally assessed by other audiences (students, other teachers, parents).
- Avoid making assumptions about student behavior, and separate the behavior from the person.
- Point out positive aspects of your students' work.
- Shake hands with students, especially when you greet them.

- Allow students to explore different learning options (Internet, resource works, interviews, video clips, DVDs, etc.).
- Display student work (with the student's permission).
- Give each student a responsibility in the classroom.
- Avoid criticizing a student's question.
- Provide multiple opportunities for students to be successful in your classroom, especially when giving tests. Could the students give oral presentations to tell you what they have learned?
- Help students turn failure into a positive learning experience.
- Celebrate your students' achievements, no matter how small.
- Allow students to make decisions about some aspects of class work (what kind of report to do, what color something can be, what medium to use, etc.).
- Try to get to know about the student's life outside of school (without prying).
- Provide opportunities for students to work in productive groups.
- Spend extra time with struggling students.
- Ask students about their other activities (e.g., sports, music, and drama groups).
- Encourage students to take *appropriate* risks.
- Allow students to suffer the consequences of their behavior, and avoid being overprotective.

Strategies to Consider

WORKING WITH STUDENTS IN GROUPS

Chapter 1 discusses the value of rehearsal. Group activities are effective means for students to rehearse by talking to each other about their learning. However, teachers are often concerned that students with special needs may remain passive, drift off-task, or disrupt the group process.

Research studies report that group activities, especially if they include cooperative learning strategies, are particularly effective in getting struggling students to participate in the general education classroom setting (e.g., Slavin, Lake, Chambers, Cheung, & Davis, 2009). Group work is often a more effective alternative to the more traditional assignment of having a student read the text and answer questions at the end of the chapter—a practice that special needs students find frustrating. For example, speaking in front of a small group is less intimidating than speaking in front of the entire class. The following suggest some of the many ways to implement this strategy. Remember to make appropriate adjustments for the age of the students.

- Assign Students to Heterogeneous Groups
  - Divide the class into three sections—high, middle, and low—based on their mastery of the subject matter. Assign one student from each section to a group.

- If necessary, switch students so that each group is made up of students who can benefit from each other but not so different that they are intimidated by other members of the group.
- Give the group assignment and stress the importance of working together. Students can read to each other, answer questions, discuss what they already know, or show a partner how to do something. The object is for all members of the group to accomplish the learning objective successfully.

- Use the Retelling Strategy in Each Group

  - Ask the students to read a portion of their text, either silently or whispering to their partners. When finished, allow some think time and ask them to tell their partners what they learned and what they remembered about the text.
  - If necessary, model this retelling strategy by telling aloud something you have read. Include analogies, personal anecdotes, and other imagery to embellish your retelling. Demonstrate how imagery and metaphors help in memory. This establishes a clear model for students to follow.
  - Keep moving among the groups while they are retelling, asking questions to assess their progress and to assist where needed.
  - After the students complete their retelling sessions, call on them to relate what they have read and learned. Look for opportunities to ask "What if . . . ?" questions.
  - Write the student responses on the board or overhead transparency so that all can see. Point out any differences in the responses and ask students to discuss them.

- Some Options to Consider

  - Encourage students to gather information from other sources in addition to the text, such as the Internet, pictures, and charts.
  - Within groups, give struggling students material to use that is written at an easier level.
  - Follow-up activities can include going on a field trip, watching a video, observing an experiment, or listening to a guest speaker.

Using strategies in addition to reading is especially helpful to struggling learners, whose difficulties with reading may become overly frustrating and turn them away from the learning experience.

3

Attention Disorders

Tell me and I forget. Teach me and I remember. Involve me and I learn.

—Benjamin Franklin

As brain research reveals more of how the brain learns, educators gain renewed hope in understanding problems that can arise during this complex process. Most learning requires the brain's attention (also called *focus*). Because emotions often drive attention, this activity occurs first in the brain's limbic area (Chapter 1) and requires the coordinated effort of three neural networks: *alerting, orienting,* and *executive control* (Posner, Rothbart, & Rueda, 2013). Alerting occurs first in the brainstem (Figure 3.1) and helps the brain to suppress background stimuli, inhibit ongoing activity, and focus on the alerting signal. In the central cortex and limbic areas, orienting mobilizes neural resources to turn the individual toward the signal and process the expected additional input while inhibiting the transmission of all other input. Executive control links the limbic centers with the rational areas of the cerebrum, directing the various neural processes needed to decide how to respond to the specific stimulus. Problems can arise anywhere within these three systems, and the resulting loss of attention may be accompanied by hyperactivity and impulsivity.

Let's use a simple example. Say you are taking an evening stroll, chatting with a friend, and suddenly you hear the rustling of bushes behind you. The alerting system detects the sounds, interrupts your speech, and inhibits the processing of your friend's conversation. Meanwhile, the orienting system determines the direction of the noise, turns your head to locate the source, and rapidly processes the sound information. Deciding what to do next is the job of executive control. If a frightened squirrel raises its head and runs away, your frontal lobe tells you there is no threat and to continue your walk and talk. However, if an angry dog shows itself, the executive, limbic, and other brain areas work together so you can make a quick retreat.

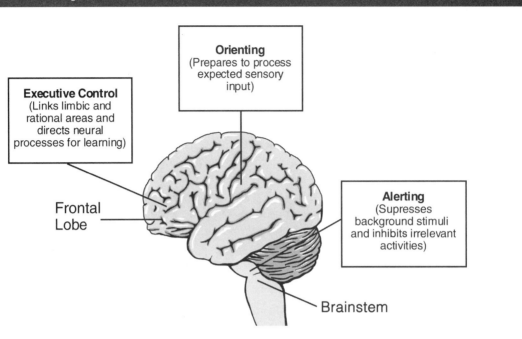

Figure 3.1 Attention for learning requires the coordinated efforts of three neural networks: alerting, orienting, and executive control.

SOME INDICATORS OF ADHD

(Not all indicators may be present in the same individual. Indicators should appear before the age of 7 and persist for at least 6 months in at least two of the child's environments.)

Inattention: Fails to attend to details; difficulty sustaining attention; does not seem to listen; fails to finish; has difficulty organizing tasks; avoids sustained effort; loses things; is distracted by extraneous stimuli; is forgetful.

Hyperactivity: Talks incessantly; leaves seat in classroom; may dash around or climb; difficulty playing quietly; fidgets with hands or feet; motor excess.

Impulsivity: Blurts out answers; difficulty waiting for turn; interrupts or intrudes.

RESEARCH FINDINGS

What Is Attention-Deficit Hyperactivity Disorder (ADHD)?

Attention-deficit hyperactivity disorder (ADHD) is a syndrome that interferes with an individual's ability to focus (inattention), regulate activity level (hyperactivity), and inhibit behavior (impulsivity). It is one of the most common learning disorders in children and adolescents. It affects an estimated five percent of youths ages 9–17. About three times more boys than girls are diagnosed. ADHD usually becomes evident in preschool or early elementary years, frequently persisting into adolescence and adulthood. Most adults outgrow the hyperactivity part of ADHD.

Although most children have some symptoms of hyperactivity, impulsivity, and inattention, there are those in whom these behaviors persist and become the rule rather than the exception. These individuals need to be assessed by health care professionals with input from parents and teachers. The diagnosis results from a thorough review of a physical examination, a variety of psychological tests, and the observable behaviors in the child's everyday settings. These behaviors are compared to a list of symptoms contained in the fifth edition of the *Diagnostic and Statistical Manual of Mental Disorders* (DSM-5, 2013). A diagnosis of ADHD requires that six or more of the symptoms for inattention or for hyperactivity-impulsivity be present for at least six months, appear before the child is seven years old, and be evident across at least two of the child's environments (e.g., at home, in school, on the playground). ADHD has been classified into three subtypes: predominantly inattentive, predominantly hyperactive-impulsive, and the combined type.

What Is the Difference Between ADD and ADHD?

Some children have no trouble sitting still or inhibiting their behavior, but they are inattentive and have great difficulty focusing. They tend to be withdrawn, polite, and shy. Because they lack the hyperactivity-impulsivity symptoms, these children are often referred to as having Attention Deficit Disorder (ADD) without hyperactivity (i.e., predominantly inattentive). Children with several symptoms of both the inattentive and hyperactive type are diagnosed as "combined type."

ADHD and ADD are categorized as different but related disorders because there are some symptomatic differences. Table 3.1 shows some of the differences in the causes as well as the behaviors observed in students diagnosed with ADHD compared with those diagnosed with ADD. The descriptions may seem simplistic, but they do help discriminate between two conditions that are very closely related. Although ADHD and ADD without hyperactivity are considered separate disorders, many of the strategies suggested in this chapter can apply to both groups of students.

Video: For information on ADHD and ADD, see:

https://www.youtube.com/watch?v=RMaCE5RT54c

ADHD and Intelligence

One persistent idea often found in lay publications is that children with ADHD might have unusually high IQs. But several studies focusing on this notion have shown that children with ADHD are no more likely to have an above average IQ than other children. In other words, intelligence in ADHD children can run the gamut from below average to gifted (e.g., Cordeiro et al., 2011). Of course, it is not uncommon for some students with ADHD to also have other learning difficulties. These additional difficulties can pose a problem when trying to obtain an accurate measure of the IQ of a student with ADHD. A meta-analysis of studies looking at this dilemma found that the influence of ADHD on IQ probably amounts to no more than two to five IQ points (Jepsen, Fagerlund, & Mortensen, 2009).

Table 3.1 Some Differences Between ADHD and ADD

	ADHD	ADD Without Hyperactivity
Cause	The size of several brain areas differ, especially in the frontal and temporal lobes. Structures in limbic area and cerebellum are smaller, likely affecting neurotransmitter flow and coordinated movement.	Cause may reside primarily in parietal lobe. The frontal lobe processes seem intact.
Primary Indicators	Persistent problems with attention, impulsivity, and hyperactivity	Low brain energy leads to difficulty with attention; seems not to listen, unorganized, forgetful in the short-term, makes careless mistakes, has problems following instructions
Decision Making	Impulsive. Race from task to task	Sluggish
Attention Seeking	Shows off. Egotistical. Relishes in being the worst. Intolerant and can become abusive. Manipulative. Needs instant gratification. Constantly frustrated.	Modest. Shy. Often socially withdrawn. Conversation is difficult. Does not need instant gratification. Becomes impatient only after repeated attempts to complete task.
Sense of Time	Time is poorly planned. Often late.	Time is poorly planned. Often late.
Assertiveness	Bossy. Often irritating.	Underassertive. Overly polite and docile.
Recognizing Boundaries	Intrusive. Occasionally rebellious.	Honors boundaries. Usually polite and obedient.
Popularity	Attracts new friends but has difficulty bonding. Reacts strongly to criticism.	Bonds but does not easily attract friends. Fearful of others' displeasure.
Associated Diagnoses	Oppositional Defiance Conduct Disorder (though rare).	Depression
Positive Attributes	These individuals really do well those things they know they can do.	Willing to pursue areas others are afraid to try. Can do well if self-employed.

What Causes ADHD?

The exact causes of ADHD remain unknown. But accumulating scientific evidence indicates that this is a neurologically based medical problem, and researchers are coming closer to understanding the causes. The biological basis of the disorder appears to lie in differences in brain structure and function as well as the presence of certain genetic abnormalities.

Brain imaging studies show that, in youth with ADHD, the brain matures in a normal pattern but is delayed, on average, by about three years (Shaw et al., 2007). This delay is most noticeable in brain regions in the frontal lobe involved in thinking, paying attention, and planning. Other studies have found that the outermost layer of the brain, the cortex, shows delayed maturation overall (Shaw et al., 2012) as well as abnormal development (Montes et al., 2013). Individuals with ADHD also show abnormal growth patterns in the corpus callosum, that brain structure important for proper communications between the two halves of the brain (Gilliam et al., 2011). These delays and abnormalities may underlie the characteristic symptoms of ADHD and may help explain how the disorder develops.

Comparing high-resolution **magnetic resonance imaging (MRI)** brain scans of children and adolescents with ADHD with scans of a non-ADHD control group, researchers found that the frontal and temporal lobes on both sides of the ADHD brains were significantly reduced in size (Figure 3.2). These cerebral areas help moderate behavior and contain some components of the attention systems. Lack of development in the frontal lobes can reduce its ability to control the excesses of emotional responses. Scans also revealed that children and adolescents with ADHD had significantly smaller total brain volumes than subjects without ADHD (Castellanos et al., 2002).

Several imaging studies have shown that ADHD brains function differently when performing the same tasks as non-ADHD brains. Although the participants with ADHD performed only slightly worse than the non-ADHD controls, they appeared to activate an entirely different network of brain areas than that seen in the non-ADHD participants. This may be because the impaired function of the executive control system in ADHD reduces the ability to recruit the same brain regions and strategies needed to accomplish cognitive tasks that non-ADHD individuals would use. Researchers speculate that the brain with ADHD compensates for this deficit by relying more on visual-spatial and motor processing than on verbal strategies (Cubillo, Halari, Smith, Taylor, & Rubia, 2012; Fassbender & Schweitzer, 2006).

Video: To see a child explain his ADHD, watch:

https://www.youtube.com/watch?v=z2hLa5kDRCA

Another contributing factor may be an imbalance in certain neurotransmitters that help the brain regulate focus and behavior. Deficiencies in the neurotransmitters dopamine and norepinephrine would affect arousal and alertness. Low serotonin is linked to impulsivity and erratic behavior (Banerjee & Nandagopal, 2015). But what could cause the imbalance? Several neuroimaging studies have shown that two structures in the limbic area (the *cordate nucleus* and the *globus pallidus*) and one in the cerebellum (the *vermis*) are smaller in adults diagnosed with ADHD than in adults without the disorder (Figure 3.3). Further, it seems that these structural differences are strongly associated with a genetic defect.

The cordate nucleus and globus pallidus appear to be involved in the dopamine network. Dopamine is a neurotransmitter that, among other things, helps control attention and coordinate movement. In the individual with ADHD, the smaller size of these two structures may decrease the effectiveness of dopamine, resulting in difficulty sustaining attention (Spencer et al., 2013). The vermis is thought to contribute to smooth motor coordination. Problems with this structure may lead to the hyperactive and impulsive behaviors seen in ADHD individuals. High-resolution brain scans of individuals with ADHD have been very helpful in revealing more about possible anatomical origins of this complex disorder. Nonetheless, it is not likely that brain scans will be used as a standard diagnostic tool for ADHD in the foreseeable future.

Behavior Problems

The behavior problems associated with ADHD are a result of difficulties with the brain's executive control system (frontal lobe). Recall that the

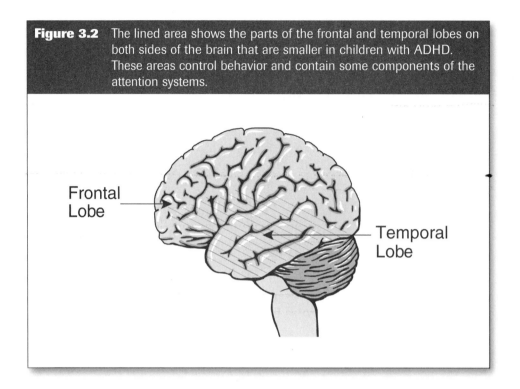

Figure 3.2 The lined area shows the parts of the frontal and temporal lobes on both sides of the brain that are smaller in children with ADHD. These areas control behavior and contain some components of the attention systems.

Frontal Lobe

Temporal Lobe

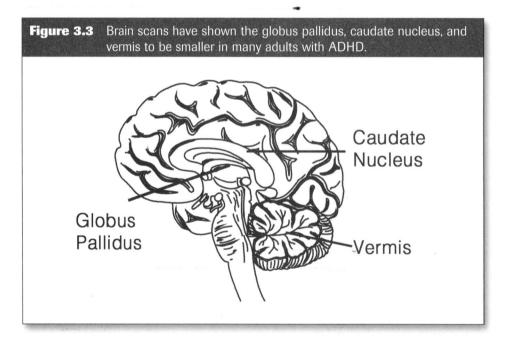

Figure 3.3 Brain scans have shown the globus pallidus, caudate nucleus, and vermis to be smaller in many adults with ADHD.

Caudate Nucleus

Globus Pallidus

Vermis

functions of this system include forethought, planning, inhibiting impulsive responses, and suppressing irrelevant stimuli. Deficits in these functions can result in behaviors that are perceived as indifferent, ill-mannered, and defiant. If these difficulties become part of a persistent pattern of behavior, the child receives frequent negative feedback, ultimately leading the child to anger or depression unless effective interventions occur. There is also evidence that motor abilities in adolescents may be affected by ADHD, leading the individual to display disruptive behavior (Van Damme, Sabbe, van West, & Simons, 2015)

Is ADHD Inherited?

Genetic predispositions for ADHD have been suspected for a long time because the disorder tends to run in families. Children with ADHD usually have at least one close relative who also has ADHD, and at least one-third of all fathers who had ADHD as a youth have children with ADHD. If one identical twin has the disorder, the other is likely to have it also. Stronger evidence of a genetic connection comes from more than 20 studies suggesting associations between ADHD and about a dozen suspected genes (Gizer, Ficks, & Waldman, 2009). One suspect cause is variations in the gene responsible for coding the neuron receptors for the key neurotransmitter dopamine (Bédard et al., 2010). As mentioned earlier, a significant function of dopamine is to help the brain focus with intent to learn. Learning about specific genes and their association with ADHD could lead to better treatments in the future.

> ADHD has probably been in the gene pool for thousands of years.

The genetic markers for ADHD behavior probably have been present in the human gene pool for thousands of years, indicating that individuals with ADHD had important roles to play in the survival of early societies. In prehistoric times, for example, individuals with ADHD behavior could have been valuable as scouts to protect a hunting party from sneak attack by predators. Success in this role required people who could rapidly scan a wide area looking for danger. Impulsiveness and quick thinking were decided advantages in a hunting society. A scout who was too deeply focused on just one interesting tree or fixated on an attractive vista would likely miss the approaching predator and get eaten. ADHD traits became a mixed blessing, however, when societies relied less on hunting and more on agriculture.

Although there are genetic predispositions for ADHD, this does not imply that parenting and schooling are unimportant. On the contrary, these are likely to be susceptible—rather than dominant—genes, so the child's environment plays a major role in determining how intensely the genetic traits emerge. How the parents and school cope with a "problem" child will shape that child's development and interaction with the world.

Other Possible Causes

Research studies have reported some other potential causes of ADHD. These include environmental factors and brain injuries.

Environmental Factors. Women who smoke cigarettes and drink alcohol during pregnancy are more likely to give birth to children with ADHD (Millichap, 2008; Nomura, Marks, & Halperin, 2010). In addition, exposure to second-hand smoke may be a contributing factor in the development of ADHD symptoms (Pagani, 2014). Preschoolers exposed to lead—still found in paint in old buildings and in plumbing fixtures—have a higher risk of developing ADHD (Kim et al., 2013).

Brain Injuries. Children who have suffered brain injuries may show behaviors similar to ADHD but not actually have the disorder. However, they may be diagnosed and treated as though they had ADHD. Research to date indicates that only a small number of children with ADHD have suffered a traumatic brain injury, and there is no substantial evidence that the injury actually *caused* the development of ADHD (Keenan, Hall, & Marshall, 2008).

Is ADHD on the Increase?

The debate continues. Although the number of children identified with the disorder has risen, it is unclear if the rise is due to greater prevalence of the disorder, to better diagnosis and identification, misdiagnosis, or all three. Certainly, heightened media interest has led to increased awareness of ADHD and the availability of effective treatments. Some scientists suggest that the changing family patterns and child-rearing problems of today may have more to do with the rise in children labeled ADHD than any biological factors. As more children are raised by total strangers, video games, and television, ADHD-like behavior may become the norm rather than the exception. Loose family structures, loss of sleep because of nighttime interactions with digital devices, lack of exercise because of too much indoor living, and addiction to electronic games are just some of the factors that could stimulate ADHD-like behaviors. One thing seems certain: parents and teachers do not cause ADHD. However, how they react to a child with ADHD symptoms may lessen or worsen the effects of the disorder.

> As more children are raised by total strangers, video games, and television, ADHD-like behavior may become the norm rather than the exception.

Is It Possible to Have ADHD-like Behavior and Not Have ADHD?

Yes. Some children diagnosed with ADHD early in life simply have the symptoms that mimic the disorder but do not have the disorder. Other factors can produce ADHD-like symptoms. Pediatric researchers are concerned about the amount of television that young children watch and the effect this viewing has on brain development. One major study showed that the more television young children watch, the more likely they are to have trouble concentrating and become restless and impulsive. The researchers noted that although ADHD has a strong genetic component, the environment also plays a key role. Hence extensive television watching may aggravate the symptoms in children who have inherited ADHD predispositions and produce ADHD-like symptoms in non-ADHD individuals (Christakis, Ebel, Rivara, & Zimmerman, 2004; Lin, Cherng, Chen, Chen, & Yang, 2015).

Some children have not learned the acceptable and unacceptable rules of behavior in certain environments, such as school. Their behavior, therefore, looks like ADHD, but these children may benefit more from being taught the appropriate behavior than from medication. Other children sometimes develop allergic reactions to certain foods that result in, among other things, hyperactive behavior. Again, these children will benefit from diet modification to control behavior. Additional factors could be stress reactions, other medical conditions, or intolerant schools.

Can Schools Inadvertently Enhance ADHD-Like Behavior?

As discussed in Chapter 1, most children are growing up in an environment that is very different from just a few years ago. But many schools haven't changed their instructional approaches to accommodate the resulting new brain. The possibility exists, therefore, that school and class-room operations can inadvertently create or enhance ADHD-like behavior in students when

- Teachers under pressure to cover curriculum move too fast (even with the realization that some students need more time)
- The main mode of instruction is teacher talk (when we know that more students have visual and kinesthetic learning preferences and want to engage with technology)
- Room arrangements allow students to hide from the teacher and create mischief (the classic row-by-row formation is more conducive to isolation than collaboration)
- Discipline is arbitrary and perceived as unfair (students in secondary schools encounter six to eight teachers daily, each with a different set of rules and expectations)
- There are few or no opportunities to get up and move around (too much material to cover, so students have to sit and listen)
- The classroom is too hot or too dark (studies show students achieve more in rooms that are well-lit with plenty of natural light)
- There are few opportunities for students to interact with each other (interactive learning reduces boredom and increases retention)
- The classroom emotional climate is neutral or tense (positive emotional climate enhances learning)

Modifying the preceding situations can often change ADHD-like behavior into more positive student participation and academic success. Please do not misinterpret my comments here. I firmly believe that children who have been correctly diagnosed with ADHD should get the appropriate treatments and therapies they need, including medication. All I am suggesting is that parents, teachers, and clinicians first examine whether other possible causes of ADHD-like behavior are at work before we resort to a clinical diagnosis of a lifelong neurological disorder. See the survey at the end of this chapter in "Strategies to Consider" on how to avoid promoting ADHD-like behavior.

The Future of ADHD Research and Treatment

Research

Additional studies will need to be conducted to differentiate individuals with true ADHD from those whose symptoms mimic the disorder. Although brain-imaging studies have documented both structural and functional abnormalities in the frontal lobe and other cerebral areas, imaging methods are not yet ready to be used as diagnostic methods. The same is true of testing for the genetic variants associated with ADHD. We can expect genetic studies to yield more information on how molecular changes in the brain lead to ADHD symptoms. Both brain imaging and genetic exploration provide insights into the causes and pathology of ADHD, but more work is needed before they can be considered diagnostically useful. In the meantime, parents and clinicians will need to rely on observational evidence. Emerging knowledge about the cause and manifestations of

ADHD should lead to an improved understanding of the brain mechanisms underlying the disorder, which should improve diagnostic and treatment strategies.

Treatment

Medications. Stimulants continue to be the most common form of treatment for ADHD. It may seem odd to give stimulants to a child with hyperactivity. However, these medications increase dopamine levels in the brain and arouse circuits that support focused and attentive behavior. They may also improve motor coordination. However, they do have side effects that include sleep problems, decreased appetite, and irritability. These effects may decrease or disappear over time or with a lower dosage.

Officially, these stimulant medications are considered safe when taken as directed by a physician. Yet, despite decades of use, concerns still linger about the *long-term* effects of stimulant drugs, such as methylphenidate (brand names: Concerta, Ritalin) and combinations of dextroamphetamine and amphetamine (brand name: Adderall). Can long-term use cause tics, delay growth, and kindle drug abuse? Longitudinal studies of long-term use of stimulant drugs used to treat ADHD show that in some children tics are possible and that slight delays in growth are evident but not significant (Swanson et al., 2006). Drug abuse actually appears less likely if the medication is taken under a physician's supervision. However, taking these stimulants in larger dosages than prescribed can lead to a rapid rise of dopamine in the brain, setting the stage for addiction. These results are not conclusive, so clinicians should continue to monitor children using stimulant medications for extended periods.

Of greater concern is the growing number of adolescents who abuse these stimulants, hoping to boost their study performance and improve their grades. Although the medications do promote wakefulness, studies have not shown that they enhance cognitive performance when taken by people who do not actually have ADHD. On the contrary, current research evidence is that students who abuse the stimulants end up with lower grades in high school and college than students who do not (National Institute on Drug Abuse, 2014).

Nonstimulant medications seem to be effective with some patients. Atomoxetine (brand name: Strattera), for example, targets norepinephrine, the other neurotransmitter believed involved in ADHD. This medication has come under increased scrutiny because there have been reports that children and teenagers taking it are more likely to have suicidal thoughts than those who do not (Food and Drug Administration, 2014). Children taking this medication should be closely monitored for unusual changes in behavior.

Psychotherapy/Behavioral Therapy. This approach aims to help children with ADHD change their behavior. It can involve helping them organize their tasks, complete homework assignments, and deal with emotionally difficult situations. Other goals are helping children monitor their own behavior, thinking before acting, and controlling anger. Learning social skills, such as asking for help, sharing toys, responding appropriately to others, and waiting their turn, are also desired goals of psychotherapy. Research studies have shown that behavioral therapies can be effective in moderating the adverse behaviors of ADHD. Studies show improvement in attention, school attendance, and family and teacher relationships after such therapy (e.g., Antshel, Faraone, & Gordon, 2014).

Parents are often included in the therapy sessions, especially when the child with ADHD displays antisocial and moody behaviors that disrupt family living (e.g., Waxmonsky et al., 2013). Parents can give positive feedback when the child behaves properly, help the child divide larger tasks into smaller ones, and control stress. Sessions with only the parents that focus on behavioral training are also a successful tool (Gerdes, Haack, & Schneider, 2012; Loren et al., 2015). It may also be appropriate for other members of the family who are in frequent contact with the child with ADHD to be part of the therapy sessions. Support groups that meet regularly can also be helpful in sharing exasperations and accomplishments, exchanging information, and talking with experts.

Among the most informative of research reports on behavioral therapy was a meta-analysis of 174 studies relating to the effectiveness of this approach (Fabiano et al., 2009). The researchers found that the treatments fell into three broad categories:

- Parent programs—these included teaching parents strategies for helping their children with ADHD succeed, such as praising their child when they catch them doing the right thing.
- Teacher programs—these offered teachers behavioral strategies for the classroom, such as giving instructions one step at a time and giving children daily report cards on how well they met desired behavioral goals.
- Therapeutic recreational programs—in these programs, children with ADHD interact with each other at summer camps and similar venues where they can participate in crafts, sports, and traditional camp activities. These interventions last longer and often include social skills training.

Effect sizes were very impressive, ranging from 0.70 for pre-post studies to a remarkable 3.78 for single-subject studies. Clearly, behavioral treatments for ADHD can be effective when properly implemented by trained personnel. Because of the success of the behavioral therapy approach, an increasing number of pediatricians are suggesting this approach for treatment before considering medication, especially with young children.

Assistive technology. A wide range of items can be used to assist students with ADHD, such as pencil grips to help them hold pencils, highlighters for marking main ideas in a reading assignment, simple timers to maintain focus, and graphic organizers or organize content and pick out essential information. More advanced technologies include clickers to record student answers, tablets, and text to speech programs.

WHAT EDUCATORS NEED TO CONSIDER

Teachers should pinpoint areas in which each student's difficulties occur. Otherwise, valuable intervention resources may be spent where they are not effective. For example, one student with ADHD may have difficulty starting a task because the directions are not clear, while another may understand the directions but may have difficulty getting organized to begin a task. These two students need different types of interventions. The research is very clear: the sooner educational interventions begin, the better. They should be started when educational performance is affected and problems persist.

Teachers of students with ADHD should be positive, upbeat, and highly organized problem solvers. Unpredictability is a classroom constant, but teachers who use sincere praise and who are willing to put in extra effort can experience success with students who have ADHD. After all, these students want to succeed. Teachers and administrators should be constantly on the alert for school structures and classroom strategies that can unwittingly provoke any student to display ADHD-like behavior. Classrooms where students sit passively and listen mainly to teacher talk are prime breeding grounds for inattention and off-task activities.

Strategies to Consider

AVOIDING INSTRUCTIONAL STRATEGIES THAT LEAD TO SCHOOL-CREATED ADHD-LIKE BEHAVIOR

Use this survey to help decide if you need to alter some of your classroom strategies.

Directions: Complete the profile below to determine whether some of your classroom or school structures can inadvertently create ADHD-like behavior in students. On a scale of 1 (lowest) to 5 (highest), circle the number that indicates the degree to which your teaching/school does the following. Connect the circles to see a profile.

1. I/We move quickly during instruction because I/we have a lot of curriculum to cover.	1	②	3	4	5
2. I/We use lecture as the main method of instruction.	①	2	3	4	5
3. I/We have classrooms arranged so it is possible for some students to be hidden from the teacher.	①	2	3	4	5
4. Each teacher determines the rules of behavior for each classroom.	1	2	③	4	5
5. I/We tend to keep students in their seats during lessons to avoid opportunities for behavior problems.	1	2	3	4	⑤
6. I/We usually turn down the lights when using the overhead projector or other visual aid.	①	2	3	4	5
7. I/We use the textbook as the main focus of instruction and classroom activity.	1	2	3	4	⑤
8. Copying information from the board is one of the main methods I/we use to give students information.	①	2	3	4	5
9. I/We tend to give more time to presenting information than to concern over students' emotional needs.	1	②	3	4	5

Scoring. If most of the circles are in the 3–5 range, there is a reasonable probability that some students who do not have true ADHD could be displaying ADHD-like behaviors. Changes in school operations and teacher behaviors that move those responses in the 3–5 range toward the 1–2 range are likely to decrease the incidence of ADHD-like behavior in students. Here's why:

1. <u>Moving too quickly can lose some students who are deep processors.</u> They want to spend more time playing with a concept before going on to the next. If the teacher does not allow time for processing, these students may nonetheless stay with the first idea and will be off task or become defiant about moving on. Slowing down and allowing processing time will lead to more retention of learning.

2. Fewer of today's students learn best by listening. They have been raised in a culture that emphasizes rapidly changing visual images and technology that requires their active participation. Too much teacher talk will drive some students to create visual representations of their own (doodling), and thus they will appear off task. <u>Using a multisensory approach and keeping students actively involved</u> is more likely to keep more students focused.

3. When some students are hidden from the teacher's sight, they can resort to off-task behavior or get into mischief, especially if there are no chances for student participation in the lesson. Classroom <u>seating arrangements should ensure that every student can be seen</u> by the teacher.

4. When teachers determine the rules of behavior in each classroom, chances are rules change from one teacher to the next (elementary) or from classroom to classroom (secondary). Students then perceive the application and enforcement of discipline as arbitrary, which can result in defiance. Schools with low disciplinary problems are generally those with <u>a few clear rules that all teachers enforce.</u>

5. Brain research shows that movement increases blood flow to the brain and opens neural pathways that retrieve memories. More students today <u>need movement to focus.</u> Keeping them in their seats for long periods of time may encourage some students to fidget, squirm, or get up on their own, typical signs of ADHD-like behavior.

6. Many secondary students come to school with less sleep than they need. Low lights will cause them to get drowsy and thus appear inattentive. How many sleep-deprived teachers might nod off under the same circumstances? Would that mean that the teachers have ADHD? Keep the lights on!

7. Textbooks are helpful instructional tools, but they are rarely novel. When texts are the main focus of instruction, students drift and resort to off-task behaviors. Using technology to access a variety of information sources, including the textbook, is far more interesting.

8. Many of today's students see the copying of information from a board as boring busywork. Discussing the information in groups with "What if . . . ?" scenarios is far more intriguing, promotes critical thinking, and will less likely lead to off-task behavior.

9. More students are coming to school hoping to get their emotional needs met, mainly because this is not happening at home. Educators must recognize the importance of maintaining a purposeful, positive emotional climate in schools and classrooms. Brain research clearly shows that survival ("Am I safe here?") and emotional needs ("Am I wanted here?") must be met before we can expect students to focus on the curriculum.

Strategies to Consider

STRATEGIES FOR WORKING WITH STUDENTS WITH ADHD/ADD

- Provide the student with a structured, predictable, and welcoming environment. As part of this environment,
  - Display rules and make sure students understand them
  - Post daily schedules and assignments in a clear manner
  - Call attention to any schedule changes
  - Set specific times for specific tasks
  - Design a quiet workspace that students can use on request
  - Seat problem students near positive peer models
  - Plan academic subjects for the morning hours
  - Provide regularly scheduled and frequent breaks during which students can stretch
  - Use attention-getting devices, such as secret signals, color codes
  - Do a countdown for the last several minutes of an activity
  - If a student starts getting disruptive, ask the student to read or answer a question
  - Sincerely praise students for constructive things they have done during the day
  - Shift the focus away from competition to contribution, enjoyment, and satisfaction
  - Contact parents to report good news and build a supportive relationship

- Modify the curriculum. Students with ADHD/ADD (like all students) can often benefit from the notion that less is more. If a student can demonstrate proficiency after 5 problems, then don't assign 10 or 20. Curriculum modification can also include the following:
  - Mixing activities of high and low interest
  - Avoiding more than 20 minutes of seat work or inactivity
  - Providing computerized learning materials
  - Simplifying and increasing visual presentations

o Teaching organization and study skills

o Using memory strategies, such as mnemonic devices

o Using visual references for auditory instruction

o Giving students simple decisions to make during the day to build this skill

o Explaining your decision to students and having them explain theirs to you

o Writing tests with easier questions dispersed throughout to keep motivation high

Strategies to Consider

GETTING, FOCUSING, AND MAINTAINING ATTENTION

The greatest challenges for the teacher of ADHD/ADD students are to get their attention, focus it toward a learning objective, and maintain that attention during the learning episode. The following are some suggested activities for each of these steps.

Getting Student Attention

- Start a lesson with enthusiasm, excitement, and an interesting question or problem.
- Use auditory signals, such as a bell, beeper, or timer, or play a bar of music on the piano.
- Use visual signals, such as raising your hand or flashing the room lights to indicate the time for silence; or say, "Everybody . . . ready."
- Use color, such as colored markers on whiteboard or on overhead transparencies or video screens. Colored paper can be used to highlight key words, steps, or patterns.
- If using a video screen, project an unfamiliar object on it to get attention.
- Use eye contact. Students should face you when you are speaking to them, especially when you are giving instructions.
- Use humor and storytelling. Add some mystery to your story and ask students to guess the ending, either orally or in writing. Consider using props or appropriate technology to stimulate and maintain interest.

Focusing Student Attention

- Use the interactive whiteboard frequently when giving direct instruction. You can write in color, project objects on it for interest, frame important points, and cover up irrelevant information. Be sure to remove any distracting material from the screen to avoid confusion. Use a stick or laser pointer to draw attention to the material on which you want students to focus.

- Use multisensory strategies during your presentation. Maintain your visibility and make sure you can be heard by all students. Incorporate demonstrations, technology, and hands-on activities whenever possible.
- Be aware of competing sounds in your environment, such as noisy ventilators or outside traffic, and try to limit their distraction.
- Use illustrations and encourage students to draw as much as possible. The drawings do not have to be accurate or sophisticated, just clear enough to understand a concept. Have fun with this. Even silly illustrations can help students remember a series of events, key points, steps in problem solving, or abstract information.
- Position all students so they can easily see the board or screen. Encourage them to readjust their seating whenever their view is blocked.

Maintaining Student Attention

- Present with a lively, brisk pace, keep moving to maintain your visibility, and avoid lag time. Use pictures, diagrams, manipulatives, gestures, video clips, and high-interest materials.
- Talk less. Talk is a powerful memory device, so give students opportunities to converse with each other about what they are learning. Maintain accountability by asking them to share with you what they learned from their partner.
- Ask higher order thinking questions that are open-ended, require reasoning, and stimulate critical thinking and discussion.
- Vary the way you call on students so they cannot predict who is next. Encourage them to share answers orally with a partner or a group or write them down in a journal.
- Use the proper structure of cooperative learning groups. ADHD students do not usually function well without the clearly defined structures and expectations that cooperative learning techniques provide.
- Allow students to use individual chalk or dry-erase boards, which are motivating and effective in checking for understanding and determining who needs extra help and practice.
- Use motivating computer programs that provide frequent feedback and self-correction for skill building and practice.

Strategies to Consider

STRATEGIES FOR SPECIFIC ADHD/ADD BEHAVIORS

For Excessive Activity	For Inability to Wait	For Failure to Sustain Attention to Routine Tasks and Activities	For Noncompliance and Failure to Complete Tasks	For Difficulty at the Beginning of Tasks	For Completing Assignments on Time
Channel activity into acceptable avenues. For example, rather than attempting to reduce a student's activity, encourage directed movement in classrooms when this is not disruptive. Allow standing during seat work, especially at the end of a task.	Give the student substitute verbal or motor responses to make while waiting. This might include teaching the student how to continue on easier parts of the task (or a substitute task) while waiting for the teacher's help.	Decrease the length of the task. There are many ways to do this, including breaking one task into smaller parts to be completed at different times or just assigning fewer tasks or problems.	Make sure the tasks fit within the student's learning abilities and preferred response style. Students are more likely to complete tasks when they are allowed to respond in various ways, such as with a computer, on a tablet, on tape. Make sure that disorganization is not the reason the student is failing to complete tasks.	Increase the structure of the tasks and highlight the important parts. This includes encouraging more note taking, giving directions orally as well as in writing, clearly stating the standards for acceptable work, and pointing out how tasks are structured (e.g., topic sentences, headers, table of contents, index).	Increase the student's use of lists and assignment organizers (notebook, folders, digital devices). Write assignments on the board and make sure that the student has copied them.

(Continued)

(Continued)

For Excessive Activity	For Inability to Wait	For Failure to Sustain Attention to Routine Tasks and Activities	For Noncompliance and Failure to Complete Tasks	For Difficulty at the Beginning of Tasks	For Completing Assignments on Time
Use activity as a reward. For example, allow the student to run an errand, prepare technology for student use, or organize the teacher's desk.	When possible, permit daydreaming or planning while the student waits. For example, the student might be allowed to doodle or play with some objects while waiting. Another option is to show the student how to underline or record relevant information.	Make tasks interesting. For example, allow students to work with partners or in small groups, use a tablet or other device, or alternate high- and low-interest activities. Novelty can often sustain interest. Make a game out of checking students' work, and use games to help in learning rote material.	Find ways to increase the choice and specific interest of tasks for the student. Consider allowing the student with ADHD a selection of specific tasks, topics, and activities. Determine which activities the student prefers, and use these as incentives.	Ask the student to write down the steps needed to get the task started, and have the student review the steps orally.	Establish routines for placing and retrieving commonly used objects, such as books, assignments, and clothes. Pocket folders are helpful because new work can be placed on one side and completed work on the other. Parents can be encouraged to establish places for certain things (e.g., books, homework) at home. Students can be encouraged to organize their desk or locker with labels and places for certain items.
Use active responses in instruction. Teaching activities that encourage active responses (e.g., moving, talking, organizing, writing in a diary, painting, or working at the board) are helpful to ADHD students.	When inability to wait becomes impatience, encourage leadership. Do not assume that impulsive statements or behavior are aggressive in intent. Cue the student when an upcoming task will be difficult and extra control will be needed.				Teach students that, on leaving one place for another, they will ask themselves, "Do I have everything I need?"

Strategies to Consider

TIPS FOR PARENTS OF CHILDREN WITH ADHD/ADD

Parents of children with ADHD/ADD often feel overwhelmed by the challenges associated with these disorders. The following tips, suggested by the Center for Parent Information and Resources, may help parents in dealing with their children. Teachers and parents should work together to develop a consistent plan for responding to the child's needs.

- Learn about ADHD/ADD. The more you know, the more you can help yourself and your child.
- Praise your child when he or she does well. Help your child identify strengths and talents. Encourage your child's special interests and enroll your child in extracurricular activities.
- Be clear, consistent, and positive, even when disciplining the child. Set rules that tell your child what to do, not just what not to do. Be clear about what will happen if the rules are not followed. Praise good behavior and reward it.
- Create opportunities for success, no matter how large or small.
- Learn about strategies for managing your child's behavior. These include the techniques of charting, having a reward program, ignoring behaviors, natural consequences, logical consequences, and time-out. Using these strategies will lead to more positive behaviors and cut down on problem behaviors.
- Talk with your doctor about whether medication will help your child, getting second opinions if your questions go unanswered. Pay attention to your child's mental health—and your own! Be open to counseling. It can help you deal with the challenges of raising a child with ADHD/ADD. It can also help your child deal with frustration, have greater self-esteem, and learn more about social skills.
- Talk to other parents whose children have ADHD/ADD and share practical advice and emotional support. Look at the resources and organizations at the end of this book for more help.
- Meet with school officials to develop an individual educational plan (IEP) to address your child's needs. Both you and your child's teacher should get a written copy of this plan.
- Keep in touch with your child's teacher to find out how your child is doing in school. Offer support. Tell the teacher how your child is doing at home. Remember that as researchers continue their investigations, we may gain new knowledge that could change some of our current understandings and beliefs about the nature of ADHD and ADD, resulting in the development of alternative treatments. Keep abreast of what is happening in this field through some of the organizations listed in the "Resources" section of this book.

4

Speech Difficulties

We speak not only to tell other people what we think, but to tell our-selves what we think. Speech is a part of thought.

—Oliver Sacks, *Seeing Voices*

Human beings have developed an elaborate and complex means of spoken communication that many say is largely responsible for our place as the dominant species on this planet. Spoken language is truly a marvelous accomplishment for many reasons. At the very least, it gives form to our memories and words to express our thoughts. The human voice can pronounce about 200 vowel and 600 consonant sounds that allow it to speak any of the nearly 7,000 languages (not counting dialects) that exist today. With practice, the voice becomes so fine-tuned that it makes only about one sound error per million sounds and one word error per million words (Pinker, 1994).

Before the advent of imaging technologies, we explained how the brain produced spoken language on the basis of evidence from injured brains. In 1861, French surgeon Paul Broca noted that damage to the left frontal lobe induced language difficulties generally known as aphasia, wherein patients muttered sounds or lost speech completely. Broca's area is located just behind the left temple (Figure 4.1). A person with damage to Broca's area, for example, could understand language but could not speak fluently. In 1871, German neurologist Carl Wernicke described a different type of aphasia—one in which patients could not make sense of words they spoke or heard. These patients had damage in the left temporal lobe. Wernicke's area is situated above the left ear. Those with damage to Wernicke's area could speak fluently, but what they said was quite meaningless. The inferences, then, were that Broca's area stored vocabulary, grammar, and probably syntax of one's native language, while Wernicke's area was the site of native-language sense and meaning.

Recent research, using scanners, indicates that spoken-language production is a far more complex process than previously thought. When preparing to produce a spoken sentence, the brain not only uses Broca's and Wernicke's areas but also calls on several other neural networks scattered throughout the left hemisphere. Nouns are processed through one set of patterns; verbs are processed by separate neural networks. The more complex the sentence structure, the more areas that are activated, including some in the right hemisphere.

LEARNING SPOKEN LANGUAGE

Is Language Prewired in the Brain?

In the 1950s, MIT linguist Noam Chomsky theorized that young children could not possibly learn the rules of language grammar and syntax merely by imitating adults. He proposed that nature endowed humans with the ability to acquire their native language by attaching what they hear to a language template that is prewired in the brain by birth—just as baby tigers are prewired to learn how to hunt. Other linguists now suggest that language acquisition may be the result of a genetic predisposition coupled with the baby brain's incredible ability to sort through the enormous amount of information it takes in—including language—and to identify regular sound patterns from background noise. Additional studies in recent years now support the notion that the ability to acquire spoken language is encoded in our genes (e.g., Clowry, 2014; Graham & Fisher, 2013).

> The human brain is prewired at birth to learn all the languages on this planet.

Figure 4.1 Broca's area and Wernicke's area, located in the left hemisphere in most individuals, are the two major language-processing centers of the brain. The visual cortex, across the back of both hemispheres, processes visual stimuli.

Visual Cortex

Broca's Area

Wernicke's Area

Learning Sounds Called Phonemes

The neurons in a baby's brain are capable of responding to the sounds of all the languages on this planet. At birth (some say even before) babies respond to the **prosody**—the rhythm, cadence, and pitch—of their mother's voice, not the words. Spoken language consists of minimal units of sound, called **phonemes**, which combine to form syllables. For example, in English, the consonant sound "p" and the vowel sound "o" are both phonemes that combine to form the syllable *po-* as in *potato*.

Each language has its own set of phonemes. The total number of basic phonemes used by all the world's languages is hard to measure because it is difficult to compare sounds across languages. Nonetheless, guesses by competent linguists range from 300 to 600. Although the infant's brain can perceive this entire range of phonemes, only those that are repeated get attention, and the neurons reacting to the unique sound patterns get continually stimulated and reinforced.

By the age of 10–12 months, the toddler's brain has begun to distinguish and remember phonemes of the native language and to ignore nonnative sounds. One study showed that at the age of 6 months, American and Japanese babies are equally good at discriminating between the "l" and "r" sounds, even though Japanese has no "l" sound. However, by age 10 months, Japanese babies have a tougher time making the distinction, while American babies have become much better at it (Cheour et al., 1998). During this and subsequent periods of growth, the ability to distinguish native sounds improves, while the ability to distinguish nonnative speech sounds diminishes. Meanwhile, pruning begins, and by one year of age, neural networks are focusing on the sounds of the language being spoken in the infant's environment.

From Phonemes to Words

The next step for the brain is to detect words from the stream of sounds it is processing. This is not an easy task because people don't pause between words when speaking. Yet the brain has to recognize differences between, say, *green house* and *greenhouse*. Remarkably, babies begin to distinguish word boundaries by the age of 8 months even though they don't know what the words mean (Singh, 2008; Willits, Seidenberg, & Saffran, 2014). They begin to acquire new vocabulary words at the rate of about 10 a day. At the same time, memory and Wernicke's areas are becoming fully functional so the child can now attach meaning to words. Of course, learning words is one skill; putting them together to make sense is a different, more complex skill.

Learning Grammar

Most researchers today accept linguist Noam Chomsky's (1965) theory of Universal Grammar; that is, all languages contain some common rules that dictate how sentences are constructed, and that the brain has preprogrammed circuits that respond to these rules. Modern linguists think that the brain may also be responding to statistical regularities heard in the flow of the native tongue. It soon discerns that some words describe objects while others describe actions. Toddlers detect patterns of word order—person, action, objects—so they can soon say, "Me want cookie." Other grammar features emerge, such as tense, and by the age of three years, over 90 percent of sentences uttered are grammatically correct. Errors are seldom random but usually result from following perceived rules of grammar. If "I batted the ball" makes sense, why shouldn't "I holded the bat?" Regrettably, the toddler has yet to learn that nearly 200 of the most commonly used verbs in English are irregularly conjugated.

> The more that children are exposed to spoken language in the early years, the more quickly they can discriminate between phonemes, recognize word boundaries, and detect syntactic patterns.

During the following years, practice in speaking and adult correction help the child decode some of the mysteries of grammar's irregularities, and a sophisticated language system emerges from what once was babble. No one knows how much grammar a child learns just by listening, or how much is prewired. What is certain is that the more children are exposed to spoken language in the early years, the more quickly they can discriminate between phonemes, recognize word boundaries, and detect syntactic patterns.

Effects of Watching Television

Just letting the toddler sit in front of a television does not seem to accomplish the goal of phoneme discrimination, because the child's brain needs live human interaction to attach meaning to the words. Moreover, television talk is not the slow, expressive speech that parents use with their infants, which infants like and want to hear. Although toddlers may be attracted to the rapidly changing sounds and images on a television, little or no language development is in progress. Further evidence indicates that prolonged television watching can impair the growth of young brains (Lin, Cherng, Chen, Chen, & Yang, 2015). Researchers point out that the visual system is not stimulated properly by television viewing in that there is no pupil dilation and the eyes stare at the screen and do not move from one point to the next—a skill critical for reading. The images change every 5–6 seconds (even faster during commercials) robbing the higher thought areas of the brain (in the frontal lobe) of time to process the images. The wavelengths of light produced by the television screen are very limited compared to the full spectrum of light we receive when viewing objects outdoors. Furthermore, television reduces the opportunities for the child's brain to create internal images.

Both the American Academy of Pediatrics and the National Literacy Trust in the United Kingdom recommend that parents and caregivers eliminate or strictly limit the exposure of television to toddlers under the age of two in favor of more face-to-face conversation and activities that enhance language development.

Speech and Language Patterns by Age

The human brain is programmed to learn spoken language during the child's earliest years. As language learning progresses, certain behavior patterns emerge over time, forming the building blocks of continued language growth and development. Early language development occurs in context with other skills, such as cognition (thinking, understanding, and problem solving), gross and fine motor coordination (stacking, throwing, catching, and jumping), social interaction (peer contact and group play), and taking care of one's self (washing, eating, and dressing).

The National Institute on Deafness and Other Communication Disorders (NIDCD, 2010a) has compiled from the research a list of speech and language behaviors that emerge for most children from birth through the age of six. Each child is different, but the list is a good indicator of speech and language progress for most children.

Birth to 3 Months

- Reacts to loud sounds
- Calms down or smiles when spoken to
- Recognizes your voice and calms down if crying
- When feeding, starts or stops sucking in response to sound
- Coos and makes pleasure sounds
- Has a special way of crying for different needs
- Smiles when he or she sees you

Between 4 and 6 Months

- Follows sounds with his or her eyes
- Responds to changes in the tone of your voice
- Notices toys that make sounds
- Pays attention to music
- Babbles in a speech-like way and uses many different sounds, including sounds that begin with *p, b,* and *m*
- Laughs
- Babbles when excited or unhappy
- Makes gurgling sounds when alone or playing with you

Between 7 Months and 1 Year

- Enjoys playing peek-a-boo and pat-a-cake
- Turns and looks in the direction of sounds
- Listens when spoken to
- Understands words for common items such as "cup," "shoe," or "juice"
- Responds to requests ("Come here")
- Babbles using long and short groups of sounds ("tata, upup, bibibi")
- Babbles to get and keep attention
- Communicates using gestures such as waving or holding up arms
- Imitates different speech sounds
- Has one or two words ("Hi", "dog", "Dada", or "Mama") by first birthday

Between 1 and 2 Years

- Knows a few parts of the body and can point to them when asked
- Follows simple commands ("Roll the ball") and understands simple questions ("Where's your shoe?")

- Enjoys simple stories, songs, and rhymes
- Points to pictures, when named, in books
- Acquires new words on a regular basis
- Uses some one- or two-word questions ("Where kitty?" or "Go bye-bye?")
- Puts two words together ("More cookie")
- Uses many different consonant sounds at the beginning of words

Between 2 and 3 Years

- Has a word for almost everything
- Uses two- or three-word phrases to talk about and ask for things
- Uses *k, g, f, t, d,* and *n* sounds
- Speaks in a way that is understood by family members and friends
- Names objects to ask for them or to direct attention to them

Between 3 and 4 Years

- Hears you when you call from another room
- Hears the television or radio at the same sound level as other family members
- Answers simple "Who?" "What?" "Where?" and "Why?" questions
- Talks about activities at daycare, preschool, or friends' homes
- Uses sentences with four or more words
- Speaks easily without repeating syllables or words

Between 4 and 5 Years

- Pays attention to a short story and answers simple questions about it
- Hears and understands most of what is said at home and in school
- Uses sentences that give many details
- Tells stories that stay on topic
- Communicates easily with other children and adults
- Says most sounds correctly except for a few (*l, s, r, v, z, ch, sh,* and *th*)
- Uses rhyming words
- Names some letters and numbers
- Uses adult grammar

Between 5 and 6 Years

- Uses sentences of six to eight words
- Has a vocabulary of about 2,000 words
- Defines objects by their use (you eat with a fork) and can tell what objects are made of
- Understands spatial relations such as "on top," "behind," "far," and "near"
- Understands time sequences (what happened first, second)
- Knows home address
- Identifies penny, nickel, and dime
- Understands common opposites such as big/little and same/different

- Counts ten objects
- Asks questions for information
- Distinguishes the left and right hands
- Uses complex sentences, for example, "Let's go to the park after we eat."
- Uses imagination to create stories

As a precaution, a child who is more than a year delayed should be examined by medical professionals for possible systemic problems, such as hearing loss. Remember that many children who have early speech and language delays eventually catch up to their developmental stage by the time they enter school.

Putting the Language Components Together

The successful use of oral language requires the brain to direct the voice box to produce sounds that follow a certain set of patterns and rules for

- Phonology—phonemes (the smallest sounds of language)
- Morphology—word formation
- Syntax—sentence formation
- Semantics—word and sentence meaning, especially idioms
- Prosody—intonation and rhythm of speech
- Pragmatics—effective use of language for different purposes, following rules of conversation, and staying on topic

Amazingly, most brains get it right. But problems can occur anywhere along the way. Some problems may just be a matter of time; that is, the brain needs more time to discern the patterns and figure out the rules. More persistent problems may be due to physiological difficulties (e.g., hearing loss), childhood trauma (physical or psychological), genetic influences, or other factors not yet understood.

PROBLEMS IN LEARNING SPOKEN LANGUAGE

The *Diagnostic and Statistical Manual of Mental Disorders-5* (DSM-5, 2013) changed the classification of communication disorders from the previous edition. Gone is specific language impairment (SLI), long considered too vague a term in light of modern research. Five disorders were established:

- *language disorder* (includes expressive language disorder and mixed receptive-expressive language disorder),
- *speech-sound disorder* (a new name for phonological disorder),
- *childhood-onset fluency disorder* (a new name for stuttering),
- *social (pragmatic) communication disorder* (a new condition for persistent difficulties in the social uses of nonverbal and verbal communication), and
- *unspecified communication disorder* (for those communication difficulties that do not fit in the other four categories).

Speech and Language Problems With Children and Adolescents

Speech and language are different. Speech is the sound that comes out of our mouths and how we form these sounds. Speech problems, such as mispronouncing words and stuttering, can be challenging but do not necessarily indicate a problem with language development. Language is a broader concept that includes all the neural structures that receive and express information to give it meaning. Problems in speech and language can be different, but it is not unusual for them to coexist.

Speech and Language Delays

Most toddlers begin to speak words around the age of 10–12 months. However, in delayed speech, children may not speak coherent words and phrases until nearly 2 years of age, and progress continues to be slow after that. About 7.5 percent of kindergarten children display significant delays in language learning (Tallal & Heim, 2015). There could be many causes for this developmental condition. Research evidence suggests that language delay can be caused by genetic defects, a situation not easily remedied by environmental interventions (Smith, Holden, Dwivedi, Dupont, & Lyons, 2015). Other potential causes include poor communication between the brain's language areas and the speech-producing physical apparatus (lips, tongue, and jaw). Hearing problems are sometimes related to speech and language delays because the child has difficulty distinguishing subtle differences in sounds and in imitating words. Certain environmental factors, such as stress and watching too much television as a toddler, *can* also cause language delay in some children.

LANGUAGE DELAY

Symptoms Around Age 1½ to 2:

- Uses only a few words during speech
- Uses only a few phrases during speech
- Speech is not coherent

Language Disorder

A broad range of problems in learning language are grouped in the category now referred to in the DSM-5 as language disorder. It describes a general condition in which a child's spoken language does not develop at the expected and acceptable rate, even though the person's sensory and cognitive systems appear normal and there is no apparent environmental problem. The disorder affects about seven percent of children entering school. Parents may first become aware of language disorder when their children fail to demonstrate the normal bursts of language development that occur around the age of 2 years. Many of these children will eventually achieve normal levels of language development during the subsequent two years. However, some will continue to display language difficulties at school age, having difficulty building vocabulary as well as difficulty acquiring written language.

Although most of the cognitive functions of children with language disorder are normal, verbal memory deficits often occur. Studies have tested the verbal memory of groups of children with and without language disorder on word recall and sentence comprehension (Lum, Ullman, & Conti-Ramsden, 2015; Marini, Gentili, Molteni, & Fabbro, 2014). Results show that children with language disorder had less functional verbal working memory capacity and greater difficulty managing their working memory abilities than their peers without language disorder. Other studies have found that young children with language disorder show deficits in visual working memory and problems with executive function behaviors (Vugs, Hendriks, Cuperus, & Verhoeven, 2014). Many children identified early in life with language disorder may eventually develop characteristics of **dyslexia** (severe reading disability).

The question is whether SLI has a biological or an environmental basis, or some combination of both. Early studies of children with language disorder, including identical twins, supported the notion of a biological basis through genetic influences and seem to point to deficits in the brain systems responsible for grammar and vocabulary processing (Bartlett et al., 2002; Choudhury & Benasich, 2003; O'Brien, Zhang, Nishimura, Tomblin, & Murray, 2003). Subsequent studies continue to find that gene variants contribute to deficits in speech and language (e.g., Graham & Fisher, 2013). Researchers have also found anomalies in brain structure in people with language disorder (Badcock, Bishop, Hardiman, Barry, & Watkins, 2012). Because of these findings, care must be taken in ascribing environmental factors or identifying a single intervention as a cure for language disorder. Because many of the children with language disorder have little or no cognitive deficit, it would seem that interventions should focus on cognitive strategies that help explain and practice the rules of grammar and syntax as well as acquire vocabulary in context.

LANGUAGE DISORDER

Symptoms:

- Complexity of speech not developing with age
- Little or no growth in vocabulary
- Consistently poor grammar with little or no improvement
- Difficulty remembering recently used words

Expressive Language Disorder

Children with this disorder understand language but have trouble expressing themselves in speech. They often have a weak vocabulary and difficulty recalling words, using the correct tense, and constructing complex sentences. Although the cause is unknown, cerebral damage, head traumas, and malnutrition, perhaps in combination with genetic influences, have been associated with the disorder. Some children may have no problem in simple expression but have difficulties retrieving and organizing words and sentences when expressing more complicated thoughts and ideas. This is more likely to occur when they are trying to define, describe, or explain information or retell an activity or event.

Some psychologists further classify individuals with this disorder into two groups. One is *developmental expressive language disorder*, which appears early in life and most likely results from genetic influences. It is more common in boys than in girls. The other group is *acquired expressive language disorder*, which is caused by specific damage to the brain, such as seizures, stroke, lesions, encephalitis, and traumatic brain injury.

Treatment usually involves language therapy that focuses on increasing the number of phrases a child can use. The phrases are presented as blocks, and the child practices building complex sentences from these blocks. Language therapy and similar treatments show an encouraging recovery rate, especially if interventions are started soon after diagnosis (Bellon-Harn, 2012).

EXPRESSIVE LANGUAGE DISORDER

Symptoms:

- Below average vocabulary skills
- Difficulty producing complex sentences and having a conversation
- Improper use of correct tenses
- Problems in recalling words

Receptive Language Disorder

Those with receptive language disorder have trouble understanding certain aspects of speech. They may not respond to their names, have difficulty following directions, or point to a bell when you say "ball." Their hearing is fine, but they cannot make sense out of certain sounds, words, or sentences they hear. Sometimes, they may appear inattentive. Because receiving and using speech are closely related, many people with receptive language disorder also have symptoms of expressive language disorder. The combined symptoms are referred to as Receptive-Expressive Language Disorder.

RECEPTIVE-EXPRESSIVE LANGUAGE DISORDER

Symptoms:

- Impairment in language comprehension
- Impairment in language expression
- Speech containing many articulation errors
- Difficulty recalling early visual or auditory memories

Language Problems With Adolescents

Problems with language are particularly troublesome for adolescents because language plays such a major role in secondary school subjects. The elementary years emphasize language development. The middle school grades begin to focus on specific subjects where mastery of language is assumed. But in high school, teachers expect students to have an increased vocabulary, more advanced sentence structure, and the ability to use different kinds of language for different situations.

Much effort goes into identifying and remediating language problems in young children. Yet less effort seems to be directed toward identifying adolescents with language problems. Such problems can lead to feelings of failure, low self-esteem, poor academic and social success, and a high dropout rate. Adolescents with language disorders can be those

- Who received no interventions in their early years
- Who initially received treatment through early intervention programs but who still have some language difficulties
- Who had normal language development but experienced a disruption because of some mental, physical, emotional, or traumatic event
- Who have some other learning disability

Working with adolescents who have language difficulties requires more direct instruction aimed at treating the identified language weakness. Consistent practice is important, but the practice should not be so repetitive as to be perceived as boring. Practice using computer programs creates interest, and success in mastering these programs can enhance self-esteem.

ADOLESCENT LANGUAGE DIFFICULTIES

Symptoms:

- Failure to understand or follow rules of conversation, such as taking turns and staying on topic
- Difficulty using different language for different needs of the learner or situation
- Difficulty requesting further information to aid understanding
- Incorrect use of grammar
- Poor or limited vocabulary
- Difficulty with instructions, especially those that are long or grammatically complex
- Extreme forgetfulness
- Difficulty understanding puns, idioms, jokes, riddles

Language and Cognitive Thought. Brain imaging and other studies have provided strong evidence that language and cognitive thought are separated in the brain. Some of these studies involved patients with Williams syndrome, a rare genetic disorder first described in 1961. Children with this disorder have difficulty with simple spatial tasks, and many have IQ scores in the 40–50 range and cannot read or write above the first-grade level. Despite these inadequacies, they develop extraordinary spoken-language skills. They amass large vocabularies, speak in complex, grammatically correct sentences, and display engaging personalities. Coincidentally, many children with Williams syndrome exhibit exceptional musical talent (Camp & Karmiloff-Smith, 2015).

Because evidence exists that language and cognitive thought are separated in the brain, we should not assume that students with language problems are not intelligent.

Stuttering (Childhood-Onset Fluency Disorder)

Stuttering (now called Childhood-Onset Fluency Disorder in the DSM-5) is a communication disorder that affects the fluency of speech. It begins during childhood and, in some cases, persists throughout life. The disorder is characterized by disruptions in the production of speech sounds. Sometimes words are repeated or preceded by interjections, and there are moments when a sound or period of silence is prolonged. Some speakers who stutter exhibit excessive physical tension in their speech or appear to be out of breath when talking. Stuttering can have a severe impact on a young person's emotional state, including fear of being caught stuttering in a social situation, worries about being bullied, and a loss of control during speech.

The exact cause of stuttering is not known. Developmental stuttering typically starts between the ages of 30 to 48 months. Numerous studies, especially those involving identical twins, strongly show that genetic factors play a significant role in the disorder (e.g., Han et al., 2014; Kang & Drayna, 2012). Many individuals who stutter inherit traits that impair their ability to string together the various muscle movements that are necessary to produce sentences fluently. Not everyone who is genetically predisposed to stuttering will develop the disorder. Environmental events can trigger stuttering. The acquisition of grammar skills appears to be another trigger for developmental stuttering. Between the ages of 2 and 5 years, children acquire many of the simpler rules of language. A child who is predisposed to stuttering may have no difficulty speaking fluently when the sentences are only two or three words long. However, the speech system may run into fluency problems when the child tries to produce longer, more complex sentences. After stuttering has begun, stress, teasing, embarrassment, and other factors often act to aggravate speech fluency.

Treatment. There is no known cure for stuttering, but many treatment approaches have proven successful. Young children who have been stuttering for only a short time have a high rate of natural recovery. However, it is not possible to determine which children will recover and which will continue stuttering. Most treatment programs for those who persistently stutter are designed to teach the speaker specific skills or behaviors that lead to improved oral communication. For example, speech-language pathologists teach speakers who stutter to control and monitor their rate of speech, to initiate words in a slightly slower and less physically tense manner, and to regulate and monitor their breathing. Over time, speakers learn to produce smooth speech at progressively faster rates, in progressively longer sentences, and in progressively more challenging situations. These therapies also help address the anxiety an individual who stutters may feel in speaking situations.

Assistive Technology. Electronic devices are available to help people who stutter control the fluency of their speech. One type of device, for instance, fits into the ear canal—like a hearing aid—and digitally replays a slightly altered version of the wearer's voice into the ear so that it sounds as if the wearer is talking in unison with another person. In some people, electronic devices help improve fluency in a relatively short period of time (NIDCD, 2010b). Smartphone applications can also be useful to help those who stutter monitor their speech. Currently marketed apps can be found at the web site of the Stuttering Foundation of America. See the "Resources" section for information. Because it is uncertain how long the effects from these technologies may last, researchers are continuing to study the long-term effectiveness of these and other emerging assistive technologies.

Speech Sound Disorder

This disorder is a broad term including any combination of difficulties in speech production that makes the child's speech barely intelligible. These difficulties are likely the result of problems in the processing of phonemes, speech-to-sound coding, and associated memory requirements. Another contributing factor is that they may have difficulty processing their own auditory feedback thereby lessening their ability to correct and improve their speech sounds (Terband, van Brenk, & van Doornik-van der Zee, 2014). It seems these children were unable to form stable phonological connections when they were acquiring their native language, probably also due to poor phonological memory. Brain imaging studies suggest that individuals with speech sound disorder recruit other cerebral mechanisms to compensate for dysfunctions in their phonological memory system (Tkach et al., 2011).

SPEECH SOUND DISORDER

Symptoms:

- Certain sounds are omitted or deleted
- One or more sounds are added to a word
- One or more sounds are substituted in a word
- Errors in rhythm, intonation, stress, and intensity
- Sounds are distorted

Some causes of speech sound disorder are known while others remain elusive. For example, some speech problems are caused by motor speech disorders, structural aberrations such as a cleft palate, or hearing impairments. There is research evidence that genetic variants play a role in the disorder (Newbury & Monaco, 2010). However, it is also possible that environmental factors, such a low parental education and lack of support for learning, contribute to the genetic predisposition, especially in the early years (Harrison & McLeod, 2010). The causes of articulation and phonological difficulties are not known.

Implications at Home

Given the evidence that the brain's ability to acquire spoken language is at its peak in the early years, parents should create a rich environment that includes lots of communication activities, such as talking, singing, and reading. However, the acquisition of speech and language can be affected by a number of factors, including muscular disorders, hearing problems, or developmental delays. These factors should be investigated if a child demonstrates significant delay or difficulty in speech.

Language Deficits and Learning a Second Language

Should students with language difficulties be expected to learn a second language? For students without language difficulties, learning another language can be a rewarding experience that can enrich their lives forever. But for students with language problems, it can be a stressful, perhaps painful, experience. Continued research on how the brain learns is revealing some insights into the neural systems responsible for language acquisition and how those systems are affected by language disorders.

Research studies suggest that students with language disorder can learn a second language, although they face the same language-learning challenges they had with their first language. The degree of competence that the child acquires in the second language will likely be determined by the limitations of the language disorder. These studies also found that children with language disorders did better at learning the second language when they were in an environment in which both languages had high support at home, such as Canadian children in a home where the parents spoke French and English (Paradis, 2010; Paradis, Genesee, & Crago, 2011).

Some studies have found that when students with language disorder are introduced to a second language, several different patterns appear (Kohnert, Windsor, & Ebert, 2009).

These patterns include (1) the continued growth of the first language but at a slower pace than is expected of monolingual children, (2) a leveling off of ability in the first language, or (3) a loss of previously attained proficiency in the first language. Factors that contribute to slower rates of growth, leveling off, or loss in the first language include low social status of the first language in the broader community, immersion in the second language in early childhood educational programs with few opportunities to use the first language outside the home, and the child's level of development in the first language when the second language is introduced (Kohnert, 2008).

> Language deficits that arise when learning a first language are very likely to arise when learning a second language.

In summary, the research to date suggests that many children with language disorder can successfully acquire a second language. However, the amount of effort required and degree of competency attained will be strongly influenced by both the intrinsic nature of the language disorder and environmental factors. Another consideration is how similar or dissimilar the second language is compared to the first language. The more similar the characteristics of the first language, such as **orthography** (how the second language is written), grammar and syntax rules, and pronunciation are to the first language, the fewer potential difficulties facing the learner with language disorder.

The Future of Speech-Language Disorders Research

Brain imaging technology continues to reveal more about the relationship between exposure to speech and language, brain development, and communication skills. Genetic studies indicate that at least some language problems are inherited. Scientists are trying to distinguish those speech and language problems that may be overcome by maturation alone from those that may require some intervention or therapy. Researchers are focusing on characterizing dialects that belong to certain ethnic and regional groups. This knowledge will help professionals distinguish a language dialect from a language disorder. The success of these efforts would spare children who are merely slower in developing or speaking a dialect the embarrassment of unnecessary labeling, while concentrating treatment on those who really need it. Another area of intense study is the effect of speech and language development on later school performance, especially learning to read.

Finally, some studies are exploring how the brain acquires a second language either during or after learning one's native language. Understanding which neural systems are involved in learning native and second languages can guide the development of instructional practices that will make it easier for all students to speak and read more than one language.

WHAT EDUCATORS NEED TO CONSIDER

Educators should consider all the following:

- Address any speech and language learning problems in young children quickly to take advantage of the brain's ability to rewire improper connections during this important period of growth
- Give more attention to the speech and language problems of adolescents
- Recognize that some speech and language delays are simply the result of delayed maturation and do not represent a permanent disorder
- Help secondary school teachers identify and address language weaknesses
- Accept the notion that students with language difficulties may still be able to learn a second language when taught with the appropriate instructional approaches
- Not assume that children with language learning problems are going to be limited in cognitive thought processes as well

Acquiring spoken language is a natural ability that comes more easily to some children than to others. Functional imaging technologies allow a more detailed study of the parts of the brain that are activated during the processing of spoken language. As research reveals more about the amazing process by which we learn to speak languages, parents and educators will be better able to help those with speech and language learning problems.

Strategies to Consider

DEVELOPING ORAL LANGUAGE SKILLS

Spoken language comes naturally to the young brain. But to master the language, the brain must first consistently *hear* it. Infants and young children hear the sounds of language and begin to make connections between words and objects or actions. At this point, speech is not necessary. The brain is acquiring vocabulary and making the associations that will give the child the words and patterns it will later need to speak the language. *Listening*, then, is the groundwork for speech and eventually for reading skills.

Research confirms that the young brain is fully ready to learn through tactile (touch) interaction by nine months of age. The neural networks for abstract thinking, including math and logic, are set to begin shortly thereafter. Thus the ability to process language, sounds, music, and rhythms is functional before the age of one year. The parent is the first teacher, and what the parent does to nurture oral language skills in the early years may well set the stage for the child's future success in school. Because some language deficits are eventually overcome, the sooner the child's language skills are engaged and practiced, the greater the likelihood that the time required to correct the deficits will be reduced. Parents, teachers, and staff in early childhood centers can enhance the development of the child's oral language skills through the following activities suggested by the Learning Disabilities Association of America.

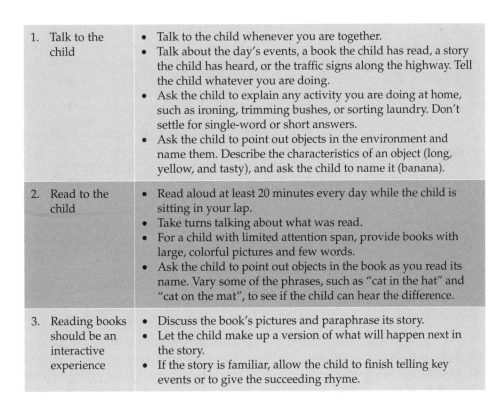

1. Talk to the child	• Talk to the child whenever you are together. • Talk about the day's events, a book the child has read, a story the child has heard, or the traffic signs along the highway. Tell the child whatever you are doing. • Ask the child to explain any activity you are doing at home, such as ironing, trimming bushes, or sorting laundry. Don't settle for single-word or short answers. • Ask the child to point out objects in the environment and name them. Describe the characteristics of an object (long, yellow, and tasty), and ask the child to name it (banana).
2. Read to the child	• Read aloud at least 20 minutes every day while the child is sitting in your lap. • Take turns talking about what was read. • For a child with limited attention span, provide books with large, colorful pictures and few words. • Ask the child to point out objects in the book as you read its name. Vary some of the phrases, such as "cat in the hat" and "cat on the mat", to see if the child can hear the difference.
3. Reading books should be an interactive experience	• Discuss the book's pictures and paraphrase its story. • Let the child make up a version of what will happen next in the story. • If the story is familiar, allow the child to finish telling key events or to give the succeeding rhyme.

(Continued)

(Continued)

		• Give the child an opportunity to correct you by purposely misreading or omitting items and events. • Have the child point out words as you read them. • Act out the story or create a puppet show. • Reinforce sequential reading by starting at the beginning of the page and showing the direction of written text, from left to right and top to bottom of page.
4.	Cultivate phonological awareness with auditory and visual word games	• Play rhyming games: If a child does not hear the rhyme, try a game with words that begin with the same sound. • Play the broken record game: Say a word very slowly and break it into syllables, then have the child repeat the word at a normal speed. • Pick a game the child enjoys, such as matching letters or copying the names of famous people. • Have the child draw pictures and make up a story while you write it down.
5.	Learning starts with a one-to-one match, followed by patterns and sequence	• Children learn to count and learn the letters of the alphabet long before they make connections to arithmetic and reading. Use activities with the child that involve counting: "Bring me one cup and two plates. Put the napkin next to one plate." Have the child repeat the instructions and match the items to the number you requested. • Have the child match letters to items in the room that begin with that letter, such as *l* for lamp and *p* for pencil. Make sure the child repeats the letter and the word aloud and walks or points to the object. • Move on to activities that involve patterns and sequence. Posters, checkers, dominoes, and playing cards are strong symbols of patterns and sequence. The child doesn't have to learn the game to be able to identify patterns and sequences in the game pieces.
6.	Provide a print-rich home and school environment	• Children with oral language difficulties are very likely to have problems learning to read. The sooner they can make connections between oral language and the written word, the better. Other media, such as videotapes, audiotapes, and the computer, can help with the effort of learning to read by making it fun and worthwhile. • Avoid television watching.

Strategies to Consider

TEACHING OTHER LANGUAGES TO STUDENTS WITH SPEECH AND LANGUAGE DISABILITIES

Research studies are identifying the problems students with language disabilities have while acquiring another language (Verhoeven, Steenge, van Weerdenburg, & van Balkom, 2011). The same problems they had learning their first language will affect their acquisition of their second language. Key among these problems are difficulties with phoneme awareness (the second language is likely to have phonemes not found in the first language), reduced capacity in the phonological working memory, and slow and inaccurate word recognition skills. Armed with this knowledge, we can design instructional approaches that address the underlying causes and increase the chances for student success. Specifically, two among successful approaches to second-language instruction for students with language disabilities are the following:

1. <u>Focusing on Phonological Awareness.</u> This approach springs from the notion that most students having difficulty in acquiring another language have phonological deficits in their native (first) language. Consequently, the following guidelines are suggested:

    o **Teach the sound system of the second language explicitly.** Present sounds in a highly structured fashion, accompanied by considerable visual, kinesthetic, and tactile practice and input. Studies using this method showed that students who were taught phonological skills in one language had improved their **phonological awareness** in the second language as well (Dixon et al., 2012).

    o **Teach the fundamentals of phonology in the student's native language before beginning instruction in the other language.** This step helps address the students' native-language deficits, which we already noted as necessary for success in acquiring the other language. Here students are taught to recognize phonemes, to read words efficiently, and to apply the sounds to the written language. They are learning the sounds and components of language structure and how these sounds and components are manipulated for meaning.

    o **Apply the fundamentals of phonology to the other language.** In this step, the sounds and components of the other language are identified. The students can then transfer the knowledge they have about phonology from their first language to the other language.

2. <u>The Course Adaptation Approach.</u> This approach adapts other language courses to conform to those principles of instruction suitable for students with learning disabilities. It can be done in two ways:

    o **Changing the instructional strategies.** Teachers in these courses reduce the syllabus to the essential components, slow the pace of instruction, reduce the vocabulary demand, provide constant review and practice, and incorporate as many multisensory activities as possible. Computer program are available on the Internet that can help with this review and practice.

    o **Design courses to address specific deficits.** Courses can be adapted to respond to the specific requests of the students who are having difficulties in their second-language classes. For example, one course might be designed for students who are strong in listening and speaking skills but weak in reading and writing, while another course might be more appropriate for students whose skills are in the reverse order. Assistive technologies can also play a big role in these course adaptions.

For either of these approaches to work effectively, students need to undergo a realistic assessment of their language learning problems. It becomes important to ensure that the learning environment is consistent with students' needs. For example, a student who is able to do oral language well should not be placed in a situation where passing grammar and translation tests is the main requirement. Nor should a student who reads and translates proficiently be placed with a teacher who values pronunciation and conversation. Reasonable accommodations need to be made.

It is perhaps unrealistic to assume that many high schools have the capacity or will to offer second-language classes solely to students with language disorder. And even if the will were there, finding teachers who are trained in the methods of instruction for these students might be more of a problem. Nonetheless, the purpose of this book is to identify what current research is telling us about the learning process and to suggest ways of providing instructional settings that translate the research into effective educational practice.

5

Reading Disabilities

Reading should not be presented to children as a chore, a duty. It should be offered as a gift.

—Kate DiCamillo, Author

Renewed emphasis in recent years on improving the basic skills of students has increased pressure to start reading instruction sooner than ever before. In many schools, reading instruction starts in kindergarten. Some neuropsychologists continue to debate whether kindergartners are developmentally ready for this challenging task. Are we creating problems for these children by trying to get them to read before their brains are ready? Because boys' brains are physiologically one or two years less mature than girls' brains at this age, are boys at greater risk of failure? To answer these questions, let's examine what researchers have discovered about how the brain learns to read and the problems that can develop. Much of what follows in this chapter is a condensed version of the in-depth discussions of reading and reading difficulties that are explained in Sousa (2014), although new information and references have been added where appropriate.

LEARNING TO READ

Is Reading a Natural Ability?

Not really. The brain's ability to acquire spoken language with amazing speed and accuracy is the result of genetic hardwiring and specialized cerebral areas that focus on this task. But there are no areas of the brain that specialize in reading. In fact, reading is probably the most difficult task we ask the young brain to undertake. Reading is a relatively new phenomenon in the development of humans. As far as we know, the genes have not incorporated reading into their coded structure, probably because reading—unlike spoken language—has not emerged over time as a survival skill.

Many cultures (but not all) do emphasize reading as an important form of communication and insist it be taught to their children. And so the struggle begins. To get that brain to read, here's what we are saying, for example, to the English-speaking child: "That language you have been speaking quite correctly for the past few years can be represented by abstract symbols called the *alphabet*. We are going to disrupt that sophisticated spoken language protocol you have already developed and ask you to reorganize it to accommodate these symbols, which, by the way, are not very reliable. There are lots of exceptions, but you'll just have to adjust." Some children—perhaps 50 percent—make this adjustment with relative ease once exposed to formal instruction. It appears, however, that for the other 50 percent, reading is a much more formidable task, and for about 20–30 percent, it definitely becomes the most difficult task they will ever undertake in their young lives.

> Reading is probably the most difficult task for the young brain to do.

Spoken Language and Reading

Before children learn to read, they acquire vocabulary by listening to others and by practicing the pronunciation and usage of new words in conversation. Adult correction and other sources help fine-tune this basic vocabulary (called the mental lexicon). Children with language impairments are at risk for problems when learning to read. One longitudinal study showed that children with language impairment in kindergarten, especially those with poor phonological awareness, were at high risk for reading disabilities in second and third grades (McNamara, Scissons, & Gutknecth, 2011). In fact, the gap in reading achievement between those students with poor phonological awareness and those with average and strong phonological awareness grew as they progressed through the grades. Another study found that how well fourth-grade students did on reading fluency and spelling fluency was a strong predictor of how successful these students would read in sixth grade (Ritchey, Silverman, Schatschneider, & Speece, 2015). These findings would indicate that it is important to assess fourth-grade students for reading and spelling fluency early in the school year and address any problems. This is particularly important because some studies indicate that up to 10 percent of native-English speakers who learned to read proficiently by third grade fall behind in reading in fourth and later grades. Fortunately, these studies also reveal that most of these students with late-emerging reading difficulties recover by seventh grade (Etmanskie, Partanen, & Siegel, 2014; Kieffer, 2010).

Because the ability to read is so strongly dependent on the word forms learned during this period, a child's beginning reading will be more successful if most of the reading material contains words the child is already using. The phoneme-grapheme connection can be made more easily and strengthened. Reading, of course, also adds new words to the child's mental lexicon. Consequently, there must be some neural connections between the systems that allow the brain to recognize spoken words and the system that recognizes written words.

Late-Talking Toddlers

If spoken language ability is closely related to success in early reading, are late-talking toddlers (ages 24–32 months) likely to be slower in developing their reading skills? Probably so. Research studies seem to indicate that late-talking toddlers show below average reading skills at age 5 (Rescorla & Turner, 2015). At age 17, late talkers continue to score lower than their peers in vocabulary, grammar, verbal memory, and reading comprehension (Rescorla, 2009). These findings suggest that slower spoken language development at an early age indicates a predisposition for slower acquisition of other language-related skills, including reading. It is uncertain whether late talking is the result of some disorder in the language processing domains, in social interaction skills, or some other factor. The good news, however, is that early intervention procedures while the late talker is age 2 appear to significantly help language skill development (e.g., Alt, Meyers, Oglivie, Nicholas, & Arizmendi, 2014).

Three Phases of Learning to Read

In simplest terms, learning to read involves connecting two cerebral capabilities that are already present in young brains: the spoken language networks with the visual recognition circuits. Trying to understand how this connection occurs in the brain has been the challenge for many researchers over the past decades. In 1985, British psychologist Uta Frith developed a three-phase model of how the brain acquires the ability to read (Frith, 1985). Much new research about how we read has emerged since Frith's model. Reading is a far more complicated process than we thought just a few years ago. Although the model's simplicity belies the complex cerebral processes that we now know are involved in learning to read, it nonetheless still provides a useful outline of what the brain experiences (Dehaene, 2009). Here is a brief summary of the three phases as shown in Figure 5.1:

- *First phase* can be considered a pictorial stage, when the children's brain photographs words and visually adjusts to the shape of the alphabet's letters.
- *Second phase* is the phonological stage, when they begin to decode the letters (graphemes) into sounds (phonemes).
- *Third phase* is the orthographic stage, when they are able to recognize words quickly and accurately.

All these phases activate several different brain circuits that, over time and with practice, eventually converge in a specialized area of the left hemisphere. This area is now referred to in the scientific literature as the **visual word form area**. Let us see how this amazing process occurs.

Decoding and Comprehension

Put very simply, successful reading involves two basic operations: *decoding* and *comprehension.* Learning to read starts with the awareness that speech is composed of individual sounds (phonemes) and a recognition that written spellings represent those sounds (called the **alphabetic principle**).

Figure 5.1 The diagram illustrates the three phases of reading. Although they generally occur in sequence, some recycling occurs when the brain needs to reassess its interpretations at any particular phase.

Of course, to be successful in acquiring the alphabetic principle, the child has to be aware of how the phonemes of spoken language can be manipulated to form new words and rhymes. The neural systems that perceive the phonemes in our language are more efficient in some children than in others. Just because some children have difficulty understanding that spoken words are composed of discrete sounds doesn't mean that they have brain damage or dysfunction. The individual differences that underlie the efficiency with which one learns to read can be seen in the acquisition of other skills, such as learning to play a musical instrument, playing a sport, or building a model.

Put very simply, reading involves two basic operations: decoding and comprehension.

Phonological and Phonemic Awareness

Phonological awareness is the recognition that oral language can be divided into smaller components, such as sentences into words, words into syllables and, ultimately, into individual phonemes. This recognition includes identifying and manipulating onsets and rimes as well as having an awareness of alliteration, rhyming, syllabication, and intonation. (Onsets are the initial consonants that change the meaning of a word; rimes are the vowel-consonant combinations that stay constant in a series. For example, in *bark*, *dark*, and *park*, the onsets are *b, d,* and *p;* the rime is *–ark*.) Being phonologically aware means having an understanding of all these levels. In children, phonological awareness usually starts with initial sounds and rhyming and a recognition that sentences can be segmented into words. Next comes segmenting words into syllables and blending syllables into words.

Phonemic awareness is a subdivision of phonological awareness and refers to the understanding that words are made up of individual sounds (phonemes) and that these sounds can be manipulated to create new words. It includes the ability to isolate a phoneme (first, middle, or last) from the rest of the word, to segment words into their component phonemes, and to delete a specific phoneme from a word. Children with phonemic awareness know that the word *cat* is made up of three phonemes, and that the words *dog* and *mad* both contain the phoneme /d/.

Phonemic awareness is different from *phonics*. Phonemic awareness involves the auditory and *oral* manipulation of sounds. A child demonstrates phonemic awareness by knowing all the sounds that make up the word *cat*. Phonics is an instructional approach that builds on the alphabetic principle and associates letters and sounds with *written symbols*. To demonstrate phonics knowledge, a child tells the teacher which *letter* is needed to change *cat* to *can*. Although phonemic awareness and phonics are closely related, they are not the same. It is possible for a child to have phonemic awareness in speech without having much experience with written letters or names. Conversely, a child may provide examples of letter-sound relationships without ever developing phonemic awareness. In fact, simply learning these letter-sound relationships during phonics instruction does not necessarily lead to phonemic awareness.

> Simply learning letter-sound relationships during phonics instruction does not necessarily lead to phonemic awareness.

Phonemic Awareness and Learning to Read

New readers must learn the alphabetic principle and recognize that words can be separated into individual phonemes, which can be reordered and blended into words. This enables learners to associate the letters with sounds in order to read and build words. Thus, phonemic awareness in kindergarten is a strong predictor of reading success that persists throughout school. Early instruction in reading, especially in letter-sound association, strengthens phonological awareness and helps in the development of the more sophisticated phonemic awareness.

Sounds to Letters (Phonemes to Graphemes)

To be able to read, the brain must memorize a set of arbitrary squiggles (the alphabet) and identify which symbols, called *graphemes*, correspond to the phonemes already stored in the mental lexicon. Many European languages use abstract letters (i.e., an alphabetic system) to represent their sounds so that the words can be spelled out in writing. The rules of spelling that govern a language are called its *orthography*. How closely a language's orthography actually represents the pronunciation of the phoneme can determine how quickly one learns to read that language correctly. Some languages, such as Spanish, Italian, and Finnish, have a very close correspondence between letters and the sounds they represent. This is known as a *shallow* orthography. Once the rules of orthography in these languages are learned, a person can usually spell a new word correctly the first time because there are so few exceptions.

English, on the other hand, has a poor correspondence between how a word is pronounced and how it is spelled. This is called a *deep* orthography. It exists because English does not have an alphabet that permits an ideal one-to-one correspondence between its phonemes and its graphemes. Consider that just when the beginning readers think they know what letter represents a phoneme sound, they discover that the same symbol can have different sounds, such as the *a*'s in *cat* and in *father*. Consider, too, how the pronunciation of the following English words differs, even though they all have the same last four letters, and in the same sequence: *bough, cough, dough, rough* and *through*. This lack of sound-to-letter correspondence makes it difficult for the young brain to recognize patterns and affects the child's confidence and ability to spell with accuracy and to read with meaning. Eventually, the brain must connect the 26 letters of the alphabet (graphemes) to the 44-plus sounds of spoken English (phonemes) that the child has been using successfully for years. But it is not easy. You may be surprised to learn that because of the complexity of English orthography, there are more than 1,100 ways to spell the sounds of the 44-plus phonemes in English.

Learning to read, therefore, starts with phoneme awareness, a recognition that written spellings represent sounds and that this combination applies phonics to the reading and spelling of words. These skills are necessary but not sufficient to learn to read the English language with meaning. The reader must acquire vocabulary and also become proficient in grasping larger units of print, such as syllable patterns, whole words, and phrases. The ultimate goal of reading is for children to become sufficiently fluent to understand what they read. This understanding includes literal comprehension as well as more sophisticated reflective understandings, such as "Why am I reading this?" and "What is the author's point?" This means, then, that beginning reading programs should include components that develop phonemic awareness, phonics, vocabulary, fluency, and comprehension.

The Neural Systems Involved in Reading

Successful decoding and comprehension in reading require the coordination of three neural networks (Figure 5.2): visual processing (orthography), phoneme recognition (phonology), and word interpretation (semantics). For example, in reading the word *dog*, the optic nerves send signals to the visual cortex, and the visual processing system puts the alphabetic symbols together. The decoding process alerts the

Figure 5.2 Successful reading requires the coordination of three neural systems: visual processing to see the word, auditory processing to hear it in the brain, and executive system processing for understanding.

Understanding:
"What does it mean?"
(Semantics)

furry animal that barks

Visual Processing:
"What do I see?"
(Orthography)

dog

Frontal Lobe

Visual Cortex

Auditory Processing:
"What do I hear?"
(Phonology)

d/aw/g

Temporal Lobe

auditory processing system that recognizes the alphabetic symbols representing the sound "d/aw/g." Other brain regions, such as Broca's and Wernicke's areas, are coordinated by the frontal lobe for comprehension. If all systems work correctly, a mental image emerges in the mind's eye of a furry animal that barks (Dehaene, 2009; Shaywitz, 2003). Problems can occur almost anywhere in the system.

The Plasticity of Neural Networks

Although Frith's model continues to be helpful, the real question is how does a brain with no innate reading center learn to accomplish this complex task? How are brain regions that are not designed to read co-opted to undertake that challenge? Psychologists and neuroscientists have wrestled with these questions for years. Now, thanks to the growing bank of thousands of brain images and other scans, as well as a large inventory of case studies, some new ideas have emerged about how the brain adjusts to the challenge of interpreting visual signals from print into sounds that have meaning.

We already mentioned that writing appeared in our culture too recently to have made alterations in our brain through the slow process of biological evolution. Yet the fact that we can read must indicate that our brain makes adjustments in its capabilities that do not require changes in the genetic code. In other words, momentous events in our culture, such as the invention of writing, can apparently cause important cerebral adaptations to occur as a result of cultural learning. These adaptions occur because of the brain's plasticity—that is, its ability to adapt to significant changes in its environment.

Recent and extensive brain imaging research indicates that reading is a complex process that requires cerebral regions to make numerous adaptations. For instance, letter analysis actually occurs in the visual word form area, while several other word processing functions are operating in parallel. Perhaps a dozen or more neural sites are involved. This updated understanding helps explain how a skilled reader can acquire the visual images of words, extract their roots, determine syntax, and ultimately find meaning in just a fraction of a second. Brain regions must be operating simultaneously and constantly exchanging information with other sites.

It is important to note that most of these areas are not exclusive to reading and may carry out other tasks. The visual word form area, however, generally responds only to written words and not to spoken words. Some areas contribute to spoken language processing while others process visual information. Signals can move in both directions between sites. Learning to read tends to be linear at the very beginning, progressing from phonemes to morphemes to graphemes, as illustrated by the three phases we discussed earlier. However, it becomes more bidirectional as reading skills, especially comprehension, develop and expand. By showing how complex the reading process is, researchers realize that our current understandings are not static and will probably evolve as newer findings emerge. In fact, some neuroscientists doubt whether we will ever fully understand how the reading brain truly works. Nonetheless, we have a lot of information to date, certainly enough to recognize what educational strategies are more likely to help children learn to read as well as what problems can arise during that process.

Surprisingly, images of an adult reading brain are substantially the same regardless of the native language or culture of the individual in the scanning device. Even for Chinese and Japanese readers who use a pictorial script, or for those who read from right to left, the location of the visual word form area in the left hemisphere is virtually identical. It is genuinely remarkable to realize that despite the vast differences among the nearly 7,000 languages on this planet, and the many forms in which those languages are expressed in writing, we all still summon the same brain areas to help us identify and comprehend the written words of our language.

To summarize: Beginning readers rely on visual recognition information and use both Broca's area and the developing visual word form area analysis region to slowly analyze each word. Intermediate and skilled readers, on the other hand, rely mainly on the visual word form area process and direct information to interconnected sites, to rapidly produce meaning from words, with only marginal help from Broca's area when needed. As we shall see later on, children and adults with reading difficulties, including dyslexia, show distinctly different patterns of brain activation when reading from those described here.

DIFFICULTIES IN LEARNING TO READ

Difficulties in reading result essentially from environmental or physical factors, or some combination of both. Environmental factors are often social and cultural and include limited exposure to language in the preschool years (resulting in little phoneme sensitivity), clashes of language in the household, letter knowledge, print awareness, vocabulary, and reading comprehension. Physical factors include speech, hearing, and visual impairments and substandard intellectual capabilities. Any combination of environmental and physical factors makes diagnosis and treatment more difficult. Brain imaging technology, however, is showing great promise as a tool for diagnosing reading and language difficulties.

> Decoding and comprehension involve the coordination of three neural networks: visual processing, phoneme recognition, and word interpretation.

Social and Cultural Causes of Reading Problems

A large number of Black and Hispanic children who are performing poorly in reading display no signs of specific learning impairments. Clearly other factors are at work. Multiple studies have identified social conditions that have an impact on the achievement of children in inner-city schools. Limited teacher training, large class sizes, the absence of literature in the home, and poor parental support for schools have all been cited as causes for lack of student progress. Although these conditions cannot be ignored, schools need to focus more on the direct connections between what we are learning about how the brain learns to read and the *linguistic* barriers interfering with that learning.

Black and Hispanic children may be performing poorly on reading tests because their home language differs substantially from the language used in reading instruction (Wheeler, Cartwright, & Swords, 2012). Black children, for example, are being immersed in a language dialect that has become known as African American Vernacular English (AAVE). Residential desegregation has increased the impact of AAVE, as has the escalating popularity of hip-hop and rap music (Alim, 2009). Meanwhile, as Spanish-speaking populations increase, children are faced with learning to read English in school while speaking Spanish at home.

> *Video:* To see a short video clip about dyslexia, go to:
>
> https://www.youtube.com/watch?v=zafiGBrFkRM

Consequently, some of the causes of poor performance by Black and Hispanic children can be attributed to impediments resulting from linguistic differences. That is, their native dialect or language is different in significant ways from what is being taught in school. They come to school with a mental lexicon whose word representations often do not match what they are trying to decode on the printed page. Learning to read involves determining which words *are* present in their mental lexicon, what they represent, and whether they can be comprehended in context. This is not a physiological deficit; it is a social and cultural problem. For these children, we should not be looking at what is wrong with them but how we can alter instruction to make them more successful in learning to read. Such alterations can be made when teachers of reading are properly trained to recognize when a child's reading problems are the result of linguistic clashes and not a pathology. Furthermore, that training should help teachers understand how they can use some of the linguistic attributes of AAVE and Spanish to help children pronounce, decode, and understand standard English.

> Teachers of reading should be trained to recognize when a child's reading problems are the result of linguistic clashes and not a pathology.

Physical Causes of Reading Problems

Recall that successful reading involves two basic processes—decoding and comprehension—that are generated by three neural systems (Figure 5.2). Problems with any one or more of these systems can cause reading difficulties. In some children, the problems occur during early brain development and affect their ability to process the sounds of language and, eventually, to decode written text. This developmental deficit appears to be the most common cause of reading difficulties and usually results in a lifelong struggle with reading. Less common are problems with reading caused by impairments in hearing and vision that can occur at any time in a person's life.

Most research studies on reading have focused primarily on developmental reading problems that scientists refer to as *developmental dyslexia*. In developmental dyslexia, the child experiences unexpected difficulty in learning to read despite adequate intelligence, environment, and normal senses. It is a spectrum disorder, varying from mild to severe. Neuroimaging studies have established that there are significant differences in the way typical brains and brains with dyslexia respond to specific spoken and written language tasks. Furthermore, there is evidence that these differences may weaken with appropriate instructional interventions.

Scientists have long been searching for the causes of reading problems. Every brain is unique, and this neurodiversity makes it difficult to determine which cerebral processes result in low reading achievement. The problem is further complicated because of the large number of sensory, motor, and cognitive systems that are involved in reading. Struggling readers may have impairments in any one or more of these systems, but not all struggling readers have dyslexia. Specifically, dyslexia seems to be caused by deficits in the linguistic regions responsible for language and phonological processing or by problems in nonlinguistic areas of the brain.

Linguistic Causes

Several potential linguistic causes of developmental dyslexia that have emerged from recent research studies, including phonological deficits, differences in auditory and visual processing speeds, the varying sizes of brain structures, memory deficits, genetics, and brain lesions. It is possible that several of these causes are related to each other and can coexist in the same individual.

- **Phonological deficits.** The ability to sound out words in one's head plays an important role in reading familiar words and sounding out new ones. Phonological information is used by the working memory to integrate and comprehend words in phrases and sentences. Extensive evidence has existed for decades that phonological operations are impaired in many individuals with dyslexia, but not all (van Ermingen-Marbach, Grande, Pape-Neumann, Sass, & Heim, 2013). The exact causes of the impairment were not clear. Because many people with dyslexia have average or above-average intelligence, researchers suspected that the phonological processing deficits appeared only when the brain was trying to decode writing. Exactly why that happens is not fully known. However, studies of

Figure 5.3   The diagram shows the linguistic causes of reading problems.

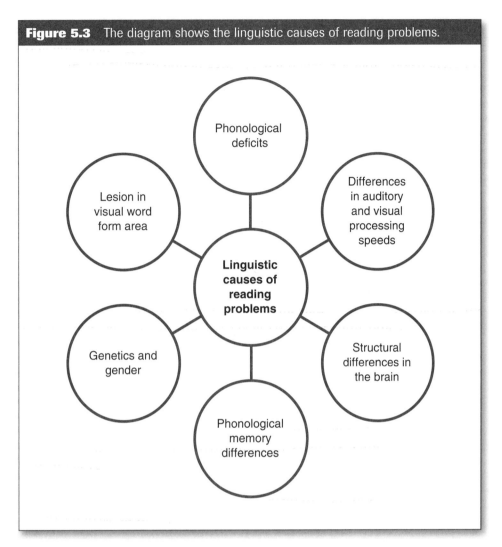

the differences in auditory and visual processing speeds as well as **functional magnetic resonance imaging (fMRI)** scans of the brain during reading are shedding new light on the possible causes of the phonological impairments.

- **Differences in auditory and visual processing speeds.** One of the more intriguing explanations of some reading difficulties, including dyslexia, has come from research studies using magnetoencephalography (MEG), a technique for measuring the electric signals emitted during brain activation as a result of mental processing. These studies noted abnormal auditory activation but normal visual activation during reading (Helenius, Salmelin, Richardson, Leinonen, & Lyytinen, 2002; Renvall & Hari, 2002; Schulte-Körne & Bruder, 2010; Steinbrink, Klatte, & Lachmann, 2014; Temple et al., 2003). Sometimes referred to as _temporal processing impairment,_ the differences in the processing speeds could explain some of the symptoms common to dyslexia.

The explanation goes like this: when reading silently, our eyes scan the words on the page (visual processing), and we sound out those words in our head. This sounding out represents the auditory processing necessary for us to decode and interpret what we are reading. To read successfully, the visual and auditory processing systems have to work together—that is, be in synchrony.

When a child begins to learn to read, it is essential that the letter (grapheme) the child sees corresponds to what the child hears (phoneme) internally. In Figure 5.3, the child with normal auditory processing (left) is looking at the letter *d* and the auditory processing system is simultaneously sounding out /*d*/ or *duh*. As the eye moves to *o*, the phoneme /*ô*/ or *awh* will sound out and then *g* produces the phoneme /*g*/ or *guh*. Later, when this child is asked to write *dog*, the /*d*/ phoneme will recall the letter *d*, the /*ô*/ phoneme will recall the letter *o*, and the /*g*/ phoneme will recall the letter *g*.

However, if the auditory processing system is impaired and lags behind the visual processing system, then the child's eye is already scanning the letter *g* while the phoneme /*d*/ or *duh* is still being processed in the auditory system. As a result, the child's brain incorrectly associates the letter *g* with the phoneme sound of /*d*/ or *duh*. Now, when we ask the child to write the word *dog*, the child hears the first phoneme /*d*/ or *duh* but incorrectly recalls the letter *g*, perhaps eventually writing the word *god*.

- If this notion is correct, then finding a way to bring the auditory and visual processing systems in closer synchrony should help remedy the problem. That is exactly what several researchers tried. They

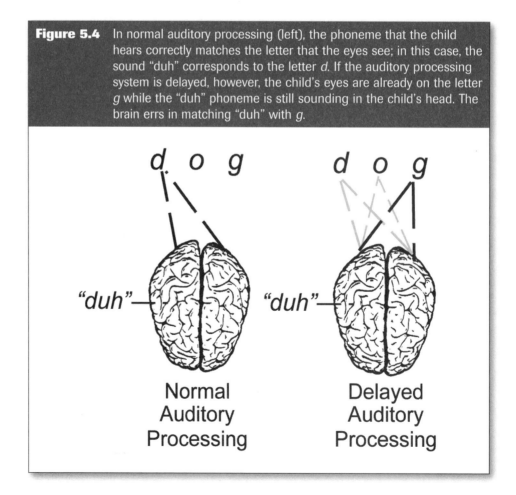

Figure 5.4   In normal auditory processing (left), the phoneme that the child hears correctly matches the letter that the eyes see; in this case, the sound "duh" corresponds to the letter *d*. If the auditory processing system is delayed, however, the child's eyes are already on the letter *g* while the "duh" phoneme is still sounding in the child's head. The brain errs in matching "duh" with *g*.

developed a computer program designed to help poor readers slow down visual processing to allow the auditory processing sufficient time to recognize the sound of the initial phoneme. Using this program with children who had reading problems produced surprisingly successful results. Furthermore, research studies suggest that temporal processing impairment may lessen as children with reading problems, including dyslexia, mature into adults (Vandermosten et al., 2011). In other words, dyslexia is much more of a phonological processing deficit and is not caused mainly by visual processing deficits—a common misconception. There are cases where visual processing is disrupted by acute astigmatism or lesions in the brain's visual cortex, but these are relatively rare.

- **Structural differences in the brain.** Some MRI studies have found that the brains of people diagnosed with dyslexia are structurally different from nondyslexic brains. In one study, the researchers noted that the brains of 16 men with dyslexia had less gray matter (surface of the cerebrum) in the left temporal lobe, the frontal lobe, and cerebellum than the brains of 14 control subjects (Brown et al., 2001; Steinbrink et al., 2008). Having less gray matter (and thus fewer neurons) in the left temporal lobe (where Wernicke's area is located) and in the frontal lobe (where comprehension occurs) could contribute to the deficits associated with dyslexia. Other studies have found that specific gene variants affect the structure and volume of the white matter—which underlies the gray matter—in the temporal lobe. Such aberrations have been shown to affect reading ability (e.g., Darki, Peyrard-Janvid, Matsson, Kere, & Klingberg, 2012).

- Another anomaly common to individuals with dyslexia has to do with the visual recognition system. It seems they are not able to recall the letters that comprise a word simultaneously, which expands their slow reading time. To compensate, they often activate regions in the right hemisphere, hoping to access the word's phonology—an inefficient and often unproductive endeavor (Laszlo & Sacchi, 2015). In sum, as the research evidence accumulates, it appears that most children with developmental dyslexia have phonological decoding areas of the brain that are insufficiently active and dysfunctional.

- **Phonological memory deficits.** Skilled reading requires an ability to retain verbal bits of information (phonemes) in working memory. Recent studies have shown distinct deficits among poor readers in this component of working memory, called phonological memory. The deficits more commonly involve serial tasks, such as holding a string of phonemes to make a word and a sequence of words to generate a sentence. Studies also indicate that memory deficits could result from difficulties with cognitive processing in the frontal lobe. However, for some children, this may represent a developmental delay, which could correct itself as they mature (Wang, Allen, Lee, & Hsieh, 2015; Wang & Gathercole, 2013).

- **Genetics and gender.** Studies of genetic composition have long shown strong associations between dyslexia and genetic mutations in twins and families (e.g., Pennington, 1990), and recent investigations have actually identified some half-dozen of the specific genes involved (e.g., Benítez-Burraco, 2010; Kere, 2014). Studies seem to indicate that the genetic mutations disrupt the migration of neurons in the fetal brain as they attempt to travel to areas of the cortex to their final position. Instead, they accumulate in disorganized tangles, often around the visual word form area (Platt et al., 2013). These tangles prevent this brain region from carrying out its normal functions of recognizing and decoding written text. As a result, the brain is forced to construct alternate and less efficient pathways to accomplish these tasks. Thus, dyslexia is a lifelong condition and not just a "phase."

- Nationwide, there are about three times more boys identified with reading problems than girls. Although this was once thought to be almost totally the result of genetic deficits, there may be other factors responsible for this disparity. It may be, for instance, that boys are overidentified, often due to their rambunctious behavior, and girls are underidentified, because they sit quietly in class and obey the rules (Beaman, Wheldall, & Kemp, 2006). It may also be that many girls are affected as well but are not getting help. Although more boys than girls do experience reading problems, the differences may be less than the 3:1 ratio represented by current enrollments (Hawke, Olson, Willcutt, Wadsworth, & DeFries, 2009). For instance, a 10-year study in Australia of the reading scores of more than one million third-grade and fifth-grade students showed ratios of poor readers to be closer to 1.5 to 1 boy-to-girl ratio in third grade, and 2.0 to 1 boy-to-girl ratio in fifth grade (Wheldall & Limbrick, 2010). A study in the United States of almost 500,000 beginning second-grade students found the poor readers to vary from a 1.6 to 1 boy-to-girl ratio for decoding and a 2.4 to 1 boy-to-girl ratio for fluency (Quinn & Wagner, 2013). Surprisingly, this study also noted that only one out of seven girls identified as reading impaired in the study was identified by the school as learning disabled.

- Another reason that boys are overidentified as poor readers may be that teachers confound competence in early reading and writing skills. They may assume that poor writing skills also mean poor reading skills. But studies show that boys are almost as skilled as girls in reading but do display significantly poorer writing skills (Berninger, Nielsen, Abbott, Wijsman, & Raskind, 2008).

- **Lesions in the visual word form area.** Researchers using various types of brain scans have noticed that some people with developmental dyslexia have lesions in the left occipito-temporal area of the brain (e.g., Fiez, Tranel, Seager-Frerichs, & Damasio, 2006; Rapcsak et al., 2009). This area is identified as the visual word form area most used by skilled readers to decode written text. Another discovery in these studies was that the amount of blood flowing to this brain region predicted the severity of the dyslexia (Rumsey et al., 1999). Regardless of the cause, a lesion and reduced blood flow would likely hamper the ability of this region of neurons to decode written text. In this instance, the person may display a condition known as alexia, which is difficulty in identifying a string of letters, although speech production and comprehension remain intact. However, demonstrating its impressive plasticity, when a lesion or damage from epilepsy occurs in the brain's visual word form area in the left hemisphere, an area exactly symmetrical to it, located in the right hemisphere, can take over its functions, albeit not as efficiently (Cohen et al., 2004; Lopes, Nunes, Simões, Secca, & Leal, 2015).

Nonlinguistic Causes

Some people, who are otherwise unimpaired, have extreme difficulties in reading because of deficits in auditory and visual perception not related to linguistic systems. This revelation was somewhat of a surprise because conventional wisdom held that impairments in reading (and also in oral language) were restricted to problems with linguistic processing. The following are some possible nonlinguistic causes found in the research literature.

Boys tend to be overidentified with reading problems; girls, on the other hand, tend to be underidentified.

- **Perception of sequential sounds.** The inability to detect and discriminate sounds presented in rapid succession seems to be a common impairment in individuals with reading and language disorders. These individuals also have difficulty in indicating the order of two sounds presented in rapid succession. This particular deficit

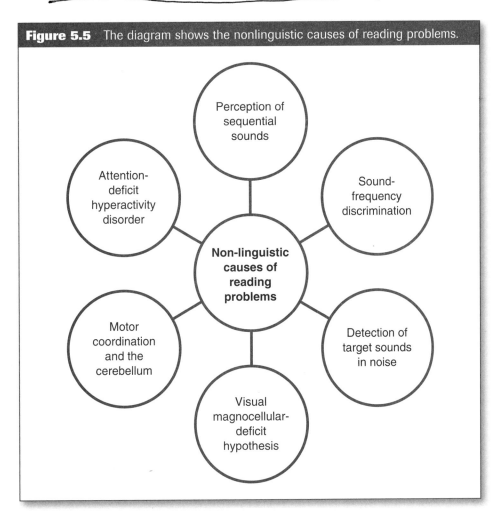

Figure 5.5　The diagram shows the nonlinguistic causes of reading problems.

is related to auditory processing of sound waves in general and is not related directly to distinguishing phonemes as part of phonological processing. Hearing words accurately when reading or from a stream of rapid conversation is critical to comprehension (Wright, Bowen, & Zecker, 2000). Little is known about the causes of this problem, and little research has been done on it.

- **Sound-frequency discrimination.** Some individuals with reading disorders are impaired in their ability to hear differences in sound frequency. This auditory defect can affect the ability to discriminate tone and pitch in speech. At first glance, this may seem like only an oral language-related impairment. However, it also affects reading proficiency because reading involves sounding out words in the auditory processing system (Hakvoort, van der Leij, Maurits, Maassen, & van Zuijen, 2015).

- **Detection of target sounds in noise.** The inability to detect tones within noise is another potential nonlinguistic impairment. Individuals who have difficulty detecting specific phoneme sounds from background noise often have problems carry on a conversation in a noisy environment and display dyslexic behaviors when reading (Chait et al., 2007). When added to the findings in the two deficits mentioned above, this evidence suggests that auditory malfunctions may play a much greater role in reading disorders than previously thought. It also suggests that the evaluation of children who have reading difficulties should include a thorough assessment of their auditory processing skills.

- **Visual magnocellular-deficit hypothesis.** The interpretation of some research studies has led to a hypothesis that certain forms of reading disorders are caused by a deficit in the visual processing system, leading to poor detection of coherent visual motion and poor discrimination of the speed of visual motion. This part of the visual system involves large neurons and so is referred to as the *magnocellular* system. Impairment in this system may cause letters on a page to bundle and overlap or appear to move—common complaints from some struggling readers and those with dyslexia. Current studies continue to show a strong correlation between deficits in the visual magnocellular system and developmental dyslexia (e.g., Giraldo-Chica, Hegarty II, & Schneider, 2015; Laycock, Crewther, & Crewther, 2012). This correlation is also found in Chinese children with dyslexia, lending further credence to the notion that deficits in detecting visual motion and outlines do affect one's ability to read different orthographic symbols (e.g., Wang, Bi, Gao, & Wydell, 2010).

- **Motor coordination and the cerebellum.** Several imaging studies have shown that many readers with dyslexia have processing deficits in the cerebellum of the brain (e.g., Nicolson & Fawcett, 2011; Stoodley & Stein, 2011). Another study determined that nearly 75 percent of the subjects with dyslexia had smaller lobes on the right side of the cerebellum than control participants (Eckert et al., 2003). The cerebellum is located at the rear of the brain just below the occipital lobe (see Figure 5.6). It is mainly responsible for coordinating learned motor skills. Deficiencies in this part of the brain could result, according to researchers, in problems with reading, writing, and spelling. Problems in reading may result if cerebellar deficits delay the time when an infant sits up and walks and begins babbling and talking. Less motor skill coordination can mean less articulation and fluency in speech. This, in turn, leads to less sensitivity to onset, rime, and the phonemic structure of language.

Figure 5.6

Cerebellum

- **Attention-Deficit Hyperactivity Disorder (ADHD).** We discussed attention-deficit hyperactivity disorder (ADHD) in Chapter 3. Children with ADHD are often assumed to also have developmental reading problems. But that is not necessarily the case. ADHD and developmental dyslexia are separate disorders, although some brain regions may be affected by both. Estimating the exact percentage of ADHD children who also have dyslexia is difficult because of the inconsistency of criteria used for diagnosis. The accepted range for the moment is from 18 to more than 40 percent (Sexton, Gelhorn, Bell, & Classi, 2012).

The possibility of deficits in visual and auditory perception and memory as well as in motor coordination on various reading tasks accounts for the wide range of individual differences observed among those with reading disorders. Analyzing these differences leads to a better understanding of the multidimensional nature of reading disorders and possible treatment.

Is Dyslexia Present in Readers of Other Languages?

Dyslexia appears in all languages, including those that are read from right to left, such as Hebrew and Arabic. People with dyslexia who speak highly phonetic languages with shallow orthography, such as Spanish, Italian, and Finnish, are usually identified with the disorder later than those who speak deep morphological languages such as English, where the linguistic demands of the language are more challenging. The key seems to be the degree to which there is a one-to-one correspondence between letters and sounds. Italians with dyslexia, for example, have an easier time because there are only 25 letters or combination of letters to represent Italian's 33 phonemes. French people with dyslexia have more difficulty because the 32 phonemes in French can be represented by about 250 letter combinations. But English has more than 1,100 ways to spell its 44 phonemes and English speakers experience this complex phonetic structure early on in their schooling.

Readers can also experience difficulties in logographic languages, such as Chinese, because of visual confusion of the more than 3,000 characters or to problems with working memory and recall (Siok, Spinks, Jin, & Tan, 2009). For example, look at this Chinese character that means "special" (特) and this one that means "grasp" (持). They look almost alike, except that the "special" character has a small extra stroke on the left side, and the "grasp" character has an extra tiny line at the bottom. These differences are difficult for the untrained eye to spot. The two characters also have very different pronunciations. "Special" is pronounced "te" with a falling tone, while "grasp" is pronounced "chi" with a rising tone. As a result, developmental dyslexia in Chinese is really two disorders: a visual-spatial deficit affecting the ability to distinguish among complex Chinese characters and a phonological disorder affecting the ability to pronounce each character correctly. In fact, the demand on the brain to recognize and process these complex symbols orthographically and phonetically actually seems to increase the amount of gray matter in these processing areas of Chinese children with dyslexia compared to typically developing children (Liu et al., 2013). Studies also show that Western and Chinese children with dyslexia have brain abnormalities in different brain regions. These findings suggest that dyslexia may not have a universal origin in all humans, but that the biological abnormality of impaired reading is dependent on the phonology and orthography of a culture.

SOME INDICATORS OF DYSLEXIA

(Few individuals exhibit all symptoms.)

- Difficulty recognizing written words
- Difficulty rhyming or sequencing syllables
- Difficulty determining the meaning or main idea of a simple sentence
- Difficulty encoding words—spelling
- Poor sequencing of letters or numbers
- Delayed spoken language
- Difficulty separating the sounds in spoken words
- Difficulty in expressing thoughts verbally
- Confusion about right- or left-handedness
- Difficulty with handwriting
- Possible family history of dyslexia

DETECTING READING PROBLEMS

In recent years, researchers have made significant progress using fMRI scans to understand how novice, skilled, and dyslexic brains read. Yet, despite these advancements, fMRI scans are not a practical tool at present for diagnosing dyslexia in a single individual. That is because the results of fMRI studies are usually reported for groups rather than for individuals. Researchers have found some variations in the activated areas of the brain among individuals within both the dyslexic and control groups. More research is needed to clarify these differences before fMRI or any other imaging techniques can be used for diagnostic purposes. Until that time, however, researchers can use the information gained from imaging studies to develop other kinds of diagnostic tests that more closely align with our new understanding of dyslexia.

For the moment, critical observation of a child's progress in learning to speak, and eventually in learning to read, remains our most effective tool for spotting potential problems. Most difficulties associated with reading do not go away with time. Therefore, the earlier that parents and teachers can detect reading problems in children, the better. The problems often begin to reveal themselves first in spoken language and later while learning to read.

Spoken Language Difficulties

Learning to read is closely connected to fluency in spoken language. Both speaking and reading rely on the proper functioning of the phonologic areas of the brain where sounds are combined to form words and words are broken down into their basic sounds. Consequently, difficulties that children have with spoken language are often clues to potential reading problems. Parents and teachers should remember that it is normal for all children to make occasional language errors while speaking. But frequent language errors, stemming from any one or a combination of the following conditions, could indicate that a child may run into trouble when beginning to learn to read. Some of the spoken language difficulties may involve any one or more of the following (Dehaene, 2009; IDA, 2015b; NAEYC, 2009):

- **Delay in speaking.** Children generally say their first words at about 12 months of age and follow with phrases when between 18 and 24 months old. Studies show that about one-fourth of children born preterm—less than 34 weeks of gestation—experience language delays at about 22 month of age (Mossabeb, Wade, Finnegan, Sivieri, & Abbasi, 2012). Language delays are also evident in 4-year-old children living in poverty where home literacy may be marginal (Nelson, Welsh, Trup, & Greenberg, 2011). Because learning to read is closely linked to a child's phonologic skills in spoken language, delays in speaking may be an early indication of potential reading problems, especially in a family that has a history of dyslexia.
- **Difficulties with pronunciation.** Children should have little difficulty pronouncing words correctly by 5 or 6 years of age. Difficulties in pronouncing words (sometimes referred to as "baby talk") may be an indication of future reading problems. Such trouble pronouncing long or complicated words could signal a snag in the parts of the brain that generate spoken language, causing a mix-up in the processing of the phonemes. Mispronunciations often involve mixing syllables within words (*aminal* for animal) and leaving off the beginning syllables (*luminum* for aluminum).
- **Difficulty in learning the letters of the alphabet.** Learning the names of the letters of the alphabet is an important, though not essential, step in learning to read. Marked difficulties in learning the letters could indicate a potential reading problem.
- **Recalling incorrect phonemes.** A child looks at a picture of a donkey and recalls the word *doggie,* a word similar in sound but not in meaning. This recall of incorrect phonemes may cause a child to talk about a word without actually recalling it. The child may get frustrated

because of the inability to say the word. As these children get older, they may resort more to vague words in order to mask their difficulties in retrieving specific words. They use general words such as *things* and *stuff*, making their conversations hard to follow. It is important to remember that the problem here is not with their thinking but with their ability to use expressive language—that is, to recall a word on command.

- **Insensitivity to rhyme.** Part of a young child's enjoyment of spoken language is playing with rhyme. Hearing and repeating rhyming sounds demonstrates how words can be separated into smaller segments of sound and that different words may share the same sound. Children with good rhyming skills are showing their readiness for learning to read. Those with little sensitivity to rhyme, on the other hand, may have reading problems because they are unable to detect the consonant sound that changes the meaning of closely rhyming words.

- **Genetics.** We mentioned earlier that heredity is a key factor in dyslexia. Looking at the family tree for signs of dyslexia in close relatives is a clue because about 25–50 percent of the children born to a parent with dyslexia will also be dyslexic (Darki et al., 2012; Schumacher et al., 2006). Whether the child actually displays dyslexia depends somewhat on that child's environment. This revelation came from studies of identical twins. Because they share the same genes, if one twin has dyslexia, so should the other. But in reality, in 30–35 percent of the cases, one twin has dyslexia while the other does not (Fisher & DeFries, 2002). Apparently, even though these children had a genetic predisposition for dyslexia, differences in the home and school environments played important roles in determining how successful these children would be at learning to read.

Early Indicators of Reading Problems

Until the time that brain imaging becomes a standard diagnostic tool, researchers will continue to look for ways to accurately identify students with reading problems as early as possible. Multiple research studies have sought to find indicators of reading problems that are more valid than solely the professional judgment of the evaluating team. The obvious problem here is that the application of professional judgment is only as good as the training and competence of the team members. This approach can often lead to considerable variability in identification from district to district and even from state to state. Using more objective measures would reduce this variability. Research studies have found that letter fluency is a useful measure in kindergarten, while response to interventions can be a valuable measure in second grade.

Even though children have a genetic predisposition for dyslexia, differences in the home and school environment can determine how successful these children will be at reading.

Letter Fluency Tasks as Kindergarten Indicators

The earlier that children who are at risk for reading problems can be identified, the better. Trying to carry out such identification procedures in kindergarten is difficult because of the broad range of background experience these children bring to the classroom. Nonetheless, studies involving kindergarten children do seem to indicate that letter-name fluency and nonsense-word fluency can be valid indicators of early reading skills, such as oral reading fluency (ORF).

One early study tested 39 kindergartners in the spring in several language skill areas, including receptive vocabulary, phonological awareness, letter-name knowledge, letter-sound knowledge, letter-name fluency, and nonsense-word fluency (Speece & Mills, 2003). These same children were again tested one year later in first grade in similar skills, plus oral reading fluency. Nonsense-word fluency and letter-word fluency, respectively, were the highest predictors of oral reading fluency. In fact, the fluency measures were more accurate at predicting ORF than national normed measures of reading and phonological awareness, which identified only 33 percent of the poor readers in this study. Subsequent studies have found similar results (e.g., Burke, Hagan-Burke, Kwok, & Parker, 2009).

Using Response to Intervention

Another technique for avoiding the misidentification or nonidentification of students with reading problems is to place increased emphasis on measures of school performance, especially in the primary grades. The Response to Intervention (RTI) model identifies students based on low achievement, application of certain criteria for exclusion, and their response to varying degrees of interventions. The goal is to screen all students to identify those who, despite a strong general education in their classroom, are still failing. In Tier 1, they receive careful monitoring and special assistance as needed. Students who do not make adequate progress in Tier 1 move to Tier 2 where they receive targeted evidence-based interventions, usually from a team of educators. If more assistance is needed, the student moves to Tier 3, which involves more frequent and intensive interventions by a multidisciplinary team. Some schools and districts also have a fourth tier, while in others students in Tier 3 are identified as being in need to special education services. All students in the RTI model can move between tiers according to their rate of progress.

Major steps in carrying out the Response to Intervention approach are as follows (National Center on Response to Intervention, 2010).

Monitor student progress. Progress monitoring is used to assess students' performance over time, to quantify student rates of improvement or their responsiveness to instruction, and to evaluate instructional effectiveness. For those students who are least responsive to effective instruction, progress monitoring also helps formulate effective individualized programs. The tools used in progress monitoring should accurately represent students' academic development and should be useful for instructional planning and for assessing student learning. In addition, in tertiary prevention, educators use progress monitoring to compare a student's expected and actual rates of learning. If a student is not achieving the expected rate of learning, the educator then experiments with instructional components in an attempt to improve the rate of learning.

Adjust the intensity and nature of interventions depending on a student's responsiveness. Progress monitoring data are used to determine when a student has or has not responded to instruction at any level of the prevention system. Increasing the intensity of an intervention can be accomplished in a number of ways, such as lengthening instructional time, increasing the frequency of instructional sessions, reducing the size of the instructional group, or adjusting the level of instruction. Also, the school can increase intensity by providing intervention support from a teacher with more experience and skill in teaching students with learning or behavioral difficulties (e.g., a reading specialist or a special education teacher).

Identify students with learning disabilities or other disabilities. If a student fails to respond to intervention, the student may have a learning disability or other disability that requires further evaluation. Progress monitoring and other data collected over the course of the intervention should be examined during the evaluation process, along with data from appropriately selected measures (e.g., tests of cognition, language, perception, and social skills). In this way, effectively implemented RTI frameworks contribute to the process of identifying a disability by reducing misidentification of students who might appear to have a disability because of inappropriate or insufficient instruction.

Use data to inform decisions at the school, grade, or classroom levels. School personnel can aggregate screening and progress monitoring data and use them to compare and contrast the adequacy of the core curriculum as well as the effectiveness of different instructional and behavioral strategies for various groups of students within a school. For example, if 60 percent of the students in a particular grade score below the cut point on a screening test at the beginning of the year, school personnel might reconsider the appropriateness of the core curriculum or whether differentiated learning activities need to be added to better meet the needs of the students in that grade.

Persistent Reading Difficulties

Remember that all children make errors in spoken language and while reading. But the number of errors should decrease with time, and there should be clear evidence of growth in vocabulary and reading comprehension. Determining whether a child has consistent problems with reading requires careful and long-term observation of the child's fluency in speaking and reading. Most children display obvious improvements in their speaking and reading skills over time. Researchers, clinicians, and educators who study dyslexia and who work with poor readers look for certain clues that will show whether a child's reading ability is progressing normally.

WHAT EDUCATORS NEED TO CONSIDER

It is important to remember that children with dyslexia have a reading disability, but not all children with reading difficulties have dyslexia. Developmental dyslexia is a neurological disability that affects the skills necessary to achieve fluency in word reading and spelling. It is not related to intelligence. Reading difficulties in children who do not have developmental dyslexia can be caused by systemic abnormalities (e.g., poor vision or hearing) or environmental factors (e.g., living with constant stress).

Remember the Strengths of Struggling Readers

Remember that struggling readers frequently have strengths in other areas, such as higher order cognitive thinking that can help them manage or overcome their difficulties with reading. Many students with dyslexia are able to go on to higher education and be successful. But their phonologic reading deficits do not go away. One study looked at more than 100 college students with and without dyslexia and compared their reading ability (Kirby, Silvestri, Allingham, Parrila, & LaFave, 2008). Not surprisingly, the students with dyslexia reported that they continued to experience reading difficulties, especially in word reading, despite their average mental ability. They scored lower than the students without dyslexia on tests of selecting the main idea and on test-taking strategies. Students with dyslexia also reported using more study aids and time management strategies, and they were more likely to use a deep approach to learning than students without dyslexia. But the differences between the two groups were weaker in other reading measures, suggesting that those with dyslexia were able to compensate for their persistent word reading difficulties with phonological processing and become sufficiently competent readers to survive successfully in a university.

Growing scientific evidence continues to support the notion that most dyslexia is caused by deficits in phonological processing. It is important to recognize that dyslexia does not reflect an overall impairment in language, intelligence, or thinking skills. Many smart people are dyslexic. Rather, for most people it reflects an overall problem with the ability of a specific brain system, referred to earlier as the visual word form area, to put together the sounds of language to form words and to break words down into their basic sounds. This focus allows research to examine more closely the nature of these deficits and to explore methods for remediation. Other research evidence suggests that dyslexia may have multiple causes that require different forms of intervention. No doubt, some individuals display dyslexic symptoms because of visual and auditory problems not directly associated with phonological processing, but their numbers are small.

Because reading does not come naturally to the human brain, children learning to read have to put much effort into associating their spoken language with the alphabet and with word recognition. To do this successfully, phonemic awareness is essential. In light of this research, educators should have second thoughts about reading programs that delay phonemic awareness or that treat it as an ancillary skill to be learned in context with general reading.

Educators should also become more aware of the scientific research into dyslexia and be able to recognize when students are having persistent reading problems. Early identification of struggling readers leads to early intervention. Researchers agree that a systematic, intensive, and comprehensive approach to early intervention can significantly reduce the number of students reading below the Basic level of proficiency.

What Teachers Should Know About Teaching Reading

- How the brain learns to read
- The relationship between spoken language and reading
- Direct instruction in phonics
- Direct instruction in the alphabetic principle
- How to diagnose spelling and reading skills
- How to build vocabulary
- How to develop fluency and comprehension
- How to use a variety of reading intervention strategies

What Beginning Readers Need to Learn

- Phonological awareness: Rhyming, alliteration, deleting and substituting sounds, sound patterns
- Phonemic awareness: Segmenting words into individual sounds, manipulating phonemes
- Alphabetic principle: Correlating letter-sound patterns with specific text
- Orthographic awareness: Understanding spelling rules and writing conventions
- Comprehension monitoring strategies: Identifying the main idea, making inferences, using study skills that assist reading

Some Effective Reading Intervention Programs

Educators are surrounded by all kinds of reading programs claiming to be effective, scientifically-based, and research-based. Several suggest that they are using the brain research on reading and reading difficulties to help design their program. Because purchasing materials for a school district's reading program is one of the costliest curriculum-related expenses, it is important to make a thoughtful choice based on evidence of the program's effectiveness. Help in making this decision comes from the Institute for Education Sciences, an arm of the U.S. Department of Education. The Institute is charged with identifying studies that provide reliable evidence of the effectiveness of practices, programs, and policies relating to the education of students. It disseminates this information through the What Works Clearinghouse. The Clearinghouse is a reliable resource for evaluating the effectiveness of reading programs. As of this printing, here is what the Clearinghouse reports about a few of the popular reading programs currently available (What Works Clearinghouse, 2015). Their term *alphabetics* refers to the alphabetic principle.

- *Cooperative Integrated Reading and Composition®* was found to have potentially positive effects on comprehension for students in Grades 1–4, with an average percentile gain of 12.
- *Corrective Reading* was found to have potentially positive effects on alphabetics and fluency in Grade 3, with an average percentile gain of 11 for reading fluency and 9 for alphabetics.

- *Early Intervention in Reading*® was found to have potentially positive effects on alphabetics and comprehension in Grade 1, with an average percentile gain.
- *Earobics*® was found to have positive effects on alphabetics and potentially positive effects on reading fluency for students in Grades K–3, with an average percentile gain of 25 in alphabetics and 15 in reading fluency.
- *Fast ForWord*® *Beginning Reading* was found to have positive effects on alphabetics and mixed effects on comprehension for beginning readers in Grades K–3, with an average percentile gain of 6 in alphabetics and 6 in reading comprehension.
- *Adolescent Literacy* was found to have potentially positive effects on reading fluency and comprehension for adolescent learners in Grades 3–10, with an average percentile gain of 17 in reading fluency and 8 in reading comprehension.
- *Open Court Reading*© was found to have potentially positive effects on general reading achievement and comprehension for beginning readers, including Grades 1–3, with an average percentile gain of 12 for general literacy achievement and 10 for reading comprehension.
- *READ 180* was found to have potentially positive effects on comprehension and general literacy achievement for adolescent learners in Grades 4–9, with an average percentile gain of 12 in reading achievement and 4 in reading comprehension.
- *Reading Apprenticeship*® was found to have potentially positive effects on comprehension for adolescent learners in Grade 9, with an average percentile gain of 2 in reading comprehension.
- *Reading Mastery* was found to have potentially positive effects on reading fluency in Grades 4 and 5, with an average percentile gain of 19 in reading fluency.
- *Reading Recovery*® was found to have positive effects on general reading achievement and potentially positive effects on alphabetics, reading fluency, and comprehension for beginning readers in Grade 1, with an average percentile gain of 46 in reading fluency, 27 in reading achievement, 21 in alphabetics, and 14 in reading comprehension.
- *Success for All*® was found to have positive effects on alphabetics, mixed effects for comprehension, and potentially positive effects on general reading achievement for students in Grade PK–3, with an average percentile gain of 13 for alphabetics, 10 for reading achievement, and 8 for reading comprehension.
- *Waterford Early Reading Program*™ was found to have potentially positive effects on alphabetics for students in kindergarten, with an average percentile gain of 19 in alphabetics.

Check the Clearinghouse site periodically for updates on research studies that look at the effectiveness of these and other reading programs.

Assistive Technology for Students With Dyslexia

Assistive technology provides students with dyslexia opportunities to save time and overcome some of the issues they encounter because of their dyslexia, such as slow note taking or unreadable handwriting. Essentially, it allows them to use their time for all the things in which they are proficient. For students with dyslexia, technology give them a chance to demonstrate their knowledge in ways that were not practicable in the past. Here are a few of the successful technologies that support students with dyslexia are the following:

- Tablets: Tablets are helpful because they have text-to-speech capabilities as well as access to a wide variety of apps that support students with dyslexia, such a Voice Dream Reader. They also have speech recognition allowing users to speak into the tablet and see their words appear as text (Meersma, 2015).
- The Livescribe Smartpen: This device is an assistive technology aid that facilitates the note-taking and learning process. It captures everything that the user writes and speaks. Inside the pen is a camera that takes a picture of notes as the user writes them, and it can record what is being said. This way, if the user chooses not to take notes, the device can record the audio and then replay the session. By recording classroom discussions and taking fewer notes, students with dyslexia can spend more time listening and learning. When students return to the material later, they have an opportunity to listen to important information for a second time, add anything that may be of significance to their notes, and rehearse what they have already written (Frankenberger, 2015).
- Dragon NaturallySpeaking: This is a speech-recognition program that can be used with students who have learning difficulties, especially those with word-retrieval problems and muscle-motor limitations affecting typing or writing. Several studies have found this technology to be particularly helpful for students with learning disabilities (e.g., Fahsl & McAndrews, 2012).

Recent research on dyslexia and other reading difficulties is encouraging. Effective interventions are already here and more may come in the near future.

DYSLEXIA MAY IMPART OTHER COGNITIVE STRENGTHS

Although dyslexia certainly causes reading difficulties and other learning challenges, it may also impart some cognitive strengths that scientists are beginning to explore. Several studies, for example, have shown a higher incidence of dyslexia among entrepreneurs than in the general population (e.g., Logan, 2009). Scientists at the Massachusetts Institute of Technology have found that people with dyslexia have sharper peripheral vision than others and can give their attention to multiple auditory inputs at once (Geiger et al., 2008). Other researchers report that people with dyslexia are faster at picking out impossible figures, such as etchings by M. C. Escher, from similarly drawn illustration than those without dyslexia (Schneps, 2015). In another study, children with dyslexia were significantly more accurate at recognizing whether they had seen a previous image than their nondyslexic peers (Hedenius, Ullman, Alm, Jennische, & Persson, 2013). These findings seem to indicate that dyslexia conveys certain advantages, such as being able to literally see the big picture, that others may miss. These advantages could be very helpful in certain occupations, such as a scientist.

Although no one knows exactly what causes these visual and auditory advantages, we do know a lot about how the brain learns to read. Researchers speculate that strong readers are skilled in the focused attention needed to read fluently. Consequently, the brain suppresses awareness of its surroundings. Individuals with dyslexia may not be able to focus attention so intently and thus become more globally aware, making them better able to perform tasks such as discriminating figures and seeing the big picture. In other words, impairments in one area, such as reading, may lead to advantages in other areas. Parents and educators need to be aware of what those advantages may be and how to use them to enhance the student's learning.

Strategies to Consider

STRATEGIES FOR TEACHING STUDENTS WITH READING PROBLEMS

It is usually the general education classroom teacher who works the most with struggling readers and who helps them learn to read. The following strategies may make the instructional process somewhat easier and more successful for all students.

General Strategies

- Make your classroom expectations clear and in language the students will easily understand. Students with reading difficulties also have problems with vocabulary and meaning.
- Ensure that classroom procedures are orderly, structured, and predictable.
- Use explicit teaching strategies, such as presenting an advanced organizer, demonstrate the new skill, provide for guided practice, and give immediate and specific feedback.
- Rewrite directions if necessary to make them simpler and reduce the reading workload. Consider putting direction on a voice recorder so the student can replay the recording to clarify directions or concepts.
- Remember that many struggling readers *can* learn to read. They just need different kinds of instructional strategies.
- Recognize that struggling readers will take up to three times longer to complete work and will tire quickly. Give them additional time to complete their assignments.
- Use age-appropriate paper or computer-generated graphic organizers whenever possible because these help students recognize important information and see the relationships among concepts.

- Present work in smaller amounts to reduce the students' anxiety about the total amount of work to be done.
- Materials often do not provide enough practice for students with reading difficulties. Supplement the material with additional practice activities, such as instructional games, computer software programs, and peer teaching activities.
- Provide an age-appropriate glossary of content-related terms to help students understand what they are reading.
- Avoid appeals to "try harder." The brains of struggling readers are already expending extra effort while decoding print, and these appeals will not improve performance. What is needed is slower speed with clearer comprehension.
- Determine and then compliment these children's abilities and teach through their strengths. Plan lessons so the students experience a sense of accomplishment rather than failure.
- Use peer-mediated reading by pairing peers of different reading ability to read aloud to each other, write stories, review their notes, or study for a test.

In the Elementary Classroom

- Get a complete explanation of the child's history of problems encountered when learning to read.
- Select scientifically researched reading strategies, and use a multisensory approach.
- Recognize the frustration that these students feel as they struggle to read.
- Recognize that performance may be well below the child's potential.
- Realize that the child may have behavioral and self-esteem problems.
- Maintain contact with the child's parents and give them periodic progress reports. Make suggestions of what they can do with the child at home to complement your classroom strategies.
- Ensure that other classmates understand the nature of dyslexia so that the child is not bullied or mocked.
- Assign a buddy to help the struggling reader in the class and school.
- Encourage the child to point out talents and strengths.

In the Secondary Classroom

- Get a complete explanation of the student's history of reading problems.
- Use a multisensory approach in classroom instruction. Use visuals and technology to maintain student attention.
- Recognize the compounded frustrations of a teenager with dyslexia. Seat any student with attention problems closer to you or near a work area away from distracting materials or sounds.
- Realize that these teenagers may have problems with their self-esteem.
- Realize that these students often have a significant gap between their performance and their potential.

- Maintain contact with the student's parents and give them periodic progress reports. Make suggestions of what they can do with the student at home to complement your classroom strategies.
- Ensure that these students' legal rights are adhered to when they take tests.
- Students with mild dyslexia often develop coping strategies in elementary school. Be aware that these strategies may be inadequate for the complex and multifaceted secondary curriculum.
- Ensure that any remedial materials are relevant to the maturity and not the academic level of the student.
- Be aware that struggling readers can have great difficulty reading an unseen text aloud in class.
- Some Suggestions for Testing
  - Avoid true/false tests whenever possible because their wording can be difficult to interpret.
  - In multiple choice tests, ask questions in complete sentences and limit the number of possible answers to no more than three.
  - In an essay test, allow students to choose among several possible topics. Ensure that the directions are clear and explicit. Provide lined paper for the students' answers.
  - For fill-in-the-blank tests, do not deduct points for spelling because this is a problem for students with reading difficulties. Put the blank line near the end of the question, and its length should mirror the length of the answer.

Strategies to Consider

DEVELOPING PHONOLOGICAL AWARENESS

Phonological awareness is the ability to hear the sounds that make up language. It includes deciding whether words begin or end with the same sounds, separating words into their individual sounds, recognizing rhymes, and how to manipulate sounds to make new words. Training in phonological awareness needs to be more intense for children who are at risk for reading disabilities. Reading programs are filled with activities for separating words into phonemes, synthesizing phonemes into words, and deleting and substituting phonemes. Research suggests that the development of phonological awareness is more likely to be successful if it follows these general principles (Botts, Losardo, Tillery, & Werts, 2014; Kantor, Wagner, Torgesen, & Rashotte, 2011; Noe, Spencer, Kruse, & Goldstein, 2014):

Video: For a video clip on phonological awareness, see:

https://www.youtube.com/watch?v=LucNw_2G_FU

- Continuous Sounds Before Stop Sounds. Start with continuous sounds such as /s/, /m/, and /f/ that are easier to pronounce than the stop sounds of /b/, /k/, and /p/.

- **Modeling.** Be sure to model carefully and accurately each activity when it is first introduced. Modeling should start with the teacher demonstrating the desired behavior so that students hear what is expected of them. Then the teacher and students perform the behavior together.
- **Simple to Complex Tasks.** Move from simpler tasks, such as rhyming, to more complex tasks, such as blending and segmenting. Blending helps children decode unfamiliar words. Segmenting words into phonemes helps children in spelling unfamiliar words and retaining those spellings in memory.
- **Larger to Smaller Units.** Move from the larger units of words and onset-rimes to the smaller units of individual phonemes.
- **Teacher Feedback.** Teacher feedback is important and should be immediate and explicit for both correct and incorrect responses. For incorrect responses, the teacher should model the correct response and ask the student to say the response with the teacher. The teacher should then ask the student to make the response alone.
- **Additional Strategies.** Use additional strategies to help struggling readers, such as concrete objects (e.g., bingo chips or blocks), or computer-based programs to represent sounds.

Strategies to Consider

PHONEMIC AWARENESS AND GUIDELINES

Research studies have long indicated that early phoneme awareness is a strong indicator of later reading success (Fuchs, Compton, Fuchs, Bouton, & Caffrey, 2011; National Reading Panel, 2000; Yurick, Cartledge, Kourea, & Keyes, 2012). Further, the research on interventions clearly demonstrates the benefits of explicitly teaching phonemic awareness skills. No students benefit more from this instruction than those already burdened with reading problems. The development of phonemic awareness occurs over several years. It is the last step in a developmental continuum that begins with the brain's earliest awareness of rhyme. Figure 5.6 illustrates the continuum from rhyming to full phoneme manipulation.

The first four steps, from rhyming to onset-rime blending, can occur during the preschool years in the appropriate environment. If the parent sings rhyming songs and reads to the child from rhyming books, the child's brain begins to recognize the sounds that comprise beginning language. However, many children begin school with a very weak phonological base. Teachers must then assess where students lie on the phonological continuum and select appropriate strategies to move them toward phoneme awareness. Here are some guidelines to consider when selecting strategies to help students recognize and successfully manipulate phonemes (Martens, Werder, Hier, & Koenig, 2013; McGee & Ukrainetz, 2009; Pieretti, Kaul, Zarchy, & O'Hanlon, 2015).

Figure 5.7 The development of phonological awareness is a continuum that begins with simple rhyming and ends with the manipulation of individual phonemes.

Rhyming ▶ Sentence Segmentation ▶ Syllable Segmentation and Blending ▶ Onset-Rime Blending ▶ Blending and Segmenting Individual Phonemes

Simple ─────────────────────────────▶ Complex

General Guidelines

- **Be specific.** Identify the specific phonemic awareness task and select the activities that are developmentally appropriate and that keep the students engaged in the task. Select words, phrases, and sentences from curricular materials to make this meaningful. Look for ways to make activities enjoyable so students see them as fun and not as monotonous drills.

- **Avoid letter names.** Use the phoneme sounds of the alphabet when doing activities and avoid letter names. Letters sounded as they are named can confuse the learner. Keep in mind that one sound may be represented by two or more letters. Target specific sounds and practice beforehand so students can hear them clearly.

- **Treat continuant and stop sounds differently.** Continuant sounds are easier to manipulate and hear than the stop sounds. When introducing each type, treat them differently so students become aware of their differences. Exaggerate continuant sounds by holding on to them: *sssssssing* and *rrrrrrun*. Use rapid repetition with the stop consonants: */K/-/K/-/K/-/K/-/K/-/K/-athy*.

- **Emphasize how sounds vary with their position in a word.** Generally, the initial position in the word is the easiest sound. The final position is the next easiest, and the middle position is the most difficult. Use lots of examples to make this clear, such as *mop*, *pin*, and *better*.

- **Be aware of the sequence for introducing combined sounds.** When introducing the combined sounds, a consonant-vowel pattern should come first, then a vowel-consonant pattern, and finally, the consonant-vowel-consonant pattern. For example: first *tie*, next *add*, and then *bed*.

- **Teach nursery rhymes.** Including nursery rhymes helps children develop the ability to rhyme. Read them aloud or say them in groups in songs and chants. Set up a listening station that includes nursery rhymes on audio CDs.

- **Create a sound box in the classroom.** When discussing a new sound, ask the students to bring in objects from home that begin with the new sound and place them in the box. For instance, if introducing the /b/ sound, students may bring in a ball, a toy boat, or a balloon.

- **Draw attention to rhyming words in classroom activities.** Take advantage of rhyming words in normal classroom activities. If a student says "ball" and "fall" in the same sentence, ask the students to identify the rhymes and think of additional rhyming words, such as "tall" and "wall."

Onset and Rime

The brain's awareness of onsets, rimes, and syllables develops before an awareness of phonemes. Onsets are the initial consonants that change the meaning of a word; rimes are the vowel-consonant combinations that stay constant in a series. For example, in *bend*, *lend*, and *send*, the onsets are *b*, *l*, and *s*; the rime is *-end*. Using literature, word families, and direct instruction are strategies that focus on word play designed to enhance onset and rime recognition (Gray, Reiser, & Brinkley, 2012; Petersen, Allen, & Spencer, 2014).

- **Literature.** Books with rhyming patterns (such as many books by Dr. Seuss) are easily recalled through repeated exposure. Almost any literary source that plays with word sounds is valuable. Books that particularly develop awareness of sound patterns associated with onset and rime are those using alliteration (the repetition of an initial consonant across several words, e.g., *Peter Piper picked a peck of peppers*) and assonance (the repetition of vowel sounds within words, e.g., *The rain in Spain stays mainly in the plain*).
- **Word Families Charts.** Using words from a story or book, construct a chart that places a different beginning letter in front of a rhyme. For example, start with the rhyme
- *-at* and add *f*, *h*, *b*, and *s* to form *fat*, *hat*, *bat*, and *sat*. Ask the students to make up a storyline whenever the word changes, for example, "The fat cat chased a hat." Encourage the students to make their own charts with different rimes and to keep them for future reference.
- **Direct Instruction.** Students who have difficulties distinguishing the sounds among rhyming words need more direct instruction. Model rhyming pairs (e.g., *sun-fun* and *hand-band*), using flash cards so students match what they see with what they hear. Be sure they repeat each rhyming pair several times to reinforce auditory input. Another activity includes three cards, only two of which have rhyming words. Ask students to pick out and say the two that rhyme or the one that does not. Later, change the rhyming words to two rhyming pictures out of three (e.g., a nose, a rose, and a horse).

Strategies to Consider

SIMPLE PHONEMIC AWARENESS

Young students are usually unaware that words are made of sounds that can be produced in isolation. This leaves it up to the teacher to find ways to emphasize the concept of speech sounds through *systematic* and *direct* instruction. An effective reading program should include activities that help children manipulate phonemes. Here are some ways to do this (Los Angeles County Office of Education, 2015):

- **Recognizing Isolated Sounds.** Associate certain speech sounds with an animal or action that is familiar to the students. For example, the buzzing sound of a bee or snoring in sleep is *zzzzzzzz–*, the hissing of a snake, *sssssss–*, the sound of asking for quiet, *shhhhhhhh–*, or the sound of a motor scooter or motor boat, *pppppppp–*. Alliteration also helps with this task. Talking about Peter Piper picking a peck of peppers affords the valuable combination of sound recognition, storytelling, and literary context. It also provides self-correcting cues for initial-sound isolation and for sound-to-word matching.

- **Counting Words, Syllables, and Phonemes.** It is easier for a child's brain to perceive words and syllables than individual phonemes. Thus word and syllable counting is a valuable exercise for sound recognition that can lead later to more accurate identification of phonemes. Start with a sentence and say it aloud. Do not write it out because the students should focus on listening. Ask the students to count the number of words they think are in the sentence. They can use markers or tokens to indicate the word number. Then show or write the sentence, and have the students compare the number of words to their own count. Syllable counting can be done in many ways. Students can count syllables in the same way they identified the word count. Also, they can march around the room while saying the syllables; they can clap hands, tap pencils, or do any overt activity that indicates counting.

- **Synthesizing Sounds.** Sound synthesis is an essential yet easily performed skill for phonemic awareness. Start with using the initial sound and then saying the remainder of the word. For example, the teacher says, "It starts with *b* and ends with *-and*; put it together, and it says *band*." The students take turns using the same phrasing to make up their own words. Variations include limiting the context to objects in the classroom or in the school, or to a particular story that the class has recently read. Guessing games can also be productive and fun activities for playing with sounds. One game involves hiding an object in a bag or other place and giving clues to its name sound-by-sound or syllable-by-syllable. When a student guesses the word correctly, you reveal the object. Songs can also be used. Blending the music with the sounds of words increases the chances that the phonemes will be remembered.

- **Matching Sounds to Words.** This activity asks the learner to identify the initial sound of a word, an important skill for sound segmentation. Show a picture of a kite and ask, "Is this a *dddd-ite,* or a *llll-ite,* or a *kkkk-ite?*" You could also ask, "Is there a *k* in *kite?*" or "Which sound does *kite* start with?" This allows students to try three onsets with three rimes and to mix and match until they get it correct. Consonants are a good beginning because they are easier to emphasize and prolong during pronunciation. Ask students to try other words in threes. Be sure to use the phoneme sound when referring to a letter, not the letter name.

- **Teaching Sound Substitution.** Try some rhyming riddles using onset and rime, such as asking children for riddles that require them to manipulate sounds in their heads. The easiest are the ones that ask for endings. The next easiest are the ones that ask for a single consonant substitution at the beginning. The most difficult are the ones that ask for a consonant blend or digraph at the beginning. For example, what rhymes with pig and starts with /d/? *dig.* What rhymes with book and starts with /c/? *cook.* What rhymes with sing and starts with /r/? *ring.* What rhymes with dog and starts with /fr/? *frog.*

- **Identifying the Position of Sounds.** Segmenting whole words into their components is an important part of phonemic awareness. This ability is enhanced when learners recognize that sounds occur in different positions in words: initial, medial, and final. Explain that words have beginning, middle, and end sounds just like a train has a beginning (engine), middle (passenger car), and end (caboose). Slowly articulate a consonant-vowel-consonant (CVC) word at this time, such as *c-a-t,* and point to the appropriate train part as you sound out each phoneme. Then ask the students to sound out other CVC words from a list or recent story, pointing to each train part as they say them.

- **Segmenting Sounds.** One of the more difficult phonemic tasks for children is to separately pronounce each sound of a spoken word in order. This process is called sound segmentation. Developing this skill should start with isolating the initial phonemes. The previous activities—matching sounds to words and identifying the position of sounds—help the learner identify and recognize initial phonemes. Visual cues can also play an important part in segmenting sounds. Select words that are familiar to the students (or ask the students to select the words) so that they can use contextual clues for meaning. After sufficient practice, eliminate the cards so that students can perform the sound segmenting task without visual cues.

- **Associating Sounds With Letters (Alphabetic Principle).** For successful reading, the brain must associate the sounds it has heard during the prereading years of spoken language with the written letters that represent them. This is particularly difficult for students with disabilities that hamper the learning of reading. Consequently, extensive practice is essential. Nearly all the activities mentioned above—especially those involving visual cues—can be modified to include associations between sounds and letters. As students master individual sounds, their corresponding letter names can then be introduced. A type of bingo game can also be used to practice sound-with-letter association. Each student gets a card with letters placed into a bingo grid. Draw a letter from a container and call out the phoneme. Students place tokens on the letter that corresponds to the phoneme. The student who first gets "phoneme bingo" names the letters aloud. Teachers can devise all types of variations to this fun bingo game.

Strategies to Consider

COMPOUND PHONEMIC AWARENESS

In compound phonemic awareness, the learner must hold one sound in memory and match it to a second sound. For example, "Do *dog* and *deer* begin with the same sound?" Two activities that develop compound phonemic awareness involve matching one word to a second word and the deleting of sounds in a word.

- **Matching One Word to Another Word.** Byrne (1991) has suggested three games for developing phonemic word matching skills that are still used successfully today. The words and pictures used in each of these games should relate to themes and readings done in the classroom. One involves making a set of dominoes that have two objects pictured on each tile. The students have to join the tiles that share the same beginning or ending sounds.

A second game uses picture cards that are placed face down in a pile. Each student draws a card from the pile and places it face up. Students continue to draw cards and place them in the face-up pile. The first student to match the beginning or ending sound of a drawn card with the top card on the face-up pile says the match aloud and collects the pile.

The third game is a variation of bingo. Each bingo card contains pictures, which the students mark when their picture has the same beginning or ending sounds as the word said by the caller (student or teacher).

- **Deleting Sounds.** Deleting sounds from words and manipulating phonemes within words are more difficult tasks for the young brain to accomplish. Furthermore, segmentation skills and letter names must be mastered before sound-deletion tasks can be successfully learned.

Three tasks seem to be particularly important to mastering this skill: deleting parts of a compound word, identifying a missing sound, and deleting a single sound from a word.

- *Deleting parts of a compound word.* To illustrate deleting parts of a compound word, point to a picture or an object that is a compound word and demonstrate how each word can be said with one part missing. For example, "This is a classroom. I can say *class* without the *room*. And this is a farmhouse (or greenhouse). I can say *farm* (*green*) without *house*. Now you try it. This is a playground." Use other common examples, such as *lighthouse, airplane, grandmother, seashore, sandbox, toothpaste,* and *night-light.*
- *Identifying the missing sound.* In this task, focus on deleting the initial and final sounds instead of the medial sounds, which

is the first step to master for the young brain. Take word pairs, such as *ate-late,* and ask "What's missing in *ate* that you hear in *late*?" Other examples are *ask-mask, able-table,* and *right-bright.* After a few trials, have the students make up their own word pairs, preferably from lesson material.

- *Deleting a single sound from a word.* This task should begin with segmentation practice. First, separate the sound for deletion. For example, separate *g* from *glove.* "Glove. It starts with *g* and ends with *love.* Take the first sound away and it says *love.*" Use words for which a sound deletion results in another real word. Other examples are *spot-pot, train-rain, scare-care,* and *snap-nap.* After practicing this skill, say a word aloud and ask students to say the word with the initial sound missing: "Say *mother* without the *m.*" Visual clues can help those who have difficulty saying a word with the deleted sound.

Strategies to Consider

READING STRATEGIES FOR FLUENCY AND COMPREHENSION

Studies have shown that children with reading problems are able to master the learning strategies that improve reading comprehension skills. For students with learning problems, learning to use questioning strategies is especially important because these students do not often spontaneously self-question or monitor their own reading comprehension.

Here are three strategies that researchers and teachers have found particularly effective. Some of the strategies have been around for over 20 years, but research continues to reaffirm their fundamental premises (e.g., Scammacca, Roberts, Vaughn, & Stuebing, 2015; Stricklin, 2011; Vaughn et al., 2011).

Questioning and Paraphrasing: Reciprocal Teaching

Reciprocal teaching is a strategic approach that fosters student interaction with the text being read (Palincsar & Brown, 1984). In reciprocal teaching, students interact deeply with the text through the strategies of questioning, summarizing, clarifying, and predicting. Organized in the form of a discussion, the approach involves one leader (students and teacher take turns being the leader), who, after a portion of the text is read, first frames a question to which the group responds. Second, participants share their own questions. Third, the leader summarizes the gist of the text, and participants comment or elaborate on that summary. At any point in the discussion, either the leader or participants may identify aspects of the text or discussion that need to be clarified, and the group joins together to clarify the confusion. Finally, the leader indicates

Video: For a video clip explaining reciprocal teaching, see:

https://www.youtube.com/watch?v=My68SDGeTHI

that it is time to move on and solicits predictions about what might come up next in the text.

Paraphasing, self-questioning, and finding the main idea are well-researched strategies having much value. Students divide reading passages into smaller parts, such as sections, subsections, or paragraphs. After reading a segment, students are cued to use a self-questioning strategy to identify main ideas and details. The strategy requires a high level of attention to reading tasks because students must alternate their use of questioning and paraphrasing after reading each section, subsection, or paragraph. Furthermore, it incorporates all modes of communication, including reading, writing, speaking, and listening. Consequently, students are more likely to find meaning in what they are reading, thereby increasing the likelihood they will remember it. Although paraphrasing for comprehension does not have to be used in every reading situation, it is another effective strategy designed to increase students' understanding of text (Williams, 2010).

Questioning to Find the Main Idea

This self-questioning strategy focuses primarily on identifying and questioning the main idea or summary of a paragraph. Here's how it works. Students are first taught the concept of a main idea and how to do self-questioning. Students then practice, asking themselves questions aloud about each paragraph's main idea. They can use a cue card for assistance. Following the practice, the teacher provides immediate feedback. Eventually, following successful comprehension of these short paragraphs, students are presented with lengthier passages, and the cue cards are removed. Continuing to give corrective feedback, the teacher finishes each lesson with a discussion of students' progress and of the strategy's usefulness. Studies show that students with learning disabilities who were trained in a self-questioning strategy performed significantly higher (i.e., demonstrated greater comprehension of what was read) than untrained students (Berkeley, Marshak, Mastropieri, & Scruggs, 2011).

Story Mapping

One major challenge for older struggling readers is their difficulty in determining the relative importance of the material they are reading. They often cannot pick out the main ideas from text or identify the information that leads to the main idea. Story maps can help. Studies show story mapping to be an effective strategy with struggling readers (e.g., Edmonds et al., 2009), including those with emotional and behavioral problems (Vannest, Harrison, Temple-Harvey, Ramsey, & Parker, 2011).

In this strategy, students read a story, generate a map of its events and ideas, and then answer questions. Figure 5.8 is one example of a story map. To fill in the map, students have to identify the setting, characters, time, and place of the story; the problem, the goal, and the action that took place; and the outcome. The teacher models for students how to fill in the map, then gives them many opportunities to practice the mapping technique for themselves and receive corrective feedback. The map is an effective visual

Figure 5.8   This is just one example of a story map. By filling in the information, students get a vivid visual representation that helps them understand, conceptualize, and remember important aspects of the story.

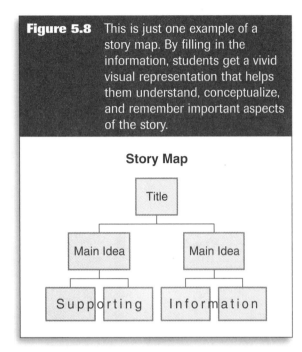

tool that provides a framework for understanding, conceptualizing, and remembering important story events. The reading comprehension of students can improve significantly when the teacher gives direct instruction on the use of the strategy, expects frequent use of the strategy, and encourages students to use the strategy independently. The story map in Figure 5.8 focuses on story content, but some story maps are designed to also help students with reading difficulties enhance their understanding of story grammar and syntax.

For older students who have reading difficulties, more specific story maps can be very effective, such as the one shown in Figure 5.9 (Hennes, Büyüknarci, Rietz, & Grünke, 2015). The students respond to the questions on the story map as they proceed through their reading.

Figure 5.9   Here is an example of a story map suitable for middle and high school students. It has been used successfully with students who have reading and other learning difficulties (Adapted from Li, 2007).

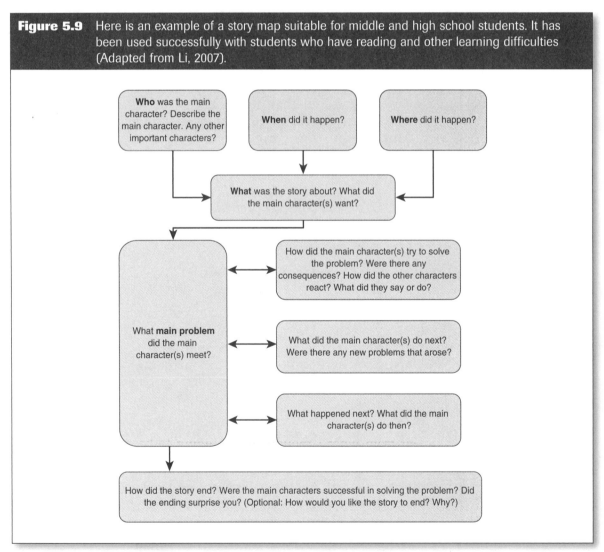

Strategies to Consider

TEACHING FOR READING COMPREHENSION

Students with reading disorders often have difficulty deriving meaning from what they read. If little or no meaning comes from reading, students lose motivation to read. Furthermore, meaning is essential for long-term retention of what they have read. Strategies designed to improve reading comprehension have been shown to improve students' interest in reading and their success (Scammacca et al., 2015).

The PASS Process

One such successful brain-friendly strategy, suggested by Deshler, Ellis, and Lenz (1996), is a four-step process called by the acronym **PASS** (**P**review, **A**sk, **S**ummarize, and **S**ynthesize). Although there are not any research studies carried out on this specific strategy, there have been a number of studies showing that the individual PASS *components* (that is, predicting, questioning, summarizing, and integrating new and past learning) do increase reading achievement in students with reading problems (e.g., Solis et al. 2012; Vaughn et al., 2011; Williams, 2010). The synergy resulting from putting these four effective components together in a coherent sequence helps students with reading difficulties to improve their reading comprehension.

The teacher guides the students through the four steps, ensuring that they respond orally or in writing to the activities associated with each step. Grouping formats, such as cooperative learning, can be used to encourage active student participation and reduce anxiety over the correctness of each student's response.

1. **P***review, Review, and Predict:*

   - Preview by reading the heading and one or two sentences.
   - Review what you already know about this topic.
   - Predict what you think the text or story will be about.

2. **A***sk and Answer Questions:*

   - Content-focused questions:

     Who? What? Why? Where?
     How does this relate to what I already know?

   - Monitoring questions:

     Does this make sense?
     Is my prediction correct?
     How is this different from what I thought it was going to be about?

   - Problem-solving questions:

     Is it important that it make sense?
     Do I need to reread part of it?
     Can I visualize the information?

Does it have too many unknown words?
Should I get help?

3. **S**ummarize:

- Explain what the short passage you read was all about.

4. **S**ynthesize:

- Explain how the short passage fits in with the whole passage.
- Explain how what you learned fits in with what you knew.

If students have difficulty with any particular step, they can go back to the previous step to determine what information they need in order to proceed.

Preview

Ask

Summarize

Synthesize

Collaborative Strategic Reading

Video: For a video clip explaining collaborative strategic reading, see:

https://www.youtube.com/watch?v=nYWt5WSSSDg

Another excellent technique for helping students comprehend what they read and build vocabulary is called *collaborative strategic reading* (CSR). It is particularly effective in classrooms where students have many different reading abilities and learning capabilities. The strategy is compatible with all types of reading programs. Longitudinal and other studies show that students in CSR classrooms improved significantly in reading comprehension compared to students in control groups (Beyers, Lembke, & Curs, 2013; Klingner, Vaughn, Arguelles, Hughes, & Leftwich, 2004; Vaughn et al., 2011).

CSR uses modified reciprocal teaching and the collaborative power of cooperative learning groups to accomplish two phases designed to improve reading comprehension. The first phase is a teacher-led component that takes students through four parts of a reading plan: Preview, Click and Clunk, Get the Gist, and Wrap-Up. The second phase involves using cooperative learning groups to provide an interactive environment where students can practice and perfect their reading comprehension skills.

Phase One

Teacher-Led Activities

- **Preview the reading.** Students know that previews in movies give some information about coming events. Use this as a hook to the new reading. The learners preview the entire reading passage in order to get as much as they can about the passage in just a few minutes' time. The purpose here is to activate their prior knowledge about the topic and to give them an opportunity to predict what they will learn.

  Refer to student experiences about a movie, television program, or a prior book that might contain information relevant to the new reading. Also, give clues to look for when previewing. For example, pictures, graphs, tables, or call-out quotes provide information to help predict what students already know about the topic and what they will learn.

- **Click and clunk.** Students with reading problems often fail to monitor their understanding while they read. Clicks and clunks are devices to help students with this monitoring. Clicks are parts of the reading that make sense; clunks are parts or words that don't.
- Ask students to identify clunks as they go along. Then the class works with the teacher to develop strategies to clarify the clunks, such as
  - Rereading the sentences while looking for key words that can help extract meaning from the context
  - Rereading previous and following sentences to get additional context clues
  - Looking for a prefix or suffix in the word that could help with meaning
  - Breaking the word apart to see if smaller words are present that provide meaning
- **Get the gist.** The goal of this phase is twofold. First, ask the readers to state in their own words the most important person, place, or thing in the passage. Second, get them to tell in as few words as possible (i.e., leaving out the details) the most important *idea* about that person, place, or thing. Because writing often improves memory, occasionally ask the students to write down their gists. Students can then read their gists aloud and invite comments from the group about ways to improve the gist. This process can be done so that all students benefit by enhancing their skills.
- **Wrap-up.** Wrap-up is a closure activity that allows students to review in their minds what has been learned. Focus students on the new learning by asking them to generate questions whose answers would show what they learned from the passage. They should also review key ideas.

  Start with questions that focus on the explicit material in the passage, such as who, what, where, and when. Afterward, move to questions that stimulate higher order thinking, such as "What might have happened if . . . ?" and "What could be another way to solve this problem?" Writing down the response will help students sort out and remember the important ideas.

Phase Two

Cooperative Learning Groups

This phase puts the students into cooperative learning groups to practice CSR in an interactive environment. True cooperative learning groups are usually made up of about five students of mixed ability levels who learn and perform certain roles in the group to ensure completion of the learning task (Johnson & Johnson, 1989). The roles rotate among the group members so that every student gets the opportunity to be the leader and use the various skills needed to perform each task. Although there are many roles that students can perform, here are the most common (assuming four members per group):

- **Leader.** Leads the group through CSR by saying what to read next and what strategy to use.
- **Clunk Expert.** Reminds the group what strategies to use when encountering a difficult word or phrase.
- **Announcer.** Calls on different group members to make certain that everyone participates and that only one person talks at a time.
- **Gist Expert.** Guides the group toward getting the gist and determines that the gist contains the most important ideas but no unnecessary details.

Other suggestions for using the cooperative learning groups with this strategy are as follows:

- **Cue Sheets.** Giving all group members a cue sheet to guide them through the CSR provides a structure and focus for the group. The cue sheet should be specific for each role. For example, the leader's sheet contains statements that steer the group through each step of CSR (e.g., "Today's topic is . . . " "Let's predict what we might learn from this." "Let's think of some questions to see if we really understand what we learned.") and also direct other group members to carry out their role (e.g., "Announcer, please call on others to share their ideas." "Encourager, tell us what we did well and what we need to do better next time.").
- **CSR Learning Logs.** Recording in logs helps students keep track of what was learned. Students can keep separate logs for each subject. The log serves as a reminder for follow-up activities and can be used to document a student's progress as required by the individualized education plan.
- **Reading Materials.** CSR was originally designed for expository text but has also been used successfully with narrative text. For the strategy to be successful, select reading passages that are rich in clues, that have just one main idea per paragraph, and that provide a context to help students connect and associate details into larger ideas.

Strategies to Consider

REPEATED READING WITH A MODEL

- Simultaneous, repeated reading with a tutor is an effective method for improving the fluency of reluctant readers (e.g., Ring, Barefoot, Avrit, Brown, & Black, 2013; Therrien, Kirk, & Woods-Groves, 2012). By carefully adjusting the timing and control of the repeated readings, the tutor helps the student foster independent reading skills. Here are the three steps to this approach.

Step One: Introduction

- Start with a passage that will take 3–5 minutes for the student to read aloud.
- Read the title.
- Give a general description of the topic.
- Ask if the student knows anything about the topic.
- Give a reason or purpose for reading the topic.
- Explain that the passage may be difficult so you will read it together.

Step Two: Simultaneous Reading

- Read the passage with the student, sitting slightly behind so as not to be a visual distraction.
- Read slowly in a clear, soft voice as the student reads aloud at the same time.
- Regulate your speed of reading to allow the student to keep up.
- The student and you should move your fingers under the printed text as you read.
- Listen carefully as to whether the student is following, with, or leading your reading of difficult words. Most students will initially follow the tutor. But with greater confidence, they will read more nearly with the tutor, and eventually will lead.
- As the student comes closer to your reading speed, soften your voice. As the student leads more, soften your voice further and slow your pace slightly to allow the student to lead even more.

Step Three: Simultaneous Repeated Readings

- After a short break, begin rereading. From two to five readings will be beneficial, depending on the student's motivation and age.
- With each rereading, maintain a smooth pace and encourage the student to read with you and to lead by softening your voice and slowing your pace slightly.

6

Writing Disabilities

Let every young man and woman be warned by my example, and understand that good handwriting is a necessary part of education.

—Mahatma Gandhi

Once the enormous challenge of learning to read is undertaken, the brain is faced with the daunting task of directing fine muscle movements to draw the abstract symbols that represent the sounds of language. For many years, researchers thought that the mental centers responsible for speech and writing were located in the same (left) side of the brain. Imaging studies, however, have indicated that these two processes are related yet separate, sometimes residing in different cerebral hemispheres (Richards et al., 2015). This finding, which suggests that spoken and written language develop differently, is not surprising when we realize that human beings have been speaking for well over 100,000 years but writing for only about 5,000 years (Perreault & Mathew, 2012). Thus spoken language has become innate and usually develops with ease, but writing usually does not develop without instruction.

IS THIS CHAPTER EVEN RELEVANT?

Some may question whether this chapter about writing difficulties is even relevant given the recent initiatives to abandon the teaching of cursive handwriting in elementary schools. The Common Core State Standards for English Language Arts, which most of the states have adopted in some form, set aside cursive writing in favor of keyboarding and other technology-based literacy learning. Supporters of the anticursive initiative argue that it is no longer relevant in an increasingly digital society, and it is not a skill needed for success in the 21st century. They also contend that teaching cursive writing is a waste of valuable class time, which should be used instead to focus on the broader communication skills (e.g., grammar and sentence structure) that are needed to succeed on state standardized tests.

Proponents of cursive writing say that cursive handwriting requires a different skill set from block printing and it helps develop motor skills while activating areas of the brain that do not play a part in learning keyboarding. Learning cursive writing, they say, allows children to improve their memory and critical thinking as well as their reading, spelling, and composition. They further note that a student moving from block printing to cursive is analogous to the way that student learns to read, namely by first sounding out a word before moving on to speaking fluently. Contrary to what the opponents suggest, supporters argue that legible handwriting is still a modern-day necessity as a back-up skill in situations where technology is not available. Also, students unable to read cursive could be at a disadvantage when faced with their teachers' handwritten feedback or when researching an old document written in cursive.

What Does the Research Say?

Research evidence to date supports the teaching of cursive for several reasons. Brain imaging studies of young children find that handwriting recruits areas of the brain known to be involved in successful reading, while typing does not (e.g., James & Engelhardt, 2012). It also activates more cerebral areas involved in fine motor skills, leading to automaticity in grapho-motor skill development (e.g., Harralson, 2013). Several studies show that handwriting is positively linked to academic performance (e.g., Dinehart & Manfra, 2013; Feder & Majnemer, 2007; Grissmer, Grimm, Aiyer, Murrah, & Steele, 2010). A study of preschoolers found that those who already had practice in handwriting words were better able to identify letters in words than preschoolers who typed the same words on a keyboard (Longcamp, Zerbato-Poudou, & Velay, 2005).

> Despite the push from technology to abandon cursive writing, the research supports cursive writing as an important device for improving motor skills, attention, reading, and academic achievement.

Recall from Chapter 2 that three separate studies compared high school students and college freshmen who wrote teacher lecture notes on paper to those who took laptop notes (Mueller & Oppenheimer, 2014). After testing both groups of students, those who took handwritten notes were better able to recall, integrate, and apply their new learning compared to the students who took their notes on a laptop. Writing by hand is slower than typing, forcing the student to listen, process, and then jot down a summary of the teacher's statements. Handwriting also requires a greater focus of attention than the automaticity of typing (MacMahon & Charness, 2014). As a result, these interacting cerebral processes lead to deeper understanding and retention of learning. In summary, despite the push from digital technology to abandon cursive writing in favor of keyboarding, research studies to date support cursive writing as an important device for improving fine motor skills, attention, reading, and academic achievement. There is no reason why students cannot learn both cursive *and* keyboarding.

LEARNING TO WRITE

Learning to write consists of integrating two components: the consolidation of mental functions that select the content of the writing (the writing process) with the physical act of moving a writing instrument across a surface to form words (handwriting). This is not an easy accomplishment, especially for young children whose executive thought processes and fine motor skills are at early stages of development.

Writing is a highly complex operation requiring the coordination of multiple neural networks. It involves the blending of attention, fine motor coordination, memory, visual processing, language, and higher order thinking. When an individual is writing, the visual feedback mechanisms are at work checking the output, adjusting fine motor skills, and monitoring eye-hand coordination. Meanwhile, kinesthetic monitoring systems are conscious of the position and movement of fingers in space, the grip on the pencil, and the rhythm and pace of the writing. Cognitive systems are also busy, verifying with long-term memory that the symbols being drawn will indeed produce the sounds of the word that the writer intends. Accomplishing this task requires visual memory for symbols, whole-word memory, and spelling rules. Hence, the phoneme-to-grapheme match is a continuous feedback loop ensuring that the written symbols are consistent with the oral language protocols the writer has previously learned.

Brain imaging studies have shown the labor-intensive nature of writing. The parietal lobe, which includes the motor cortex, and the occipital lobe, where visual processing occurs, were the areas of highest activity (Figure 6.1) when an individual was writing (Planton, Jucla, Roux, & Démonet, 2013; Wing, 2000). Not surprising was the discovery that spoken-language areas in the left hemisphere were also activated. Writing relies heavily on speech because most of us sound out words in our head as we write them down.

After reviewing numerous scanning studies on the writing process, Alan Wing (2000) pieced together a complex flow diagram illustrating the relationships between the neurological networks responsible for both speech and writing. Figure 6.2 is a simplified version of Wing's diagram. The visual systems analyze the spelling and grammar as it is written out on paper (orthography) and adjust the motor output to form the letters correctly. Simultaneously, the auditory system is sounding out the words in the brain (phonological output), associating and converting the sounds to letters (phoneme-to-grapheme conversion) for writing (motor output). Other studies lend support to Wing's design (e.g., Alonso, 2015; Planton et al., 2013).

At a minimum, the ability to write requires a properly functioning central nervous system, intact receptive and expressive language skills, and the related cognitive operations. To write accurately and clearly also requires emotional stability; application of the concepts of organization and flow; an understanding of the rules of pronunciation, spelling, grammar, and syntax; visual and spatial organization; and simultaneous processing.

When all these operations fall into place, writing becomes a valuable tool for learning. Writing focuses attention, encourages mental rehearsal,

Figure 6.1 In a right-handed individual, writing involves mainly the left parietal lobe. For a left-handed person, the right parietal lobe is the area of main activation. Regardless of which hand is used, the visual cortex involvement is the same.

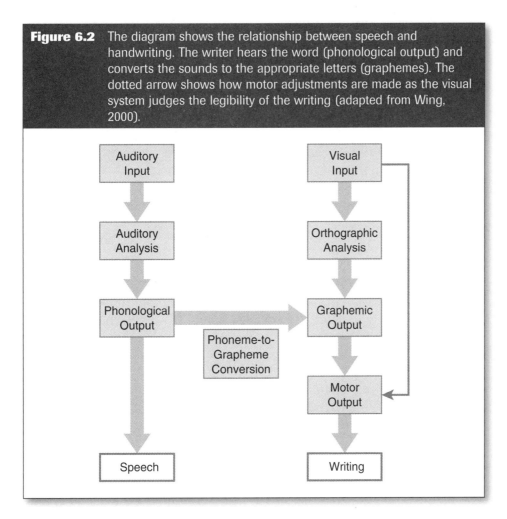

Figure 6.2 The diagram shows the relationship between speech and handwriting. The writer hears the word (phonological output) and converts the sounds to the appropriate letters (graphemes). The dotted arrow shows how motor adjustments are made as the visual system judges the legibility of the writing (adapted from Wing, 2000).

reinforces long-term memory, and helps the mind sort and prioritize information. However, for some students, the process of writing becomes an arduous task that actually interferes with learning.

DIFFICULTIES IN WRITING

Environmental Causes

Difficulties with writing can be environmental—that is, too little time was spent in the child's early years on practicing correct writing—or they can stem from deficits within one or more of the neural networks needed for legible and clear writing to occur. Let's deal first with how the school environment may contribute inadvertently to writing problems.

Teachers of writing should realize that, like reading, the brain does not perceive writing to be a survival skill. That is, the brain has no "writing centers" comparable to those for spoken language. Instead, writing requires the coordination of numerous neural networks and systems, all which have to learn new skills. Learning to write therefore requires direct instruction; it is not innate to the brain. Hard work and lots of practice are needed just to learn the fine motor skills for reproducing the printed and cursive letters of the alphabet. In some schools, little time is given to formal instruction in handwriting. To conserve time, it is often taught as an activity ancillary to other learning tasks. Some of the difficulties students experience with writing may be due to an unfortunate combination of learning the difficult skills of writing with very little practice time. Furthermore, students are questioning the need to write well because they have access to computers at an early age and typing into a word processing program seems so much easier. Therefore, teachers should explain to their students that writing may help them learn some information better than typing.

> There are no areas of the brain specialized for writing.

Invented Spelling

In Chapter 5, we noted that learning to read English is more of a challenge than many other languages because of its deep orthography—that is, the numerous ways in which its 44-plus phonemes can be represented in the alphabet. As a consequence, learning to spell English words is a difficult task because the rules have so many exceptions. Take the most commonly expressed rule: *"I" before "e" except after "c" or sounded as "a" as in "neighbor" or "weigh."* Yet, a very common word such as "science" violates the rule. It is no wonder, then, that children learning to write often spell words the way they sound them out, irrespective of any rules of spelling.

Spelling is closely linked to reading because it involves breaking apart a spoken word into its sounds and encoding them into the letters representing each sound. While learning to read words, children also learn how to spell those words. As children try to represent words in writing with the alphabet, they often encode words by their initial consonants, followed by their ending sounds. Middle sounds, usually vowels, are omitted at first. Thus, *horse* might be written as *hrs* and *monster* as *mstr*. The pronunciation of this *invented spelling* is very close to that of the intended word. Invented spelling allows children to practice applying the alphabetic principle and gain in phonemic awareness. It serves as a transitional step and assists in the development of reading and writing.

Studies on early literacy development have shown that invented spelling is a reliable measure of early reading achievement. Preschool children who were inventive spellers performed significantly better on word reading and that invented spelling was the best predictor of how well kindergartners could match, through finger-point reading, spoken words to printed words (Niessen, Strattman, & Scudder, 2011). Other studies confirm that invented spelling is developmentally based and can increase a child's achievement in spelling, reading, and writing.

When their invented spelling is accepted, children feel empowered to write more and with purpose, communicating their messages from the very beginning of school. Writing slows down the process of dealing with text, allowing children more time to recognize and learn about sound-letter relationships. For some children, writing may be an easier way to literacy than reading. In reading, the process involves changing letter sequences to sounds, whereas in writing the process is reversed—going from sounds to letters. Accordingly, writing may be a simpler task because it involves going from sounds in the child's head that are already known and automatic to letters rather than from the unknown letters in reading to what is known.

Some educators and parents in the past have raised concerns about whether the persistent use of invented spelling leads to confusion and the formation of bad spelling habits. But research studies indicate that, with appropriate teacher intervention, the invented spellings gradually come closer to conventional forms. Consequently, spelling errors should not be seen as an impediment to writing but as an indication of the child's thought processes while making sense of letter-sound relationships. From that perspective, the errors could yield important information about a child's internal reading patterns (Sipe, 2001). On the other hand, remember that practice eventually makes permanent. The consistent repetition of incorrect spellings will, in time, lead to their storage in long-term memory. Therefore, teachers should use strategies that will help children transform invented spelling into conventional spelling. Furthermore, as children begin to use word processing programs with a spell-check feature, they will become more familiar with the correct spelling of the words in their vocabulary.

> Invented spelling allows children to practice applying the alphabetic principle and gain in phonemic awareness.

Neurological Causes

Given that such a complex order of operations is necessary for accurate writing, difficulties can arise anywhere within the neural systems involved. Because writing is so dependent on the brain's parietal lobes, for instance, a lesion or stroke in this area would be especially significant. Another possible source of writing difficulty could result from problems with receptor cells located in the skin, muscles, tendons, and joints. These specialized cells, called **proprioceptors** (meaning "receptors for self") provide continuous information to the brain about the position of the limbs and head in space. Any deficits in the proprioceptor pathways could interfere with the intricate muscle coordination needed for legible and fluent writing (de Nooij, Doobar, & Jessell, 2013)

Although researchers admit that eye problems could contribute to poor handwriting, there is little research evidence to support a connection between poor eyesight and persistently poor penmanship. It is more likely that any visual deficit results from problems in the visual processing system deep within the brain (Vlachos & Karapetsas, 2003). Furthermore, if corrective glasses improve the handwriting, then it is likely the individual does not have a writing disability.

Whatever the neurological cause of writing difficulties, some children struggle because so much time is spent on the transcribing *process* that they often lose track of the *content* they are working on. The persistent condition of not being able to put thoughts into writing or accomplish other parts of the writing process (such as letter formation) is known as *developmental dysgraphia*.

DYSGRAPHIA

Symptoms:

- Inconsistencies in letter formation; mixture of upper and lower cases, of print and cursive letters
- Unfinished words or letters
- Generally illegible writing (despite time given to the task)
- Talking to self while writing
- Watching hand while writing
- Inconsistent position on page with respect to margins and lines
- Slow copying or writing
- Omitted words in writing
- Inconsistent spaces between letters and words
- Struggle to use writing as a communication tool
- Cramped or unusual grip on pencil
- Unusual body, wrist, or paper position

Dysgraphia

Dysgraphia (also known as *agraphia*) is a spectrum disorder describing major difficulties in mastering the sequence of movements necessary to write letters and numbers. The disorder exists in varying degrees and is seldom found in isolation without symptoms of other learning problems.

Many students have difficulty with writing as they progress through the upper elementary grades. But those with dysgraphia are inefficient at *handwriting* more than anything else, and this inefficiency establishes a barrier to learning. Their handwriting is usually characterized by slow copying, inconsistencies in letter formation, mixtures of different letters and styles, and poor legibility. Specific symptoms of the disorder are shown in the box titled *Dysgraphia*. Teachers must realize that dysgraphia is a disorder and is *not* the result of laziness, not caring, not trying, or just carelessness in writing.

What Causes Dysgraphia?

Dysgraphia is a neurological disorder that can stem from several causes. Although there are many individual variations, dysgraphia can be broadly classified into the following three types (Table 6.1) (Berninger & May, 2011; Heilman, 2002; IDA, 2015a; Kushki, Schwellnus, Ilyas, & Chau, 2011; Martins et al., 2013; Rapcsak et al., 2009).

Dyslexic Dysgraphia. Handwriting requires the ability to convert the sounds of language into the letters that represent them. The inability to make this phoneme-to-grapheme conversion usually results in poorly legible written text and severely abnormal spelling. Individuals with dyslexic dysgraphia may be able to write most simple words such as *dog* or *hat*, but run into trouble writing words such as *tomb*. If they had no prior exposure to *tomb*, they may write *toom*. However, these individuals can draw and copy written text adequately because little or no phoneme-to-grapheme conversion is required.

MRI studies have shown that individuals with dyslexic dysgraphia often have lesions in the brain's left parietal lobe in or near the visual word form area. You may recall from Chapter 5 that this is the region actively involved in decoding and matching phonemes and graphemes.

Motor Dysgraphia. Problems with muscles controlling motor output to the hands, wrists, and fingers lead to a motor clumsiness that also produces poorly legible handwriting, drawing and copying. Students may also have memory deficits that interfere with their ability to remember the motor patterns of letter forms. Spelling, however, is generally good because the phoneme-to-grapheme systems are unaffected.

Spatial Dysgraphia. Sometimes, deficits in the spatial processing functions of the brain's right hemisphere cause poorly legible text, but with accurate spelling. Copying is poor to legible, depending on the spatial complexity of the original text.

Diagnosing Dysgraphia

Dysgraphia cannot be diagnosed just by looking at a sample of handwriting. A qualified clinician must directly test the individual. Determining which type of writing disorder a child has requires the assessment of various factors, such as fine motor coordination,

Video: For a brief description of dysgraphia and helpful hints see:

https://www.youtube.com/watch?v=jmBg_BvDL-c

Table 6.1 Different Types of Dysgraphia

Type	Symptoms			Possible Cause
	Legibility	Spelling	Copying	
Dyslexic Dysgraphia	Poor	Poor	Satisfactory	Deficits/lesions in phoneme-to-grapheme conversion
Motor Dysgraphia	Poor	Satisfactory	Poor	Deficits in muscle control of motor output to fingers, wrist, and hand
Spatial Dysgraphia	Poor	Satisfactory	Satisfactory	Deficits/lesions in spatial processing systems of the brain's right hemisphere

Sources: Berninger & May, 2011; Heilman, 2002; IDA, 2015a.

writing speed, organization, knowledge and use of vocabulary, spelling, and the degree of attention and concentration. Based on the work of Berninger and May (2011) and other researchers, clinicians examining children for dysgraphia should consider administering tests from among the following collection:

- University of Washington Alphabet Writing I 5
- Weschler Individual Achievement Test—Second Edition in Spelling
- Weschler Individual Achievement Test—Second Edition in Written Expression
- Weschler Individual Achievement Test—Second Edition in Word Reading
- Weschler Individual Achievement Test—Second Edition in Pseudoword Reading
- Weschler Individual Achievement Test—Second Edition in Reading Comprehension
- Woodcock Johnson III in Writing Fluency
- Process Assessment of the Learner (PAL) in Finger Succession
- Process Assessment of the Learner (PAL) in rapid automatic naming
- Process Assessment of the Learner (PAL) in rapid automatic switching
- Clinical Evaluation of Language Fundamentals, Fourth Edition in Formulated Sentences
- Tests of working memory
- Tests of emotional control
- Behavior Rating Inventory of Executive Function (BRIEF)
- Test of Word Reading Efficiency (TOWRE)
- Family history

We now know that the centers for processing spoken language and written language are separated in the brain. Teachers should not assume, therefore, that a student with symptoms of dysgraphia will have other language problems as well. In fact, students with dysgraphia but who are otherwise linguistically talented find enormous frustration when trying to convert their thoughts into written expression. Their frustration can eventually turn them away from writing. Teachers sometimes misinterpret this behavior as laziness, carelessness, or poor motivation. Administering assessment instruments will be useful in determining whether the cause of poor writing is of neurological or some other origin.

> Students with dysgraphia have problems with the writing process. They are often frustrated and are not necessarily lazy or unmotivated.

Associating Dysgraphia With Other Disorders

Students with dysgraphia sometimes have other learning difficulties as well. This condition is known as **comorbidity**. The following are the more common comorbid associations.

Dyslexia (Severe Reading Impairment). Studies show that many children with dyslexia often have poor handwriting and spelling. This strong correlation probably exists because deficits in the brain's visual word form area (located in the left hemisphere) affect the child's ability to match phonemes to graphemes and vice versa. Successful interventions for dyslexia frequently result in improvements in handwriting and spelling as well (Rapcsak et al., 2009; Richards et al., 2015).

Sequencing Problems. Some individuals have a deficit in the cerebellum that makes it difficult for them to process sequential and rational information (Leggio, Chiricozzi, Clausi, Tedesco, & Molinari, 2011). Students with this difficulty will have problems with the sequence of letters, numbers, and words as they write. Usually they slow down their writing to focus on the mechanics of spelling, punctuation, and word order. As a result, they may get so bogged down with the details of writing that they lose the thoughts they are trying to express.

Attention-Deficit Hyperactivity Disorder (ADHD). Students with ADHD (Chapter 3) often have difficulty with writing in general and with handwriting in particular. They are impulsive and process information at a very rapid rate, and they do not possess the fine motor skills needed to write down their thoughts legibly (Nicolson & Fawcett, 2011).

Auditory Processing Disorders. Students who have language disorders (Chapter 4) as a result of auditory processing deficits will usually have difficulty with writing. Those with expressive language disorder are particularly weak at writing because it is the most difficult form of expressive language.

Visual Processing Disorders. Most students with dysgraphia do not have visual processing problems. However, the small percentage of students who *do* will have difficulty with writing speed and legibility simply because they are not able to fully process the visual information as they are transferring it to paper.

WHAT EDUCATORS NEED TO CONSIDER

One of the main goals of writing is to help individuals express their knowledge and ideas. Students with dysgraphia have writing problems that lead to excessively rapid or slow writing, messy and illegible papers, and frustration. It is wrong to label them as lazy or unmotivated. Rather, educators should look for ways to help these students cope with their writing difficulties.

All teachers should emphasize that writing is more than *hand*writing. The notion of transferring thoughts and ideas from inside the brain to an outside device—paper or computer—requires teaching how to organize thoughts, analyze material, and sort out material differently, depending on whether students plan to relate an incident or persuade another person. To write an initial draft requires instruction in penmanship and learning the rules of written language, including spelling, capitalization, punctuation, and sentence structure. Unfortunately, complex rules in the English language are loaded with exceptions and require substantial practice for mastery. Even after the initial draft is written, students need to learn how to edit and revise their material for clarity.

The point here is that students who demonstrate difficulty with writing need a full assessment to determine whether their obstacles are environmental or systemic. Teachers should look first at the learner's background knowledge of writing and assess the type and degree of writing instruction that has been provided in the past. Simply by providing more and sustained practice of writing skills and written language rules, teachers can help many students eventually overcome their writing difficulties.

Characteristics of Good Writing

Students with difficulties in the process of writing need help understanding what constitutes effective writing. The Northwest Regional Educational Laboratory in Portland, Oregon, developed a popular model in the early 1990s that identifies the following six common traits of good writing:

- *Ideas*, the main theme of the writing piece
- *Organization*, the internal structure of the piece
- *Voice*, the personal tone and message of the author
- *Word choice*, the vocabulary the writer chooses to convey meaning
- *Sentence fluency*, the rhythm and flow of the language
- *Conventions*, the mechanical correctness of the piece

Now used in many schools in North America, the model, originally called the *Six Traits Writing Project*, eventually added the seventh trait of *presentation*, which refers to how visual and verbal elements are combined in the piece. As a result, the model has been renamed *6+1 Trait Writing* (NWREL, 2006).

Several research studies have found that this model can be effective with students who have writing difficulties (Spandel, 2009; Zheng, Warschauer, & Farkas, 2013). For more information, see the "Resources" section.

Helping Students With Dysgraphia

Students with writing disorders often lack confidence in their ability to overcome the frustrations they experience when writing. Educators working with these students need to help them regain confidence by developing three types of strategies for helping students with dysgraphia: accommodation (also called compensation) strategies, modification strategies, and remediation strategies. Accommodations bypass the problem by avoiding the difficulty and by reducing the impact that writing has on learning. Modification looks to change the types and the expectations of assignments. Remediation strategies focus on reteaching the concept or skill or providing additional structural practice that more closely matches the student's needs and learning preferences.

To help students, educators must first determine the point at which a student begins to struggle. Does the problem occur as the student begins to write, or does it appear later in the writing process? Is there a problem with organization of thoughts? Is the struggle more evident when the student changes from just copying material to generating complex ideas and trying to commit those to writing? Is the struggle because of confusion over printed and cursive letters, over grammar, or because of punctuation? Once the struggle area is identified, then it becomes a matter of selecting the appropriate combination of accommodation, modification, and remedial techniques for the student. See "Strategies to Consider" at the end of this chapter for ways to build confidence and for techniques that help students with writing difficulties.

Assistive Technology

Many assistive technology devices can be used to help struggling writers increase both the content and mechanics of their writing. Generally, students use a combination of assistive technology devices to meet their needs. Here are just a few:

- Contrast aids, such as highlighter tapes and pens and colored overlays
- Handheld word identification aids, such as a talking dictionary and spell corrector
- Graphic organizers, such as *Inspiration, Kidspiration, Microsoft Word*, teacher-made and online printable organizers
- Portable word processors
- Standard word processing software, such as *Microsoft Word* and *WordPerfect*
- Voice recognition software, such as *Microsoft Speech Recognition* and *Dragon Naturally Speaking*

New assistive technology devices appear periodically, so surf the Internet on a regular basis to see what is available.

Strategies to Consider

SUGGESTIONS FOR BUILDING CONFIDENCE IN STUDENTS WITH WRITING DISORDERS

Lack of confidence is one of the major difficulties of students with writing disorders. Here are a few suggestions to give to students with dysgraphia to help them regain confidence and overcome the frustrations they often experience when writing.

- **Organize Your Thoughts.** First try to get your major ideas down on paper. Then go back and fill in the details.
- **Use a Voice Recorder.** If you are feeling frustrated with your writing, stop and dictate what you want to write into a voice recorder. Listen to the recording later and write down your major ideas.
- **Use the Computer.** Even if you are not great at the beginning, it is important to practice your keyboarding skills. You will get better and faster at it once you have learned the pattern of the keys. Word processing programs can help you organize your thoughts, put them in the proper sequence, and even check your spelling. In the long run, it will be faster and clearer than handwriting.

- **Continue to Practice Handwriting.** No matter how frustrating handwriting is, you will need to be able to write things down in the future. Like any other skill, your handwriting will get better with continued practice.
- **Talk While Writing.** Talk to yourself while writing. This auditory feedback is a valuable tool for helping you monitor what and how you write.
- **Use Visual Aids.** Drawing a picture or filling in a diagram can help you organize your thoughts. Some computer programs, such as *Inspiration Software*, have the capability of producing all types of graphic organizers.

Strategies to Consider

PREVENTION OF AND INTERVENTION IN WRITING DIFFICULTIES

Students with writing difficulties need special attention to help them become good writers. Sometimes, instruction for these students focuses mainly on lower level writing skills, such as handwriting and spelling, with few opportunities to actually write. Researchers believe that writing instruction must emphasize both prevention and intervention; respond to the specific needs of each child; maintain a healthy balance between meaning, process, and form; and employ both formal and informal learning methods. They suggest that such instruction consider the following six principles (Dudley-Marling & Paugh, 2009; Graham & Harris, 2005):

- **Provide effective writing instruction.** An important strategy in preventing writing difficulties, for children with and without learning disabilities, is to provide effective writing instruction. Such a program of instruction would contain the following features:
  - A welcoming and literate classroom environment where students' written work is prominently displayed, the room is filled with writing and reading material, and word lists adorn the walls
  - Daily writing assignments, with students working on a wide range of writing tasks for multiple audiences, including writing at home
  - Extensive efforts to make writing motivating by setting an exciting mood, creating a risk-free environment, allowing students to select their own writing topics or modify teacher assignments, developing assigned topics compatible with students' interests, reinforcing children's accomplishments, and specifying the goal for each lesson
  - Periodic teacher/student conferences about the writing topic the student is currently working on, including the establishment of goals or criteria to guide the child's writing and revising efforts

o A predictable writing routine where students are encouraged to think, reflect, and revise

o Overt teacher modeling of the process of writing and positive attitudes toward writing

o Cooperative learning arrangements where students help each other plan, draft, revise, edit, or publish their written work

o Group or individual sharing where students present work in progress or completed papers to their peers for feedback

o Instruction covering a broad range of knowledge, skills, and strategies, including phonological awareness, sentence-level skills, text structure, the functions of writing, handwriting and spelling, writing conventions, and planning and revising. Follow-up instruction as needed

o Integration of writing activities across the curriculum and the use of reading to support the development of writing

o Frequent opportunities for students to self-regulate their behavior during writing, including working independently, arranging their own space, and seeking help from others

o Teachers and students working together to assess writing progress, strengths, and needs

o Periodic conferences with parents and frequent communications with home about the writing program and students' progress as writers

- **Tailor instruction to meet individual needs.** A critical aspect of tailoring writing instruction is finding the right balance between formal and informal instruction and between meaning, process, and form. Each of these factors should be emphasized when developing a writing program. Teachers should adjust the emphasis placed on each, depending on an individual student's needs. Tailoring instruction for individual students includes many different personalized strategies, such as

o Devoting more attention to the development of critical skills, more explicit teaching of these skills, and more individually guided assistance

o Using scaffolding and guidance designed to help students refine and extend their writing skills—for example, with struggling writers receiving additional support with spelling, and extra time explicitly teaching letter-sound relationships

o Giving more attention to teaching handwriting, phonics for spelling, and punctuation and capitalization skills to weaker writers than to average writers

o Providing mini-lessons responsive to individual needs and follow-up conferencing

o Using adult tutors or volunteers or older and same-age peers (including collaborative planning, writing, or revising with a peer)

o Developing personalized spelling lists for weaker writers, directly helping them spell words they don't know, or providing resources (e.g., word banks) designed to facilitate correct spelling

- Allowing weaker writers to dictate their compositions or write with a keyboard
- Supporting the thinking and creative processes involved in writing by having weaker writers talk out their story before writing, using webs or graphic organizers to generate and sequence ideas, or drawing pictures depicting what would happen in the story
- Supporting the students' revising efforts by using revising checklists or through direct help from the teacher or a peer
- Providing additional personalized help by selecting writing topics, offering shorter or easier writing assignments, small-group instruction, additional homework assignments, and extra instruction on grammar and sentence writing skills

- **Intervene early.** Early supplementary instruction or intervention to prevent or alleviate writing difficulties yields more benefits than remediating problems in later grades. The basic goal is to help struggling writers catch up with their peers early, before their difficulties become more resistant to improvement. Such programs typically seek to accelerate the progress of struggling writers by providing them with additional instruction, either in a small group or through one-on-one tutoring.

  A few studies have examined the effectiveness of early intervention programs in writing. In each study, young children received extra instruction in either handwriting or spelling from an adult tutor, classroom aide, or a parent volunteer. The studies demonstrated that early intervention programs that provide instruction in either handwriting or spelling can have a positive effect on struggling writers' fluency of composition, as measured by the children's ability to either craft sentences or generate text when writing. These results have important implications for the prevention of writing problems because researchers have found that impaired compositional fluency in the primary grades may serve as the developmental origin of writing problems in later grades.

  Early intervention practices that are likely to be effective include allocating additional time for writing, providing individually guided assistance when writing, and supplying additional help in mastering critical skills, such as planning, revising, and sentence construction.

- **Expect that each child will learn to write.** Teachers sometimes set low expectations for students with writing and learning difficulties. These low expectations may lead to fewer interactions with the teacher, less attention and praise, more criticism, and less informative feedback. But many of these students can be taught to write, and recognizing that they are capable is a critical element for success. With this positive approach, teachers

  - Ignore negative expectations
  - Set high but realistic goals for each student's writing performance
  - Help students develop a positive attitude about their capabilities

○ Plan writing lessons so that all children can accomplish tasks successfully

○ Monitor and improve the quality of classroom interactions for struggling writers

○ Build a positive relationship with each child, accepting students as individuals and showing enthusiasm for their interests

- **Identify and address roadblocks to writing.** Another critical element in helping struggling writers is to identify and address obstacles that impede their success in learning to write. Children with learning disabilities may exhibit one or more inhibiting behaviors, including a low tolerance for failure, attention difficulties, and problems in activating and orchestrating the processes involved in learning. Other roadblocks include difficulties such as impulsivity, disorganization, inflexibility, lack of persistence, frequent absences, and poor home support. Teachers need to address these or any other roadblocks that might impede the writing development of struggling students. For example, not only teach students a planning strategy that will help them improve their written work but also include a component that addresses their roadblocks. Students should be encouraged to attribute their success to their efforts as well as to the use of the planning strategy.

- **Take advantage of technological tools for writing.** A wide assortment of technological devices provides new options for minimizing the writing difficulties experienced by students with writing difficulties, allowing them to circumvent some problems and obtain support in overcoming others. These devices make the process of writing easier as well as more motivating. Thanks to word processing programs, for example, revising can be done without tedious recopying, the resulting paper can be presented in a wide range of professional-looking formats, and typing provides an inherently easier means for producing text.

○ Technological tools can also provide support for planning and revising through the use of outlining and graphic mapping software and multimedia applications. In addition, spell checkers, word prediction programs, grammar and style checkers, and speech synthesis all help make text production easier. Finally, the use of computer networks allows students to collaborate and communicate easily with audiences that extend beyond their classroom.

○ It is important to keep in mind that although technology can help students with learning difficulties write, it does not make writing instruction superfluous. For instance, many of these students fail to take advantage of word processing when revising because they continue to revise in the same old way, mostly trying to correct mechanical errors. By teaching them to focus their attention on substantive changes when revising, students gain much greater use of the editing features of word processing and are more likely to make additions and rewrite parts of their text. Similarly, a spell checker will not eliminate spelling errors or the need for spelling instruction.

Strategies to Consider

ACCOMMODATION STRATEGIES FOR STUDENTS WITH WRITING DISORDERS

Accommodation strategies help bypass writing difficulties and reduce the impact that writing has on the learning process so that students can focus more on the content of their writing. The accommodations can adjust the rate and volume of writing, the complexity of the task, and the tools used to create the final product. Here are some accommodation strategies in each of these areas (Jones, 2015).

Accommodating the Rate of Work Produced

- **Allow more time** for students to complete written tasks, such as note taking, written tests, and copying. Also, allow these students to begin written projects earlier than others. Consider including time in the student's schedule for acting as an aide, and then have the student use that time for making up or starting new written work.
- **Encourage developing keyboarding skills and using the computer and other digital devices.** Students can begin to learn keyboarding in first grade. Encourage them to use word processing programs. Teaching handwriting is still important, but students may produce longer and more complex writing with the computer.
- **Have students prepare worksheets in advance**, complete with the required headings, such as name, date, and topic. Provide a standard template with this information already on it.

Accommodating the Volume of Work Produced

- **Provide partially completed outlines** and ask students to fill in the missing details. This is a valuable, but not burdensome, exercise in note taking.
- **Allow students to dictate to another student.** One student (scribe) writes down what another student says verbatim and then allows the dictating student to make changes without help from the scribe.
- **Correct poor spelling in first drafts**, but do not lower the grade because of it. However, make clear to the students that spelling does eventually count, especially in assignments completed over time.
- **Reduce copying of printed work.** Avoid having students copy over something already printed in a text, such as entire mathematics problems. Provide a worksheet with the text material already on it, or have the students just write down their original answers or work.
- **Allow students to use abbreviations** in some writing, such as *b/4* for *before*, *b/c* for *because*, and *w/* for *with*. These are also helpful shortcuts during note taking.

Accommodating the Complexity of the Work Produced

- **Allow students to use print or cursive writing.** Many students with dysgraphia are more comfortable with print (manuscript) letters. However, students should still be encouraged to use cursive writing. It eliminates the need to pick up a pencil and deciding where to replace it after each letter. Cursive has very few reversible letters, a typical source of confusion for students with dysgraphia. It eliminates word-spacing problems and allows the writing process to flow more easily.
- **Teach and model for students the stages of writing,** such as brainstorming, drafting, editing, and proofreading.
- **Encourage students to use a spell checker.** Using the spell checker decreases the demands on the writing process, lowering frustration and diverting more energy to thought production. For students who also have reading difficulties, concurrently using a computer reading program also decreases the demands on the writer.
- **Have students proofread after a delay in time** when they are more likely to catch writing errors. This way, they will see what they *actually* wrote rather than what they *thought* they wrote.

Accommodating the Tools of the Work Production

- **Allow students to use lined and graph paper.** Lined paper helps students keep their writing level across the page. Have younger students use graph paper for mathematics calculations to keep columns and rows straight. Older students can turn lined paper sideways for column control.
- **Allow students to use different writing instruments.** Students should use the writing instrument they find most comfortable. Some students have difficulty writing with ballpoint pens, preferring thin-line marker pens that have more friction with the paper. Others prefer mechanical pencils.
- **Have pencil grips available** in all styles. Even high school students enjoy these fun grips, and some like the big pencils usually associated with primary school.
- **Allow some students to use speech recognition programs.** For students with very difficult writing problems, using a speech recognition program within a word processing program allows them to dictate their thoughts rather than type them. However, this is not a substitute for learning handwriting.

Strategies to Consider

MODIFICATION STRATEGIES FOR STUDENTS WITH WRITING DISORDERS

For some students, accommodation strategies will not remove the barriers that their writing difficulties pose. Teachers may need to make modifications in these students' assignments. Here are some suggested modifications in the volume, complexity, and format of written work (Jones, 2015).

Modifying the Volume of Work Produced

- **Limit the amount of copying that students do.** For example, to copy definitions, have the students rewrite and shorten them without affecting the meaning. Another option is to have them use drawings or diagrams to answer questions.
- **Reduce the length** of written assignments. Emphasize that students should be spending more time improving the quality of their work rather than increasing its length.

Modifying the Complexity of the Work Product

- **Prioritization of tasks.** Stress or de-emphasize certain tasks for a complex activity. For example, students could focus on complex sentences in one activity and on using descriptive words in another. Evaluate the assignment based on the prioritized tasks.
- **Use cooperative learning groups** to give students a chance to play different roles, such as brainstormer, encourager, information organizer, and so forth.
- **Provide intermittent deadlines** for long-term assignments. Work with other teachers when setting due dates, especially those involving writing assignments. Parents may also be able to monitor the student's work at home so that it can comply with deadlines.
- **Encourage graphic organizers.** Preorganization strategies such as the use of graphic organizers will help students get their main ideas in line before tackling the writing process. On the following page are just a few examples of the many different types of graphic organizers.

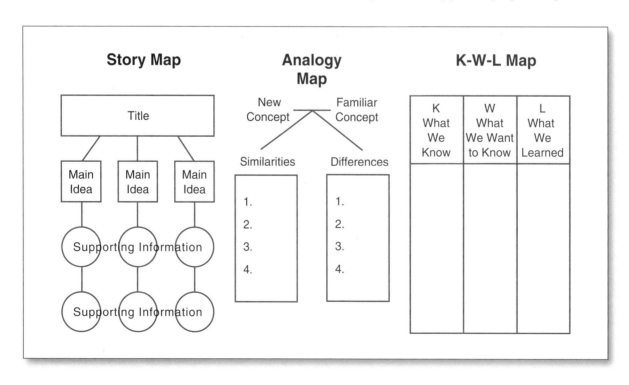

Modifying the Format of the Work Produced

- **Allow students to submit alternative projects,** such as an oral report or visual project. Ask for a short written report to explain or expand on the oral or visual work. However, these alternatives should not replace all writing assignments.
- **Allow students to use information directly from the Internet** in their term papers and other projects. Retrieved information still needs to be fully cited, but this method reduces the amount of copying.

Strategies to Consider

REMEDIATION STRATEGIES FOR STUDENTS WITH WRITING DISORDERS

Students should not be allowed to avoid the process of writing, no matter how severe their dysgraphia. Writing is an important skill that they will eventually use to sign documents, write checks, fill out forms, take messages, or make grocery lists. Thus they need to learn to write even if they can do so for just a short time.

Remediation strategies focus on reteaching information or a particular skill to help students acquire mastery and fluency. Substantial modeling of all strategies is essential for the students to be successful. Here are some suggested areas for remediation (Jones, 2015; Peterson, 2014).

- **Teaching Handwriting Continuously.** Many students would like to have better handwriting. Build handwriting instruction into the students' schedule. Provide opportunities to teach them this, keeping in mind the age, aptitude, and attitude of each student.
- **Helping With Spelling.** Spelling difficulties are common for students with dysgraphia, especially if sequencing is a major problem. The students with dysgraphia who also have dyslexia need structured and specific instruction in learning to spell phonetically. This skill can help them use technical tools that rely on phonetic spelling to find a word.
- **Correcting the Pencil Grip.** Young children should be encouraged to use a proper pencil grip from the beginning of their writing experience. Descriptive research indicates that, for the best results, the grip should be consistently between 3/4 inch to 1 inch from the pencil tip. Moderate pressure should be applied, and the angle of the pencil to the paper should be about 45 degrees and slanted toward the student's writing arm. Accomplishing the proper slant will be difficult for left-handed writers.

  A poor pencil grip can be changed to the appropriate form by using plastic pencil grips, which are commercially available. Obviously, it is easier to encourage the correct grip as soon as the student begins writing; older students with poor grip posture find it very difficult to make changes. The teacher needs to consider whether it is worth the time and effort to get the student to change the grip to be more efficient. If not, identify compensatory strategies that are available for the student.

- **Writing a Paragraph.** Students can be taught this eight-step process for writing a paragraph.

  1. Plan the paper by thinking about the ideas that you want to include in it.
  2. Organize the ideas with a graphic organizer. Place the main idea in the center and supporting facts on lines coming out from the center, much like the spokes of a wheel.
  3. Analyze the graphic organizer to ensure that all your ideas have been included. Check your spelling.
  4. Write a draft of the paragraph, focusing on the main ideas.
  5. Edit your work for punctuation, capitalization, grammar, and spelling.
  6. Use the corrections made in Step 5 to revise the paragraph.
  7. Proofread again, editing and revising as needed.
  8. Develop a final product in written or typed form.

Accept whatever the students are able to write on their own and provide immediate and specific feedback as well as direct instruction to help them improve their initial efforts.

- **Increasing the Speed of Writing.** Many students with dysgraphia write very slowly. To identify the appropriate remediation strategy, teachers need to determine the cause of the slowness.

  o Is it the actual formation of the letters? If so, the students need more practice on this skill, perhaps by saying the letters aloud while writing. Air writing can be helpful because it uses many more muscles to form the letters. Also, have the students write large letters on a big surface, such as a chalkboard or dry-erase board.
  o Is it in the organization of ideas? If so, provide the students with graphic organizers to help them sort and prioritize their thoughts and facts.

- **Motivating the Students.** Students are more likely to write about topics they find personally meaningful and that allow them to experience success.

  o Offer choices. Give the students a limited array of choices of topics, characters, or points of view that are interesting to them.
  o Provide background knowledge to help them make effective choices in their writing. Introduce students to real-world examples of writing genres and discuss why the authors wrote their text and how their choice of genres allowed them to achieve their literary goal.
  o Provide students with both concrete and vicarious experiences through videos, photographs, and field trips to help them give

substance to their writing. Ask them to discuss these experiences in class to encourage reflection and to enrich their writing.

- Give students opportunities to write for an authentic audience. By sharing a piece of writing with an audience, they are more likely to continue their commitment to the writing process through drafting, revising, and editing their work.

- Encourage a view of writing as a social tool. Studies show that students often use their writing to improve their social status or to build new friendships by including characters with the names of their peers or by creating plays that they can perform with their classmates.

- **Dealing With Fatigue.** Poor motor sequencing or an incorrect pencil grip can lead to fatigue with the writing process. The following can help students relieve the stress of writing and relax the writing hand.

  - Take writing breaks at regular intervals. Students should realize that it is permissible to stop occasionally and relax the muscles of the hand. This break also gives them a chance to review what has been written and to continue to organize their thoughts.

  - Shake the hands quickly to relax the muscles. This increases blood flow to the finger and hand muscles.

  - Rub the hands on some texture, such as the carpet or clothes.

  - Rub the hands together and focus on the feeling of warmth. The rubbing also helps restore blood flow to the area.

- **Giving Praise, Being Patient, and Encouraging Patience.** Genuinely praise the positive aspects of students' work. Be patient with their efforts and problems, and encourage them to have patience with themselves.

Strategies to Consider

EXPRESSIVE WRITING FOR STUDENTS WITH LEARNING DISABILITIES

One of the goals of teaching writing is to help students express their thoughts and ideas in personal narratives and persuasive essays. Students whose learning disabilities include problems with writing often have great difficulty with this. Note that in the DSM-5 expressive writing disorder has now been included under the umbrella term of "specific learning disorder." Finding ways of helping these students has been the subject of considerable research. Most studies have found that interventions to help students with expressive writing difficulties are effective (Travagin, Margola, & Revenson, 2015).

A meta-analysis studied the effectiveness of research-based instructional approaches for teaching expressive writing to students with learning disabilities. The following three components of instruction consistently led to improving student success in learning expressive writing (Baker, Gersten, & Graham, 2003; Cook & Bennett, 2014):

PLANNING THINK SHEET

TOPIC: _____

Who am I writing for?

Why am I writing this?

What do I already know about this?

How can I group my ideas?

How will I organize my ideas?

---

1. Adhering to a basic framework of planning, writing, and revision

Most of the successful interventions used a basic framework of planning, writing, and revision. Each step was taught explicitly, followed by multiple examples and the use of memory devices, such as prompt cards or mnemonics.

Planning. Planning results in better first drafts. One way of helping students develop a plan of action is to provide a planning think sheet that uses structured and sequential prompts. It specifies the topic and poses questions to guide the student's thought processes. See the sample sheet at the right.

Creating a First Draft. The planning think sheet helps students create first drafts by serving as a guide through the writing process. The guide also gives the student and teacher a common language for an ongoing discussion about the assignment. This student-teacher interaction emphasizes cooperative work rather than the recent method of writing mainly in isolation.

Revising and Editing. The skills of revising and editing are critical to successful writing. Some researchers found a peer editing approach to be particularly effective. Here's how it works:

- Pairs of students alternate their roles as student-writer and student-critic.
- The student-critic identifies ambiguities and asks the writer for clarification. The writer then makes revisions, with the teacher's help if needed.
- Once the clarifications are made, the student pair then moves on to correct capitalization, punctuation, and spelling.
- Throughout the process, the student writers have to explain the intent of their writings and continue revising their essays to reflect their intent accurately. These clarifying dialogues help the student pairs understand each other's perspectives.

2. Teaching explicitly the critical steps in the writing process

Because different types of writing (e.g., personal narrative or persuasive essay) are based on different structures, explicitly teaching text structures provides the students with a specific guide to completing their writing task. For example, writing a persuasive essay requires a thesis and supporting arguments. Narrative writing focuses on character development and a story climax. Teach these structures, using explicit models of each text type.

3. Providing feedback guided by the information explicitly taught

The researchers found that successful interventions always included frequent and specific feedback to the students on the quality of their overall writing, strengths, and missing elements. Combining feedback with instruction strengthens the dialogue between student and teacher, thereby helping students to develop a sensitivity to their own writing style. This sensitivity may lead students to reflect on, realize, and correct writing problems as well as perceive their ideas from another's perspective. The research studies also showed that student gains were more likely to occur when the teachers and other students provided feedback mainly in the areas of organization, originality, and interpretation.

> Researchers found that frequent feedback was a powerful tool for improving students' writing.

7

Mathematical Disabilities

Pure mathematics is, in its way, the poetry of logical ideas.

—Albert Einstein

More than 50 years ago, Tobias Dantzig (1967) introduced the term *number sense* in 1954 to describe a person's ability to recognize that something has changed in a small collection when, without that person's knowledge, an object has been added or removed from the collection. Research has shown that toddlers have a sense of numbers and can already deal with limited arithmetic operations (e.g., simple adding and subtracting) before the age of one year (Lee, Kotsopoulos, Tumber, & Makosz, 2014). By the age of two years, most toddlers can recognize the greater-than and less-than relationships (the concept of *ordinality*) between numerical values as large as 4 and 5, even though they have not yet learned the numbers' verbal labels (Brannon & van der Walle, 2001).

Early numerical capability makes sense in terms of our past development as a species. In primitive societies, a youngster going for a stroll out of the cave needed to determine quickly if the number of animals in an approaching pack might spell danger or just an opportunity for play. Young hunters had to determine how *many* individuals would be needed to take down a large animal. Mistakes in these calculations could be fatal. Recognizing that three apples provide more nourishment than one was also a valuable survival asset. Numeration, then, persisted in the genetic code. Let us take a look at how we learn to calculate and the problems that can arise in this complex process. Much of what follows in this chapter is a condensed version of the in-depth discussions of mathematics and mathematics difficulties that are explained in Sousa (2015), although some new information and references have been added where appropriate.

LEARNING TO CALCULATE

Brain imaging studies have revealed clues about how the brain performs different types of mathematical operations. Functional MRI scans indicate that the parietal and frontal lobes (Figure 7.1) are primarily involved in basic mental mathematics (e.g., counting forward or doing exact and approximate calculations). Activation intensifies as the number size increases. Approximate calculations require larger cerebral areas than exact calculations, presumably because approximation requires more number manipulation (Dehaene, Piazza, Pinel, & Cohen, 2003; De Smedt, Holloway, & Ansari, 2011). Other areas of the brain are recruited into action when dealing with more complex mathematics, such as in algebraic calculations and geometry (Qin et al., 2004; Zamarian, Ischebeck, & Delazer, 2009).

Numerical Reasoning and Language

In the second edition of this book, I noted that brain imaging studies seemed to suggest that the brain areas responsible for calculations and numerical reasoning were different from those used in processing language.

However, in the intervening years, research studies using more sophisticated technology are now indicating that language and arithmetic processing and reasoning do involve similar neural networks. What is still uncertain is the extent of this engagement (e.g., Andin, Fransson, Rönnberg, & Rudner, 2015; Moll, Snowling, Göbel, & Hulme, 2015). Children tend to have more difficulty with language-based arithmetic tasks, such as number facts and word problems, than with those tasks requiring little language demands, such as number sense and nonverbal calculations (Jordan & Levine, 2009). Furthermore, cognitive processes,

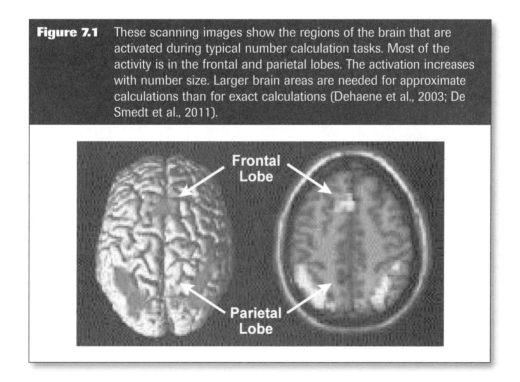

Figure 7.1　These scanning images show the regions of the brain that are activated during typical number calculation tasks. Most of the activity is in the frontal and parietal lobes. The activation increases with number size. Larger brain areas are needed for approximate calculations than for exact calculations (Dehaene et al., 2003; De Smedt et al., 2011).

such as visual-spatial and phonological skills, appear to be significantly linked to learning diverse forms of arithmetic (Zhang & Lin, 2015). Some studies show that how well primary-grade children can do phonological decoding is directly related with arithmetic achievement (e.g., Vukovic & Lesaux, 2013).

Although language may be helpful in developing mathematical ability, it is not necessary for calculation, and it is processed in different parts of the brain. The implication for schooling is to remember that there are students with mathematical difficulties who may not necessarily have difficulties with language, and those with language problems who may still be capable in mathematics.

Gender Differences in Mathematics

For decades, boys have consistently scored higher than girls on standardized mathematics tests, such as the Scholastic Aptitude Test (SAT) and the National Assessment of Educational Progress (NAEP). Those seeking to explain this gender disparity have looked to discoveries in brain science as potential explanations. They say, for example, that males' brains are about 6–8 percent larger than females' brains. But males are on average about 6–8 percent taller than females, which could explain the brain size differences. And brain imaging studies show that males seem to have an advantage in visual-spatial ability (the ability to rotate objects in their heads) (e.g., Maloney, Waechter, Risko, & Fugelsang, 2012), while females are more adept at language processing (e.g., Kaushanskaya, Gross, & Buac, 2013). But whether these differences translate into a genetic advantage for males over females in mathematical processing remains to be seen and proved.

To some extent, the belief that boys are much better at mathematics than girls is out of proportion to the data. The 2012 NAEP test results indicated that the gender gap in mathematics narrowed for 17-year-olds (NAEP, 2012). However, the 2015 NAEP results in mathematics showed a slight increase in the gap for Grades 4 and 8 (NAEP, 2015).

Stereotype Threat

Social context may play an important role in partially explaining gender differences in mathematics achievement. Studies have found that merely telling females that a mathematics test shows gender differences is enough to hurt their performance (e.g., Jamieson & Harkins, 2012). However, telling females that they have the power to do well in mathematical assessments significantly improves their performance (Van Loo & Rydell, 2013). This phenomenon is called *stereotype threat,* and it occurs when people believe they will be evaluated based on societal stereotypes about their particular group. In one typical study of stereotype threat, researchers gave a mathematics test to females and males. They told half the females that the test will show gender differences and told the rest that it would find none. Females who expected gender differences did significantly worse on the test than males, but females who were told there would not be gender differences performed as well as the males did on the test (e.g., Franceschini, Galli, Chiesi, & Primi, 2014).

Although most neuroscientists will admit to gender differences in how the brain processes information, especially in young children, they are reluctant to support the concept that these differences offer a lifelong learning advantage for one sex over the other in any academic area. It is important for educators to know about these gender differences and how they change through various stages of human development. The danger here is that people will think that if the differences are innate and unchangeable, then nothing can be done to improve the situation. Such ideas are damaging because they leave the student feeling discouraged, and they ignore the brain's plasticity and exceptional ability to learn complex information when suitably motivated. A variety of teaching approaches and strategies may indeed make up for these gender differences.

DIFFICULTIES IN MATHEMATICS

Some children are adept in mathematical calculations while others struggled despite much effort and motivation. But the percentage of school-age children who experience difficulties in learning mathematics has been growing steadily in the last three decades. Why is that? Is the brain's ability to perform arithmetic calculations declining? If so, why? Does the brain get less arithmetic practice because technology has shifted computation from brain cells to inexpensive electronic calculators?

In previous chapters, we have referred to the considerable amount of research that has been conducted to understand how the human brain learns. As a result, we also have a greater understanding of the diagnosis and remediation of learning disorders, especially in areas of language, reading, and writing. In addition, a few researchers have been studying why students have problems with learning early mathematics, despite normal intelligence and adequate instruction.

About 6–8 percent of school-age children have serious difficulty processing mathematics (Butterworth, 2010). This is about the same number as children who have serious reading problems. However, because of the strong emphasis that our society places on the need to learn reading, many more research studies have focused on problems in this area than on mathematics. Nonetheless, the growing number of students who are having trouble learning mathematics has spurred considerable research interest in how the brain does calculations and the possible causes of mathematical difficulties.

Dyscalculia

The condition that causes persistent problems with processing numerical calculations is referred to as **dyscalculia** (pronounced dis-kal-KOOL-ee-ah), from the Greek "counting badly." Dyscalculia is a difficulty in conceptualizing numbers, number relationships, outcomes of numerical operations, and estimation—that is, what to expect as an outcome of an operation. If the condition is present from birth, it is called *developmental dyscalculia*. Genetic studies of twins reveal that developmental dyscalculia is moderately inheritable (Tosto, Malykh, Voronin, Plomin, & Kovas,

Video: For a brief overview of dyscalculia by one of the researchers in this area see:

https://www.youtube.com/watch?v=imhRoqxSEhU

2013) and affects about 3–6 percent of the school-age population (Price & Ansari, 2013). If the condition results from an injury to the brain after birth, it is called *acquired dyscalculia*. Whether developmental or acquired, for most individuals, this disorder is the result of specific disabilities in basic numerical processing and not necessarily the consequence of deficits in other cognitive abilities (Landerl, Göbel, & Moll, 2013).

People with dyscalculia have difficulty

- Mastering arithmetic facts by the traditional methods of teaching, particularly the methods involving counting
- Learning abstract concepts of time and direction, telling and keeping track of time, and the sequence of past and future events
- Acquiring spatial orientation and space organization, including left/right orientation, trouble reading maps, and grappling with mechanical processes
- Following directions in sports that demand sequencing or rules and keeping track of scores and players during games such as card and board games
- Following sequential directions and sequencing (including reading numbers out of sequence, substitutions, reversals, omissions, and doing operations backward), organizing detailed information, remembering specific facts and formulas for completing their mathematical calculations

Dyscalculia can be (1) quantitative, which is a difficulty in counting and calculating; (2) qualitative, which is a difficulty in the conceptualizing of mathematics processes and spatial sense; or (3) mixed, which is the inability to integrate quantity and space.

Environmental Causes

Attitudes About Mathematics. Even individuals with normal abilities in processing numerical operations can display mathematical disorders. Because they have no inherent mathematical deficits, their difficulties most likely arise from environmental causes. In modern American society, reading and writing have become the main measures of a good student. Mathematics ability has been regarded more as a specialized function rather than as a general indicator of intelligence. Consequently, the stigma of not being able to do mathematics was reduced and became socially acceptable. Just hearing their parents say "I wasn't very good at math" allowed children to embrace the social attitudes that regard mathematics failure as acceptable and routine.

In recent years, schools have placed a heavy emphasis on raising standards in all curriculum areas. At the same time, the federal Every Student Succeeds Act still includes requirements for assessments in reading and mathematics. Despite these initiatives, student attitudes about mathematics have not improved much. Surveys show that most students (including those who like mathematics) find making nonmathematical mistakes much more embarrassing than making mathematical mistakes (Latterell, 2005). Furthermore, regardless of the efforts toward gender equity, female high school students still rate themselves as less confident in mathematics than their male peers (Nosek & Smyth, 2011).

These findings are unsettling, especially because other research studies have shown that attitudes are formed by social forces and predict academic performance. Not surprisingly, students with positive attitudes about what they are learning achieve more than students with poor attitudes. Apparently, higher standards and increased testing are not sufficient as yet to improve how students feel about learning mathematics.

> Despite higher standards and high-stakes testing, student attitudes about mathematics have not improved much.

Fear of Mathematics. Some children develop an early fear (or phobia) of mathematics because of negative experiences in their past or a simple lack of self-confidence with numbers. Studies show that this fear can appear as early as second grade but can have a significant negative effect on mathematics achievement at any grade level (e.g., Suárez-Pellicioni, Núñez-Peña, & Colomé, 2014; Wu, Willcutt, Escovar, & Menon, 2014). Mathematics anxiety conjures up fear of some type. Perhaps it is the fear that one won't be able to do the calculations, or the fear that it's too difficult, or the fear of failure, which often stems from having a lack of confidence. In people with mathematics anxiety, the fear of failure often causes their minds to draw a blank, leading to more frustration and more blanks. Added pressure of having time limits on mathematics tests also raises the levels of anxiety for many students. And teachers may inadvertently contribute to this fear. Research studies show that teacher attitudes greatly influence math anxiety and represent the most dominating factor in molding student attitudes about mathematics, especially in girls (Beilock, Gunderson, Ramirez, & Levine, 2010).

Generally, students with this phobia have a limited understanding of mathematical concepts. They may rely mainly on memorizing procedures, rules, and routines without much conceptual understanding, so panic soon sets in. Mathematics phobia can be as challenging as any learning disability, but it is important to remember that these students have typical neurological systems for computation. They need help primarily in replacing the memory of failure with the possibility of success. Students with mathematical disorders, on the other hand, have a neurological deficit that results in persistent difficulty in processing numbers

Quality of Teaching. One critical factor in how well students learn mathematics is the quality of the teaching. Studies show that student achievement in mathematics is strongly linked to the teacher's expertise in mathematics. Students of an expert teacher perform better on achievement tests than students of a teacher with limited training in mathematics (Hill & Dalton, 2013; Rolland, 2012).

MATHEMATICAL DISORDERS

General Characteristics:

- Inconsistent results with addition, subtraction, multiplication, and division
- Inability to remember mathematical formulas, rules, or concepts
- Difficulty with abstract concepts of time and direction
- Consistent errors when recalling numbers, including transpositions, omissions, and reversals
- Difficulty remembering how to keep score during games

Neurological and Other Causes

Researchers in the field of mathematics disabilities are faced with the challenge of distinguishing those factors that *cause* difficulties in mathematics from those that are the *consequences* of these factors. Because some students with moderate mathematics difficulties are of average or higher intelligence and possess good reading skills, the brain regions involved in mathematics difficulties are likely localized or modular. Thus, the neurological causes of mathematics difficulties can be limited and not affect other cognitive areas.

Because the parietal lobe is heavily involved with number operations, damage to this area can result in difficulties with computation. Studies of individuals with Gerstmann syndrome—the result of damage to the parietal lobe—showed that they had serious problems with mathematical calculations as well as right-left disorientation but no problems with oral language skills (Chen, Xu, Shang, Peng, & Luo, 2014; Lemer, Dehaene, Spelke, & Cohen, 2003; Roitman, Brannon, & Platt, 2012).

Individuals with visual processing weaknesses almost always display difficulties with mathematics. This is probably because success in mathematics requires one to mentally visualize numbers and mathematical situations, especially in algebra and geometry. Students with sequencing difficulties also may have dyscalculia because they cannot remember the order of mathematical operations or the specific formulas needed to complete a set of computations.

Genetic factors also seem to play a significant role. For example, studies of identical twins reveal close mathematics scores. Children from families with a history of mathematical giftedness or retardation show common aptitudes with other family members (Pinel & Dehaene, 2013). Girls born with Turner syndrome (a condition caused by the partial or complete absence of one of the two X chromosomes normally found in females) usually display dyscalculia, among other learning problems (Mazzocco & Hanich, 2010).

Types of Mathematical Disorders

The complexity of mathematics makes the study of mathematical disorders particularly challenging for researchers. Learning deficits can include difficulties in mastering basic number concepts, counting skills, and processing arithmetic operations, as well as procedural, retrieval, and visual-spatial deficits. As with any learning disability, each of these deficits can range from mild to severe.

Number Concept Difficulties. As mentioned before, the understanding of small numbers and quantity appears to be present at birth. The understanding of larger numbers and place value, however, seems to develop during the preschool and early elementary years. A poor understanding of the concepts involved in a mathematical procedure will delay the adoption of more sophisticated procedures and limit the child's ability to detect procedural errors. Studies show that most children with mathematical disorders nevertheless have their basic number competencies intact. However, they are often unable to use their number concept skills to solve arithmetic problems (Mussolin, Mejias, & Noël, 2010).

Counting Skill Deficits. Studies of children in the primary grades with mathematical disorders show that they have deficits in counting knowledge and counting accuracy. Some may also have problems keeping numerical information in working memory while counting, resulting in counting errors (Martin, Cirino, Sharp, & Barnes, 2014; Moeller, Neuburger, Kaufmann, Landerl, & Nuerk, 2009).

Difficulties With Arithmetic Skills. Children with mathematical disorders have difficulties solving simple and complex arithmetic problems, and they rely heavily on finger counting. Their difficulties stem mainly from deficits in both numerical procedures (solving 6 + 5 or 4 × 4) and working memory. They tend to use developmentally immature procedures, such as counting all rather than counting on. At the same time, they do not show the shift from procedure-based problem solving to memory-based problem solving that is found in typically achieving children, most likely because of difficulties in storing arithmetic facts or retrieving them from long-term memory. Moreover, deficits in visual-spatial skills can lead to problems with arithmetic because of misalignment of numerals in multicolumn addition. Although *procedural, memory,* and *visual-spatial* deficits can occur separately, they are often interconnected.

Procedural Disorders. Students displaying this disorder

- Use arithmetic procedures (algorithms) that are developmentally immature
- Have problems sequencing the steps of multistep procedures, such as 47 × 12 or 243 + 344
- Have difficulty understanding the concepts associated with procedures
- Make frequent mistakes when using procedures

The exact cause of this disorder is unknown, but research studies have yielded some intriguing findings. Children with developmental or acquired dyscalculia can still count arrays of objects, say the correct sequence of number words while counting, and understand basic counting concepts, such as cardinality. However, they have difficulties in solving complex arithmetic problems. Researchers suspect one possible cause may be a dysfunction in the brain's left hemisphere, which specializes in procedural tasks, and in working memory deficits (Roşca, 2009).

Memory Disorders. Students displaying this disorder

- Have difficulty retrieving arithmetic facts
- Have a high error rate when they do retrieve arithmetic facts
- Retrieve incorrect facts that are associated with the correct facts
- Rely on finger counting because it reduces the demands on working memory

This disorder likely involves the manipulation of information in the language system. Here again, a dysfunction of the left hemisphere is suspected, mainly because these individuals frequently have reading disorders as well (Ashkenazi, Black, Abrams, Hoeft, & Menon, 2013a; D'Amico & Guarnera, 2005). This association further suggests that memory deficits may be inheritable.

Memory disorders can be caused by two separate problems. One involves disruptions in the ability to retrieve basic facts from long-term memory, resulting in many more errors than typically achieving children. Research findings indicate that this form of memory disorder is closely linked to the language-processing system and may indicate developmental or acquired deficits in the left hemisphere.

The second possibility involves disruption in the retrieval process caused by difficulties in inhibiting the retrieval of irrelevant associations. Thus the student seems impulsive. For example, when asked what is 7 + 3, a student might quickly blurt out 8 or 4 because those numbers come next in counting. Solving arithmetic problems becomes much easier when irrelevant information is prevented from entering working memory. When irrelevant information is retrieved, it lowers working memory's capacity and competes with correct information for the individual's attention. This type of retrieval deficit may be caused by deficits in the brain's executive areas of the prefrontal cortex responsible for inhibiting working-memory operations (De Visscher, Berens, Keidel, Noël, & Bird, 2015; Geary, Hoard, & Bailey, 2012; Peng, Congying, Beilei, & Sha, 2012).

Visual-Spatial Deficits. Students with this disorder

- Have difficulties in the spatial arrangement of their work, such as aligning the columns in multicolumn addition
- Often misread numerical signs, rotate and transpose numbers, or both
- Misinterpret spatial placement of numerals, resulting in place value errors
- Have difficulty with problems involving space in areas, as required in algebra and geometry

Studies indicate that this disorder is more closely associated with deficits in the right hemisphere regions that specialize in visual-spatial tasks. Individuals with injuries to this area show a deficit in spatial orientation tasks and in the ability to generate and use a mental number line. Some studies suggest that the left parietal lobe also may be implicated (Ashkenazi, Rosenberg-Lee, Metcalfe, Swigart, & Menn, 2013b; Szucs, Devine, Soltesz, Nobes, & Gabriel, 2013).

Many students eventually overcome procedural disorders as they mature and learn to rely on sequence diagrams and other tools to remember the steps of mathematical procedures. Those with visual-spatial disorders also improve when they discover the benefits of graph paper and learn to solve certain algebra and geometry problems with logic rather than through spatial analysis alone. However, memory deficits do not seem to improve with maturity. Studies indicate that individuals with this problem will continue to have difficulties retrieving basic arithmetic facts throughout life. This finding may suggest that the memory problem not only exists for mathematical operations but may signal a more general deficit in retrieving information from memory.

Children often outgrow procedural and visual-spatial difficulties, but memory problems may continue throughout life.

Associating Dyscalculia With Other Disorders

Reading Disorders. About 50 percent of individuals with dyscalculia can also have developmental reading difficulties, or dyslexia (Ashkenazi et al., 2013a). No one knows for sure why these conditions appear simultaneously in so many children. Some research suggests this comorbidity may be because both reading and mathematics share cerebral regions responsible for working memory, processing speed, and verbal comprehension (Willcutt et al., 2013). It is also possible that students with both disorders are less successful solving mathematics problems than those who have only dyscalculia because they have difficulty translating word problems into mathematical expressions. Computer programs are now available for elementary level students that address both weaknesses. These programs focus on teaching basic mathematics and reading skills while adhering to national and state standards. They provide instruction at a student's own pace and include automatic progress tracking for each student so teachers can provide additional instruction to those who need it.

Attention-Deficit Hyperactivity Disorder (ADHD). Because many children with ADHD have difficulty with mathematics, some researchers wondered if these two conditions had related genetic components, increasing the possibility that they would be inherited together. But studies show that these two disorders are transmitted independently and are connected to distinctly different genetic regions (Monuteaux, Faraone, Herzig, Navsaria, & Biederman, 2005). No other genetic studies have appeared to date to challenge these results. Consequently, these findings underscore the need for separate identification and treatment strategies for children with both conditions.

The Future of Research in Mathematics Disorders

Numerous research studies have looked at the effectiveness of instructional strategies on improving achievement by students with mathematics difficulties. As expected, some strategies work better than others, and a particular strategy's effectiveness can depend on the nature of the learning difficulties found in the individuals being studied.

Because of this wide range of effectiveness for instructional strategies, it is usually helpful to rely on a meta-analysis of studies to determine which strategies have a significant impact of student achievement. This impact is often measured by effect size. (Note: See the "Introduction" for an explanation of effect size.) The most recent meta-analysis of instructional interventions in mathematics with students with learning difficulties was conducted by Russell Gersten and his colleagues (Gersten et al., 2009). They looked at 42 different interventions and found that the following five had significantly important effect sizes:

- Use of heuristics (experienced-based techniques for problem solving and discovery), effect size = 1.56
- Use of explicit instruction, effect size = 1.22
- Student verbalizations, effect size = 1.04
- Cross-age tutoring, effect size = 1.02
- Sequence and/or range of examples, effect size = 0.82

Among these studies, the use of heuristics had the largest effect size. A heuristic was any strategy that represented a generic approach to solving a problem. It could be as simple as asking the student to read the problem, underline key words, solve it, and then check your work. Heuristics are not problem specific. Instead, they show the student multiple ways to solve a problem, encourage reflection to assess alternate solutions, and select one to solve the problem. Explicit instruction also yielded a large effect size, a result found in earlier meta-analyses of similar studies. To be included in this meta-analysis, explicit instruction meant that the teacher demonstrated a step-by-step strategy for solving the problem that was specific for a set of similar problems, and that the teacher asked the students to use the same procedure to solve a given problem.

That student verbalization scored high as a strategy is not surprising. Encouraging the students to verbally explain their thinking processes is a form of rehearsal that helps students find sense and meaning in what they are doing. It also gives teachers the opportunity to correct question and correct student thinking, thereby leading them on a path to successfully solving a problem. Cross-age tutoring also yielded an impressive effect size. In these studies, the tutors were well-trained upper elementary students who tutored students in lower grades. Their training focused on teaching lessons to the students as well as on what type of specific feedback they should give to students who had difficulty or made mistakes.

The large effect size for sequence and/or range of examples indicates how important it is for teachers to present mathematics examples to these students in a logical pattern. That pattern could be showing the distinctive features of a particular type of problem set, or going from easy to progressively more complex and difficult problems, or finding common features to outwardly dissimilar word problems. Meta-analyses such as this one show us that we do have instructional strategies that, when appropriately implemented, can significantly help students who have difficulties in learning mathematics. The ultimate goal of research is to develop remedies to help individuals deal with their problems. Remediation becomes difficult when a disorder is not well understood. Enough is now known to suggest some strategies that are likely to help those challenged by mathematical processing. Further research can only improve on this situation.

WHAT EDUCATORS NEED TO CONSIDER

Studies show that using intense tutoring with first graders who display problems with calculations significantly improved their end-of-year achievement in mathematics (Fuchs et al., 2005). The key, of course, is early detection so that interventions can begin as soon as practicable.

Determining the Source of the Problem

The first task facing educators who deal with children with mathematics disorders is to determine the nature of the problem. Obviously, environmental causes require different interventions than developmental causes. Low performance on a mathematics test *may* indicate that a problem exists, but tests do not provide information on the exact source of the poor performance. Standardized tests, such as the *Brigance Comprehensive Inventory of Basic Skills—Revised*, are available that provide more precise information on whether the problems stem from deficits in counting, number facts, or procedures.

Educators should examine the degree to which students with mathematics difficulties possess the prerequisite skills for learning mathematical operations. What skills are weak, and what can we do about that? They also should look at the mathematics curriculum to determine how much mathematics is being taught and the types of instructional strategies that teachers are using. Are we trying to cover too much? Are we using enough visual and manipulative aids? Are we developing student strengths and not just focusing on their weaknesses?

Prerequisite Skills. Examining the nature of mathematics curriculum and instruction may reveal clues about how the school system approaches teaching these topics. A good frame of reference is the recognition that students need to have mastered a certain number of skills before they can understand and apply the principles of more complex mathematical operations. The Common Core State Standards for Mathematics (National Governors Association Center for Best Practices & Council of Chief State School Officers, 2010), which have been adopted by many states, suggest curriculum content and practices that focus on fewer topics, link topics and thinking across grade levels, and maintain rigor. Students will need to acquire certain skills in order to successfully master this content. These skills should include the ability to

1. Follow sequential directions

2. Recognize patterns

3. Estimate by forming a reasonable guess about quantity, size, magnitude, and amount

4. Visualize pictures in one's mind and manipulate them

5. Have a good sense of spatial orientation and space organization, including telling left from right, compass directions, horizontal and vertical directions

6. Do deductive reasoning—that is, reason from a general principle to a particular instance or from a stated premise to a logical conclusion

7. Do inductive reasoning—that is, come to a natural understanding that is not the result of conscious attention or reasoning, easily detecting the patterns in different situations and the interrelationships between procedures and concepts

Students, for example, who are unable to follow sequential directions will have great difficulty understanding the concept of long division, which requires retention of several different processes performed in a particular sequence. First one estimates, then multiplies, then compares, then subtracts, then brings down a number, and the cycle repeats. Those with directional difficulties will be unsure which number goes inside the division sign or on top of the fraction. Moving through the division problem also presents other directional difficulties: One reads to the right, then records a number up, then multiplies the numbers diagonally, then records the product down below while watching for place value, then brings a number down, and so on.

Diagnostic Tools for
Assessing Learning Difficulties in Mathematics

Research studies over the last 15 years suggest that five critical factors affect the learning of mathematics. Each factor can serve as a diagnostic tool for assessing the nature of any learning difficulties students may experience with mathematical processing (Augustyniak, Murphy, & Phillips, 2005; Liston, 2009; Sharma, 2006).

- **Level of Cognitive Awareness.** Students come to a learning situation with varying levels of cognitive awareness about that learning. The levels can range from no cognitive awareness to high levels of cognitive functioning. The teacher's first task is to determine the students' level of cognitive awareness and the strategies each student brings to the mathematics task. This is not easy, but it can be accomplished if the teacher does the following:

  - Interviews the students individually and observes how each one approaches a mathematical problem that needs to be solved
  - Asks "What is the student thinking?" and "What formal and informal strategies is the student using?"
  - Determines what prerequisite skills are in place and which are poor or missing
  - Determines if a mathematics answer is correct or incorrect and asks students to explain how they arrived at the answer

    Knowing the levels of the students' cognitive awareness and prerequisite skills will give the teacher valuable information for selecting and introducing new concepts and skills.

- **Mathematics Learning Profile.** Researchers agree that each person processes mathematics differently and that these differences run along a continuum from primarily quantitative to primarily qualitative.

Quantitative learners
  - Prefer entities that have definite values, such as length, time, volume, and size
  - Prefer procedural approaches to problem solving and tend to be very methodical and sequential in all they do
  - Approach mathematics as though following a recipe
  - Prefer to break down problems into their parts, solve them, and then reassemble the components to deal with larger problems
  - Are better at deductive reasoning—that is, reasoning from the general principle to a particular instance
  - Learn best when mathematics is presented as a highly structured subject and with a continuous linear focus

o Prefer hands-on materials with a counting basis, such as base-10 blocks and number lines
o Stick with one standardized way of solving problems because alternative solutions are often perceived as uncomfortable and distracting

Qualitative learners

o Approach mathematics tasks holistically and intuitively
o Describe mathematical elements in terms of their qualities rather than by separate parts
o Are social learners who reason by talking through questions, associations, and examples
o Learn by seeing relationships between concepts and procedures
o Draw associations and parallels between familiar situations and the current task
o Focus on visual-spatial aspects of mathematical information
o Have difficulty with sequences, algorithms, elementary mathematics, and precise calculations
o In their work, tend to invent shortcuts, bypass steps, and consolidate procedures with intuitive reasoning
o Often do not practice enough to attain levels of automaticity

Because both types of learning preferences are present in mathematics classes, teachers need to incorporate multiple instructional strategies. Teaching to one preference alone leaves out students with the other preference, many of whom may do poorly in mathematics as a result. In fact, some may even exhibit the symptoms of mathematics disorders.

• **Language of Mathematics.** Mathematical disorders often arise when students fail to understand the language of mathematics, which has its own symbolic representations, syntax, and terminology. Solving word problems requires the ability to translate the language of English into the language of mathematics. The translation is likely to be successful if the student recognizes English language equivalents for each mathematical statement. For example, if the teacher asks the class to solve the problem "76 take away 8," the students will correctly write the expression in the exact order stated, "76 − 8." But if the teacher says, "Subtract 8 from 76," a student following the language order could mistakenly write, "8 − 76." Learning to identify and correctly translate mathematical syntax becomes critical to student success in problem solving.

Language can be an obstacle in other ways. Students may learn a limited vocabulary for performing basic arithmetic operations, such as "add" and "multiply," only to run into difficulties when they encounter expressions asking for the "sum" or "product" of numbers. Teachers can avoid this problem by introducing synonyms for every function: "Let us *multiply* 6 and 5. We are finding the *product* of 6 and 5. The product of 6 *times* 5 is 30."

- **Prerequisite Skills.** As noted earlier, the seven prerequisite skills necessary to learning mathematics successfully are nonmathematical in nature. However, they must be mastered before even the most basic understandings of number concepts and arithmetic operations can be learned. Teachers need to assess the extent to which these seven skills are present in each student.

Teachers might consider using this simple profile diagram to assist in their assessment. After assessing the student's level on each skill, they can analyze the results and decide on a plan of action that will address any areas needing improvement.

Students with four or more scores in the 1–2 range will have significant problems learning the basic concepts of mathematics. They will need instruction and practice in mastering these skills before they can be expected to master mathematical content.

PREREQUISITE SKILLS PROFILE FOR MATHEMATICS

Student's Name: _____ Date: _____

Directions: On a scale of 1 (lowest) to 5 (highest), circle the number that indicates the degree to which the student displays mastery of each skill. Connect the circles to see the profile.

Skill

Skill					
Follows sequential directions	5	4	3	2	1
Recognizes patterns	5	4	3	2	1
Can estimate quantities	5	4	3	2	1
Can visualize and manipulate mental pictures	5	4	3	2	1
Sense of spatial orientation and organization	5	4	3	2	1
Ability to do deductive reasoning	5	4	3	2	1
Ability to do inductive reasoning	5	4	3	2	1

Action Plan: As a result of this profile, we will work together to _____

_____

_____

by doing _____

_____

- **Levels of Learning Mastery.** How does a teacher decide when a student has mastered a mathematical concept? Certainly, written tests of problem solving are one of the major devices for evaluating learning. However, they are useful tools only to the extent that they actually measure mastery rather than rote memory of formulas and procedures. Cognitive research suggests that a person must move through six levels of mastery to truly learn and retain mathematical concepts. For mastery, the student

  - Level One: Connects new knowledge to existing knowledge and experiences
  - Level Two: Searches for concrete material to construct a model or show a manifestation of the concept
  - Level Three: Illustrates the concept by drawing a diagram to connect the concrete example to a symbolic picture or representation
  - Level Four: Translates the concept into mathematical notation using number symbols, operational signs, formulas, and equations
  - Level Five: Applies the concept correctly to real-world situations, projects, and story problems
  - Level Six: Can teach the concept successfully to others or can communicate it on a test

  Too often, paper-and-pencil tests assess only level 6. Thus, when the student's results are poor, the teacher may not know where learning difficulties lie. By designing separate assessments for each level, teachers will be in a much better position to determine what kind of remedial work will help each student having difficulties.

Other Considerations

Less Is More. Another lesson that research has taught us is that students with special needs are likely to be more successful if taught fewer concepts in more time. The notion that "less is more" can apply to all students and is particularly important for those with learning problems. Studies of mathematics (as well as science) courses in the United States and other countries show that spending more time on fewer key concepts leads to greater student achievement in the long run. This is one of the main goals of both the Common Core State Standards for Mathematics and the Next Generation Science Standards. Yet our current mathematics curriculum does not challenge students to study topics in depth. We tend to present a large number of ideas but develop very few of them. Students with special needs should focus on mastering a few important ideas and learn to apply them accurately.

Use of Manipulatives. Manipulatives support the tactile and spatial reinforcement of mathematical concepts, maintain focus, and help students develop the cognitive structures necessary for understanding arithmetic relationships. In addition to physical, concrete

> Studies reveal that concrete and virtual manipulatives are equally effective in improving students' understanding of mathematical concepts.

manipulatives (e.g., Cuisenaire rods and tokens), virtual manipulatives produced by computer software programs help these learners make connections between various types of knowledge. For example, computer software can construct and dynamically connect pictured objects to symbolic representations (such as cubes to a numeral) and thus help learners generalize and draw abstract concepts from the manipulatives. Studies reveal that concrete and virtual manipulatives are equally effective in improving students' understanding of mathematical concepts (e.g., Burns & Hamm, 2011).

Search for Patterns. One of the more surprising research findings is that many children with learning disabilities—including those with mathematical disorders—can learn basic arithmetic concepts. What is needed for these children is an approach that relies less on intensive drill and practice and more on searching for, finding, and using patterns in learning the basic number combinations and arithmetic strategies.

Build on Students' Strengths. As obvious as this statement seems, teachers can often turn a student's failure into success if they build on what the student already knows how to do. Too often teachers get so focused on looking for ways to improve an area of weakness that they unintentionally overlook an individual's learning strengths. Yet many years of research into learning preferences has demonstrated effective ways of recruiting preference strengths to build up weaknesses.

Assistive Technology. Perhaps the best tool for helping students with difficulties in mathematics is the iPad or similar tablet because so many worthwhile apps are available, many of them for free. In addition, calculators, electronic mathematics games, mathematics flashcards and manipulatives, and talking calculators can all be helpful devices.

Most people learn mathematics best in the context of real-world problems. School systems will increase all their students' chances for learning mathematics successfully if they plan curriculum content and instructional strategies that enhance prerequisite skills while developing knowledge and application of mathematical concepts and operations. Students are more comfortable with mathematics when they perceive it as a practical tool and not as an end unto itself. Integrated curriculum units provide opportunities for mathematics to be threaded through diverse and relevant topics. Finally, if the notion that babies are born with a sense of number logic continues to be supported by further research, then educators will need to reconsider how and when we teach mathematics in elementary schools.

Strategies to Consider

GENERAL GUIDELINES FOR TEACHING MATHEMATICS

What we have learned about how students in general education learn mathematics can apply as well, with appropriate modifications, to students with mathematical disorders. Here are some recommendations gleaned from the research.

- **Help students develop conceptual understanding and skills.** These students need time to look at concrete models, understand them, and link them to abstract numerical representations. Allow them more time for mathematics study and for completing assignments.
- **Consider giving more oral and fewer written tests.** The stress of written tests increases the mental burden on these students, who often are better at telling you what they know than writing it.
- **Develop meaningful (relevant) practice exercises.** No one questions the value of practice—it makes permanent! But extensive practice that has little meaning for students is perceived as boring and may lead to disengagement. Practice solving problems that are purposeful and meaningful. Also, provide guided practice with feedback before independent practice so that students can understand what to do for each step and why.
- **Maintain reasonable expectations.** If we really want all students to have basic competencies in mathematics, then we must establish expectations that are reasonable. This should include problem-based learning, solving authentic problems, and showing the applications of mathematics to other subject areas, such as science. Similarly, setting expectations that are too low—explicitly or implicitly—increases the burden that children with all types of special needs may need to carry as adults.
- **Build on children's strengths.** In all areas of learning, teachers can often turn a student's failure into success if they build on what the student already knows how to do. Many years of research into learning preferences has demonstrated effective ways of recruiting preference strengths to build up weaknesses.
- **Use manipulatives appropriately.** Manipulatives can be valuable tools if students are able to connect what they are handling with what they are thinking. Have students explain aloud the connections they are making, and make sure they refer to the mathematical concepts and skills they are learning. Virtual manipulatives can be just as effective as concrete ones.
- **Help students make connections.** Students perceive meaning when they are able to connect what they are learning to prior knowledge or to future usefulness. Help students connect symbols to verbal descriptions. Find ways to link social situations to solving practical mathematical problems (e.g., splitting a restaurant check, determining an appropriate tip).
- **Determine and build on a student's informal learning strategies.** All learners develop informal strategies for dealing with their world. Determine what strategies the student is using and build on them to develop concepts and procedures.
- **Accommodate individual learning preferences as much as is practicable.** Use as many multisensory approaches as possible. Include modeling, role-playing, demonstrations, simulations, and cooperative learning groups to provide variety and maintain student interest. Use mnemonic devices (Chapter 2) and games to help students remember number combinations and other important facts. Limit direct instruction (i.e., teacher talk) and use more interactive teaching strategies.

- **Use technology appropriately.** All students should have access to electronic tools. They can use them to understand mathematical concepts as well as how to benefit their adult lives. Using computer software that includes speech recognition and three-dimensional design, for instance, can be very helpful for students with special needs.

Strategies to Consider

TEACHING STRATEGIES IN MATHEMATICS FOR DIFFERENT LEARNING PREFERENCES

Cognitive researchers are suggesting that students approach the study of mathematics with different learning preferences that run the gamut from primarily quantitative to primarily qualitative (Augustyniak et al., 2005; Farkas, 2003; Liston, 2009; Sharma, 2006). The implication of this research is that students are more likely to be successful in learning mathematics if teachers use instructional strategies that are compatible with this range of preferences. Tables 7.1 and 7.2 illustrate teaching strategies that are appropriate for the mathematical behaviors exhibited by quantitative and qualitative learners, respectively. Table 7.3 suggests a sequence for using inductive and deductive approaches when introducing a new mathematical concept.

Tables 7.1 and 7.2 are meant to help teachers address specific mathematical behaviors that they identify in individual students. Such strategies target specific needs and, with practice, can strengthen a student's weakness. It is

Table 7.1   Teaching Strategies for Learners With Quantitative Preference

Mathematical Behaviors	Teaching Strategies to Consider
Approaches situations using recipes	Emphasize the meaning of each concept or procedure in verbal terms.
Approaches mathematics in a mechanical, routine-like fashion	Highlight the concept and overall goal of the learning.
Emphasizes component parts rather than larger mathematical constructs	Encourage explicit description of the overall conceptual framework. Look for ways to link parts to the whole.
Prefers numerical approach rather than concrete models	Use a step-by-step approach to connect the model to the numerical procedure.
Prefers the linear approach to arithmetic concept	Start with the larger framework and use different approaches to reach the same concept.
Has difficulty in situations requiring multistep tasks	Separate multiple tasks into smaller units and explain the connections between the units.

Table 7.2 Teaching Strategies for Learners With Qualitative Preference

Mathematical Behaviors	Teaching Strategies to Consider
Prefers concepts to algorithms (procedures for problem solving)	Connect models first to the concept and then to procedures before introducing algorithms.
Perceives overall shape of geometric structures at expense of missing the individual components	Emphasize how the individual components contribute to the overall design of the geometric figure.
Difficulties with precise calculations and in explaining procedure for finding the correct solution	Encourage explicit description of each step used.
Can offer a variety of approaches or answers to a single problem	Use simulations and real-world problems to show application of concept to different situations.
Prefers to set up problems but cannot always follow through to a solution	Provide opportunities for the student to work in cooperative learning groups. To ensure full participation, give the student one grade for problem approach and setup and one grade for exact solution.
Benefits from manipulatives and enjoys topics related to geometry	Provide a variety of manipulatives and models (e.g., Cuisenaire rods, tokens, or blocks) to support numerical operations. Look for geometric links to new concepts.

unrealistic, however, to expect teachers to identify and select individual strategies for problems encountered by all their students during a single learning episode. Moreover, students can shift their preference if sufficiently motivated to do so.

Table 7.3 suggests an instructional sequence for introducing a new mathematical concept. The order first accommodates qualitative learners and then moves to techniques for quantitative learners.

Table 7.3 Inductive to Deductive Approach for Introducing a New Concept

Steps of the Inductive Approach for Qualitative Learners	• Explain the linguistic aspects of the concept • Introduce the general principle or law that supports the concept • Provide students opportunities to use concrete materials to investigate and discover proof of the connection between the principle and the concept • Give many specific examples of the concept's validity, using concrete materials • Allow students to discuss with each other what they discovered about how the concept works • Demonstrate how these individual experiences can be integrated into a general principle or rule that applies equally to each example
Steps for the Deductive Approach for Quantitative Learners	• Reemphasize the general principle or law that the concept relates to • Demonstrate how several specific examples obey the general principle or law • Allow students to state the principle and suggest specific examples that follow it • Ask students to explain the linguistic elements of the concept

By understanding the different approaches to the learning of mathematics, teachers are more likely to select instructional strategies that will result in successful learning for all students.

Strategies to Consider

USING THE CONCRETE-REPRESENTATIONAL-ABSTRACT (CRA) APPROACH

Students who have difficulties with mathematics can benefit significantly from lessons that include multiple models that approach a concept at different cognitive levels. Mathematics educators have recognized a substantial body of research showing that the optimal presentation sequence for new mathematical content is concrete-representational-abstract, or the CRA approach. This approach has also been referred to as concrete-pictorial-abstract or concrete-semiconcrete-abstract. Regardless of the name, the instructional approach is similar and originally based on the work of Jerome Bruner (1960). Concrete components include manipulatives (e.g., Cuisenaire rods, foam-rubber pie sections, and markers), measuring tools, or other objects the students can handle during the lesson. Pictorial representations include drawings, diagrams, charts, or graphs created by the students or provided for the students to read and interpret. The abstract aspect refers to symbolic representations, such as numbers or letters that the student writes or interprets to demonstrate understanding of a task. This approach continues to be successful with students who have difficulties learning mathematics (e.g., Mancl, Miller, & Kennedy, 2012; Sealander, Johnson, Lockwood, & Medina, 2012; Strickland & Maccini, 2013).

Video: For a brief explanation of the CRA model, see:

https://www.youtube.com/watch?v=OOa3dZCPeRM

When using the CRA approach, the sequencing of activities is critical. Activities with concrete materials should come first to impress on students that mathematical operations can be used to solve real-world problems. Pictorial examples show representations of the concrete manipulatives and help students visualize mathematical operations during problem solving. It is important here that the teacher explain how the pictorial examples relate to the concrete examples. Finally, formal work with symbols is used to demonstrate how they provide a shorter and more efficient way to represent numerical operations. Ultimately, students need to reach that final abstract level by using symbols proficiently with many of the mathematical skills they master; however, the meanings of those symbols must be firmly rooted in experiences with real objects. Otherwise, their performance of the symbolic operations will simply be rote repetitions of meaningless memorized procedures.

The CRA approach benefits all students but has been shown to be particularly effective with students who have mathematics difficulties, mainly because it moves gradually from actual objects to pictures and then to symbols. These students often get frustrated when teachers present mathematics problems only in the abstract. Mathematics teachers need to organize content into concepts and provide instruction that allows students to process the new learning in meaningful and efficient ways.

Research studies support the effectiveness of this approach. Witzel and his colleagues have conducted several studies of students identified as having difficulties in learning algebra. Students who learned how to solve algebra transformation equations through the CRA approach scored higher on postinstruction and follow-up tests than did the control peers receiving traditional instruction. Furthermore, students who used the CRA sequence of instruction performed fewer procedural errors when solving for algebraic variables (Witzel, 2005; Witzel, Mercer, & Miller, 2003).

Teachers of mathematics in elementary schools have recognized the importance of using concrete and pictorial activities when introducing new concepts. Yet despite newer research in cognitive neuroscience lending support to the CRA method, it is not in widespread use in middle and high school mathematics classrooms and is seldom mentioned in textbooks. Perhaps teachers at the secondary level feel that concrete objects may be perceived by students as too elementary, or it may be that the content demands of the curriculum push teachers directly to the abstract level to save time. But students with difficulties in learning mathematics are encouraged when concrete and pictorial representations eventually lead them to interpret abstract concepts accurately (Walkowiak, 2014).

To help teachers implement CRA, Witzel has developed a seven-step process that uses the mnemonic CRAMATH as a guide (Witzel, Riccomini, & Schneider, 2008).

1. **Choose a topic in mathematics.** The teacher looks for a broad idea that may join apparently dissimilar items together. A middle school topic might involve working with algebraic equations, such as $24 = 10 - 4x$.

2. **Review procedures for solving the problem.** For example, when solving equations, the teacher lists the steps, such as identifying the variable and coefficient, balancing across the equal sign, calculating according to the order of operations, continuing until the coefficient is 1, determining the answer, and, finally, checking the answer.

3. **Adjust the steps to eliminate notation or calculation tricks.** After presenting the steps, the teacher eliminates any tricks or shortcuts so students do not spend time learning tricks or shortcuts that work only in specific situations and not in others. For example, take the equation, $x - 9 = 14$. Students might assume that this can be easily solved by just adding nine to both sides. However, the first step should be to make the coefficient of the unknown equal to 1. Thus, the student should first divide each side of the equation by the coefficient of 1. Otherwise, when presented with the equation, $3x - 4 = 17$, the teacher has to tell the students that if there is a coefficient greater than 1, they must divide by that coefficient after adding 4 to both sides.

4. **Match the abstract steps to the appropriate concrete manipulative.** The teacher should choose objects that apply to multiple skills

to help students recognize the generalizability of the rules, procedures, and concepts in mathematics. For example, algebra blocks are helpful for simple equations involving whole-number coefficients, such as $5x = 30$, but not helpful for equations with fractional coefficients, such as $3/5 \, x = 18$. Here, it is more useful to use concrete objects representing groupings, such as containers. (See the Resources section at the end of this book for a website that suggests concrete/virtual representations for mathematics topics at different grade levels.)

5. **Arrange concrete and representational lessons.** After completing the work with concrete objects, the teacher creates pictorial representations that mimic the concrete ones. For example, subtraction using toothpicks involves removing the toothpicks from the desktop. Pictorially, this could be represented by drawing an X over the toothpicks that were subtracted.

6. **Teach each concrete, representational, and abstract lesson to mastery.** Teachers use frequent and accurate assessments to evaluate their students' progress as they transition from one stage to the next toward mastering the learning objectives. Transitioning from the representational to the abstract stage is the most difficult for students with learning difficulties in mathematics. Therefore, teachers should use clear and appropriate terminology and language related to the mathematical principle. For example, a coefficient may be called a cup in the concrete stage, a group in the representational stage, but a coefficient in the abstract stage.

7. **Help students apply what they learned through word problems.** Students with learning difficulties in mathematics do not usually apply concepts or skills to new settings without appropriate guidance and explicit instruction. Teachers should present instructional activities that improve students' ability to generalize across different scenarios. Using real-world examples in word problems can help students recognize the practical applications of mathematics to new settings and understand the value of learning mathematics skills.

Concrete and pictorial representations should be used at all grade levels. By using cognitive strategies such as CRA, teachers provide students with a technique for tackling mathematics problems rather than just searching for an answer.

Emotional and Behavioral Disorders

While physics and mathematics may tell us how the universe began, they are not much use in predicting human behavior because there are far too many equations to solve.

—Stephen Hawking, Theoretical Physicist

In recent years researchers have recognized the contribution that the emotions make not only to the development of the human brain but also the impact they have on the learning process. Although these contributions are not always considered to be positive, understanding their impact can help parents and educators make appropriate decisions to meet the emotional needs of children and adolescents.

EMOTIONS, BEHAVIOR, AND LEARNING

The brain is genetically programmed to gather information and to develop skills that are likely to keep its owner alive. Among other things, human survival depends on the family unit, where emotional bonds increase the chances of producing children and raising them to be productive adults. Consequently, the human brain has learned over thousands of years that survival and emotional messages must have high priority when it filters through all the incoming signals from the body's senses.

The brainstem monitors and regulates survival functions, such as body temperature, respiratory rate, and blood pressure (Chapter 1). Emotional messages are carried through and interpreted in the limbic area, usually with the help of the frontal lobe (Figure 8.1). These survival and emotional messages guide the individual's behavior, including directing its attention to a learning situation. Specifically, emotion drives attention, and attention drives learning.

But even more important to understand is that emotional attention often comes before cognitive recognition. You see a letter from the Internal Revenue Service in the mail, and within a few seconds your palms are sweating, your breathing is labored, and your blood pressure rises—all this before you even know what is in the letter. That is your amygdala acting up, the part of the limbic system responsible for emotional responses, and it can act without input from the cognitive parts of the brain (frontal lobe). In this instance, the brain is responding emotionally to a situation without the benefit of cognitive information and processing, such as thinking, reasoning, and consciousness.

Pathways of Emotional Signals

In Chapter 1, we learned that the thalamus receives all incoming sensory impulses (except smell) and directs them to other parts of the brain for further processing. Incoming sensory information to the thalamus can take two different routes to the amygdala. The quick route (called the *thalamic pathway*) sends the signals directly from the thalamus to the amygdala (pathway A in Figure 8.2). The second possibility (called the *cortical pathway*) is for the thalamus to direct the signals first to the cerebral cortex (in the cerebrum) for cognitive processing and then to the amygdala (pathway B).

The time it takes for signals to travel along the two pathways is different. For example, it takes sound signals about 12 milliseconds (a millisecond is 1/1,000th of a second) to travel pathway A and about twice as long to travel pathway B. Which pathway the signals take could mean the difference between life and death. If the sound from a car blasting its horn travels along pathway A, it will probably be fast enough to get you to jump out of the way even though you are not sure what is coming. Only later does your cerebral cortex provide the explanation of what happened. Survival is the first priority, an explanation second.

Figure 8.1   Survival functions are controlled from the brainstem. Emotional signals are processed and interpreted in the limbic area and frontal lobe.

Disturbances in this dual pathway system can explain some abnormal behaviors. Anxiety disorders, for example, can result whenever a certain action, such as walking into a crowd, is associated with fear. If this activity always takes pathway A, then a phobia develops that cannot be easily moderated through rational discussion. This probably explains why psychotherapy alone is rarely successful in treating many phobias and anxiety disorders.

Different Brain Areas for Different Emotions

Although the amygdala is the center of emotional processing and response, neuroscientists now believe that different areas of the brain interpret specific emotions. The frontal cortex of the left hemisphere deals with positive emotions; the right frontal cortex is concerned with negative emotions (Figure 8.3) (Álvarez et al., 2014). Damage to the front of the left hemisphere results in feelings of hopelessness and bouts of depression.

Figure 8.2 Sensory information travels to the thalamus, where it can be routed directly to the amygdala (thalamic pathway, A), or first to the cerebrum and then to the amygdala (cortical pathway, B).

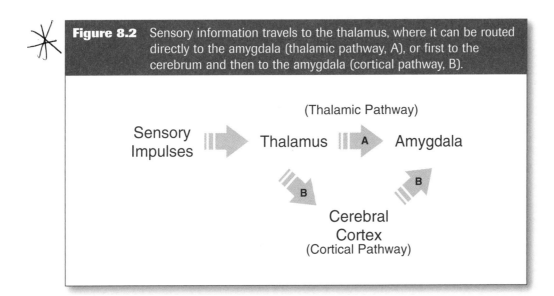

Figure 8.3 The left hemisphere's frontal cortex processes positive emotions. The right hemisphere's frontal cortex processes negative emotions and nuance.

However, if the front right side is damaged, the individual often expresses inappropriate cheerfulness, even denying the injury.

Studies using scanning techniques have identified specific brain regions that respond to emotions associated with fear, disgust, and happiness. Their inputs are processed by the amygdala, which influences the individual's subsequent cognitive and motor responses (e.g., Meaux & Vuilleumier, 2015; Tettamanti et al., 2012). However, the more complex the emotional input, the more these brain regions interact (Oosterwijk et al., 2012).

The Nature of Anxiety

Anxiety serves a useful purpose in that it signals us that something needs to be corrected in our environment. The anxious feelings you got when seeing the letter from the Internal Revenue Service were soon tempered when cognitive reflection reminded you that this is the time of year estimated-tax forms are sent out. This return to emotional stability is the result of the interactions between the emotion-generating amygdala and the emotion-inhibiting left frontal cortex. Both the amygdala and left frontal cortex need to be functioning properly for this balance to be maintained and, thus, for good mental health. If either one of these components is malfunctioning, then the person's behavior is likely to be abnormal.

> Students must feel physically safe and emotionally secure before they can focus on the curriculum.

First Survival and Emotions, Then the Textbook

The typical human brain is programmed to deal first with its owner's survival and emotional needs. Therefore, the brain is unlikely to attend to any other task until it is assured that these needs have been met and that the environment poses no threat. If we transfer this notion to schools, it means that students are not going to care about the curriculum unless they feel physically safe and emotionally secure.

Physical Safety. For students to feel physically safe, schools must be free of weapons and violence. A student will have trouble concentrating on the lesson if a nearby student displays a weapon or threatens physical harm. Physical safety also refers to the safe condition of the student's body. Has the student had enough sleep and an adequate breakfast? Rest and fuel are important requirements for attention and learning.

Emotional Security. Emotional security refers to the degree to which a student feels accepted as a valued member of a group. In my view, the emotional needs of children can be met in just three places:

- In the home (and those entities to which the family belongs, such as religious or community groups)
- In school, through the formal organization of educators and school groups
- Outside the school, from an informal organization of peers

In years past, the emotional needs of children and adolescents used to be met mainly at home and in the neighborhood. The family dined together nightly, spending quality time to strengthen emotional bonds through reassurances, caring, and love. Neighbors watched out for each other's children at play, and it was a safer world.

In today's fast-paced lifestyle, many families dine together only once or twice a week. Hectic family schedules mean that parents and children have less time together. When the children *are* at home, they spend more time in their own bedrooms—playing computer games, calling on their cell phones, interacting with social media, and watching television—than with their parents. According to surveys conducted recently by the Pew Research Center, 91 percent of teens between the ages of 13 and 17 are using media and sending or receiving an average of 30 texts a day (Lenhart, 2015). When do they have time for meaningful conversation with their family?

Because the amount of quality time at home is so small, many students are not getting their emotional needs met. Consequently, they come to school looking for emotional support from the formal organization through teachers and other professionals in the school environment. Finding emotional support in the primary grades is easy because those teachers are trained to provide it. But it is an entirely different matter in secondary schools. High school teachers are trained to deliver curriculum efficiently and effectively. Few have had training in how to deal with the emotional needs of students, and even fewer ever believed that such training would be necessary. Furthermore, many were not prepared for the formidable impact that technology and social media have had on the classroom culture, climate, and student behavior. However, high school teachers are now well aware that they must meet the emotional needs of their students before they can be successful at presenting the curriculum.

If the students' emotional needs are not met in the home or in school, then some students resort to the third alternative—joining an informal organization of peers, commonly called a gang, either real or virtual. These are family-like units that have a name, a set of values, and a system of rewards and punishments. Regrettably, their behavior is too often directed toward deviant, rather than socially acceptable, goals.

EMOTIONAL AND BEHAVIORAL DISORDERS

Because emotions and behavior affect each other and are so closely intertwined, disorders of these areas are usually discussed together. Although a few of these disorders can appear in early adulthood or later, many appear in childhood and adolescence. Some are more common than others, and conditions can range from mild to severe. Often, a person has more than one disorder. Nearly all these disorders can seriously affect memory in children and adolescents, especially verbal memory.

The causes of all the types of disorders can be biological, environmental, or a mixture of both. Biological factors include genetics, chemical imbalances in the body, and damage to the central nervous system, such as a head injury. Environmental causes can include

Video: For a description of the causes, symptoms, and treatments for emotional and behavioral disorders, see:

https://www.youtube.com/watch?v=4OVtxwpFx-8

exposure to violence, extreme stress, or the loss of an important person, such as by death or divorce.

An in-depth discussion of all types of emotional and behavioral disorders that afflict humans is beyond the scope of this book. Rather, the following describes those emotional and behavioral disorders that are most common among children and adolescents and that educators are likely to encounter in almost any school.

ANXIETY DISORDERS

- Social anxiety disorder (Social Phobia)
- Generalized anxiety disorder
- Panic disorder
- Obsessive-compulsive disorder
- Post-traumatic stress disorder

Anxiety Disorders

In the DSM-5's chapter on anxiety disorders, some have been redistributed among other chapters. Obsessive-compulsive disorder (OCD) has been given its own chapter with related disorders, and post-traumatic stress disorder (PTSD) is included in the chapter on trauma- and stressor-related disorders. Despite this redistribution, the fact that these chapters are in sequential order reflects the close relationship among these conditions. For that reason, OCD and PTSD and included here as anxiety disorders.

Most people experience feelings of anxiety before an important event, such as a business presentation, big test, or first date. But people with anxiety disorders have anxiety and fears that endure longer than six months, are chronic and unrelenting, and can grow progressively worse. Sometimes their anxieties are so bad that people become housebound.

Anxiety disorders are the most common of childhood disorders, affecting an estimated 13 percent of the 9- to 17-year-old population. These young people experience excessive worry, fear, or uneasiness that interferes with daily routines. Anxiety disorders include the following (NIMH, 2015a):

- **Social anxiety disorder:** This disorder (also called social phobia) is characterized by an overwhelming fear of scrutiny, embarrassment, or humiliation when with their peers. Their fear may be so severe that it interferes with schoolwork and other ordinary activities. Social phobia can be limited to only one type of situation, such as a fear of speaking, eating, or writing in front of others. In its most severe form, people experience symptoms almost anytime they are around others. Physical symptoms include blushing, profuse sweating, trembling, nausea, and difficulty talking. Social phobia usually begins in childhood or early adolescence, and there is some evidence that genetic factors are involved. Social phobia can be treated successfully with carefully targeted psychotherapy or medications.

- **Generalized anxiety disorder (GAD):** This disorder is a pattern of unrealistic and excessive worry not attributable to any recent experience but disruptive to routine life and events. Those with GAD have incessant fears about the future and almost always anticipate the worst even though there is little reason to expect it. Their worries are accompanied by fatigue, headaches, muscle tension, muscle aches, difficulty swallowing, trembling, twitching, irritability, and sweating. Children with GAD may seem unable to relax, and they may startle more easily than others. They tend to have difficulty concentrating and often have trouble falling or staying asleep.

  The disorder comes on gradually, though the risk is highest between childhood and middle age. Females are more than twice as afflicted as males, and there is evidence that genes play a modest role. GAD is commonly treated with psychotherapy, medication, or both.

- **Panic disorder:** Individuals with this condition experience repeated episodes of terrifying attacks of panic that strike without warning. They develop intense anxiety between episodes, worrying when and where the next one will strike. Physical symptoms include rapid heartbeat, chest pain, numb or tingling hands, nausea, abdominal distress, and dizziness. Panic attacks can occur at any time, even during sleep. An attack generally peaks within 10 minutes, but some symptoms may last much longer. Studies of twins indicate that the risk of developing panic disorder can be inherited.

  Panic disorder most often begins during late adolescence or early adulthood. People often avoid any situation in which they would feel helpless if a panic attack were to occur. When people's lives become so restricted, as happens in about one-third of those with panic disorder, the condition is called *agoraphobia*. Early treatment of panic disorder can often prevent agoraphobia.

- **Obsessive-compulsive disorder (OCD):** This disorder involves patterns of repeated thoughts and behaviors that are impossible to control or stop. Although rare in young children, the occurrence of the disorder increases in adolescents. Distinguishing OCD from developmentally normal childhood behavior involves assessing how often the child engages in the behavior, how much the behavior disrupts the child's daily routine, and how distressed the child becomes when the behavior is interrupted or prevented (NIMH, 2015b).

  Individuals with OCD may be obsessed with germs or dirt, so they wash their hands over and over, or they may be filled with doubt and feel the need to check things repeatedly. Some have frequent thoughts of violence and fear that people close to them will harm them. They may spend long periods touching things or counting or be preoccupied by order or symmetry. Children with OCD may not realize that their behavior is out of the ordinary.

  The course of the disorder varies in that symptoms may come and go, they may ease over time, or they can grow progressively worse.

Research evidence suggests that OCD runs in families. Depression or other anxiety disorders may accompany OCD, and some people with OCD also have eating disorders. OCD generally responds well to treatment with medications that regulate serotonin (called selective serotonin reuptake inhibitors) or to carefully targeted behavioral therapy. The earlier children with OCD are treated, the better the chances of lessening the undesirable symptoms of the disorder (e.g., Anderson, Freeman, Franklin, & Sapyta, 2015; Melin, Skärsäter, Haugland, & Ivarsson, 2015).

- **Post-traumatic stress disorder (PTSD):** A debilitating condition involving a pattern of flashbacks and other symptoms that occur in children who have experienced a psychologically distressing event (e.g., physical and sexual abuse, being a witness or victim of violence, or exposure to some other traumatic event, such as a hurricane, flood, or bombing). <u>Nightmares, numbing of emotions, and feeling angry or irritable are common symptoms.</u> PTSD can occur at any age. There is evidence that susceptibility may run in families, which would explain why only certain individuals exposed to similar traumatic events develop full-blown PTSD. In those who do develop PTSD, symptoms usually begin within three months of the trauma, and the course of the illness varies. Some people recover within six months; others have symptoms that last much longer. The disorder is often accompanied by depression, substance abuse, or one or more other anxiety disorders. PTSD can be treated with medications and carefully targeted psychotherapy (NIMH, 2015c).

Causes of Anxiety Disorders

Normal emotional behavior relies on the integrating balance between the emotions initiated by the amygdala and the mediating effect of our thoughts. If either one of these components malfunctions, problems arise. Brain imaging has helped neuroscientists gain a greater understanding of the source of these problems and thus the causes of anxiety disorders. For example, if a malfunction causes nonthreatening sensory signals to always take the thalamic pathway (Figure 8.2), panic attacks result because the signals are not benefiting from the mediating effect of cognitive thought. Here is an example: To most of us, the sound of a car backfiring is annoying, but we usually would not mistake it for a gunshot. However, to an adolescent brought up in a neighborhood where gunfire has killed a friend or family member, that backfiring could activate a full-fledged stress response. This post-traumatic stress response might send the adolescent diving for cover and in full panic. Apparently, the sounds of the backfiring went directly to the amygdala (thalamic pathway), triggering the panic behavior. No input from the cerebral cortex was present to curtail the post-traumatic response.

Treating Anxiety Disorders

For many years, psychiatrists thought that obsessive-compulsive disorder had psychological roots and attempted to treat it with psychoanalysis.

Brain imaging studies, however, suggest that obsessive-compulsive behavior is the result of hyperactivity in a circuit of the brain that connects the frontal lobe to a part of the limbic area called the caudate nucleus. Activity in this circuit decreases between obsessive-compulsive episodes and after treatment. The disorder responds to a combination of drugs that increases the action of the neurotransmitter serotonin, followed by psychotherapy that addresses the specific nature of the behavior. Researchers are now looking at some new treatment approaches, such as deep brain stimulation, for those who do not respond well to the usual therapies.

Depressive Disorders

Children and adolescents with learning disabilities are susceptible to chronic depression. About 3.3 percent of 13- to 18-year-olds have major depression. The onset of depressive disorders is occurring earlier in life today than ever before (NIMH, 2015d). Depressed children do not necessarily look like depressed adults. They are more often irritable rather than sad and withdrawn.

In the DSM-5, some of the depressive disorders have been reclassified. Persistent depressive disorder now includes major depressive disorder (unipolar depression) and dysthymia (a less severe type of major depression). Bipolar disorder (manic-depression) is a separate category. Because of the risk of overdiagnosis and overtreatment of bipolar disorder in children, the DSM-5 included a new diagnosis. Disruptive mood regulation disorder now applies to children up to 18 years of age who exhibit continuing irritability and frequent occurrences of extreme lack of behavioral control. All types can have far-reaching effects on the functioning and adjustment of young people. Children and adolescents with depressive disorders are at an increased risk for illness and interpersonal and social difficulties. These adolescents also have an increased risk for substance abuse and suicidal behavior.

Unfortunately, depressive disorders in adolescents often go unrecognized because their signs are interpreted as normal mood swings typical of this age group. For example, instead of communicating how bad they feel, they may act out and be irritable toward others, which may be interpreted simply as misbehavior or disobedience. Parents are even less likely to identify major depression in their adolescents than are the adolescents themselves.

DEPRESSIVE DISORDERS

Depression: Symptoms common to all ages

- Persistent sad or irritable mood
- Loss of interest in activities once enjoyed
- Significant change in appetite or body weight
- Difficulty sleeping or sleeping too much
- Psychomotor agitation or retardation
- Loss of energy

(Continued)

(Continued)

- Feelings of worthlessness, helplessness, or inappropriate guilt
- Difficulty concentrating, remembering details, and making decisions
- Recurrent thoughts of death or suicide

Bipolar Disorder: Symptoms for preteens and older

- Severe changes in mood
- Overly inflated self-esteem
- Increased energy
- Able to go without much sleep
- Talks too fast and too much, cannot be interrupted
- Excessive involvement in risk behaviors

Symptoms of Depressive Disorders

The symptoms of major depressive disorders are common to children, adolescents, and adults. Five or more of these symptoms must persist for an extended period of time before a diagnosis of depression is indicated. Because of the difficulty in diagnosing younger people using just the common symptoms, clinicians often look for other signs that are usually associated with the disorder.

Disruptive mood regulation disorder in children and adolescents is marked by exaggerated mood swings between extreme lows (depression) and highs (excitedness or manic behavior). Periods of quiet may occur in between. The mood swings may recur throughout life. This illness is often confused with attention-deficit hyperactivity disorder.

Causes of Depressive Disorders

Depressive disorders are disorders of the brain and can be caused by any of the following conditions (or combination): genetics, psychological factors, events occurring in a person's environment and biological events occurring inside the body (NIMH, 2015d). Brain-imaging technologies show that the brains of people who have depression look different from those of people without depression. The parts of the brain involved in mood, thinking, sleep, appetite, and behavior appear different (e.g., Papmeyer et al., 2015). But these images do not reveal why the depression has occurred. They also cannot be used to diagnose depression. Some types of depression run in families, suggesting that a biological vulnerability can be inherited (e.g., Goswami et al., 2013). This seems to be the case with bipolar disorder. Studies of families in which members of each generation develop bipolar disorder found that those with the illness have a somewhat different genetic makeup than those who do not get ill (King et al., 2006). However, the reverse is not true: Not everybody with the genetic susceptibility to bipolar disorder will have the illness.

Apparently, environmental factors are involved in the disorder's onset. A serious loss, divorcing parents, accident, trauma, or any drastic change in life patterns can trigger a depressive episode. Studies show that children who were raised in homes where they were exposed to high levels of parental depression and family discord had significantly higher rates of depressive disorders than their counterparts (e.g., Batten et al., 2012; Jacobs, Warner, & Weissman, 2013).

Physical changes in the body can be accompanied by mental changes as well. Medical illnesses, such as stroke, a heart attack, cancer, and hormonal disorders, can cause depressive illness, making the sick person apathetic and unwilling to care for physical needs. Very often, a combination of genetic, psychological, and environmental factors is involved in the onset of a depressive disorder.

Whether inherited or not, major depressive disorder is often associated with changes in brain structures or brain function. Below-normal concentrations of one or more neurotransmitters, such as serotonin, have been shown to be an underlying cause of depression (e.g., Haase & Brown, 2015; Stamm et al., 2013).

Treating Depressive Disorders

Treatment for depressive disorders involves short-term psychotherapy, medication, or the combination of both plus targeted interventions involving the home and school environment. Certain types of short-term psychotherapy, particularly cognitive-behavioral therapy (CBT), can help relieve depression in children and adolescents, as well as adults. CBT is based on the premise that people with depression have cognitive distortions in their views of themselves, the world, and the future. CBT, designed to be a time-limited therapy, focuses on changing these distortions. CBT targets higher functioning areas in the frontal lobe, which in turn influence other brain regions (Fujino et al., 2015; Kaufman, Rohde, Seeley, Clarke, & Stice, 2005).

Antidepressant medications act on the more primitive structures in the limbic area involved in mood and temperament. These in turn feed back to the frontal lobe through complex chemical pathways. Thus, CBT and antidepressant medications work differently in the brain. In Figure 8.4, representative scans show the changes that occur in the brain after treatment with CBT in the top image and the antidepressant medication paroxetine (brand name: Paxil **positron emission tomography (PET)** in the bottom image. Note that the CBT treatment primarily affected the frontal lobes, while the drug treatment centered on the limbic and more primitive areas (Seminowicz et al., 2004).

Because separate depression therapies affect the brain differently, more clinical practitioners suggest using a combination of drug and psychotherapy rather than one or the other. Studies have shown antidepressant medications to be effective in treating children and adolescents with depression. Because of the potential side effects of antidepressant drugs, children given both therapies need to be monitored closely by a physician.

DEPRESSIVE DISORDERS

Signs associated with depressive disorders in children and adolescents

- Frequent, nonspecific complaints of headaches, tiredness, and stomach and muscle aches
- Frequent absences from school or poor performance in school
- Talking about running away from home
- Outbursts of crying, shouting, and complaining
- Being bored
- Lack of interest in playing with friends
- Alcohol or substance abuse
- Social isolation, poor communication
- Fear of death
- Extreme sensitivity to rejection or failure
- Increased hostility and irritability
- Reckless behavior
- Difficulty with relationships
- Self-mutilation

Other Emotional and Behavioral Disorders

A number of other emotional and behavioral disorders are found in the school population, such as the following:

Attention-Deficit Hyperactivity Disorder (ADHD). The significant increase in the number of children diagnosed with this disorder has received much attention from the media and from researchers. ADHD is discussed fully in Chapter 3.

Oppositional-Defiant Disorder. All children are occasionally oppositional by arguing, talking back, or defying their parents, teachers, and other adults. However, persistent and openly hostile behavior that interferes with a child's daily functioning is called oppositional-defiant disorder. It is characterized by deliberate attempts to annoy others, excessive arguing with adults, frequent temper tantrums, and refusal to comply with adult requests.

In the DSM-5, four refinements were made to this disorder. First, the symptoms have been grouped into three types: angry/irritable mood, argumentative/defiant behavior, and vindictiveness. This change emphasizes that the disorder displays both behavioral and emotional symptoms. Second, the exclusion criterion for conduct disorder has been removed. Third, specific attention is given to the frequency of the behavior so as to distinguish it from the oppositional-defiant behavior of typically developing children. Fourth, the criteria now have a severity rating to reflect research indicating that the degree of pervasiveness of the symptoms in different settings is a critical indicator of the severity of the disorder.

This disorder can look like ADHD, but these children are not only unruly, they harm animals, beat up on others, and destroy property. The cause is unknown, but recent imaging studies have found disruptions in the neutral networks connecting the brain's amygdala to areas in the frontal lobe (e.g., Finger et al., 2012). Medications alone generally are not used for this disorder unless another disorder coexists. Treatment centers on psychotherapy that usually includes training to help parents in reinforcing their child's positive behavior, individual counseling to show the child how to manage anger, and social skills training to help the child interact more positively with peers. If the child does not respond to treatment, the behavior may worsen and become a general conduct disorder.

Conduct Disorder. This disorder usually begins with the appearance of hostile and defiant behavior during the preschool years, known as oppositional-defiant disorder. (See the previous section.) As the child gets older, conduct disorder may appear, causing children and adolescents to act out their feelings or impulses toward others in destructive ways. Young people with conduct disorder consistently violate the general rules of society and basic rights of others. The offenses they commit get more serious over time and include lying, aggression, theft, truancy, setting fires, and vandalism. However, most young people with conduct disorder do not have lifelong patterns of conduct problems or antisocial behavior.

The origin of conduct disorder is complicated by the interaction of numerous biological and environmental factors. There may be a genetic link that causes problems in the brain's limbic area (Haberstick, Smolen, & Hewitt, 2006). Studies using fMRI have shown impairment in the systems that recognize emotional stimuli and cognitively control emotional behavior (e.g., Fairchild et al., 2015; Passamonti et al., 2010; Sterzer, Stadler, Krebs, Kleinschmidt, & Poustka, 2005). Youths with conduct disorder also show less responsiveness in the frontal lobe during stimulus-reinforcement and reward tasks (Finger et al., 2011). This may explain why youths with this disorder are more likely to repeat poor decision making. Furthermore, individuals with conduct disorder have reduced levels of cortisol and serotonin, as well as reduced autonomic nervous system functions (Cappadocia, Desrocher, Pepler, & Schroeder, 2009). As a result of these reductions, individuals may respond less to fear and anxiety, be unable to regulate their mood and impulsive behaviors, and possess low self-esteem.

Persistent family conflicts, drugs and alcohol use by parents, and child abuse are also linked to conduct disorder. Males are diagnosed with this disorder far more frequently than females. But this difference in prevalence may be because the criteria used for diagnosis focus on more overt behaviors, such as fighting and aggression, which are often exhibited by males. Females are more likely to be diagnosed using covert behaviors, such as running away from home and stealing.

This is one of the most difficult behavior disorders to treat because of the interplay of numerous possible causes. Even so, progress can be made with cognitive-behavioral therapy, parent management training, and the use of community support services. No specific medication is formally approved to treat this disorder, but various drugs are available to treat some of the distressing symptoms.

Eating Disorders. Eating disorders involve serious disturbances in eating behavior, such as extreme and unhealthful reduction of food intake or severe overeating, as well as feelings of distress or extreme concern about body shape or weight. The main types of eating disorders are *anorexia nervosa* (the compulsive need to continually lose weight) and *bulimia nervosa* (the compulsion to eat large amounts of food and to take subsequent radical measures to eliminate it). A third type, binge-eating disorder, has been approved as a formal psychiatric diagnosis in the DSM-5.

Eating disorders frequently develop during adolescence or early adulthood, but some reports indicate their onset can occur during childhood or later in adulthood. People who suffer from eating disorders can experience a wide range of physical health complications, including serious heart conditions and kidney failure, which may lead to death. Females are much more likely than males to develop an eating disorder, but males can also have eating disorders. No generally accepted view of the causes of these disorders exists at present, although most experts believe the problem to be a mix of genetic, behavioral, biological, psychological, and social factors. Neuroimaging studies have shown different patterns of brain activity between women with bulimia nervosa and healthy women (NIMH, 2015e). Adolescents displaying the symptoms of these disorders need immediate medical attention because these disorders are life-threatening. Various forms of treatment are available, such as psychotherapy (individual, group, or family), counseling, self-help groups, and medication. Medications do not cure eating disorders, but they may relieve the symptoms of depression and anxiety that are frequently associated with these disorders.

Autism. Autism is a spectrum disorder that usually appears before the child's third birthday. Children with autism have difficulty communicating with others and display inappropriate and repeated behaviors over long periods of time. Autism is discussed in Chapter 9.

CONDUCT DISORDER

Symptoms:

- Shows aggressive behavior that harms or threatens to harm other people or animals
- Damages or destroys property
- Deceitfulness, lying, or stealing
- Truancy or other violation of rules

Impact of Childhood Abuse

Child welfare agencies report over a million instances a year of childhood neglect and abuse. For years, mental health professionals thought that emotional, sexual, and physical mistreatment of children led to psychological problems that could be treated successfully with therapy. Yet, many children and adolescents did not respond to psychotherapy, and researchers wondered if the mistreatment led to more damaging changes in the developing brain. Brain imaging studies and other experiments have confirmed that child abuse can cause permanent damage to the neural structure and function of the brain itself (e.g., Beauchamp et al., 2011; van Rijn & Spevak, 2011). Typically, the brains of adolescents with a history of abuse showed less blood flow to the cerebellum, a smaller corpus callosum, and reduced integration of activity between the left and right hemispheres. Researchers now suspect that the stress associated with childhood abuse triggered hormonal changes that rewired the child's brain to deal with a malevolent world (Coghlan, 2011; Sousa et al., 2011). This may explain why victims of child abuse can become abusers themselves as they age (e.g., Kolla, Gregory, Attard, Blackwood, & Hodgins, 2014).

The consequences of childhood abuse can appear in many ways. Victims may suffer anxiety, depression, suicidal thoughts, or posttraumatic stress. Outwardly, they may display aggression, delinquency, hyperactivity, or impulsivity. During adolescence, they are at high risk for *borderline personality disorder* (BPD). Individuals with this disorder experience episodes of impulsive aggression, self-injury, and drug or alcohol abuse. They may feel unfairly misunderstood or mistreated, bored, empty, and have little idea who they are. Although they may form an immediate attachment and idealize another person, a slight conflict can cause them to switch unexpectedly to the other extreme and angrily accuse the other person of not caring for them at all. Suicide threats and attempts may occur along with anger at perceived abandonment and disappointments. Psychotherapy and medications have shown promise as treatments for this disorder.

The Future of Research in Emotional and Behavioral Disorders

As the number of children and adolescents with emotional and behavioral problems continues to increase, more resources will be devoted to searching

Figure 8.4 These images of representative PET scans show how different areas of the brain are affected after treatment with cognitive-behavioral therapy (top) and the antidepressant drug paroxetine (bottom).

out the underlying genetic and environmental causes of these disorders. Brain imaging studies will give us more information on the neural and chemical mechanisms involved. New knowledge about causes often brings suggestions for new treatments. In the meantime, parents, educators, and clinicians need to work together to improve the identification and education of affected students.

WHAT EDUCATORS NEED TO CONSIDER

Educators should consider three areas for improving the identification and treatment of students with emotional and behavioral disorders. The first area is *developmental psychopathology*, which holds that the course of these disorders is determined by a variety of early genetic, biologic, psychological, environmental, and social factors. Parents and teachers may have noticed these earlier signs but did not necessarily view them as potential problems. Yet, early detection and prevention are more effective than just early identification and early intervention. Primary prevention or classroom-wide interventions in preschool can significantly improve both functional behavior and the symptoms in children at risk and possibly forestall the disorders in youngsters at highest risk (Feil et al., 2014). Training in early detection is essential for all personnel who work with these students.

The second area involves *psychiatric comorbidity*, the recognition that emotional and behavioral disorders may be preceded by other psychiatric problems. For example, children with disruptive disorders often have comorbid depression or anxiety disorders. Treatment for simple disruptive behavioral disorders does not work with children who have mixed disorders. Rather, differential treatment involving much more emphasis on cognitive-behavioral therapy and emotional-regulation approaches will be more effective.

A third area for consideration is *psychopharmacology*. Special education teachers and general educators should be aware of how medication for psychiatric disorders has become an effective intervention, especially when combined with behavioral interventions. Selective serotonin reuptake inhibitors (SSRI), for example, can help up to 70 percent of cases on average. But collaboration among teachers, therapists, prescribing physicians, and families is critical for these medications to work effectively (Iftene, Predescu, Stefan, & David, 2015).

Bullying

Some students with emotional and behavioral disorders can become bullies. Bullying is a repeated pattern of aggressive behavior over time that involves unwanted and undesirable actions. People bully for a variety of reasons. It may be because they have strong needs for power, or find satisfaction in causing injury to others, or are psychologically rewarded for their behavior. Regardless of the reasons, bullying is a serious problem that can take many forms. Bullying can occur through threats of physical harm, verbal insults, social exclusion, derogatory racial and sexual comments, taking or damaging property, or through cyberbullying. Educators and parents should be watchful of students with emotional and behavioral problems for signs of bullying, and such actions should be immediately addressed.

School-Wide Positive Behavioral Interventions and Supports (SWPBIS)

Several formats and approaches have emerged over the years for helping schools deal with students who have emotional and behavioral disorders. One successful approach that has been around for more than a decade is School-Wide Positive Behavioral Interventions and Supports (SWPBIS). Similar in approach to the Response to Intervention model, SWPBIS is a set of interventions routines for establishing a school social culture and individual behavior supports that allow all students to achieve. It uses a multitier approach. The first tier of primary prevention focuses on supporting all students before behavioral problems emerge. It emphasizes teaching school-wide behavioral expectations, rewarding appropriate student behavior, minimizing the natural rewards for inappropriate behavior while establishing the consequences for inappropriate behavior, and collecting data about student behavior to guide school-based decisions (Scott, Anderson, & Alter, 2011).

A second tier includes interventions that are implemented for students who do not respond to the primary prevention procedures. The third tier of support, tertiary prevention, usually involves individualized support based on a behavioral, academic, social, and medical assessment of a student. In a recent study that looked at seven states with a history of implementing SWPBIS, researchers found that, when properly implemented with sufficient state resources, the program was effective in promoting positive student behaviors (Horner et al., 2014). SWPBIS has also been shown to improve behavior and attendance in high schools (Freeman et al., 2015). See the "Resources" section for more information on the SWPBIS approach.

Strategies to Consider

ESTABLISHING A POSITIVE EMOTIONAL CLIMATE IN THE CLASSROOM

All students—especially those with emotional and behavioral disorders—need to be in an emotionally secure setting before they can be expected to give attention to curriculum. The classroom climate is set by the teachers, and the school climate is set by the administration. Teachers and administrators need to recognize that many more students than ever come to school wanting to get at least some of their emotional needs met. Working together, faculty and staff should take *purposeful* steps to ensure that a positive emotional climate be established and maintained in the school and in all classrooms. Some ways to set a positive emotional climate are as follows:

- **Use humor, but not sarcasm.** Humor is a very effective device for getting attention and for establishing a warm climate. Laughter is common to us all, and it helps diverse people bond and feel good about being with each other. Sarcasm, on the other hand, is destructive. It hurts, no matter how familiar a teacher is with students. Occasionally, a teacher has said, "Oh, the student knows I was only kidding." In fact, we don't know that, and we need to wonder whether the student's sly grin means the brain is laughing or plotting revenge. Besides, there is so much good humor available that there is no need for sarcasm.

- **Insist on respect among students.** Not only is it important for teachers to respect students, and vice versa, but teachers must also ensure that students show respect for each other. This includes

    o listening to each other's class contributions (as opposed to just waiting for their turn to speak),
    o respecting different and opposing opinions,
    o acknowledging other students' comments,
    o complimenting and helping each other when appropriate,
    o asking others for their opinions, and
    o refraining from sarcasm.

- **Have just a few rules that all teachers enforce.** Students with emotional problems are very likely to get upset when they believe that they are not being treated fairly. Studies on school discipline show that schools with few discipline problems tend to be those with just a few rules (five to seven) that all teachers enforce uniformly. Keep in mind that secondary students usually see six to eight teachers during the school day. Perhaps one teacher allows gum chewing, but it drives the next period's teacher to distraction. An absent-minded, gum-chewing student going from the first to the second teacher's class may be headed for trouble.

- **Get training in how to handle emotional situations.** Most secondary teachers were not trained to deal with the emotional scenarios that appear in today's classrooms, mainly because emotional needs of adolescents are expected to be addressed in the family. But the reality is that more students are turning to the school setting for emotional fulfillment, and teachers must be trained to cope effectively with this situation.

- **Look for opportunities to teach students how to handle their emotions.** With training, teachers can use classroom and school opportunities to teach students how to handle their emotions. Look for ways to help them delay gratification, control impulses, express their feelings, and conduct themselves in their in-school relationships.

- **Use genuine praise.** Students with emotional problems often have low self-esteem. Genuinely praising their productive efforts can go a long way in helping them improve their self-image. Use "you" statements rather than "I" statements. For example, "You should be proud of the work you accomplished" is more effective for building a student's self-esteem than "I am pleased with what you accomplished."

- **Reduce test anxiety.** Test anxiety affects many students, but it can be potentially serious when it leads to high stress in students who already have emotional and behavioral difficulties. Find ways to reduce test anxiety. Cognitive-behavioral treatments to reduce test anxiety have proven effective in several studies. With these treatments, students were less anxious about the tests and felt more confident about their academic work.

Strategies to Consider

INTERVENTIONS FOR STUDENTS WITH BEHAVIORAL PROBLEMS

Research on programs designed to help students with behavioral problems covers a wide variety of students, situations, and settings. As a result, there is a broad range of possible approaches that teachers and schools can take to make a difference in students' behavior. Here are some suggestions:

- **Identifying the cause of the misbehavior.** Problem behavior is obvious, but the reasons for it might not be. Schools need to investigate *why* the student is exhibiting undesirable behavior. As more is known about the cause, appropriate interventions can be identified and implemented.
- **Selecting classroom management and teaching strategies.** Blaming, punishing, and threatening students work only in the short term. Effective teachers rely instead on proactive strategies, such as reinforcing social behavior and teaching social problem solving. For difficult students, they use point or token systems, time-out, contingent reinforcement (reinforcement that is contingent on the display of acceptable behavior), and response cost (students lose points or tokens for unacceptable behavior) strategies.
- **Adapting curriculum and instruction.** Disruptive behavior is sometimes the result of inappropriate curriculum and ineffective teaching. When investigating the cause of student misbehavior, check whether curricular and instruction modifications have been made to accommodate these students. Are there visual aids to support lesson content? Are classes small enough so that there is sufficient teacher-student interaction?
- **Addressing social skills.** Students with behavioral problems often lack the social skills needed to maintain successful relationships with their peers and teachers. As a result, they experience teacher rejection, school failure, and social rejection. When teachers help students build social competence, they increase the likelihood that these students will succeed in school. Kathleen Lane and her

colleagues suggest a six-step research-based method for designing, implementing, and evaluating a social skills intervention for elementary students (Lane, Menzies, Barton-Arwood, Doukas, & Munton, 2005). Schools using this approach have noticed fewer disruptive behaviors in the classroom, increased time on academic tasks, and improved social interactions on the playground. Here is a summary of the method.

- *Step 1. Identify students for participation.* Use observations, behavioral instruments (e.g., Systematic Screening for Behavior Disorders), and rating scales (e.g., Student Risk Screening Scale) to select students who can best benefit from the interventions. These instruments have been particularly effective at the high school level (Kalberg, Lane, Driscoll, & Wehby, 2011).
- *Step 2. Identify specific skill deficits and design the intervention program.* Use the data gathered from the first step to identify the skill strengths, skill deficits, performance deficits, and interfering problem behaviors for each student. Develop the social skills lessons, which will be presented as 30- to 60-minute sessions, two days a week, to groups of three to five students.
- *Step 3. Organize intervention groups.* Place students into intervention groups based on skill deficits, demographics (age or gender), or randomly (for larger groups).
- *Step 4. Prepare intervention leaders.* Initial and ongoing training of intervention leaders ensures that the intervention is implemented as intended and that best practices in social skills instruction are being followed.
- *Step 5. Implement the intervention.* Each lesson uses effective instructional strategies in a role-play format that contains five stages: tell, show, do, follow through and practice, and generalization. Use behavior checklists to monitor the extent to which the intervention plan is implemented as originally designed. Select rules for how the group functions so as to prevent problem behaviors from interfering with instruction.
- *Step 6. Monitor student progress.* Use teacher ratings, self-reporting, and direct observations to monitor and assess student progress.

- **Teaching social problem solving.** Effective programs for preventing discipline problems include the direct teaching of social problem solving. Although the interventions vary, they usually teach thinking skills that students can use to avoid and resolve interpersonal conflicts, resist peer pressure, and cope with their emotions and stress. The most effective programs also include a broad range of social competency skills taught over a long period of time.
- **Adopting schoolwide and districtwide programs.** School and district policies should make clear that appropriate behavior is a precondition to learning. Rules of behavior should be clear and communicated to staff, parents, and students. It is important that they be consistently enforced so students perceive the system as fair. The staff should also be trained to teach alternatives to vandalism and disruptive behavior.

- **Getting parental involvement.** Effective programs to control behavior almost always have a parental component. Parental management training and family therapy are two promising approaches for controlling student behavior. Parental management training teaches techniques such as strategic use of time-out, rewards, praise, and contingency contracting. Parents have ongoing opportunities to discuss, practice, and review these techniques. Family therapy is designed to empower parents with the skills and resources to solve their own family problems. Although parental management training and family therapy are very effective approaches, less intensive parental training should suffice for most children and adolescents (Durand, Hieneman, Clarke, Wang, & Rinaldi, 2013).

- **Using auditory processing strategies.** Researchers have noted that students with behavior problems and low achievement in literacy may have *auditory processing* problems. Auditory processing is the ability to hold, sequence, and process accurately what is heard. Kathy Rowe and her colleagues in Australia have found that training teachers in strategies that support auditory processing resulted in a significant improvement in student attentiveness, behavior, and literacy (Rosen, Cohen, & Vanniasegaram, 2010; Rowe, Pollard, & Rowe, 2005). The training focused on five strategies:

  - Attracting the child's attention
  - Speaking slowly, using short sentences, eye contact, and visual cues
  - Pausing between sentences and repeating when necessary
  - Using visual cues, such as blank looks, and repeating instructions as needed
  - Creating hearing, listening, and compliance routines for students

Strategies to Consider

REDUCING THE RISK OF ANTISOCIAL BEHAVIOR

Behavior is the result of the interaction of environmental influences and genetic predispositions. Schools can do nothing to alter the genetic coding. But recent research seems to indicate that genes affecting personality traits are either activated or repressed by the individual's environment. Consequently, if schools undertake comprehensive efforts to provide supportive structures and reduce risk factors, then fewer children may fall victim to emotional and behavioral problems that can seriously interfere with their schooling and life. These efforts that will encourage prevention of problem behaviors fall into the broad areas of school organization and effectiveness, student achievement and early intervention, parent and community involvement, and professional development for staff (LDA, 2006).

School Organization and Effectiveness	The school should • Have high expectations for learning and behavior for all students and help all children achieve them • Clearly communicate expectations for learning and behavior to all students • Include staff, students, parents, and community members in the decision-making process • Promote student engagement and attachment • Have a consistent system of reinforcement and recognition to shape student behavior • Provide alternatives to suspension and expulsion • Conduct risk assessment as part of safe schools improvement plans
Student Achievement and Early Intervention	The school should • Intervene early to identify and assist students who fail to meet expectations for learning and behavior • Evaluate students' social, emotional, and adaptive functions, as well as cognitive function • Include special education students in general education classrooms • Not disproportionately discipline students with disabilities
Parent and Community Involvement	The school should • Work with parents and community groups to educate and care for children • Involve parents and community groups in developing the safe schools improvement plan • Provide information to parents about how to help their children learn and behave appropriately in school • Collaborate with other agencies to meet family and community needs
Professional Development for Staff	The school should • Train teachers to use a variety of instructional and classroom management strategies to prevent academic failure and problem behavior for all students • Encourage preservice programs in teacher-training institutions to provide this training • Encourage state departments of education to include this training in their inservice programs

9

Autism Spectrum Disorder

It is never too late to expand the mind of a person on the autism spectrum.

—Temple Grandin, Autism Rights Activist

Since the publication of the second edition of this book in 2007, the number of children in the United States diagnosed with an autism spectrum disorder (ASD) has risen from 1 in 166 to 1 in 68, according to the Centers for Disease Control and Prevention. Four out of five of those affected are males. Researchers and clinicians still debate whether the rapid rise in the number of diagnosed cases is due to an actual increase in the incidence of ASD or to the broadened standards that physicians use to make a diagnosis. Are more children developing ASD, or are we just getting better at finding those who already have it? Many experts say it is both.

This rapid increase in the number of cases of ASDs in recent years has prompted more research into their causes and into the effectiveness of past and newer treatments. It is not possible in this one chapter to explore in detail all the research pathways currently being pursued or to assess the efficacy of the many forms of treatment. Rather, my purpose here is to describe the conditions included in ASD, their diagnoses, possible causes, and considerations that educators should keep in mind when dealing with students who have ASD. Those who want to pursue this topic in greater depth will find support organizations and additional references listed in the "Resources" section at the end of this book.

> Autism spectrum disorder affects as many as one in 68 people, and four out of five of those affected are males.

MULTIPLE CONDITIONS ON ONE SPECTRUM

In previous chapters we discovered how the brain acquires language, learns to read and write, calculates, and generates the emotions to interact and communicate with other human beings. Different neural networks must work in harmony to carry out these activities successfully. When several networks malfunction early in a child's life, developmental disorders appear. In the DSM-5, four previously separate developmental disorders are classified as a single condition called *autism spectrum disorder.* This classification now includes *autistic disorder* **(classic autism)**, **Asperger syndrome**, *pervasive developmental disorder—not otherwise specified (PDD-NOS)*, and *childhood disintegrative disorder.* The DSM-5 change reflects a consensus among researchers and practitioners that the four previously separate disorders are actually a single condition with varying levels of severity in two basic areas. ASD is now characterized by (1) deficits in social communication and social interaction and (2) restrictive repetitive behaviors, interests, and activities. Both components are required for an ASD diagnosis. If the restrictive repetitive behaviors are not present, the diagnosis becomes social communication disorder (DSM-5, 2013). ASD is a lifelong condition and can run the gamut from mild to severe.

What Is Autism Spectrum Disorder?

Autism spectrum disorder is more common in the child population than some better-known disorders, such as diabetes, spina bifida, or Down syndrome. This prevalence demonstrates the importance of early and more accurate screening for the symptoms of ASD. The earlier the disorder is diagnosed, the sooner the child can be helped through treatment interventions. Early intervention has a dramatic impact on reducing symptoms and increasing a child's ability to grow and learn new skills.

Symptoms of Autism Spectrum Disorder

All children with ASD demonstrate deficits in (1) social interaction, (2) verbal and nonverbal communication, and (3) repetitive behaviors or interests. In addition, they will often have unusual responses to sensory experiences, such as certain sounds or the way objects look. Each of these symptoms will appear in individual children differently. For instance, a child may have little trouble learning to read but exhibit extremely poor social interaction. Each child will display communication, social, and behavioral patterns that are individual but fit into the overall diagnosis of ASD.

The symptoms usually appear before three years of age. In some children, parents may notice the hints of future problems from birth. Problems in communication and social skills become more noticeable as the child lags further behind other children the same age. Usually between 12 and 36 months old, the differences in the way they react to people and other unusual behaviors become apparent. Some parents report the change as being sudden, and that their children start to reject people, act strangely, and lose language and social skills they had previously acquired. In other cases, there is a leveling off of progress so that the difference between the child with ASD and other children the same age becomes more noticeable.

Other indicators of ASD. The following are possible indicators of ASD (NIMH, 2015f):

- Does not babble, point, or make meaningful gestures by 1 year of age
- Does not speak one word by 16 months
- Does not respond to name or other verbal attempts to get attention
- Does not combine two words by 2 years
- Does not seem to know how to play with toys
- Excessively lines up toys or other objects
- Is attached to one particular toy or object
- Avoids eye contact
- Has poor language or social skills
- Rarely smiles
- Seems to be hearing impaired at times

Social symptoms. Typically developing infants are social beings. Early in life, they gaze at people, turn toward voices, grasp a finger, and even smile. In contrast, most children with ASD seem to have tremendous difficulty learning to engage in the give-and-take of everyday human interaction. Even in the first few months of life, many do not interact and they avoid eye contact. They seem indifferent to other people and often seem to prefer being alone. They may resist attention or passively accept hugs and cuddling. Later, they seldom seek comfort or respond to parents' displays of anger or affection in a typical way. Research has suggested that although children with ASD are attached to their parents, their expression of this attachment is unusual and difficult to interpret. To parents, it may seem as if their child is not attached at all. Some children with ASD also tend to be physically aggressive at times, particularly when they are in a strange or overwhelming environment. Occasionally, they will break things, attack others, or harm themselves.

Communication difficulties. Some children with ASD remain mute throughout their lives. Others will only parrot what they hear (a condition known as *echolalia*). Those who do speak tend to confuse pronouns such as "I," "my," and "you," and may use the same phrase, such as "milk and cookies," in many different situations. Some children only mildly affected may exhibit slight delays in language, or even seem to have precocious language and unusually large vocabularies, but have great difficulty in sustaining a conversation. The give and take of normal conversation is hard for them, although they often carry on a monologue on a favorite subject, giving no one else an opportunity to comment.

It is very difficult to understand the body language of people with ASD. Most of us smile when we talk or shrug our shoulders when we cannot answer a question. But the facial expressions and movements of children with ASD rarely match what they are saying. In addition, their tone of voice does not usually reflect their feelings. Without meaningful gestures or the language to ask for things, these children are at a loss to communicate their needs. Consequently, they may simply scream or grab what they want.

Repetitive and unusual behaviors. Most children with ASD appear physically normal and have good muscle control. But they can also exhibit repetitive actions, such as flicking their fingers, rocking back and forth, or running from room to room turning lights on and off. Others demand consistency in their environment and develop fixations with certain objects, such as eating the same foods at the same time and sitting in the same place every day. Repetitive behavior sometimes takes the form of a persistent, intense preoccupation. For example, the child might be obsessed with learning all about refrigerators, train schedules, or lighthouses. Often there is great interest in numbers, symbols, or science topics.

Does this repetitive-obsessive behavior have the same underlying neurological cause as obsessive-compulsive disorder (OCD)? Several studies have found that about 17 percent of individuals with ASD who have high rates of repetitive behaviors also meet the criteria for OCD (van Steensel, Bögels, & Perrin, 2011). Moreover, children with ASD are significantly more likely to have one or both parents with latent obsessive-compulsive traits, suggesting a strong genetic link for this behavior (Delorme et al., 2007).

Sensory symptoms. When children's perceptions are accurate, they can learn from what they see, feel, or hear. On the other hand, if sensory information is faulty, the child's experiences of the world can be confusing. In ASD, the brain seems unable to balance the senses appropriately. Many children with ASD are highly attuned or even painfully sensitive to certain sounds, textures, tastes, and smells. For some children, even the feel of clothes touching their skin is almost unbearable. Loud and intrusive sounds, such as from a vacuum cleaner, a ringing telephone, or a sudden storm, will cause these children to cover their ears and scream. They may have no reaction to intense cold or pain.

Intellectual disability. Many children with ASD have some degree of intellectual impairment. When tested, some areas of ability may be normal, while others, such as language and cognitive abilities, may be especially weak. For example, a child with ASD may do well on the parts of the test that measure visual skills but earn low scores on the language subtests. However, some individuals with ASD (such as those previously diagnosed with Asperger syndrome) have average to above average language skills and show no delays in cognitive abilities.

Fragile X syndrome. This disorder is the most common inherited form of inherited intellectual ability. It was so named because one part of the X chromosome has a defective piece that appears pinched and fragile when viewed under a microscope. It results from a mutation in a single gene that turns the gene off. Fragile X syndrome affects about two to five percent of people with ASD. It is important to have a child with ASD checked for Fragile X, especially if the parents are considering having another child. If a child with ASD also has Fragile X, there is a one in two chance that boys born to the same parents will have the syndrome. Other members of the family who may be contemplating having a child may also wish to be checked for the syndrome (NIMH, 2015f).

Memory and recall. A few studies have looked at long-term memory and how well children with ASD learn information, encode it accurately, and retrieve it correctly. The results showed that most children with ASD had greater difficulty recalling verbal information compared to typically developing children. However, in studies involving working memory, individuals with high-functioning ASD solved problems involving spatial working memory at least as well as, or better than, the control group. These findings suggest that working memory deficits in ASD appear to affect verbal memory systems more than visual-spatial memory (Kercood, Grskovic, Banda, & Begeske, 2014).

AUTISM SPECTRUM DISORDER

Major Symptoms:

- Social interaction impairments characterized by nonverbal behaviors, inappropriate peer relationships, failure to interact with others, and poor social or emotional reciprocity
- Communication impairments characterized by a delay in, or lack of, spoken language development, stereotyped or repetitive language use or idiosyncratic language, and lack of developmentally appropriate spontaneous or social imitative play
- Repetitive and restricted stereotyped patterns of behavior characterized by abnormally intense preoccupation with one or more restricted patterns, inflexible adherence to nonfunctional routines, repetitive motor movements, and persistent preoccupation with objects

---

Diagnosis of Autism Spectrum Disorder

No two children display ASD in exactly the same way. Further, some children can exhibit symptoms that look like ASD but may indicate other disorders and not ASD. These possibilities also need to be investigated. Children with ASD can generally be reliably diagnosed by age 2, although some screening tests have been shown to be helpful at 18 months of age. The diagnosis requires a two-stage process. The first stage involves a screening process using parental questionnaires and clinical observations. Several screening instruments have been developed to quickly gather information about a child's social and communicative development within medical settings. If the screening process shows possible indicators of ASD, further evaluation is needed.

The second stage entails a comprehensive evaluation by a multidisciplinary team that includes a psychologist, a neurologist, a psychiatrist, a speech therapist, or other professionals who diagnose children with ASD. Specialists evaluate language and social behavior, talk with parents about the child's developmental milestones, and test for certain genetic and neurological problems. A hearing test should also be performed. Although hearing loss can occur with ASD, some children with ASD may be incorrectly thought to have such a loss.

Causes of Autism Spectrum Disorder

The exact causes of ASD remain unknown. But researchers in the past 20 years have made impressive gains in understanding the impaired abilities of people with ASD

Memory deficits in autism spectrum disorder affect verbal memory systems more than visual-spatial memory.

and in using this understanding to develop theories about its causes. Most experts now agree that ASD is associated with abnormal brain developments that occur in part as a result of both genetic and environmental factors. Here are some of the major areas of research looking into the causes of this complex set of disorders.

Brain structure studies. Brain imaging tools compare the structure and functioning of typical brains to those with ASD. Postmortem and MRI studies have shown that major brain structures seem to be implicated in ASD. This includes the cerebellum, cerebral cortex, limbic area, corpus callosum, basal ganglia, and brainstem (e.g., Barbeau et al., 2015; Itahashi et al., 2015; Richter et al., 2015; Xiang et al., 2016).

Abnormal brain growth. Recent neuroimaging studies have shown that a contributing cause for ASD may be abnormal brain development beginning in the infant's first months. This is called the "brain growth dysregulation hypothesis" and it suggests that the anatomical abnormalities seen in ASD are caused by genetic defects controlling brain growth. Researchers found that the head measurements of children with ASD were smaller at birth than the national norms. However, their heads grew dramatically during the first two months of infancy and between 6 and 14 months. Faster growth predicted greater impairment (e.g., McKeague et al., 2015).

The MRI scans of the children with ASD showed more brain tissue in both the cerebrum and cerebellum. By contrast, body weight and length developed normally in the children with ASD. The researchers also found that around the age of 5 years, the head size of a child with ASD was about the same as a typical teenage brain. However, by adulthood, the brain size was no different in those with or without ASD (Chaste et al., 2013). The unusually rapid increase in brain growth during infancy is particularly perplexing given the behavioral abnormalities that define ASD. One would assume that more brain tissue would lead eventually to advantages rather than deficits. But white matter contributes disproportionately to this brain volume increase and in a nonuniform pattern. At some point it becomes impossible to interconnect so many extra brain cells, resulting in functional abnormalities (Green, Dissanayake, & Loesch, 2015). This condition seems to be more prevalent in infant males than in infant females (Fukumoto et al., 2011).

It is possible that sudden, rapid head growth in an infant may be an early warning signal that someday will lead to early diagnosis and effective biological intervention or possible prevention of ASD. But some scientists caution that rapid head growth could also indicate tumors, hydrocephalus, or nothing at all.

Parental similarities. MRIs of parents of children with ASD showed brain regions in the parent group that were either larger or smaller than in adults with no family history of ASD. For example, in the frontal lobes, the researchers found more gray matter but significantly less white matter. This is an executive-control area that plays a major role in understanding other people's mental states and acting accordingly. These findings offer hints at which brain abnormalities might be inherited with ASD (Parr, Gray, Wigham, McConachie, & Le Couteur, 2015).

Genetic studies. Studies of twins and families suggest that genetic factors play a dominant role in the causes of ASD. Scientists are now hunting for the genes involved, but it is a difficult process. Unlike Down syndrome or Huntington's disease, in which a single gene or an entire chromosome is inherited, many gene mutations are involved in ASD (e.g., El-Fishawy & State, 2010; Krumm, O'Roak, Shendure, & Eichler, 2014). Researchers suspect that mutations in these genes may affect the activity of certain neurotransmitters as well as the brain's plasticity during development, thereby altering neural connections as a result of specific experiences. In an effort to explain the rapid rise in the number of children diagnosed with ASD, researchers are exploring whether various combinations of genetic mutations could be interacting with unknown environmental factors, resulting in the wide variety of symptoms that appear in children affected with ASD (Dickerson et al., 2015). Such environmental factors could be affecting the way genes are expressed while not affecting the gene sequence itself, an interaction called *epigenetics* (Hall & Kelley, 2014). Further research is needed in this area.

Gaze avoidance. One strategy for tracking down specific genes is to compare children with ASD to their unaffected family members and look for any overlap in behavior or brain function. Of particular interest to researchers was whether the siblings of children with ASD exhibited signs of *gaze avoidance.* This tendency to avoid eye contact is a key feature of ASD and often one of the earliest indications that a child may have the disorder (Akechi et al., 2010). A few years ago, researchers thought that gaze avoidance resulted from deficits in the part of the brain associated with face perception, called the *fusiform gyrus.* These deficits, it was thought, led to less responsiveness to faces, a central cause of the social impairment observed in ASD. But subsequent studies indicate that this structure is normal in most individuals with ASD (e.g., Nomi & Uddin, 2015).

In a study using new technology that tracks a person's eyes when gazing at a photograph, researchers found that the unaffected siblings showed the same pattern of gaze avoidance for eyes as did the youths with ASD (Figure 9.1). The low eye contact occurred even when they looked at pictures of family and friends, so the behavior did not reflect inherited shyness.

While the youths were looking at the photographs, MRI machines scanned the amygdala, because this brain structure is associated with emotions and the interpretation of facial expressions. The amygdala was smaller in both groups. Yet the smaller amygdala did not result in ASD symptoms. Apparently, other brain systems must compensate for this abnormality in the non-ASD siblings. Whenever the youths with ASD did gaze at the eyes in the picture, higher activity was detected in the amygdala, indicating the presence of negative feelings. When the individuals with ASD looked away from the image's eyes, they showed reduced activity in the amygdala. Gaze avoidance, then, may be serving the functional purpose of lowering the anxiety levels created by the stimulated amygdala (Tottenham et al., 2014).

Neurotransmitter studies. Numerous studies have looked at a wide array of neurotransmitters to determine how they may affect ASD. These studies are complicated by the fact that ASD varies over a broad spectrum and is often present with other behavioral problems. Of all the neurotransmitters studied, serotonin has the most empirical evidence for a role in ASD (e.g., Kolevzon et al., 2014; Yang et al., 2015). Genetic studies of families with ASD reveal that they often have mutations within a specific gene that regulates serotonin levels in the brain. About 25 percent of people with ASD have elevated serotonin levels. Some researchers suggest that elevated serotonin levels could be used as a biomarker to help diagnose children who display behaviors associated with ASD (e.g., Gabriele, Sacco, & Persico, 2014; Hammock et al., 2012). Drugs that are selective serotonin reuptake inhibitors (SSRIs) have eased the symptoms of ASD in some people.

The "Theory of Mind" hypothesis and mirror neurons. One of the neurological signs of people with ASD is their failure to construe the mental states of others—a deficit in what has been called the "theory of mind." This theory refers to the everyday ability to infer what others are thinking or believing in order to explain and predict their behavior. Researchers are investigating how theory of mind develops in the brain, but they suspect it is independent of other skills. Individuals with ASD have difficulty viewing situations from another person's perspective and predicting other people's emotions and motives. This may explain why they have such difficulty with simple behaviors such as attending to a situation and playing games with others (Pelligra, Isoni, Fadda, & Doneddu, 2015).

> Individuals with ASD have difficulty viewing situations from another person's perspective and predicting other people's emotions and motives.

Some researchers are attempting to identify the brain structures associated with theory of mind, where fast intuitions are combined with slower, deliberate judgments. One idea centers around a type of neuron found in the cortex of the frontal and temporal lobes. Known as Von Economo neurons (named after their discoverer), these cells are distinguished by having larger and fewer dendrites extending from the cell body than typical neurons in the cortex. They develop after birth and are particularly vulnerable to dysfunction. Because these neurons have many receptors for dopamine and serotonin, they are believed to be strongly linked to the formation of social bonds, rewards and punishments, and intuitive responses to complex situations. Imaging studies of individuals with ASD found that they contained either a significantly higher or a significantly lower number of Von Economo neurons than non-ASD controls. Furthermore, the areas in the white matter that carry these neurons' axons were in disarray. The failure of these neurons to develop normally may be partially responsible for the social impairments and faulty intuition typical of individuals with ASD (Allman et al., 2011).

In Chapter 1 we discussed mirror neurons, which allow us to re-create the experience of others within ourselves and to understand others' emotions and empathize. Researchers suspect that the inability of individuals with ASD to empathize may be due to deficits in mirror neuron systems. However, the results of studies on mirror neurons and ASD using fMRI and EEG are mixed and inconclusive (Hamilton, 2013). Mirror neurons are not located in the same brain areas as Von Economo neurons, and they are structurally different.

The extreme male brain theory of ASD. The observation that four out of five people with ASD are males has led some researchers to try to explain the reasons for this gender discrepancy. One possible explanation is that some of the genetic mutations associated with ASD may be located on the X chromosome. Because males inherit only one copy of this chromosome, they are more susceptible to the consequences of its defects.

Another explanation comes from Simon Baron-Cohen, director of the Autism Research Center in Cambridge, England, who studies the differences between male and female brains. Baron-Cohen says males have a greater tendency than females to analyze, construct, control, and predict the behavior of systems—a mental domain he calls "systemizing." Boys are more interested than girls in toy cars, building blocks, and mechanical toys. They are better at reading maps, paying attention to relevant detail, judging the behavior of moving objects, constructing with building blocks, and converting 2-D diagrams into 3-D models. Females, on the other hand, have a greater tendency to identify other people's emotions and respond accordingly—a mental domain that Baron-Cohen calls "empathizing." He believes that genetics and culture drive systemizing and empathizing and that most people have components of both domains.

> Could Individuals with ASD merely be displaying the extremes of normal male traits?

According to Baron-Cohen, people with ASD display the extremes of normal male systemizing traits. They are very poor at empathizing yet can show special abilities in mathematical calculations, music, chess, mechanical knowledge, and other areas involving systemizing. Not much is known about the neural circuits associated with systemizing, but research in this area may lead to greater understanding of ASD and treatment (Baron-Cohen, 2003; Baron-Cohen et al., 2014). This theory has its share of critics.

Mercury toxicity. In 1998, a British physician reported that his study of 42 children with ASD revealed that they all had intestinal problems and autistic-like symptoms after receiving the measles, mumps, and rubella (MMR) vaccine. Subsequent articles compared these autistic-like symptoms to those of mercury poisoning and suggested that they were caused by thimerosal, a mercury-based preservative contained in the vaccines (Bernard, Enayati, Redwood, Roger, & Binstock, 2001; Rimland, 2000). As a precaution, thimerosal-containing vaccines for children were phased out in the United States starting in 1999.

Several large studies, including hundreds of thousands of children, have shown the rate of ASD to be about the same for *both* vaccinated (including children who received vaccine containing thimerosal) and unvaccinated children (e.g., Taylor, Swerdfeger, & Eslick, 2014; Uno, Uchiyama, Kurosawa, Aleksic, & Ozaki, 2015). Medical researchers believe that the emergence of ASD symptoms after a MMR vaccination is most likely coincidental because ASD symptoms usually appear between 18 and 24 months, which is shortly after the age when the MMR vaccination is typically administered at 12 to 15 months. Meanwhile, public health officials fear that parents worried over the potential link might be reluctant to get their children vaccinated against these potentially fatal diseases (Centers for Disease Control and Prevention, 2015). Some scientists suggest that children with ASD may also inherit a genetic fault that makes them far more susceptible to mercury poisoning. Mothers could pass mercury to the fetus during pregnancy from the heavy consumption of fish.

Figure 9.1 Children without ASD tend to look at another person's eyes and keep their gaze there, as seen by the representations of eye movements and fixations on the left. But children with ASD avoid looking into another person's eyes, as indicated on the right. The lines show the eye movements. Where the eyes stop is indicated by the circles, which grow larger the longer the eye gazes at a certain spot (adapted from Tottenham et al., 2014).

Unusual Abilities

About 10 percent of people with ASD display remarkable abilities and skills. This percentage includes those with high-functioning ASD, formerly called Asperger's Syndrome. At a time when other children are drawing lines or scribbling, some children with ASD can draw detailed, realistic pictures with proper dimensional perspective. Some begin to read before they speak or play musical instruments without being taught. Others can make mathematical calculations incredibly rapidly, or memorize enormous amounts of information, such as pages from a phone book, many years of sport scores, and entire television shows. Such abilities are known as *savant skills,* and the extreme forms are rare. Not all people with savant skills have ASD. Six savant skills typically occur in ASD (Waterhouse, 2013):

- rapid mental mathematical calculations
- drawing a scene or image with detail accuracy after viewing it only once
- mental calendar calculations
- accurately playing a musical piece after hearing it just once
- extraordinary memory for numbers and facts
- extraordinary autobiographical memory

Researchers have been trying to explain why certain people with ASD possess savant skills. Several studies have explored the executive functions in savants with ASD. Their findings are encouraging, but not conclusive, because there are numerous possible explanations for the savant skills. One notion is that those brain areas that are not affected by the general cognitive deficits of ASD are able to enhance their abilities (Crane, Pring, Ryder, & Hermelin, 2011).

About 10 percent of people with ASD display remarkable abilities known as savant skills.

Another possibility is that individuals with ASD free up both time and mental resources that non-ASD people typically use for social interactions and devote these resources to developing a talent. Moreover, individuals with ASD often display exceptional creativity. This may be the result of not being susceptible to the social pressures that typically developing children experience in middle school as they attempt to conform to their peer group's expectations, often resulting in a stifling of their originality (Happé & Vital, 2009).

One intriguing description of savant skills attempts to explain how some savants clearly know things they never learned, such as calendar calculating, a talent that seems to be universally present in savants. Researcher Darold Treffert suggests that savants may inherit knowledge through "genetic memory," the transfer of knowledge and skills through genes (Treffert, 2010). He maintains that brain regions damaged by the effects of ASD provoke the recruitment of still intact tissue in another area of the brain. That new area is then rewired to allow the release of the dormant knowledge and skill capacity stored in the individual's genetic memory.

Treatment for Autism Spectrum Disorder

At present, there is no cure for ASD nor do children outgrow it. Nonetheless, more than ever before, people with ASD can be helped. A combination of early intervention, special education support, and medication is helping children and adolescents with ASD lead more normal lives. Medications can alleviate some of the symptoms and therapy can help a child learn, communicate, and interact with others in productive ways.

An effective treatment program builds on the child's interests, offers a predictable schedule, teaches tasks as a series of simple steps, actively engages the child's attention in highly structured activities, and provides regular reinforcement of desirable behavior. Parental involvement has emerged as a major factor in treatment success. Parents work with teachers and therapists to identify the behaviors to be changed and the skills to be taught. Recognizing that parents are the child's earliest teachers, more programs are beginning to train parents to continue the therapy at home.

One of the effective methods available for treatment of people with ASD is applied behavior analysis (ABA). Nearly 40 years of research have demonstrated the efficacy of applied behavioral methods in reducing inappropriate behavior and in increasing communication, learning, and appropriate social behavior in individuals with ASD. The goal of behavioral management is to reinforce desirable behaviors and reduce undesirable ones. This technique is tedious and time-consuming, calling for hours of daily instruction (up to 40 hours per week) to break learning into very basic components and reward students for each positive step. If started at an early age, some experts believe, the process could actually help rewire the young brain. Numerous studies attest to ABA's effectiveness when appropriately implemented by properly trained educators or parents (e.g., Heitzman-Powell, Buzhardt, Rusinko, & Miller, 2014; Solis, El Zein, Vaughn, McCulley, & Falcomata, 2015).

Elementary school. In elementary school, the child should receive help in any skill area that is delayed while being encouraged to grow in areas of strength. Where possible, the curriculum should be adapted to the individual child's needs. Many schools today have an inclusion program in which the child is in a general education classroom for most of the day, with special instruction for a part of the day. This instruction should include such skills as learning how to act in social situations and in making friends. Although higher functioning children may be able to handle academic work, they too need help to organize tasks and avoid distractions.

The adolescent years. During middle and high school years, instruction should address such practical matters as work, community living, and recreational activities. This should include work experience, using public transportation, and learning skills that will be important in community living. Adolescence is a time of stress and confusion, and it is no less so for teenagers with ASD. The teenage years are also a time when children become more socially sensitive. At the age that most teenagers are concerned with acne, popularity, grades, and dates, teens with ASD may become painfully aware that they are different from their peers. They may notice that they lack friends, and unlike their schoolmates, they aren't dating or planning for a career. For some, the sadness that comes with such realization actually motivates them to learn new behaviors and acquire better social skills.

Medications used in treatment. Medications are often used to treat behavioral problems, such as aggression, self-injurious behavior, and severe tantrums that keep the person with ASD from functioning more effectively at home or school. The medications used are those that have been developed to treat similar symptoms in other disorders. For example, selective serotonin reuptake inhibitors are the medications most often prescribed for symptoms of anxiety, depression, and/or obsessive-compulsive disorder. Antipsychotic medications have been used to treat severe behavioral problems. These medications work by reducing the activity in the brain of the neurotransmitter dopamine.

Seizures are found in one in four persons with ASD, most often in those who have low IQ or are mute. They are treated with one or more of the anticonvulsant medications, which usually reduce the number of seizures but cannot always eliminate them. Stimulant medications used in persons with attention-deficit hyperactivity disorder have also been prescribed for children with ASD. These medications may decrease impulsivity and hyperactivity, especially in higher functioning children.

Sleep Problems

Regardless of age, individuals with ASD often have problems falling asleep or staying asleep. Consistent loss of sleep can lead to difficulties in paying attention, in physically and cognitively functioning, and in maintaining acceptable behavior. This may be one of the less difficult problems to solve by establishing a sleep schedule and establishing a bedtime routine that is free of distractions, such as digital devices. Medication can also help. One possibility is melatonin, available without a prescription. This hormone is responsible for regulating the body's sleep-wake cycle and may help the individual with ASD get into a regular sleep pattern. Be sure to check this out first with a physician, because melatonin does have some side effects.

The Future of Research on Autism Spectrum Disorders

Researchers and clinicians have launched an all-out effort to track down the causes and triggers for ASD. Medical researchers and physicians from leading medical centers in the United States have formed the Autism Treatment Network, a cooperative effort to develop reliable criteria for diagnosing ASD, to test medical treatments, and to prepare scientists and physicians for careers in ASD study and treatment. Meanwhile, the U. S. Centers for Disease Control and Prevention are supporting efforts to diagnose children with ASD earlier, by 18 months of age instead of age 3, hoping that earlier diagnosis and intervention will alter the disorder's course. Currently, children with ASD may be labeled high functioning or low functioning, but little is known about what causes these functional variations. Discovering physiological differences could help physicians diagnose different subgroups of ASD and develop more effective and personalized forms of treatment for each child with ASD.

ASD has long been defined by its behavioral symptoms, but researchers are now focusing on what goes wrong in the brain to cause those behaviors. Research continues to identify genetic variants associated with ASD in the hope that this may provide a more accurate diagnostic tool for the future, at least in terms of estimating the chances that the children of siblings of a person with ASD may inherit the disorder. It may even lead to early interventions during infancy.

Another development is the Autism Tissue Program. Studies of the postmortem brain with imaging methods will help scientists learn why some brains are large, how the limbic system develops, and how the brain changes as it ages. Tissue samples can be stained and show which neurotransmitters are being made in the cells and how they are transported and released to other cells. Focusing on specific brain regions will make identifying susceptibility genes easier.

Scientists continue to explore the role that neurotransmitters may play in ASD. Individuals with ASD often show lower levels of neurotransmitters, such as acetylcholine, dopamine, serotonin, and GABA, in several areas of the brain. These findings suggest that multiple neurotransmitter systems are affected in ASD. Researchers may be able to develop drugs that specifically target these neurochemical imbalances.

Because many fMRI studies have found the synchronization of brain activation consistently lower in people with ASD than in those without ASD, some researchers are proposing that ASD may be the result of poor interconnections between brain areas responsible for problem solving, language, and social behavior. This theory, known as *underconnectivity*, is consistent with other findings. For example, as explained earlier, larger brain size may interfere with critical connections between neuron networks (e.g., Just, Keller, Malave, Kana, & Varma, 2012). More study is needed, but researchers are hopeful that pursing underconnectivity will lead to a better understanding of ASD and improved treatments.

Other researchers are looking at whether abnormalities in the immune system contribute to ASD. Genetic studies have indicated a link between ASD and the genes associated with the immune system (Careaga, Van de Water, & Ashwood, 2010). About one third of children with ASD have unexplained gastrointestinal problems. Researchers have found that children with ASD have about one half the amount of glutathione (an antioxidant critical for the immune system) in their brain and stomach lining as children without ASD (e.g., Gu, Chauhan, & Chauhan, 2013). Natural body chemicals that help make glutathione were also abnormal. Studies are investigating whether this glutathione abnormality can be reversed by administering certain vitamins, such as B_{12} and folic acid.

As researchers learn more about the development of the human brain, they will be better able to unlock the genetic, biochemical, psychological, and physiological mysteries of ASD.

WHAT EDUCATORS NEED TO CONSIDER

The growing numbers of students diagnosed with ASD pose an enormous challenge to educators who are expected to provide the best environment for helping these students succeed. Clearly, the more that educators know about ASD and appropriate intervention strategies, the more successful they will be in that mission. ASD is a neurological disorder that affects children's overall ability to communicate and interact socially. Their behavior may be difficult to control at times. Teachers should be adequately trained to use interventions that will preserve a positive educational climate in the classroom for these students and their peers.

Adolescents diagnosed with ASD have to bear both the burden of coping with the teenage years and the recognition that they are different from their peers. They typically lack friends and neither date nor plan for the future. Awareness of this often drives them to learn new and unacceptable behaviors. Success in school for students with ASD should be measured not so much by whether they succeed at algebra as by whether they acquire the knowledge and skills that will make them more self-sufficient as adults.

Strategies to Consider

ENHANCING LEARNING IN STUDENTS WITH AUTISM SPECTRUM DISORDER

The items listed here are for consideration by any educator responsible for helping students with ASD successfully cope with their situation and become self-sufficient adults.

- **Different learning style.** Students with ASD learn differently in that they have difficulty understanding the perceptions of others, experience sensory overload, and use intellect instead of emotion to guide their social interactions. Use visual aids whenever possible to help them organize their work and day.

- **Need for structure.** These students need structure. Their activities should

  o Organize their materials
  o Give clear instructions
  o Provide stability
  o Establish patterns
  o Provide consistency and predictability
  o Increase independence

- **Social interaction.** These students need to learn ways to interact socially with their peers and adults. When teaching them about social interaction, use

  o A predictable sequence of interactions (no surprises)
  o A planned set of conversational scripts
  o Lots of repetition
  o Messages linked to what the student is doing
  o Speech and visual cues simultaneously
  o Messages mixed with ongoing activities

Strategies to Consider

INTERVENTIONS FOR YOUNG CHILDREN WITH AUTISM SPECTRUM DISORDER

A 2006 study examined interventions conducted with young children with ASD to determine their effectiveness. The researchers found that interventions that included parent involvement, targeted various developmental areas, and extended over a long period of time (for 1 year or more) were the most effective. Their findings are described in the six categories listed below.

- **Parent involvement** (e.g., Harrop, 2015; Hock, Kinsman, & Ortaglia, 2015; Schultz, Schmidt, & Stichter, 2011). Researchers have demonstrated the ability of parents to implement a variety of interventions, including a focus on areas such as language and behavior. Parents are effective intervention agents because they can increase the number of hours of intervention that children receive, and they can intervene throughout the child's life span. Furthermore, parents who serve as intervention agents often report that they have increased feelings of support and competence and fewer feelings of stress and depression. To be most effective, however, parents must be trained in how to implement the interventions properly. School districts could operate these parent-training workshops. Here are some interventions that worked:

○ Parents who implemented language and speech interventions with behavior modifications to their children for a period of 10 weeks found that the children mastered significantly more speech skills than prior to the intervention.

○ Parents trained to teach language, imitation, and preacademic skills by using structured teaching and visual aids to their children found that after 10 weeks the children scored better on subtests of a developmental profile.

○ Parents trained in behavior management had a significant reduction in their children's problem behaviors after 3 months of intervention.

○ Parents trained in language, social development, functional behavior assessment, and problem solving taught language and social skills to their children for 12 weeks. Children in the intervention group performed significantly better in language skills over time.

- **Intensive behavioral intervention** (e.g., Klintwall, Eldevik, & Eikeseth, 2015; Kovshoff, Hastings, & Remington, 2011). Several studies in which children with ASD received intensive intervention (40 or more hours per week) in language, behavior, and social and emotional areas, ranging from 16 months to 2 years, all reported positive outcomes.

- **Multicomponent early intervention** (e.g., Yakubova & Taber-Doughty, 2015). In these studies, children received multicomponent early intervention in language, social and emotional, cognitive, and behavior areas for periods of 43 weeks to 1 year. After the intervention, the children showed significantly improved scores in fine motor, cognitive, language (both receptive and expressive), and social and emotional areas. They also displayed a decrease in autistic behavior.

- **Language and speech treatments** (e.g., Ricketts, Dockrell, Patel, Charman, & Lindsay, 2015; Van der Paelt, Warreyn, & Roeyers, 2014). Children who received specific language training for periods of 1 to 2 years performed significantly better than the control group in auditory comprehension, nonverbal imitation, vocal imitation, and communicative speech.

- **Other interventions.** Other studies have shown some promise for the following interventions:

○ Children who received intensive behavioral interventions when under the age of 60 months had significantly better outcomes than those who received the interventions after the age of 60 months (e.g., Boyd, Odom, Humphreys, & Sam, 2010).

○ Children using a computer program with a teacher-directed behavior training on vocabulary acquisition significantly increased their learning of vocabulary as well as their attention and motivation scores (e.g., Khowaja & Salim, 2013).

Strategies to Consider

INTERVENTIONS FOR CHILDREN AND ADOLESCENTS WITH AUTISM SPECTRUM DISORDER

There are literally dozens of interventions and treatments currently being used or suggested for children and adolescents with ASD, ranging from behavior analysis to megavitamin therapy. Which are the most effective? Which have enough empirical evidence to be considered scientifically based practices? Researchers have reviewed many of these interventions and treatments and found four that have been rigorously researched and that repeatedly yield significantly positive outcomes for students with ASD. Because every individual with ASD exhibits a unique combination of strengths and weaknesses in various areas, no one technique should be adopted at the exclusion of others. Here is a brief description of each:

- **Applied Behavior Analysis (ABA)** (e.g., Heitzman-Powell et al., 2014). ABA emphasizes a proactive approach, using effective strategies for intervening after a behavior has occurred. It involves a comprehensive analysis of the student's environment, including adaptive and meaningful curriculum, appropriate instructional activities, appropriate stimulus control, and a positive classroom structure that increases the student's desired behaviors. The ABA techniques have been refined over more than 35 years to teach a variety of skills in multiple settings, including social skills in natural settings, one-to-one instruction, and group instruction. The effectiveness of ABA is enhanced because decisions related to this approach are driven by data collected through observation, either live or by videotaping. Researchers generally agree that starting ABA before age 5 increases the likelihood of successful outcomes.

    Because of the complexities involved in administering ABA, it is important that individuals who provide behavior analysis services be properly qualified and thoroughly trained. A national certification process has been established.

- **Discrete Trial Teaching (DTT)** (e.g., Downs & Downs, 2013; Gongola & Sweeney, 2012). DTT is related to applied behavior analysis and is a strategy for teaching new skills. The *trial* is a single teaching unit consisting of three components: an instructional piece, the student's response to the instruction, and the consequences. The teacher's instructions are given (e.g., "Tell me which one of these objects is a cube"). Then comes the student's answer ("This one is the cube"), which is evaluated as correct ("That right. Good for you"), incorrect, or no response. As a consequence of the student's response, the teacher decides the next step, which may involve reteaching, modeling, prompting, or moving on. DTT uses techniques such as errorless learning, modeling, shaping, correction procedures, and reinforcement to promote skill acquisition. It can be used to teach new behaviors, such as motor skills, imitation and play skills, language skills, and emotional expression. DTT can also be used to reduce aggressive behaviors. Most educators can implement DTT with training and supervision, but special and extensive training is needed to develop DTT curricula and to supervise DTT programs.

- **Pivotal Response Training (PRT)** (e.g., Minjarez, Mercier, Williams, & Hardan, 2013; Suhrheinrich, 2015). PRT focuses on pivotal areas that can improve other important areas and have a widespread impact on the child's development. It aims to provide individuals with ASD with the educational and social skills they need to function independently and successfully in inclusive settings. PRT uses the principles of applied behavior analysis (ABA) to help students respond to multiple cues and stimuli, improve motivation, increase response to natural cues in the environment, and improve self-management. PRT should be used in inclusive settings, such as general education classrooms and homes. This approach stresses the importance of inclusion as contrasted with the traditional ABA approach of one-on-one training. PRT is also effective for lowering the level of stress and raising the level of empowerment in parents of children with ASD.

- **Learning Experiences: An Alternative Program for Preschoolers and Parents (LEAP)** (e.g., Sanders et al., 2015; Strain & Bovey, 2011). LEAP is an early childhood (ages 3 to 5) intervention approach that uses peer mediation and is designed to occur in inclusive preschool settings. A speech language therapist assists the children with ASD and their parents in the classroom and at home. Children without ASD are taught interventions that help them develop the social skills of their peers with ASD. The LEAP curriculum aims to develop language and communications abilities, increase choice making, facilitate independence in work and play activities, and generally enhance social and emotional growth. Family members receive training in teaching strategies and behavior management to ensure that the interventions are supported throughout the day. Studies have shown that students who attended LEAP schools for 15 hours per week and remained for two to three years improved in their social interaction, language and communication skills, cognitive function, and behavior, and a reduction in their autistic characteristics. Furthermore, the studies suggested that these improvements were maintained over time.

Strategies to Consider

HELPING STUDENTS WITH HIGH-FUNCTIONING AUTISM SPECTRUM DISORDER

Children and adolescents diagnosed with high-functioning ASD (formerly Asperger syndrome) usually have average or above average cognitive abilities. They tend to have excellent rote memory skills and often exhibit a precocious vocabulary. However, they have problems with abstract thinking. They frequently do not understand the logic of classroom instruction and discussion and are easily distracted. Educational structure and classroom management strategies become important. Instructional approaches have to be concrete and varied. Support and discipline strategies need to be clear and nonthreatening. Here are a few points to consider that could help students diagnosed with high-functioning ASD (Fienup, Shelvin, & Doepke, 2013; Lorenzo, Pomares, & Lledó, 2013; Palm, 2012/2013; Willard-Holt, Weber, Morrison, & Horgan, 2013).

- Educational Structure and Classroom Management
  - Provide a predictable environment and routine and prepare students for any upcoming changes
  - Ensure that each student is seated in a position of least distraction and close to the teacher or other source of information to which the student must respond
  - Be consistent and do not ask for an option if there is none
  - Avoid doing for the students what they can do for themselves
  - Give clear, precise, concrete instructions, and do not assume that mere repetition means that the student has understood
  - Find ways to tie new situations to old ones that students have experienced
  - State expectations clearly and allow each student time to process the information
  - Concentrate on changing unacceptable behaviors, and do not worry about those that are simply odd
  - Break tasks up into manageable segments, and plan a completion schedule with the student
  - Teach students how to complete a task, such as taking a multiple-choice test
  - Do not rely on emotional appeals by assuming students want to please you

- Instructional Approaches
  - Support verbal information with visual aids, such as blank graphic organizers, to help record and organize information
  - Incorporate 3-D models and manipulatives whenever possible
  - Consider tape recording information so students can take notes later at their own pace and refer back to the tape recording when needed
  - Model the action you want students to use, and maintain the behavior with visual cues
  - Use cooperative learning groups, but teach appropriate social responses to use in this activity
  - Minimize assigned written work because these students do not understand the logic of repetitive activities
  - Use larger print on paperwork, and include only a few items on each page

- o Assign enrichment activities related to the students' interests because they will be more satisfied and productive gathering facts about a subject they like
- o Avoid abstract language (e.g., metaphors and irony), and fully explain any constructions that you do use
- o Work with students to determine the appropriate and interesting means for each to demonstrate knowledge of the topic (e.g., design and make a poster, give an oral presentation, write a story or poem, draw or paint a picture, make a collage, act out information, write a song, make a board game, or take a test)
- o Seek out computer programs that use immersive virtual reality systems, which have been shown to improve social competencies and executive functioning

- • Support and Discipline Strategies

  - o Have a strategy ready in case the students cannot cope because of overstimulation or confusion
  - o Have a time-out area for discipline when needed, and make sure the time-out is not more appealing than the curricular activity
  - o Look for stressors in their environment and try to reduce or eliminate them
  - o Explicitly teach the rules of social conduct
  - o Inform parents on a regular basis of the students' successes and failures, and ask for parental advice when appropriate
  - o Give students some space, and avoid cornering or trapping them
  - o Use an unemotional tone of voice when telling them what they need to do, and give sincere praise when they do it correctly
  - o Try not to confuse lack of tact with rudeness
  - o Protect them from teasing and bullying
  - o Teach them how to meet someone, how to recognize when someone will not talk to them, and how to tell when someone is teasing them

Putting It All Together

Children are apt to live up to what you believe in them.

—Lady Bird Johnson (1912–2007),
First Lady of the United States

The preceding chapters have described some of the recent research on the human brain that sheds light on problems affecting learning. Some of the problems may result from genetic mutations, fetal brain injury during gestation, or environmental impact. Whatever the cause, teachers represent the essential link between the students with learning problems and the strategies and services selected to help them.

HELPING STUDENTS WITH LEARNING DIFFICULTIES

We know that students with learning problems *can* learn when teachers spend the time and use their expertise to find the appropriate ways to teach these students. To that end, let's look at four important areas that ought to be considered when working with students who have learning difficulties. Those areas are

- Identification: How do we assess students for learning difficulties?
- Accommodation: How do we modify the instructional environment to help these students?
- Motivation: How do we encourage students with learning difficulties to achieve?
- Communication: How do we ensure that parents stay involved?

Identifying Students With Learning Difficulties

Very often, the general education classroom teacher is the first to recognize a potential learning problem. Although many students encounter learning problems at one time or another, these problems are usually temporary and quickly overcome. For others, the problems persist and result in a lag in academic achievement compared to their learning potential. These students need help.

The question now is whether the learning problem can be addressed in the general education classroom. Asking older students to take an inventory similar to the one below will help you and them learn from their perceptions of how well they perform certain tasks. Working with a student on the comments section can provide useful insights on instructional approaches to consider. For younger students, a verbal discussion of these areas may be more effective than the written inventory.

The results of the inventory, teacher observations, and student performance may indicate that a more formal assessment of the student's achievement is needed to determine if a learning disability exists. Only a few schools continue to use an ability (IQ)-achievement discrepancy model to identify the presence of a learning disability; that is, <u>students with learning disabilities show an unexpected gap between their potential and achievement</u>. Rather, most schools use the Response to Intervention (RTI) method for identifying learning disabilities (NCLD, 2015). In RTI, students who do not respond to intensive intervention would be identified as having a learning disability. Educators should carefully weigh the advantages and disadvantages of these and other identification methods.

The Ability-Achievement Discrepancy

Some educators still believe in the use of the discrepancy model, saying that it has a valid basis in that it provides psychometric evidence of the unexpected underachiever. It is a simple system that uses data from long-validated assessments, so teachers do not need to spend a great deal of time in the identification process. The model indicates the presence of underachievement but only the *possibility* of a disability and can thus serve as the first step in the identification process. Other educators say that even if the model is flawed, we should still use it but with greater integrity.

Assessment Inventory			
Area	Strengths	Challenges	Comments
Attention			
Speaking			
Reading			
Writing			
Calculating			
Memory			
Emotional/Behavioral			

Arguments against the discrepancy method continue even with its declining use. One argument is that the <u>high number of students identified as learning disabled through this method is suspect</u>. IQ tests, they say, can be biased against certain racial groups or those who are indigent. Furthermore, results are not consistent from state to state, or even from one school district to another: One district may have a high number of students with learning disabilities while another has few. Some studies report that the same team using the discrepancy model will not identify the same students as having a learning disability. But proponents of the discrepancy approach say that these misidentifications are not because of a flawed model but due rather to the lack of rigor in its implementation.

One of the most pressing arguments against the discrepancy model is what some critics see as its "<u>wait-to-fail</u>" aspect. Because assessments of achievement are not sensitive enough to detect learning problems in the primary grades, students must be in third or fourth grade to have a discrepancy large enough to be identified as having a learning disability. But supporters counter that this criticism is not really valid because early identification has long been a major focus.

Video: For a brief explanation of the problems associated with the ability(IQ)-achievement discrepancy model, see:

https://www.youtube.com/watch?v=hgj2sqXtr6U

Response to Intervention (RTI)

With RTI, low achievers are identified as quickly as possible and provided intensive and validated instruction though the multiple-tier protocol described in Chapter 2. The model replaces traditional psychometric measures with an approach that emphasizes student outcomes rather than student deficits. Most states have some form of RTI operating to support local districts in meeting the demands of closing the achievement gap for students with special needs. RTI has proven to be effective when appropriately implemented. Such implementation means that the school's RTI framework includes data-based decision making, effective screening of students, monitoring of student progress, and a multilevel prevention system. Research studies offer evidence of effective use of RTI with preschool children (Carta et al., 2014), in primary grades reading (Harlacher, Potter, & Weber, 2015), in intervention blocks (Averill, Baker, & Rinaldi, 2014), with middle school students (Dulaney, 2013; Vaughn & Fletcher, 2012), and with high school students (Fisher & Frey, 2013). There are also suggestions for using the RTI model with gifted students who have learning problems (Crepeau-Hobson & Bianco, 2013).

There are, of course, cautions that experience is showing must be observed to maintain the effectiveness of RTI. An analysis of studies focusing on these cautions cites the following (Noll, 2013):

- Allow teachers to have access to research-based strategies for implementing the reading program.
- Ensure that there is high-quality instruction in Tier 1 that includes differentiation and small-group instruction, thereby lowering the number of students who will need more intervention.
- Provide effective on-site professional development so teachers have help implementing literacy instruction in their own classrooms.

- Avoid quick fixes and seek strategies that actually improve reading achievement.
- Rely more on highly trained and knowledgeable teachers than on commercially produced intervention programs to improve reading.
- Use assessments that measure the effects of instruction and intervention on reading full texts rather than word lists.
- Assist teachers with the support they need to effectively analyze assessment data.

With these cautions in mind, educators can devise effective RTI programs to help their students with learning problems achieve success.

The Neuropsychological Component

Some researchers are recommending that the RTI multitier model be expanded to a more complex framework that includes findings from neuroscience on how the brain develops and learns. They suggest, for example, that the expanded neuropsychological model could include a method for evaluating reading skills that also reveals whether the child can generalize learning or complete more abstract or inferential tasks. What do these evaluations tell us about the child's executive (frontal lobe) functions? This is important to know because the extent of executive function has implications for learning to read as well as for content courses, such as mathematics, science, and social studies.

The expanded model must also be able to differentiate among learners with different needs. The instruments should separate a child with reading difficulties because of attentional problems from one with reading difficulties because of problems with decoding. These two children need different interventions. With this approach, screening would include measures of attention, working memory, auditory processing ability, executive functions, processing speed, and other functions that affect learning (Feifer, 2008).

Of course, the inclusion of a neuropsychological component can only be successful if teachers are sufficiently knowledgeable to accurately assess these elements. All we are discovering about how the brain learns and how to address learning difficulties should now be a mandatory part of every teacher's knowledge base. Although some of that information has been included in this book, new research is continually emerging that may further help educators and parents address a child's learning difficulty. Teacher training institutions and school districts have a responsibility to regularly provide educators with the most recent research on teaching and learning from *all* areas of scientific inquiry, including **educational neuroscience**. Only then will we be better able to identify children with learning difficulties earlier and more accurately so that we can provide them with the most appropriate strategies they need to achieve success.

A Combined Model

Based on the research and experiences associated with identifying students with learning difficulties as soon as possible, it seems appropriate to develop a combined model that

- Avoids the disadvantages of the ability-achievement discrepancy in the primary grades

- Incorporates the advantages of a multitier framework similar to that used in RTI
- Includes findings from neuroscience research about brain development and function
- Eliminates other potential conditions that could resemble a learning difficulty

Such a model would include the work of various researchers (e.g., Carta et al., 2014; Fuchs, Fuchs, & Compton, 2012; Kavale & Forness, 2000; Lovett & Sparks, 2013; Semrud-Clikeman, 2005) and consist of five tiers that include these components. The advantages of the combined model shown in Figure 10.1 are that it

- Uses measures for early identification of learning difficulties in the lower primary grades
- Ensures that the underachievement is occurring in a basic skill area
- Examines the student's ability to acquire and organize information
- Includes an assessment of neuropsychological processes associated with learning
- Eliminates other conditions that could be responsible for the underachievement

The identification process stops when the student cannot meet the criteria at any level. The designation of a *learning disability* occurs when the student passes successfully through each level.

Figure 10.1 This model combines a multilevel approach that includes early identification and assessments of neuropsychological processes.

Level 5	***Eliminate Other Conditions*** Eliminating the following conditions leaves learning difficulty as the sole designation: **Cultural differences**　　**Emotional or behavioral disorder** **Sensory impairment**　　**Mild intellectual impairment** **Insufficient instruction**
Level 4	***Assess Neuropsychological Processes*** The student is assessed in psychological processes to determine if any deficits exist. Those processes include: **Attention**　　**Working memory**　　**Linguistic processing** **Executive functions**　　**Social cognition**
Level 3	***Examine Learning Efficiency*** This level examines the student's ability to structure and organize learning tasks as well as the rate of acquiring information. The goal is to determine the student's awareness about learning and whether tasks are being organized efficiently and efforts are being constantly sustained.
Level 2	***Analyze Standard Achievement Test Scores in Major Academic Areas*** To ensure that the potential learning difficulty is based on a deficit in basic skill areas, analyze the student's total standardized achievement test scores in: **Language**　　**Reading**　　**Writing**　　**Mathematics**
Level 1	***Early Identification*** For students in primary grades, use instruments such as the *Get Ready to Read* early literacy screener, and the Picture Naming and Sound Identification measures in the *Individual Growth and Development Indicators*.

Accommodating Students With Learning Difficulties

Here are some suggestions for teachers to consider when making accommodations for students with learning difficulties. Not all these suggestions apply to every student, and individual strategies should be developed to address the needs of individual students. Implementing accommodations such as those listed here can improve the academic achievement of students with learning disabilities. In mainstreamed classrooms, take care to balance these accommodations so as not to appear unfair to the students who are not in need of these strategies.

- **Learn about learning.** Educators in all areas can be empowered by updating their knowledge of what neuroscience is revealing about how the brain learns. These discoveries and insights can help explain problems and improve instructional skills. Teachers should draw on the knowledge of special educators and researchers to address specific problems.

Design a learning profile for each student with learning problems. For students with learning problems, keep a simple record of their

- Reasoning ability
- Learning profile
- Classroom participation
- Comprehension
- Work level
- Progress

Design the profile to spot trends in each area. Use this information to build on students' existing strengths and identify areas needing improvement.

Use assistive technology. Computers and other forms of advanced technology are useful tools for helping students with various types of learning problems. Stanberry and Raskind (2009) suggest some types of assistive technology:

- **Abbreviation expanders.** Add-ons to word processing programs, allowing a student to create, store, and re-use abbreviations for frequently-used words or phrases, thereby saving keystrokes and ensuring the proper spelling of words and phrases that were coded as abbreviations.
- **Alternative keyboards.** Special overlays that customize the appearance and function of a standard keyboard, such as grouping keys by color and location, thereby helping students who have difficulty typing.
- **Audio books and publications.** Books recorded on CDs and MP3 downloads allow students to listen to text.
- **Electronic mathematics worksheets.** These software programs help students organize and work through mathematics problems on a computer screen. Numbers that appear on the screen can be read aloud through a speech synthesizer.

- **Graphic organizers and outlining.** These programs help students who have difficulty when they begin a writing project by allowing them to organize their information into appropriate order and categories.
- **Information/data managers.** These portable, hand-held devices help a student plan, organize, store, and retrieve calendar entries, task lists, contact data, and other information in electronic form.
- **Optical character recognition.** A student can scan printed material into a computer or handheld unit that is read aloud via a speech synthesis/screen reading system.
- **Personal FM listening systems.** This tool transmits a speaker's voice via a wireless transmitter and microphone directly to the student's ear via a receiver and earphone, thereby helping the listener focus on what the speaker is saying.
- **Proofreading programs.** These software programs help students who struggle with writing (e.g., spelling, grammar, punctuation, word usage, and sentence structure) by alerting them to possible errors.
- **Speech-recognition programs.** The student speaks into a microphone, and the spoken words appear on the computer screen as text, thereby helping students whose oral language abilities are better than their writing skills.
- **Talking calculators.** A built-in speech synthesizer reads aloud each number, symbol, or operation key a student presses and vocalizes the answer to the problem, thereby providing the auditory feedback needed to check the accuracy of the keys that were pressed and verifying the answer.
- **Talking spell checkers and electronic dictionaries.** These tools help a poor speller to select or identify appropriate words and correct spelling errors during the process of writing and proofreading. Talking devices say as well as display the selected words onscreen, so the student sees and hears the words.
- **Word-prediction programs.** This software helps a student during word processing by predicting a word the student intends to type, thereby aiding those who struggle with writing to use proper spelling, grammar, and word choices, with fewer keystrokes. Predictions are based on spelling, syntax, and frequent/recent use.

Deciding which assistive technologies to use should be based on the student's specific learning difficulty and needs. Our goal should be to apply the technology that uses the student's abilities while compensating for the disability.

Modify the learning environment. Just a few changes in the learning environment can sometimes make a significant difference in student achievement. Consider which students might benefit if you

- Seat student in an area free of distractions
- Consider using study carrels
- Keep the student's work area free of unnecessary materials
- Use a checklist to help get the student organized
- Stand near the student when giving directions

- Provide organizational strategies such as charts and time lines
- Assist in organizing the student's notebook
- Use materials that address the students' learning profile
- Provide opportunities for movement

Modify instructional strategies. Consider modifying instructional strategies to meet the various learning styles and abilities of students with learning problems. Here are some strategies to consider:

- Allow students to audio record lectures
- Break assignment into shorter tasks
- Adjust the reading level of the classroom material
- Teach the concrete before the abstract
- Relate the new learning to students' experiences
- Reduce the number of concepts presented at one time
- Give an overview of the lesson before beginning
- Periodically check the student's comprehension of the language used for instruction
- Monitor the rate at which you present material
- Require verbal responses from the student to check for comprehension
- Provide clear and concise directions for homework assignments
- Allow word-processed assignments
- Consider the oral administration of tests and open book tests
- Provide practice test questions for study
- Allow use of dictionary (book or electronic) or calculator during test
- Provide extra time to finish a written test

Modify the curriculum materials. Modifications to curriculum materials will vary depending on the nature of the student's learning problem. For those with *spoken language* difficulties, you can

- Paraphrase complex information
- Slow the rate of presentation
- Provide written directions to supplement verbal directions
- Keep sentence structures simple
- Avoid the use of abstract language such as puns, idioms, and metaphors
- Get the student's attention before expressing key points
- Use visual aids such as charts and graphs
- Call student by name before asking questions

For those with *written language* difficulties

- Allow student to use cursive or manuscript writing
- Permit student to type, record, or give oral answers instead of writing
- Provide copies of class notes
- Avoid the pressure of speed and accuracy
- Reduce the amount of copying from the textbook or board
- Establish realistic standards for neatness
- Accept key word responses instead of complete sentences

For those with organizational problems

- Establish clear rules and consistently enforce them
- Provide an established daily routine
- Consider making contracts with students and use rewards when the contract is completed
- Ensure that due dates are clearly understood
- Provide a specific place for turning in assignments

Get the reluctant starter going. Some students have difficulty getting started and need the teacher's guidance to move forward. For them, consider the following:

- Give a personal cue to begin work
- Check progress often, especially after the first few minutes of work
- Provide immediate feedback and reinforcers
- Divide work into smaller units
- Suggest time periods for each task
- Ensure that the student understands the instructions
- Present the assignment in sequential steps
- Provide a checklist for multitask assignments

Maintain attention. Because some students with learning problems can be easily distracted, look for ways to maintain attention during the lesson.

- Seat the students close to you
- Provide praise for correct answers
- Relate new learning to students' experiences
- Give an advance warning when a transition is going to occur
- Use physical proximity and appropriate touch to help student refocus
- Remove any technology that can be a distraction

Use group instruction and peers. Although some students with learning problems do not always work well in groups, persistence and guidance can often result in a productive experience.

- Assign a peer tutor to record material dictated by the student
- Use cooperative learning strategies when appropriate
- Assign a peer helper to read important directions and information to the student and to check for understanding

Adjust time demands. Meeting time lines and deadlines is not always easy for some students with learning problems. Some get involved in minute details, while others dart from one idea to another and lose track of time.

- Increase time allowed for the completion of tests or assignments
- Reduce the amount of work or length of tests
- Introduce short breaks or change of tasks

- Follow a specific routine and be consistent
- Alternate active and quiet tasks
- Help students prioritize the steps needed to complete an assignment
- Set time limits for completing specific tasks

Deal with inappropriate behavior. Inappropriate behavior is not acceptable. But keep in mind that the misbehavior may not have been intentional.

- Provide clear and concise classroom expectations and consequences
- Enforce rules consistently
- Avoid confrontational techniques because they often escalate the situation
- Provide the student with alternatives
- Avoid power struggles
- Designate a cooling-off location in the classroom
- Ignore attention-getting behavior for a short time (extinction)
- Assign activities which require some movement
- Deal with the behavior and avoid criticizing the student
- Speak privately to the student about inappropriate behavior
- Check for levels of tolerance and be aware of signs of frustration

Modify homework assignments. Homework can be a valuable learning tool for students with learning problems if it is relevant and not excessive.

- Consider allowing student to work on homework in school
- Give frequent reminders about due dates
- Give short assignments
- Allow for extra credit assignments
- Develop an award system for in-school work and homework completed

Motivating Students With Learning Difficulties

Teachers are always looking for ways to motivate their students to learn. But motivating students with learning difficulties can be particularly challenging because these students have doubts about their abilities and often experience failure in the classroom. They get caught up in an unfortunate cycle where low expectations lead to poor performance, resulting in low motivation. The low motivation keeps their expectations low, and so the cycle continues. Eventually, these students can develop a negative self-concept, which can be frustrating for teachers to overcome. Low motivation among students is directly related to their fear of academic failure. Here are some basic strategies that teachers should consider to help motivate students with learning difficulties (Bruster, 2015; Dweck, 2014/2015; Hattie, 2011; Hossain & Wiest, 2013; Morgan, 2015; Waugh, 2002).

Structure activities for success. The old saying that nothing succeeds like success is appropriate for all students but especially so for those who have not had the exhilaration that comes with successful academic experiences. Students are more likely to experience this success when teachers

- Distribute an outline in advance of a lesson or unit that clearly describes assignments and the level of performance expected. This approach lowers the anxiety that often leads to poor performance.
- Break assignments into logical and sequential instructional steps and give feedback to the student regarding performance of each step. If the instructional goal is clear and the teacher provides guidance and encouragement, then students are more motivated to complete the task and less apt to go off course and get frustrated.
- Set assignments at the correct level of difficulty for each student. If the task is too easy, the student gets little satisfaction from completing it. However, if the task is too difficult, the student can become frustrated and give up.
- Establish a blog to facilitate teacher-to-student and student-to-student discussions about the curriculum content.

Set realistic expectations. When students have few successful learning experiences, they have no way of knowing what skills are needed or how much effort to apply to accomplish a learning task. Consequently, they often set unrealistic goals, resulting in failure. Teachers can help students set realistic goals by

- Discussing with the student a task which the student had performed poorly and determining the reasons for the poor performance. Point out that a little more effort may have made the difference. The goal is to identify the causes of failure so that the student can set realistic and attainable goals.
- Helping the student devise an action plan outlining how the student will use time and effort to accomplish a specific learning task.

Link success to effort. Students who generally experience failure in school tend to attribute their occasional successes to luck. This is known as a fixed mindset; that is, these students believe their abilities are predetermined by nature and cannot be improved. Teachers should reinforce with students the notion of a growth mindset, namely, that successful classroom work is the direct result of their effort and not luck. Give students genuine praise for their successful work, and congratulate them on completing the task. To be successful in this strategy, teachers must believe in their own growth mindset, accepting that they can continually improve their instruction for the benefit of all students.

Communicate positive expectations and frequent feedback. Research studies have long shown that teacher expectations can have a powerful influence on a student's self-expectations and performance. For example, teachers communicate negative expectations when they call on and praise low-achieving students less often than high-achieving students and when they smile and maintain eye contact more often with high-achieving students. It is also important to recognize the power of frequent, clear, and specific feedback to students about their work. These informal assessments go a long way in helping students develop a growth mindset and in understanding how much progress they are making toward their achievement goals. Teachers are often unaware that they behave differently toward students of various ability levels. By occasionally asking themselves the following questions, they may become more conscious of their behavior and communicate positive expectations to all students:

- Do I give positive feedback to low-achieving students as often as I do to high-achieving students?
- Am I unduly critical of the performance of low-achieving students?
- Do I interact with low-achieving students as often as I do with high-achieving students?

Demonstrate noncontingent acceptance. Consistent failure in school erodes not only students' self-expectations but also their self-worth. Teachers can help these students improve their self-worth by

- Telling them that their acceptance is not contingent on their levels of performance in the classroom
- Showing students that they genuinely care about their well-being
- Talking regularly with students about concerns and problems that are unrelated to their schoolwork
- Exhibiting an understanding of their students' problems and a willingness to listen and offer advice
- Helping students deal with their frustrations and reassuring them they have the ability to overcome difficult challenges

When teachers carefully structure classroom assignments and provide guidance and encouragement, students with learning difficulties can change their expectations from failure to success. Because the traditional approaches to understanding learning differences focus on detecting and fixing deficits, teachers can get so concerned about the students' problems that they miss the opportunity to capitalize on the students' latent talents and strengths. Many studies indicate that using an individual's strengths to mitigate areas of weakness results in improved motivation and performance and boost to that person's self-esteem.

Communicating With Parents

Raising a child with a learning disability can be stressful. Some families are more resilient than others in adapting to this stress. Many parents report benefits and positive outcomes for their families, including improved coping skills, family harmony, shared parental duties, spiritual growth, and better communications. Other parents, however, report that anger, guilt, blame, and frustration are often the cause of conflict in the home. The level of the child's disability, the type of family structure, family income, and ethnic and cultural factors all contribute to how a family adapts to raising a child with a learning disability.

School personnel can help ease parental stress by meeting personally with parents as soon as learning problems are detected. Several meetings may be needed before the parent gets past the emotional reactions and responds calmly and constructively. They should be encouraged to ask questions, which should be answered fully and openly. Some parents just need reassurance that they can overcome any feelings of helplessness and that there are resources available that can help them understand and manage their child's difficulties. Frequent communication with parents is important so that all are working together to assist the student in meeting expectations. Teachers can consider

- Developing a daily and weekly journal and sharing it with the parents
- Scheduling periodic parent-teacher meetings
- Providing a duplicate set of textbooks that they can use at home during the school year
- Providing weekly progress reports to parents
- Mailing (or e-mailing) the parents a schedule of class and homework assignments
- Explaining clearly the school's grading policy and any adaptations that were made for the student. Surveys indicate that parents of students with learning difficulties want the grading system to be sensitive to an individual's progress and to communicate their children's strengths and needs, as well as offer suggestions for improvement.

Schools can also help by providing parents with contact information about local support groups, Internet sites, and organizations that assist parents of children with learning disabilities.

Future Trends in Special Education

New research in educational neuroscience and innovative ideas about how to structure schools and revise curriculums will no doubt have an impact on special education. School leaders and special education practitioners should be aware of new ideas and strategies that can improve how we help students with learning difficulties. Here are some present and possible future trends (Cook & Tankersley, 2013; Dukes, Darling, & Doan, 2014; Gordillo, 2015; Kauffman, 2015; Walker & Gresham, 2014).

- **Focus on Evidence-Based Strategies and Standards-Based IEPs.** Despite come controversy, the Common Core State Standards are generating more pressure to develop individualized education programs (IEPs) that are aligned with the language arts and mathematics standards.
- **Autism Spectrum Disorder (ASD).** Autism will continue to be a major focus of special education programs because of the rapid and continuing rise in the number of children diagnosed with this disorder. Expect a stronger push from national advocates to ensure that schools are preparing students with ASD for life after high school and to find appropriate settings and services to meet their ongoing needs.
- **Emotional and Behavioral Disorders (EBD).** Managing the problematic behavior of students with emotional and behavioral disorders (EBD) has always been a major challenge for both special and general education teachers. But recent encouraging developments offer promise for greater success with these students. These include modifying certain aspects of instruction, such as pace, intensity, structure,

repetition, reinforcement, and progress monitoring, for learners with EBD. Another is to recognize the success of positive behavioral interventions and supports and to implement them as standard practice. Still another is to ensure that any methods teachers use in working with students with EBD are firmly rooted in scientific evidence rather than in personal beliefs, anecdotes, or speculation.

- **Professional Development.** There will be a greater attention given to ongoing and job-embedded professional development for all educators to ensure that evidence-based practices and interventions are part of each student's IEP.

- **Preparing Special Education Teachers.** It is critical that teacher preparation institutions thoroughly incorporate the emerging evidence-based approaches for working with students who have special needs into their course work. They have an obligation to ensure that new teachers are fully prepared academically and emotionally to meet the challenges ahead. This preparation should include substantial field experiences, pre- and postgraduate mentoring, and performance-based assessment.

- **Greater Program Accountability.** Federal and state initiatives are beginning to move toward accountability that centers on results-driven indicators to improve the outcomes for students with disabilities. This will require many school districts to take action to ensure that their practices are aligned with this results-driven shift.

- **Providing and Maintaining a Multitiered System of Support.** More than a decade of experience with multitiered models of support, such as response to intervention (RTI), demonstrates their success with students who have learning difficulties and whose needs can often be served in general education settings. More educators will shift to these models and find ways to refine and enhance their effectiveness.

- **Assistive Technology.** Assistive technology will continue to have an impact on special education instruction. It has already proven effective in enabling greater instructional flexibility in the classroom and by the learning opportunities of students with special needs. As the technology advances, so will the need for professional development programs that provide teachers with the skills they need to use the emerging technology effectively and efficiently.

- **Impact of Charter Schools.** Charter schools are increasing at a steady rate and will do so for the foreseeable future. Although parents may find this an attractive option, they should realize that charters usually take money away from the public schools, an increasing number of which have closed because of this reallocation of funding. Data from the National Center for Education Statistics (2015) reveal that charter schools have a disproportionately small number of students with special needs than their local public schools. Moreover, the students with learning difficulties enrolled in charters continue to be those with mild disabilities and do not reflect the disability categories in the public noncharter schools. Local school districts will need to ensure that the services provided to students with learning difficulties in publically funded charter schools are provided the services required by current laws and regulations.

- **Crowdfunding.** As public schools' money to purchase teaching supplies, materials, and equipment continues to decrease, more general and special education teachers are now and will be turning to online donors for financial support. Crowdfunding sites, such as *AdoptAClassroom.org* and *Donorschoose.org,* can provide the financial means to help teachers obtain the most basic materials needed for instruction.

Although children with learning difficulties present unique challenges, they also encourage educators to seek out the best science-based and evidence-based programs to successfully address those challenges. This requires that both general education and special education teachers be prepared to operate in an environment that builds their expertise and provides the best intervention models and support for children with learning difficulties. We cannot ever think about doing less.

Resources

Organizations

(Note: All Internet sites were active at time of publication.)

American Speech-Language-Hearing Association (ASHA)
2200 Research Boulevard
Rockville, MD 20850-3289
(800) 638-8255
Web: www.asha.org

Anxiety and Depression Association of America
8701 Georgia Ave, Suite 412
Silver Spring, MD 20910
(240) 485-1001
Web: www.adaa.org

Asperger Autism Spectrum Education Network (ASPEN)
9 Aspen Circle
Edison, NJ 08820
(732) 321-0880
Web: www.aspennj.org

Attention Deficit Disorder Association
P.O. Box 7557
Wilmington, DE 19083-9997 (800) 939-1019
Web: www.add.org

Autism Society
4340 East-West Hwy
Suite 350
Bethesda, MD 20814
(800) 3-AUTISM or
    (800) 328-8476
Web: www.autism-society.org

Autism Speaks
1 East 33rd St, 4th Floor
New York, NY 10016
(212) 252-8584
Web: www.autismspeaks.org

Children and Adults with Attention Deficit Hyperactivity Disorder
   (CHADD.)
4601 Presidents Drive, Suite 300
Lanham, MD 20706
(301) 306-7070
Web: www.chadd.org

Council for Exceptional Children
2900 Crystal Drive Suite 1000
Arlington, VA 22202-3557
(888) 232-7733
Web: www.cec.sped.org

Council for Learning Disabilities (CLD)
P.O. Box 405
Overland Park, KS 66210
   (913) 491-1011
Web: www.cldinternational.org

Dyscalculia.org
7420 Calhoun Street
Dearborn, Michigan 48126
Web: www.dyscalculia.org

International Association of Special Education
Web: www.iase.org

International Dyslexia Association
40 York Rd., 4th Floor
Baltimore, MD 21204
(410) 296-0232
Web: www.eida.org

International Literacy Association
800 Barksdale Road
P.O. Box 8139
Newark, DE 19714-8139
(800) 336-READ or (800) 336-7323
Web: www.literacyworldwide.org

International OCD Foundation
P.O. Box 961029
Boston, MA 02196
(617) 973-5801
Web: www.iocdf.org

Learning Disabilities Association of America
4156 Liberty Road
Pittsburgh, PA 15234-1349
(412) 341-1515
Web: www.ldaamerica.org

Mental Health America
2000 N. Beauregard St., 6th Floor
Alexandria, VA 22311
(800) 969-6642
Web: www.nmha.org

National Center for Learning Disabilities
32 Laight St., 2nd Floor
New York, NY 10013
(888) 575-7373
Web: www.ncld.org

National Center for
    Special Education Research
555 New Jersey Ave., NW
Washington, DC 20208
(202) 219-1385
www.ies.ed.gov/ncser/

National Center on Response to Intervention
1000 Thomas Jefferson Street, NW
Washington, DC 20007
(877) 784-4255
Web: www.rti4success.org

National Eating Disorders Association
165 West 46th Street, Suite 402
New York, NY 10036
(212) 575-1650
Web: www.nationaleatingdisorders.org

National Institute on Deafness and Other Communication Disorders
1 Communication Avenue
Bethesda, MD 20892-3456
(800) 241-1044
Web: www.nidcd.nih.gov

National Institute of Mental Health
6001 Executive Boulevard, Room 6200, MSC 9663
Bethesda, MD 20892-9663
(866) 615-6464
Web: www.nimh.nih.gov

Nonverbal Learning Disorders Association
507 Hopmeadow St.
Simsbury, CT 06070
(860) 658-5522
Web: www.nlda.org

Positive Behavioral Interventions and Supports:
    Technical Assistance Center
Web: www.pbis.org

Reading Recovery Council of North America
500 W. Wilson Bridge Rd., Suite 250
Worthington, OH 43085 (877) 883-7323
Web: www.readingrecovery.org

Stuttering Foundation of America
1805 Moriah Woods Blvd., Suite 3
Memphis, TN 38117
(800) 992-9392
Web: www.stutteringhelp.org

U.S. Department of Education
400 Maryland Avenue SW
Washington, DC 20202
(800) USA-LEARN (872-5327)
Web: www.ed.gov

Glossary

Alexia. A form of dyslexia whereby the individual has difficulty identifying a string of letters.

Alphabetic principle. The notion that written words are composed of letters of the alphabet that intentionally and systematically represent segments of spoken words.

Amygdala. The almond-shaped structure in the brain's limbic system that encodes emotional messages to long-term storage.

Aphasia. The loss of language function.

Apoptosis. The genetically programmed process in which unneeded or unhealthy brain cells are destroyed.

Ascertainment bias. The failure to represent equally all classes of individuals in a sample. For instance, the tendency to more likely refer males for evaluation of reading problems than females with comparable reading problems.

Asperger syndrome. A disorder within the autism spectrum that results in social and communication, but not intellectual, impairments.

Assistive technology. Any item, piece of equipment, or product system that is used to increase, maintain, or improve the functional capabilities of a person with a disability.

Attention-deficit hyperactivity disorder (ADHD). A syndrome that interferes with an individual's capacity to regulate activity level, inhibit behavior, and attend to tasks in developmentally appropriate ways.

Autism. A spectrum disorder that affects an individual's ability to communicate, form relationships with others, and relate appropriately to the environment.

Brainstem. One of the major parts of the brain, it receives sensory input and monitors such vital functions as heartbeat, body temperature, and digestion.

Broca's area. A region in the left frontal lobe of the brain believed responsible for generating the vocabulary and syntax of an individual's native language.

Cerebellum. One of the major parts of the brain, it coordinates muscle movement and is thought to play a role in long-term memory.

Cerebrum. The largest of the major parts of the brain, it controls sensory interpretation, thinking, and memory.

Comorbidity. The simultaneous appearance of two or more disorders within an individual, such as the co-occurrence of attention-deficit hyperactivity disorder and dyslexia. The association may reflect a causal relationship between one disorder and another, or reveal an underlying susceptibility to both disorders.

Corpus callosum. The bridge of nerve fibers that connects the left and right cerebral hemispheres and allows communication between them.

Cortex. The thin but tough layer of cells covering the cerebrum that contains all the neurons used for cognitive and motor processing.

Dendrite. The branched extension from the cell body of a neuron that receives impulses from nearby neurons through synaptic contacts.

Dopamine. A neurotransmitter believed to control mood, behavior, and muscle coordination.

Dyscalculia. A condition that causes persistent problems with processing numerical calculations.

Dysgraphia. A spectrum disorder characterized by difficulty in mastering the sequence of movements necessary to write letters and numbers.

Dyslexia. Also known as severe reading disability, this is a learning disorder characterized by problems in reading and writing.

Educational neuroscience. A field of scientific inquiry that examines how findings from neuroscience can affect the curricular, instructional, and assessment decisions of educational practitioners.

Frontal lobe. The front part of the brain that monitors higher order thinking, directs problem solving, and regulates the excesses of the emotional (limbic) system.

Functional magnetic resonance imaging (fMRI). An instrument that measures blood flow to the brain to record areas of high and low neuronal activity.

Glial cells. Special "glue" cells in the brain that surround each neuron providing support, protection, and nourishment.

Gray matter. The thin but tough covering of the brain's cerebrum also known as the cerebral cortex.

Hippocampus. A brain structure that compares new learning to past learning and encodes information from working memory to long-term storage.

Immediate memory. A temporary memory where information is briefly processed and then either discarded or sent on to working memory.

Limbic area. The structures at the base of the cerebrum that control emotions.

Magnetic resonance imaging (MRI). An instrument that uses radio waves to disturb the alignment of the body's atoms in a magnetic field to produce computer-processed, high-contrast images of internal structures.

Mental lexicon. The collection of vocabulary words that one has and can readily access.

Mirror neurons. Clusters of neurons in the brain that fire not only when experiencing a task or emotion but also when seeing someone else experience the same task or emotion.

Mnemonic. A word or phrase used as a device for remembering unrelated information, patterns, or rules.

Motor cortex. The narrow band across the top of the brain from ear to ear that controls movement.

Myelin. A fatty substance that surrounds and insulates a neuron's axon.

Neuron. The basic cell making up the brain and nervous system, consisting of a globular cell body, a long fiber, called an axon, which transmits impulses, and many shorter fibers, called dendrites, which receive them.

Neuroplasticity. The brain's ability to continually reorganize itself based on input from the environment.

Neurotransmitter. One of about 100 chemicals stored in axon sacs that transmit impulses from neuron to neuron across the synaptic gap.

Orthography. The written system for a language.

Phonemes. The minimal units of sound in a language that combine to make syllables.

Phonemic awareness. The ability to deal explicitly and segmentally with sound units smaller than the syllable (i.e., the phoneme).

Phonological awareness. The ability to recognize the production and interpretation of the sound patterns (rather than the meaning) of language.

Positron emission tomography (PET) scanner. An instrument that traces the metabolism of radioactively tagged sugar in brain tissue producing a color image of cell activity.

Proprioceptors. Sensory cells in the skin, muscles, tendons, and joints that monitor the position of the limbs and head in space.

Prosody. The rhythm, cadence, accent patterns, and pitch of a language.

Rehearsal. The reprocessing of information in working memory.

Response to intervention. A method of determining whether students have learning difficulties by assessing their responses to the methods, strategies, curriculum, and interventions they encounter.

Retention. The preservation of a learning in long-term storage in such a way that it can be identified and recalled quickly and accurately.

Reticular activating system (RAS). The dense formation of neurons in the brainstem that controls major body functions and maintains the brain's alertness.

Synapse. The microscopic gap between the axon of one neuron and the dendrite of another.

Thalamus. A part of the limbic system that receives all incoming sensory information, except smell, and shunts it to other areas of the cortex for additional processing.

Transfer. The influence that past learning has on new learning, and the degree to which the new learning will be useful in the learner's future.

Visual magnocellular-deficit. A disorder of the visual processing system that leads to poor detection of visual motion, causing letters to bunch up or overlap during reading.

Visual word form area. Located at the boundary of the temporal and occipital lobes on the left side of the brain, this region plays an essential role in the visual analysis of letter and word shape.

Wernicke's area. A section in the left temporal lobe of the brain believed responsible for generating sense and meaning in an individual's native language.

White matter. The support tissue that lies beneath the cerebrum's gray matter (cortex).

Working memory. The temporary memory wherein information is processed consciously.

References

Ackerman, J. P., Riggins, T., & Black, M. M. (2010). A review of the effects of prenatal cocaine exposure among school-age children. *Pediatrics, 125,* 554–565.

Akechi, H., Senju, A., Kikuchi, Y., Tojo, Y., Osanai, H., & Hasegawa, T. (2010, August). The effect of gaze direction on the processing of facial expressions in children with autism spectrum disorder: An ERP study. *Neuropsychologia, 48*(10), 2841–2851.

Alim, S. (2009). Translocal style communities: Hip hop youth as cultural theorists of style, language, and globalization. *Pragmatics 19*(1), 103–128.

Allman, J. M., Tetreault, N. A., Hakeem, A. Y., Manaye, K. F., Semendeferi, K., Erwin, J. M., . . . Hof, P. R. (2011, April). The von Economo neurons in fronto-insular and anterior cingulate cortex. *Annals of the New York Academy of Sciences, 1225,* 59–71.

Alonso, M. A. P. (2015, February). Metacognition and sensorimotor components underlying the process of handwriting and keyboarding and their impact on learning. An analysis from the perspective of embodied psychology. *Procedia— Social and Behavioral Sciences, 176,* 263–269.

Alt, M., Meyers, C., Oglivie, T., Nicholas, K., & Arizmendi, G. (2014, November– December). Cross-situational statistically based word learning intervention for late-talking toddlers. *Journal of Communication Disorders, 52,* 207–220.

Álvarez, S., Ruiz, A., Suárez, J. A., Romero, S., Simal, P., Fernández-Liria, A., & Lahera, G. (2014). Emotion recognition deficit in patients with single right hemisphere damage. *European Psychiatry, 29,* Supplement 1, 1.

Anderson, L. M., Freeman, J. B., Franklin, M. E., & Sapyta, J. J. (2015, July). Family-based treatment of pediatric obsessive-compulsive disorder: Clinical considerations and application. *Child and Adolescent Psychiatric Clinics of North America, 24*(3), 535–555.

Andin, J., Fransson, P., Rönnberg, J., & Rudner, M. (2015, April). Phonology and arithmetic in the language–calculation network. *Brain and Language, 143,* 97–105.

Antshel, K. M., Faraone, S. V., & Gordon, M. (2014, August). Cognitive behavioral treatment outcomes in adolescent ADHD. *Journal of Attention Disorders, 18*(6), 483–495.

Ashkenazi, S., Black, J. M., Abrams, D. A., Hoeft, F., & Menon, V. (2013a). Neurobiological underpinnings of math and reading learning disabilities. *Journal of Learning Disabilities, 46*(6), 549–569.

Ashkenazi, S., Rosenberg-Lee, M., Metcalfe, A. W. S., Swigart, A. G., & Menon, V. (2013b, September). Visuo-spatial working memory is an important source of domain-general vulnerability in the development of arithmetic cognition. *Neuropsychologia, 51,* 2305–2317.

Augustyniak, K., Murphy, J., & Phillips, D. K. (2005, December). Psychological perspectives in assessing mathematics learning needs. *Journal of Instructional Psychology, 32,* 277–286.

Averill, O. H., Baker, D., & Rinaldi, C. (2014, September). A blueprint for effectively using RTI intervention block time. *Intervention in School and Clinic, 50*(1), 29–38.

Badcock, N. A., Bishop, D. V. M., Hardiman, M. J., Barry, J. G., & Watkins, K. E. (2012, March). Co-localisation of abnormal brain structure and function in specific language impairment. *Brain and Language, 120*(3), 310–320.

Baker, S., Chard, D., Ketterlin-Geller, L., Apichatabutra, C., & Doabler, C. (2009). Teaching writing to at-risk students: The quality of evidence for self-regulated strategy development. *Exceptional Children, 75,* 303–318.

Baker, S., Gersten, R., & Graham, S. (2003). Teaching expressive writing to students with learning disabilities: Research-based applications and examples. *Journal of Learning Disabilities, 36,* 109–123.

Banerjee, E., & Nandagopal, K. (2015, March). Does serotonin deficit mediate susceptibility to ADHD? *Neurochemistry International, 82,* 52–68.

Barbeau, E. B., Lewis, J. D., Doyon, J., Benali, H., Zeffiro, T. A., & Mottron, L. (2015). A greater involvement of posterior brain areas in interhemispheric transfer in autism: fMRI, DWI and behavioral evidences. *NeuroImage: Clinical, 8,* 267–280.

Baron-Cohen, S. (2003). *The essential difference: The truth about the male and female brain.* New York: Basic Books.

Baron-Cohen, S., Cassidy, S., Auyeung, B., Allison, C., Achoukhi, M., Robertson, S., . . . Lai, M. C. (2014, July). Attenuation of typical sex differences in 800 adults with autism vs. 3,900 controls. *PLoS One, 9*(7). doi: 10.1371

Bartlett, C. W., Flax, J. F., Logue, M. W., Vieland, V. J., Bassett, A. S., Tallal, P., & Brzustowicz. (2002, July). A major susceptibility locus for specific language impairment is located on 13q21. *American Journal of Human Genetics, 71,* 45–55.

Batten, L. A., Hernandez, M., Pilowsky, D. J., Stewart, J. W., Blier, P., Flament, M. F., . . . Weissman, M. M. (2012, November). Children of treatment-seeking depressed mothers: A comparison with the Sequenced Treatment Alternatives to Relieve Depression (STAR*D) child study. *Journal of the American Academy of Child & Adolescent Psychiatry, 51*(11), 1185–1196.

Baumeister, R. F., Campbell, J. D., Krueger, J. I., & Vohs, K. D. (2005, January). Exploding the self-esteem myth. *Scientific American, 292,* 84–91.

Beach, K. D., & O'Connor, R. E. (2015, March/April). Early response-to-intervention measures and criteria as predictors of reading disability in the beginning of third grade. *Journal of Learning Disabilities, 48*(2), 196–223.

Beaman, R., Wheldall, K., & Kemp, C. (2006). Differential teacher attention to boys and girls in the classroom. *Educational Review, 58,* 339–366.

Beauchamp, M. H., Ditchfield, M., Maller, J. J., Catroppa, C., Godfrey, C., Rosenfeld, J. V., . . . Anderson, V. A. (2011, April). Hippocampus, amygdala and global brain changes 10 years after childhood traumatic brain injury. *International Journal of Developmental Neuroscience, 29*(2), 137–143.

Bédard, A-C., Schulz, K. P., Cook Jr., E. H., Fan, J., Clerkin, S. M., Ivanov, I., . . . Newcorn, J. H. (2010, November). Dopamine transporter gene variation modulates activation of striatum in youth with ADHD. *NeuroImage, 53*(3), 935–942.

Beilock, S. L., Gunderson, E. A., Ramirez, G., & Levine, S. C. (2010). Female teachers' math anxiety affects girls' math achievement. *Proceedings of the National Academy of Sciences, 107*(5), 1860–1863.

Bellon-Harn, M. L. (2012, June). Dose frequency: Comparison of language outcomes in preschool children with language impairment. *Child Language Teaching and Therapy, 28*(2), 225–240.

Benítez-Burraco, A. (2010). Neurobiology and neurogenetics of dyslexia. *Neurología* [English edition], *25*(9), 563–581.

Berkeley, S., Marshak, L., Mastropieri, M. A., & Scruggs, T. E. (2011, March/April). Improving student comprehension of social studies text: A self-questioning strategy for inclusive middle school classes. *Remedial and Special Education, 32*(2), 105–113.

Bernard, S., Enayati, A., Redwood, L., Roger, H., & Binstock, T. (2001). Autism: A novel form of mercury poisoning. *Medical Hypotheses, 56,* 462–471.

Berninger, V. W., & May, M. O. (2011, March/April). Evidence-based diagnosis and treatment for specific learning disabilities involving impairments in written and/or oral language. *Journal of Learning Disabilities, 44*(2), 167–183.

Berninger, V. W., Nielsen, K. H., Abbott, R. D., Wijsman, E., & Raskind, W. (2008, April). Gender differences in severity of writing and reading disabilities. *Journal of School Psychology, 46*(2), 151–172.

Betancourt, L. M., Yang, W., Brodsky, N. L., Gallagher, P. R., Malmud, E. K., Giannetta, J. M., . . . Hurt, H. (2011, January-February). Adolescents with and without gestational cocaine exposure: Longitudinal analysis of inhibitory control, memory and receptive language. *Neurotoxicology and Teratology, 33*(1), 36–46.

Beyers, S. J., Lembke, E. S., & Curs, B. (2013, September). Social studies progress monitoring and intervention for middle school students. *Assessment for Effective Intervention, 38*(4), 224–235.

Bonifacci, P. (2004, September). Children with low motor ability have lower visual-motor integration ability but unaffected perceptual skills. *Human Movement Science, 23,* 157–168.

Borragán, G., Urbain, C., Schmitz, R., Mary, A., & Peigneux, P. (2015, April). Sleep and memory consolidation: Motor performance and proactive interference effects in sequence learning. *Brain and Cognition, 95,* 54–61.

Botts, D. C., Losardo, A. S., Tillery, C. Y., & Werts, M. G. (2014, August). A comparison of activity-based intervention and embedded direct instruction when teaching emergent literacy skills. *The Journal of Special Education, 48*(2), 120–134.

Boudah, D. J. (2014, January). The main idea strategy: A strategy to improve reading comprehension through inferential thinking. *Intervention in School and Clinic, 49*(3), 148–155.

Boutin, A., Panzer, S., & Blandin, Y. (2013, December). Retrieval practice in motor learning. *Human Movement Science, 32*(6), 1201–1213.

Boyd, B. A., Odom, S. L., Humphreys, B. P., & Sam, A. M. (2010, March). Infants and toddlers with autism spectrum disorder: Early identification and early intervention. *Journal of Early Intervention, 32*(2), 75–98.

Brannon, E. M., & van der Walle, G. (2001). Ordinal numerical knowledge in young children. *Cognitive Psychology, 43,* 53–81.

Brown, W. E., Eliez, S., Menon, V., Rumsey, J. M., White, C. D., & Reiss, A. L. (2001). Preliminary evidence of widespread morphological variations of the brain in dyslexia. *Neurology, 27,* 781–783.

Bruner, J. S. (1960). *The process of education.* Cambridge, MA: Belknap Press.

Bruster, B. (2015, Fall). Poetry and writing: Improving fluency and motivation for students with developmental dyslexic traits. *Reading Improvement, 52*(3), 93–99.

Buckner, R. L., Kelley, W. M., & Petersen, S. E. (1999, April). Frontal cortex contributions to human memory formation. *Nature Neuroscience, 2,* 311–314.

Burke, M. D., Hagan-Burke, S., Kwok, O., & Parker, R. (2009, February). Predictive validity of early literacy indicators from the middle of kindergarten to second grade. *Journal of Special Education, 42*(4), 209–226.

Burns, B. A., & Hamm, E. M. (2011). A comparison of concrete and virtual manipulative use in third- and fourth-grade mathematics. *School Science and Mathematics, 111*(6), 256–261.

Butterworth, B. (2010). Foundational numerical capacities and the origins of dyscalculia. *Trends in Cognitive Sciences, 14*(12), 534–541.

Byrne, B. (1991). Experimental analysis of the child's discovery of the alphabetic principle. In L. Riehen & C. Perfetti (Eds.), *Learning to read: Basic research and its implications* (pp. 75–84). Hillsdale, NJ: Erlbaum.

Camp, J. S., & Karmiloff-Smith, A. (2015). Williams Syndrome. *International Encyclopedia of the Social & Behavioral Sciences* (2nd ed.), 579–583.

Cappadocia, M. C., Desrocher, M., Pepler, D., & Schroeder, J. H. (2009, August). Contextualizing the neurobiology of conduct disorder in an emotion dysregulation framework. *Clinical Psychology Review, 29*(6), 506–518.

Careaga, M., Van de Water, J., & Ashwood, P. (2010, July). Immune dysfunction in autism: A pathway to treatment. *Neurotherapeutics, 7*(3), 283–292.

Carta, J. J., Greenwood, C. R., Atwater, J., McConnell, S. R., Goldstein, H., & Kaminski, R. A. (2014, December). Identifying preschool children for higher tiers of language and early literacy instruction within a response to intervention framework. *Journal of Early Intervention, 36*(4), 281–291.

Castellanos, F. X., Lee, P. P., Sharp, W., Jeffries, N. O., Greenstein, D. K., Clasen, L. S., . . . Rapoport, J. L. (2002, October). Developmental trajectories of brain volume abnormalities in children and adolescents with attention-deficit hyperactivity disorder. *Journal of the American Medical Association, 288,* 1740–1748.

Centers for Disease Control and Prevention (CDC). (2015). *Measles cases and outbreaks.* Atlanta, GA: Author.

Chait, M., Eden, G., Poeppel, D., Simon, J. Z., Hill, D. F., & Flowers, D. L. (2007, July). Delayed detection of tonal targets in background noise in dyslexia. *Brain and Language, 102*(1), 80–90.

Chaste, P., Klei, L., Sanders, S. J., Murtha, M. T., Hus, V., Lowe, J. K., . . . Kim, S.-J. (2013, October). Adjusting head circumference for covariates in autism: Clinical correlates of a highly heritable continuous trait. *Biological Psychiatry, 74*(8), 576–584.

Chen, Z., Xu, M., Shang, D., Peng, G., & Luo, B. (2014, July). Distinct representations of symbolic ordinality and quantity: Evidence from neuropsychological investigations in a Chinese patient with Gerstmann's syndrome. *Brain and Cognition, 88,* 14–20.

Cheour, M., Ceponiene, R., Lehtokoski, A., Luuk, A., Allik, J., Alho, K., & Naatanan, R. (1998, September). Development of language-specific phoneme representations in the infant brain. *Nature Neuroscience, 1,* 351–353.

Chomsky, N. (1965). *Aspects of the theory of syntax.* Cambridge: MIT Press.

Choudhury, N., & Benasich, A. A. (2003, April). A family aggregation study: The influence of family history and other risk factors on language development. *Journal of Speech, Language, and Hearing Research, 46,* 261–272.

Chow, B. W.-Y., Ho, C. S.-H., Wong, S. W.-L., Waye, M. M. Y., & Bishop, D. V. M. (2013, March). Generalist genes and cognitive abilities in Chinese twins. *Developmental Science, 16*(2), 260–268.

Christakis, D. A., Ebel, B. E., Rivara, F. P., & Zimmerman, F. J. (2004, November). Television, video, and computer game usage in children under 11 years of age. *Journal of Pediatrics, 145,* 652–656.

Cipolli, C., Mazzetti, M., & Plazzi, G. (2013, April). Sleep-dependent memory consolidation in patients with sleep disorders. *Sleep Medicine Reviews, 17*(2), 91–103.

Clowry, G. J. (2014, November). Seeking clues in brain development to explain the extraordinary evolution of language in humans. *Language Sciences, 46,* Part B, 220–231.

Coghlan, A. (2011, December). Abused children's brains work like those of soldiers. *New Scientist, 212*(2842), 12.

Cohen, L., Lehéricy, S., Henry, C., Bourgeois, M., Larroque, C., Sainte-Rose, C., . . . Hertz-Pannier, L. (2004, December). Learning to read without a left occipital lobe: Right-hemispheric shift of visual word form area. *Annals of Neurology, 56*(6), 890–894.

Cone-Wesson, B. (2005, July-August). Prenatal alcohol and cocaine exposure: Influences on cognition, speech, language, and hearing. *Journal of Communication Disorders, 38,* 279–302.

Cook, B. G., & Tankersley, M. G. (Eds.). (2013). *Research-based practices in special education*. Upper Saddle River, NJ: Pearson Education.

Cook, K. B., & Bennett, K. E. (2014, November/December). Writing interventions for high school students with disabilities: A review of single-case design studies. *Remedial and Special Education, 35*(6), 344–355.

Cordeiro, M. L., Farias, A. C., Cunha, A., Benko, C., R., Farias, L. G., Costa, M. T., . . . McCracken, J. T. (2011, August). Co-occurrence of ADHD and high IQ: A case series empirical study. *Journal of Attention Disorders, 15*(6), 485–490.

Corradini, A., & Antonietti, A. (2013, September). Mirror neurons and their function in cognitively understood empathy. *Consciousness and Cognition, 22*(3), 1152–1161.

Cortiella, C., & Horowitz, S. H. (2014). *The state of learning disabilities: Facts, trends and emerging issues*. New York: National Center for Learning Disabilities.

Crane, L., Pring, L., Ryder, N., & Hermelin, B. (2011). Executive functions in savant artists with autism. *Research in Autism Spectrum Disorders, 5*(2), 790–797.

Crepeau-Hobson, F., & Bianco, M. (2013, January). Response to intervention: Promises and pitfalls for gifted students with learning disabilities. *Intervention in School and Clinic, 48*(3), 142–151.

Cubillo, A., Halari, R., Smith, A., Taylor, E., & Rubia, K. (2012, February). A review of fronto-striatal and fronto-cortical brain abnormalities in children and adults with Attention Deficit Hyperactivity Disorder (ADHD) and new evidence for dysfunction in adults with ADHD during motivation and attention. *Cortex, 48*(2), 194–215.

D'Amico, A., & Guarnera, M. (2005). Exploring working memory in children with low arithmetical achievement. *Learning and Individual Differences, 15,* 189–202.

Dantzig, T. (1967). *Number: The language of science*. New York: Free Press.

Darki, F., Peyrard-Janvid, M., Matsson, H., Kere, J., & Klingberg, T. (2012, October). Three dyslexia susceptibility genes, DYX1C1, DCDC2, and KIAA0319, affect temporo-parietal white matter structure. *Biological Psychiatry, 72*(8), 671–676.

Datchuk, S. M., & Kubina, R. M. (2013, May/June). A review of teaching sentence-level writing skills to students with writing difficulties and learning disabilities. *Remedial and Special Education, 34*(3), 180–192.

Dehaene, S. (2009). *Reading in the brain*. New York: Viking.

Dehaene, S., Piazza, M., Pinel, P., & Cohen, L. (2003). Three parietal circuits for number processing. *Cognitive Neuropsychology, 20,* 487–506.

Delorme, R., Goussé, V., Roy, I., Trandafir, A., Mathieu, F., Mouren-Siméoni, M.-C., . . . Marion Leboyer, M., (2007, January). Shared executive dysfunctions in unaffected relatives of patients with autism and obsessive-compulsive disorder. *European Psychiatry, 22*(1), 32–38.

Dennis, E. L., Jahanshad, N., McMahon, K. L., de Zubicaray, G. I., Martin, N. G., Hickie, I. B., Toga, A. W., Wright, M. J., & Thompson, P. M. (2013, January). Development of brain structural connectivity between ages 12 and 30: A 4-Tesla diffusion imaging study in 439 adolescents and adults. *NeuroImage, 64*(1), 671–684.

de Nooij, J. C., Doobar, S., & Jessell, T. M. (2013, March). Etv1 inactivation reveals proprioceptor subclasses that reflect the level of NT3 expression in muscle targets. *Neuron, 77*(6), 1055–1068.

Denton, C. A. (2012, May/June). Response to intervention for reading difficulties in the primary grades: Some answers and lingering questions. *Journal of Learning Disabilities, 45*(3), 232–243.

Deshler, D. D. (2015, March/April). Moving in the right direction but at what speed, and how smoothly? *Remedial and Special Education, 36*(2), 72–76.

Deshler, D., Ellis, A., & Lenz, B. (1996). *Teaching adolescents with learning disabilities: Strategies and methods*. Denver, CO: Love.

De Smedt, B., Holloway, I. D., & Ansari, D. (2011, August). Effects of problem size and arithmetic operation on brain activation during calculation in children with varying levels of arithmetical fluency. *NeuroImage, 57*(3), 771–781.

De Visscher, A., Berens, S. C., Keidel, J. L, Noël, M.-P., & Bird, C. M. (2015, August). The interference effect in arithmetic fact solving: An fMRI study. *NeuroImage, 116*, 92–101.

Diagnostic and Statistical Manual of Mental Disorders-5 (DSM-5). (2013). Arlington, VA: American Psychiatric Association.

Dickerson, A. S., Rahbar, M. H., Han, I., Bakian, A. V., Bilder, D. A., . . . Baio, J. (2015, December). Autism spectrum disorder prevalence and proximity to industrial facilities releasing arsenic, lead or mercury. *Science of the Total Environment, 536*, 245–251.

Dinehart, L. H. B., & Manfra, L. (2013). Association between early fine motor development and later math and reading achievement in early elementary school. *Early Education and Development 24*(2): 138–161.

Dixon, L. Q., Zhao, J., Shin, J-Y., Wu, S., Su, J-H., Burgess-Brigham, R., . . . Snow, C. (2012, March). What we know about second language acquisition: A synthesis from four perspectives. *Review of Educational Research, 82*(1), 5–60.

Downs, A., & Downs, R. C. (2013, December). Training new instructors to implement discrete trial teaching strategies with children with autism in a community-based intervention program. *Focus on Autism and Other Developmental Disabilities, 28*(4), 212–221.

Dudley-Marling, C., & Paugh, P. C. (2009). *A classroom teacher's guide to struggling writers.* Portsmouth, NH: Heineman.

Dukes, C., Darling, S. M., & Doan, K. (2014, February). Selection pressures on special education teacher preparation: Issues shaping our future. *Teacher Education and Special Education, 37*(1), 9–20.

Dulaney, S. K., (2013, March). A middle school's response-to-intervention journey: Building systematic processes of facilitation, collaboration, and implementation. *NASSP Bulletin, 97*(1), 53–77.

Durand, V. M., Hieneman, M., Clarke, S., Wang, M., & Rinaldi, M. L. (2013, July). Positive family intervention for severe challenging behavior: A multisite randomized clinical trial. *Journal of Positive Behavior Interventions, 15*(3), 133–143.

Dweck, C. (2014, December/ 2015, January). Teachers' mindsets: "Every student has something to teach me": Feeling overwhelmed? Where did your natural teaching talent go? Try pairing a growth mindset with reasonable goals, patience, and reflection instead. It's time to get gritty and be a better teacher. *Educational Horizons, 93*(2), 10–15.

Eckert, M. M., Leonard, C. M., Richards, T. L., Aylward, E. H., Thomson, J., & Berninger, V. W. (2003). Anatomical correlates of dyslexia: Frontal and cerebellar findings. *Brain, 126*, 482–494.

Edmonds, M. S., Vaughn, S., Wexler, J., Reutenbuch, C., Cable, A., & Tackett, K. K., (2009, Spring). A synthesis of reading interventions and effects on reading comprehension outcomes for older struggling readers. *Review of Educational Research, 79*(1), 262–300.

El-Daw, B., & Hammoud, H. (2015, May). The effect of building up self-esteem training on students' social and academic skills. *Procedia—Social and Behavioral Sciences, 190*(21), 146–155.

El-Fishawy, P., & State, M. W. (2010, March). The genetics of autism: Key issues, recent findings, and clinical implications. *Psychiatric Clinics of North America, 33*(1), 83–105.

Ellis, E. S., Deshler, D. D., Lenz, B. K., Schumaker, J. B., & Clark, F. L. (1991). An instructional model for teaching learning strategies. *Focus on Exceptional Children, 23*(6), 1–24.

Environmental Protection Agency (2014, December). *Mercury.* Fact sheet retrieved from http://www.epa.gov/mercury/effects.htm.

Etmanskie, J. M., Partanen, M., & Siegel, L. S. (2014, March). A longitudinal examination of the persistence of late emerging reading disabilities. *Journal of Learning Disabilities,* 1–15.

Evans, A. C. (2006, March). The NIH MRI study of normal brain development. *NeuroImage, 30,* 184–202.

Fabiano, G. A., Pelham Jr., W. E., Coles, E. K., Gnagy, E. M., Chronis-Tuscano, A., & O'Connor, B. C. (2009, March). A meta-analysis of behavioral treatments for attention-deficit/hyperactivity disorder. *Clinical Psychology Review, 29*(2), 129–140.

Fadiga, L., Craighero, L., & Olivier, E. (2005, March). Human motor cortex excitability during the perception of others' action. *Current Opinion in Neurobiology, 15,* 213–218.

Fahsl, A. J., & McAndrews, S. L. (2012, March). Journal writing: Support for students with learning disabilities. *Intervention in School and Clinic, 47*(4), 234–244.

Fairchild, G., Toschi, N., Hagan, C. C., Goodyer, I. M., Calder, A. J., & Passamonti, L. (2015). Cortical thickness, surface area, and folding alterations in male youths with conduct disorder and varying levels of callous–unemotional traits. *NeuroImage: Clinical, 8,* 253–260.

Farkas, R. D. (2003, September-October). Effects of traditional versus learning-styles instructional methods on middle school students. *Journal of Educational Research, 97,* 42–52.

Fassbender, C., & Schweitzer, J. B. (2006). Is there evidence for neural compensation in attention-deficit hyperactivity disorder? A review of the functional neuroimaging literature. *Clinical Psychology Review, 26,* 445–465.

Feder, K., & Majnemer, A. (2007). Handwriting development, competency, and intervention. *Developmental Medicine & Child Neurology 49*(4): 312–317.

Fegen, D., Buchsbaum, B. R., & D'Esposito, M. (2015, January). The effect of rehearsal rate and memory load on verbal working memory. *NeuroImage, 105*(15), 120–131.

Feifer, S. G. (2008, November). Integrating response to intervention (RTI) with neuropsychology: A scientific approach to reading. *Psychology in the Schools, 45*(9), 812–825.

Feil, E. G., Frey, A., Walker, H. M., Small, J. W., Seeley, J. R., Golly, A., & Forness, S. R. (2014, September). The efficacy of a home-school intervention for preschoolers with challenging behaviors: A randomized controlled trial of preschool first step to success. *Journal of Early Intervention, 36*(3), 151–170.

Fienup, D. M., Shelvin, K. H., & Doepke, K. (2013, December). Increasing recall of information of children diagnosed with Asperger's Syndrome: Utilization of visual strategies. *Research in Autism Spectrum Disorders, 7*(12), 1647–1652.

Fiez, J. A., Tranel, D., Seager-Frerichs, D., & Damasio, H. (2006). Specific reading and phonological processing deficits are associated with damage to the left frontal operculum. *Cortex, 42,* 624–643.

Finger, E. C., Marsh, A., Blair, K., Reid, M., Sims, C., Ng, P., Pine, D., & Blair, R. (2011). Disrupted reinforcement signaling in the orbitofrontal cortex and caudate in youths with conduct disorder or oppositional defiant disorder and a high level of psychopathic trait. *American Journal of Psychiatry 168*(2), 152–162.

Finger, E. C., Marsh, A., Blair, K. S., Majestic, C., Evangelou, I., Gupta, K., . . . Blair, R. J. (2012, June). Impaired functional but preserved structural connectivity in limbic white matter tracts in youth with conduct disorder or oppositional defiant disorder plus psychopathic traits. *Psychiatry Research: Neuroimaging, 202*(3), 239–244.

Fisher, D., & Frey, N. (2013, March/April). Implementing RTI in a high school: A case study. *Journal of Learning Disabilities, 46*(2), 99–114.

Fisher, S. E., & DeFries, J. C. (2002). Developmental dyslexia: Genetic dissection of a complex cognitive trait. *Nature Reviews Neuroscience, 30,* 767–780.

Food and Drug Administration. (2014). *Strattera medication guide.* Retrieved from http://www.fda.gov/downloads/Drugs/DrugSafety/UCM089138.pdf.

Forsyth, D. R., Kerr, N. A., Burnette, J. L., & Baumeister, R. F. (2007). Attempting to improve the academic performance of struggling college students. *Journal of Social and Clinical Psychology, 26*(4), 447–459.

Franceschini, G., Galli, S., Chiesi, F., & Primi, C. (2014, May). Implicit gender–math stereotype and women's susceptibility to stereotype threat and stereotype lift. *Learning and Individual Differences, 32,* 273–277.

Frankenberger, C. (2015). *Technology: Livescribe smartpen.* Retrieved from http://dyslexia.yale.edu/2014TabletComparison.html.

Freeman, J., Simonsen, B., McCoach, D. B., Sugai, G., Lombardi, A., & Horner, R. (2015, April). Relationship between school-wide positive behavior interventions and supports and academic, attendance, and behavior outcomes in high schools. *Journal of Positive Behavior Interventions.* doi: 10.1177/1098300715580992

Frith, U. (1985). Beneath the surface of developmental dyslexia. In K. E. Patterson, J. C. Marshall, & M. Coltheart (Eds.), *Surface dyslexia: Cognitive and neuropsychological studies of phonological reading* (pp. 301–330). Hillsdale, NJ: Erlbaum.

Fuchs, D., Compton, D. L., Fuchs, L. S., Bouton, B., & Caffrey, E. (2011, July/August). The construct and predictive validity of a dynamic assessment of young children learning to read: Implications for RTI frameworks. *Journal of Learning Disabilities, 44*(4), 339–347.

Fuchs, D., Fuchs, L. S., Compton, D. L. (2012). Smart RTI: A next-generation approach to multilevel prevention. *Exceptional Children, 78*(3), 263–279.

Fuchs, L. S., Compton, D. L., Fuchs, D., Paulsen, K., Bryant, J. D., & Hamlett, C. L. (2005, August). The prevention, identification, and cognitive determinants of math difficulty. *Journal of Educational Psychology, 97,* 493–513.

Fujino, J., Yamasaki, N., Miyata, J., Sasaki, H., Matsukawa, N., Takemura, A., . . . Murai, T. (2015, March). Anterior cingulate volume predicts response to cognitive behavioral therapy in major depressive disorder. *Journal of Affective Disorders, 174,* 397–399.

Fukumoto, A., Hashimoto, T., Mori, K., Tsuda, Y., Arisawa, K., & Kagami, S. (2011, August). Head circumference and body growth in autism spectrum disorders. *Brain and Development, 33*(7), 569–575.

Gabriele, S., Sacco, R., & Persico, A. M. (2014, June). Blood serotonin levels in autism spectrum disorder: A systematic review and meta-analysis. *European Neuropsychopharmacology, 24*(6), 919–929.

Gautam, P., Warner, T. D., Kan, E. C., & Sowell, E. R. (2015). Executive function and cortical thickness in youths prenatally exposed to cocaine, alcohol and tobacco. *Developmental Cognitive Neuroscience, 16,* 155–165.

Geary, D. C., Hoard, M. K., & Bailey, D. H. (2012, July/August). Fact retrieval deficits in low achieving children and children with mathematical learning disability. *Journal of Learning Disabilities, 45,* 291–307.

Geiger, G., Cattaneo, C., Galli, R., Pozzoli, U., Lorusso, M., Facoetti, A., & Molteni, M. (2008). Wide and diffuse perceptual modes characterize dyslexics in vision and audition. *Perception, 37*(11), 1745–1764.

Gerdes, A. C., Haack, L. M., & Schneider, B. W. (2012, February). Parental functioning in families of children with ADHD: Evidence for behavioral parent training and importance of clinically meaningful change. *Journal of Attention Disorders, 16*(2), 147–156.

Gersten, R., Chard, D. J., Jayanthi, M., Baker, S. K., Morphy, P., & Flojo, J. (2009, September). Mathematics instruction for students with learning disabilities:

A meta-analysis of instructional components. *Review of Educational Research, 79,* 1202–1242.

Giedd, J. N. (2015, September). The amazing teen brain. *Scientific American, 312*(6), 33–37.

Giedd, J. N., Blumenthal, J., Jeffries, N. O., Castellanos, F. X., Liu, H., Zijdenbos, A., Paus, T., Evans, A. C., & Rapoport, J. L. (1999). Brain development during childhood and adolescence: A longitudinal MRI study. *Nature Neuroscience, 2,* 861–863.

Gilliam, M., Stockman, M., Malek, M., Sharp, W., Greenstein, D., Lalonde, F., . . . Shaw, P. (2011, May 1). Developmental trajectories of the corpus callosum in attention-deficit/hyperactivity disorder. *Biological Psychiatry, 69*(9), 839–846.

Giraldo-Chica, M., Hegarty II, J. P., & Schneider, K. A. (2015). Morphological differences in the lateral geniculate nucleus associated with dyslexia. *NeuroImage: Clinical, 7,* 830–836.

Gizer, I. R., Ficks, C., & Waldman, I. D. (2009, July). Candidate gene studies of ADHD: A meta-analytic review. *Human Genetics, 126*(1), 51–90.

Glover, V. (2015). Stress: Effects on neonatal and child development. *International Encyclopedia of the Social & Behavioral Sciences (Second Edition),* 556–561.

Gongola, L., & Sweeney, J. (2012, January). Discrete trial teaching: Getting started. *Intervention in School and Clinic, 47*(3), 183–190.

Gordillo, W. J. (2015). *10 trends to watch in special education.* Oakland, CA: Scientific Learning. Retrieved from http://www.scilearn.com/blog/2015-special-education-trends.

Goswami, D. B., Jernigan, C. S., Chandran, A., Iyo, A. H., May, W. L., Austin, M. C., . . . Karolewicz, B. (2013, June). Gene expression analysis of novel genes in the prefrontal cortex of major depressive disorder subjects. *Progress in Neuro-Psychopharmacology and Biological Psychiatry, 43*(3), 126–133.

Graham, S. A., & Fisher, S. E. (2013). Decoding the genetics of speech and language. *Current Opinion in Neurobiology, 23*(1), 43–51.

Graham, S., & Harris, K. R. (2005). Improving the writing performance of young struggling writers. *Journal of Special Education, 39,* 19–33.

Graves, A., Brandon, R., Duesbery, L., McIntosh, A., & Pyle, N. (2011). The effects of Tier 2 literacy instruction in sixth grade: Toward the development of a response to intervention model in middle school. *Learning Disability Quarterly, 34,* 73–86.

Gray, K. A., Day, N. L., Leech, S., & Richardson, G. A. (2005, May-June). Prenatal marijuana exposure: Effect on child depressive symptoms at ten years of age. *Neurotoxicology and Teratology, 27,* 439–448.

Gray, S., Reiser, M., & Brinkley, S. (2012, February). Effect of onset and rhyme primes in preschoolers with typical development and specific language impairment. *Journal of Speech, Language, and Hearing Research, 55*(1), 32–44.

Green, C., Dissanayake, C., & Loesch, D. (2015, June). A review of physical growth in children and adolescents with Autism Spectrum Disorder. *Developmental Review, 36,* 156–178.

Grissmer, D. W., Grimm, K. J., Aiyer, S. M., Murrah, W. M., & Steele, J. S. (2010, September). Fine motor skills and early comprehension of the world: Two new school readiness indicators. *Developmental Psychology 46* (5), 1008–1017.

Gu, F., Chauhan, V., & Chauhan, A. (2013, December). Impaired synthesis and antioxidant defense of glutathione in the cerebellum of autistic subjects: Alterations in the activities and protein expression of glutathione-related enzymes. *Free Radical Biology and Medicine, 65,* 488–496.

Haase, J., & Brown, E. (2015, March). Integrating the monoamine, neurotrophin and cytokine hypotheses of depression—A central role for the serotonin transporter? *Pharmacology & Therapeutics, 147,* 1–11.

Haberstick, B. C., Smolen, A., & Hewitt, J. K. (2006, May). Family-based association of 5HTTLPR and aggressive behavior in a general population sample of children. *Biological Psychiatry, 59,* 836–843.

Hafström, O., Milerad, J., Sandberg, K. L., & Sundell, H. W. (2005, November). Cardiorespiratory effects of nicotine exposure during development. *Respiratory Physiology & Neurobiology, 149,* 325–341.

Hakvoort, B., van der Leij, A., Maurits, N., Maassen, B., & van Zuijen, T. L. (2015, February). Basic auditory processing is related to familial risk, not to reading fluency: An ERP study. *Cortex, 63,* 90–103.

Hall, L., & Kelley, E. (2014, November). The contribution of epigenetics to understanding genetic factors in autism. *Autism,18*(8), 872–881.

Hamilton, A. F. de C. (2013, January). Reflecting on the mirror neuron system in autism: A systematic review of current theories. *Developmental Cognitive Neuroscience, 3,* 91–105.

Hammock, E., Veenstra-VanderWeele, J., Yan, Z., Kerr, T. M., Morris, M., Anderson, G., . . . Jacob, S. (2012, July). Examining Autism Spectrum Disorders by biomarkers: Example from the oxytocin and serotonin systems. *Journal of the American Academy of Child & Adolescent Psychiatry, 51*(7), 712–721.

Han, T-U., Park, J., Domingues, C. F., Moretti-Ferreira, D., Paris, E., Sainz, E., . . . Drayna, D. (2014, September). A study of the role of the FOXP2 and CNTNAP2 genes in persistent developmental stuttering. *Neurobiology of Disease, 69,* 23–31.

Happé, F., & Vital, P. (2009, April). What aspects of autism predispose to talent? *Philosophical Transactions of the Royal Society B: Biological Sciences, 364*(1522), 1369–1375.

Harlacher, J. E., Potter, J. B., & Weber, J. M. (2015, March). A team-based approach to improving core instructional reading practices within response to intervention. *Intervention in School and Clinic, 50*(4), 210–220.

Harralson, H. H. (2013). Chapter 2—The Decline of Handwriting. *Developments in Handwriting and Signature Identification in the Digital Age,* 9–24.

Harrison, L. J., & McLeod, S. (2010). Risk and protective factors associated with speech and language impairment in a nationally representative sample of 4 to-5-year-old children. *Journal of Speech, Language, and Hearing Research, 53,* 508–529.

Harrop, C. (2015, August). Evidence-based, parent-mediated interventions for young children with autism spectrum disorder: The case of restricted and repetitive behaviors. *Autism, 19*(6), 662–672.

Hattie, J. (2011). *Visible learning for teachers: Maximizing impact on learning.* New York: Routledge.

Hawke, J. L., Olson, R. K., Willcutt, E. G., Wadsworth, S. J., & DeFries, J. C. (2009, August). Gender ratios for reading difficulties. *Dyslexia, 15*(3), 239–242.

Haworth, C. M. A., Kovas, Y., Harlaar, N., Hayiou-Thomas, M. E., Petrill, S. A., Dale, P. S., & Plomin, R. (2009, October). Generalist genes and learning disabilities: A multivariate genetic analysis of low performance in reading, mathematics, language and general cognitive ability in a sample of 8000 12-year-old twins. *Journal of Child Psychology and Psychiatry, 50*(10), 1318–1325.

Hedenius, M., Ullman, M. T., Alm, P., Jennische, M., & Persson, J. (2013). Enhanced recognition memory after incidental encoding in children with developmental dyslexia. *PLoS ONE 8*(5): e63998. doi:10.1371.

Heilman, K. M. (2002). *Matter of mind: A neurologist's view of brain-behavior relationships.* New York: Oxford University Press.

Heitzman-Powell, L. S., Buzhardt, J., Rusinko, L. C., & Miller, T. M. (2014, March). Formative evaluation of an ABA outreach training program for parents of children with autism in remote areas. *Focus on Autism and Other Developmental Disabilities, 29*(1), 23–38.

Helenius, P., Salmelin, R., Richardson, U., Leinonen, S., & Lyytinen, H. (2002). Abnormal auditory cortical activation in dyslexia 100 msec after speech onset. *Journal of Cognitive Neuroscience, 14,* 603–617.

Hennes, A.-K., Büyüknarci, Ö., Rietz, C., & Grünke, M. (2015, March). Helping children with specific learning disabilities to improve their narrative writing competence by teaching them to use the story maps strategy. *Insights into Learning Disabilities, 12*(1), 35–56.

Hill, J. G., & Dalton, B. (2013, October). Student math achievement and out-of-field teaching. *Educational Researcher, 42*(7), 403–405.

Hock, R., Kinsman, A., & Ortaglia, A. (2015, July). Examining treatment adherence among parents of children with autism spectrum disorder. *Disability and Health Journal, 8*(3), 407–413.

Horner, R. H., Kincaid, D., Sugai, G., Lewis, T., Eber, L., Barrett, S., . . . Johnson, N. (2014, October). Scaling up school-wide positive behavioral interventions and supports: Experiences of seven states with documented success. *Journal of Positive Behavior Interventions, 16*(4), 197–208.

Hossain, M. M., & Wiest, L. R. (2013). Collaborative middle school geometry through blogs and other web 2.0 technologies. *Journal of Computers in Mathematics and Science Teaching, 32*(3), 337–352.

Hughes, C., & Dexter, D. D. (2015). *Field studies of RTI programs, revised.* Available online at the RTI Action Network at http://www.rtinetwork.org/learn/research/field-studies-rti-programs.

Huizink, A. C. (2014, July). Prenatal cannabis exposure and infant outcomes: Overview of studies. *Progress in Neuro-Psychopharmacology and Biological Psychiatry, 52*(3), 45–52.

Iacoboni, M., Molnar-Szakacs, I., Gallese, V., Buccino, G., Mazziotta, J. C., & Rizzolatti, G. (2005). Grasping the intentions of others with one's own mirror neuron system. *PloS Biology, 3,* e79.

Iftene, F., Predescu, E., Stefan, S., & David, D. (2015, February). Rational-emotive and cognitive-behavior therapy (REBT/CBT) versus pharmacotherapy versus REBT/CBT plus pharmacotherapy in the treatment of major depressive disorder in youth; A randomized clinical trial. *Psychiatry Research, 225*(3), 687–694.

Individuals with Disabilities Education Improvement Act (IDEA) of 2004, PL 108–446, 20 U.S.C. §§ 1400 *et seq.*

International Dyslexia Association (IDA). (2015a). *Understanding dysgraphia.* Baltimore, MD: Author.

International Dyslexia Association (IDA). (2015b). *Dyslexia basics.* Retrieved from http://www.eida.org/fact-sheet-5/.

Irwin, M. R., Olmstead, R., & Carroll, J. E. (in press). Sleep disturbance, sleep duration, and inflammation: A systematic review and meta-analysis of cohort studies and experimental sleep deprivation. *Biological Psychiatry.*

Itahashi, T., Yamada, T., Nakamura, M., Watanabe, H., Yamagata, B., Jimbo, D., . . . Hashimoto, R., (2015). Linked alterations in gray and white matter morphology in adults with high-functioning autism spectrum disorder: A multimodal brain imaging study. *NeuroImage: Clinical, 7,* 155–169.

Jacobs, R. H., Warner, V., & Weissman, M. M. (2013, January). The impact of paternal and maternal depression on internalizing and externalizing disorders among offspring. *Comprehensive Psychiatry, 54*(1), e5.

James, K. H., & Engelhardt, L. (2012, December). The effects of handwriting experience on functional brain development in pre-literate children. *Trends in Neuroscience and Education, 1*(1), 32–42.

Jamieson, J. P., & Harkins, S. G. (2012, May). Distinguishing between the effects of stereotype priming and stereotype threat on math performance. *Group Processes and Intergroup Relations, 15,* 291–304.

Jepsen, J. R. M., Fagerlund, B., & Mortensen, E. L. (2009, May). Do attention deficits influence IQ assessment in children and adolescents with ADHD? *Journal of Attention Disorders, 12*(6), 551–562.

Johnson, D.W., & Johnson, R. T. (1989). Cooperative learning: What special educators need to know. *The Pointer, 33*, 5–10.

Jones, S. (2015). Dysgraphia accommodations and modifications. *LDOnline.* Retrieved from http://www.ldonline.org/article/6202/.

Jordan, N. C., & Levine, S. C. (2009). Socioeconomic variation, number competence, and mathematics learning difficulties in young children. *Developmental Disabilities Research Reviews, 15*, 60–68.

Just, M. A., Keller, T. A., Malave, V. L., Kana, R. K., & Varma, S. (2012, April). Autism as a neural systems disorder: A theory of frontal-posterior underconnectivity. *Neuroscience & Biobehavioral Reviews, 36*(4), 1292–1313.

Kaiser, M.-L, Schoemaker, M. M., Albaret, J.-M, & Geuze, R. H. (2015, January). What is the evidence of impaired motor skills and motor control among children with attention deficit hyperactivity disorder (ADHD)? Systematic review of the literature. *Research in Developmental Disabilities, 36*, 338–357.

Kalberg, J. R., Lane, K. L., Driscoll, S., & Wehby, J. (2011, November/December). Systematic screening for emotional and behavioral disorders at the high school level: A formidable and necessary task. *Remedial and Special Education, 32*(6), 506–520.

Kaminski, E., Hoff, M., Sehm, B., Taubert, M., Conde, V., Steele, C. J., Villringer, A., & Ragert, P. (2013, September). Effect of transcranial direct current stimulation (tDCS) during complex whole body motor skill learning. *Neuroscience Letters, 552*(27), 76–80.

Kang, C., & Drayna, D. (2012, November). A role for inherited metabolic deficits in persistent developmental stuttering. *Molecular Genetics and Metabolism, 107*(3), 276–280.

Kantor, P. T., Wagner, R. K., Torgesen, J. K., & Rashotte, C. A. (2011, July/August). Comparing two forms of dynamic assessment and traditional assessment of preschool phonological awareness. *Journal of Learning Disabilities, 44*(4), 313–321.

Kauffman, J. M. (2015, January/February). Opinion on recent developments and the future of special education. *Remedial and Special Education, 36*(1), 9–13.

Kaufman, N. K., Rohde, P., Seeley, J. R., Clarke, G. N., & Stice, E. (2005, February). Potential mediators of cognitive-behavioral therapy for adolescents with comorbid major depression and conduct disorder. *Journal of Consulting and Clinical Psychology, 73*, 38–46.

Kaushanskaya, M., Gross, M., & Buac, M. (2013, October). Gender differences in child word learning. *Learning and Individual Differences, 27*, 82–89.

Kavale, K. A., & Forness, S. R. (2000). What definitions of learning disability say and don't say: A critical analysis. *Journal of Learning Disabilities, 33*, 239–256.

Keenan, H. T., Hall, G. C., & Marshall, S. W. (2008). Early head injury and attention deficit hyperactivity disorder: Retrospective cohort study. *British Medical Journal, 337*, a1984.

Kennedy, M. J., Deshler, D. D., & Lloyd, J. W. (2015). Effects of multimedia vocabulary instruction on adolescents with learning disabilities. *Journal of Learning Disabilities, 48*(1), 22–38.

Kercood, S., Grskovic, J. A., Banda, D., & Begeske, J. (2014, October). Working memory and autism: A review of literature. *Research in Autism Spectrum Disorders, 8*(10), 1316–1332.

Kere, J. (2014, September). The molecular genetics and neurobiology of developmental dyslexia as model of a complex phenotype. *Biochemical and Biophysical Research Communications, 452*(2), 236–243.

Khowaja, K., & Salim, S. (2013, September). A systematic review of strategies and computer-based intervention (CBI) for reading comprehension of children with autism. *Research in Autism Spectrum Disorders, 7*(9), 1111–1121.

Kieffer, M. J. (2010, August/September). Socioeconomic status, English proficiency, and late-emerging reading difficulties. *Educational Researcher, 39*(6), 484–486.

Killgore, W. D. (2010). Effects of sleep deprivation on cognition. *Progress in Brain Research, 185,* 105–129.

Kim, S., Arora, M., Fernandez, C., Landero, J., Caruso, J., & Chen, A. (2013, October). Lead, mercury, and cadmium exposure and attention deficit hyperactivity disorder in children. *Environmental Research, 126,* 105–110.

King, C. A., Knox, M. S., Henninger, N., Nguyen, T. A., Ghaziuddin, N., Maker, A., & Hanna, G. L. (2006, February). Major depressive disorder in adolescents: Family psychiatric history predicts severe behavioral disinhibition. *Journal of Affective Disorders, 90,* 111–121.

Kirby, J. R., Silvestri, R., Allingham, B. H., Parrila, R., & LaFave, C. B. (2008). Learning strategies and study approaches of postsecondary students with dyslexia. *Journal of Learning Disabilities, 41*(1), 85–96.

Klassen, R., & Lynch, S. (2007). Self-efficacy from the perspective of adolescents with LD and their specialist teachers. *Journal of Learning Disabilities, 40,* 494–507.

Klingner, J. K., Vaughn, S., Arguelles, M. E., Hughes, M. T., & Leftwich, S. A. (2004, September-October). Collaborative strategic reading: "Real-world" lessons from classroom teachers. *Remedial and Special Education, 25,* 291–302.

Klintwall, L., Eldevik, S., & Eikeseth, S. (2015, January). Narrowing the gap: Effects of intervention on developmental trajectories in autism. *Autism, 19*(1), 53–63.

Kohnert, K. (2008). *Language disorders in bilingual children and adults.* San Diego, CA: Plural Publishing.

Kohnert, K., Windsor, J., & Ebert, K. D. (2009). Primary or "specific" language impairment and children learning a second language. *Brain and Language, 109*(2-3): 101–111.

Kolevzon, A., Lim, T., Schmeidler, J., Martello, T., Cook Jr., E. H., & Silverman, J. M. (2014, December). Self-injury in autism spectrum disorder: An effect of serotonin transporter gene promoter variants. *Psychiatry Research, 220*(3), 987–990.

Kolla, N. J., Gregory, S., Attard, S., Blackwood, N., & Hodgins, S. (2014, February). Disentangling possible effects of childhood physical abuse on gray matter changes in violent offenders with psychopathy. *Psychiatry Research: Neuroimaging, 221*(2), 123–126.

Kooijman, M. N., Bakker, H., Franco, O. H., Hofman, A., Taal, H. R., & Jaddoe, V. W. V. (2015). Fetal smoke exposure and kidney outcomes in school-aged children. *American Journal of Kidney Diseases, 66*(3), 412–420.

Kovshoff, H., Hastings, R. P., & Remington, B. (2011, September). Two-year outcomes for children with autism after the cessation of early intensive behavioral intervention. *Behavior Modification, 35*(5), 427–450.

Krumm, N., O'Roak, B. J., Shendure, J., & Eichler, E. E. (2014, February). A de novo convergence of autism genetics and molecular neuroscience. *Trends in Neurosciences, 37*(2), 95–105.

Kushki, A., Schwellnus, H., Ilyas, F., & Chau, T. (2011, May/June). Changes in kinetics and kinematics of handwriting during a prolonged writing task in children with and without dysgraphia. *Research in Developmental Disabilities, 32*(3), 1058–1064.

Lamm, C., & Majdandžić, J. (2015, January). The role of shared neural activations, mirror neurons, and morality in empathy—A critical comment. *Neuroscience Research, 90,* 15–24.

Landerl, K., Göbel, S. M., & Moll, K. (2013, June). Core deficit and individual manifestations of developmental dyscalculia (DD): The role of comorbidity. *Trends in Neuroscience and Education, 2,* 38–42.

Lane, K. L., Menzies, H. M., Barton-Arwood, S. M., Doukas, G. L., & Munton, S. M. (2005, Winter). Designing, implementing, and evaluating social skills interventions for elementary students: Step-by-step procedures based on actual school-based investigations. *Preventing School Failure, 49,* 18–26.

Larroque, B., Ancel, P.-Y., Marret, S., Marchand, L., André, M., & Arnaud, C. (2008, March). Neurodevelopmental disabilities and special care of 5-year-old children born before 33 weeks of gestation (the EPIPAGE study): A longitudinal cohort study. *The Lancet, 371*(9615), 813–820.

Laszlo, S., & Sacchi, E. (2015, June/July). Individual differences in involvement of the visual object recognition system during visual word recognition. *Brain and Language, 145–146,* 42–52.

Latterell, C. M. (2005, Fall). Social stigma and mathematical ignorance. *Academic Exchange Quarterly, 9,* 167–171.

Lavezzi, A. M., Ottaviani, G., & Matturri, L. (2005, November). Adverse effects of prenatal tobacco smoke exposure on biological parameters of the developing brainstem. *Neurobiology of Disease, 20,* 601–607.

Laycock, R., Crewther, D. P., & Crewther, S. G. (2012, July). Abrupt and ramped flicker-defined form shows evidence for a large magnocellular impairment in dyslexia. *Neuropsychologia, 50*(8), 2107–2113.

Learning Disabilities Association of America (LDA). (2006). Preventing antisocial behavior in disabled and at-risk students. *LDOnline* [Online]. Retrieved from http://www.ldonline.org/ld_indepth/add_adha/ ael_behavior.html

Lebel, C., Warner, T., Colby, J., Soderberg, L., Roussotte, F., Behnke, M., . . . Sowell, E. R. (2013, August). White matter microstructure abnormalities and executive function in adolescents with prenatal cocaine exposure. *Psychiatry Research: Neuroimaging, 213*(2), 161–168.

Lee, J., Kotsopoulos, D., Tumber, A., & Makosz, S. (2014, March). Gesturing about number sense. *Journal of Early Childhood Research,* Online: 1476718X13510914, 1–17.

Leggio, M. G., Chiricozzi, F. R., Clausi, S., Tedesco, A. M., & Molinari, M. (2011, January). The neuropsychological profile of cerebellar damage: The sequencing hypothesis. *Cortex, 47*(1), 137–144.

Lemer, C., Dehaene, S., Spelke, E., & Cohen, L. (2003). Approximate quantities and exact number words: Dissociable systems. *Neuropsychologia, 41,* 1942–1958.

Lenhart, A. (2015, April). *Teens, social media & technology overview 2015.* Washington, DC: Pew Research Center.

Lester, B., & Lagasse, L. (2010). Children of addicted women. *Journal of Addictive Diseases 29*(2), 259–276. doi:10.1080/10550881003684921

Lewis, B. A., Singer, L. T., Short, E. J., Minnes, S., Arendt, R., Weishampel, P., . . . Min, M. O. (2004, September-October). Four-year language outcomes of children exposed to cocaine in utero. *Neurotoxicology and Teratology, 26,* 617–627.

Li, D. (2007). Story mapping and its effects on writing fluency and word diversity in students with learning disabilities. *Learning Disabilities: A Contemporary Journal, 5*(1), 77–93.

Lin, L.-Y., Cherng, R.-J., Chen, Y.-J., Chen, Y.-J., & Yang, H-M. (2015, February). Effects of television exposure on developmental skills among young children. *Infant Behavior and Development, 38,* 20–26.

Liston, M. (2009). Different learning styles in mathematics teaching. *National Center for Excellence in Mathematics and Science Teaching: Resource and Research Guides, 1*(4), 1–4.

Little, S. G., & Akin-Little, A. (2015). Stress in childhood: Effects on development. *International Encyclopedia of the Social & Behavioral Sciences (Second Edition),* 570–576.

Liu, L., You, W., Wang, W., Guo, X., Peng, D., & Booth, J. (2013, June). Altered brain structure in Chinese dyslexic children. *Neuropsychologia, 51*(7), 1169–1176.

Logan, J. (2009). Dyslexic entrepreneurs: The incidence; their coping strategies and their business skills. *Dyslexia, 15*(4), 328–346.

Longcamp, M., Zerbato-Poudou, M. T., & Velay, J. L. (2005). The influence of writing practice on letter recognition in preschool children: A comparison between handwriting and typing. *Acta Psychologica 119*(1), 67–79.

Lopes, R., Nunes, R. G., Simões, M. R., Secca, M. F., & Leal, A. (2015, May). The Visual Word Form Area remains in the dominant hemisphere for language in late-onset left occipital lobe epilepsies: A postsurgery analysis of two cases. *Epilepsy & Behavior, 46*, 91–98.

Loren, R. E. A., Vaughn, A. J., Langberg, J. M., Cyran, J. E. M., Proano-Raps, T., Smolyansky, B. H., . . . Epstein, J. N. (2015, February). Effects of an 8-session behavioral parent training group for parents of children with ADHD on child impairment and parenting confidence. *Journal of Attention Disorders, 19*(2), 158–166.

Lorenzo, G., Pomares, J., & Lledó, A. (2013, March). Inclusion of immersive virtual learning environments and visual control systems to support the learning of students with Asperger syndrome. *Computers & Education, 62*, 88–101.

Los Angeles County Office of Education. (2015). *Phonemic awareness activities*. Retrieved from http://teams.lacoe.edu/documentation/classrooms/patti/k-1/activities/phonemic.html.

Lovett, B. J., & Sparks, R. L. (2013, July/August). The identification and performance of gifted students with learning disability diagnoses: A quantitative synthesis. *Journal of Learning Disabilities, 46*(4), 304–316.

Luby, J. L. (2015). Poverty's most insidious damage: The developing brain. *Journal of the American Medical Association Pediatrics*. Retrieved from http://archpedi.jamanetwork.com/article.aspx?articleid=2381540&resultClick=3.

Lum, J. A. G., Ullman, M. T., & Conti-Ramsden, G. (2015, March). Verbal declarative memory impairments in specific language impairment are related to working memory deficits. *Brain and Language, 142*, 76–85.

MacMahon, C., & Charness, N. (2014, April). Focus of attention and automaticity in handwriting. *Human Movement Science, 34*, 57–62.

Magzamen, S., Imm, P., Amato, M. S., Havlena, J. A., Anderson, H. A., Moore, C. F., & Kanarek, M. S. (2013, November). Moderate lead exposure and elementary school end-of-grade examination performance. *Annals of Epidemiology, 23* (11), 700–707.

Maloney, E. A., Waechter, S., Risko, E. F., & Fugelsang, J. A. (2012, June). Reducing the sex difference in math anxiety: The role of spatial processing ability. *Learning and Individual Differences, 22*(3), 380–384.

Mancl, D. B., Miller, S. P., & Kennedy, M. (2012). Using the concrete-representational-abstract sequence with integrated strategy instruction to teach subtraction with regrouping to students with learning disabilities. *Learning Disabilities Research and Practice, 27*(4), 152–166.

Marini, A., Gentili, C., Molteni, M., & Fabbro, F. (2014, December). Differential verbal working memory effects on linguistic production in children with Specific Language Impairment. *Research in Developmental Disabilities, 35*(12), 3534–3542.

Martens, B. K., Werder, C. S., Hier, B. O., & Koenig, E. A. (2013, March). Fluency training in phoneme blending: A preliminary study of generalized effects. *Journal of Behavioral Education, 22*(1), 16–36.

Martin, R. B., Cirino, P. T., Sharp, C., & Barnes, M. (2014, August). Number and counting skills in kindergarten as predictors of grade 1 mathematical skills. *Learning and Individual Differences, 34*, 12–23.

Martins, M. R. I., Bastos, J. A., Cecato, A. T., Araujo, M. L. S., Magro, R. R., & Alaminos, V. (2013, January/February). Screening for motor dysgraphia in public schools. *Jornal de Pediatria, 89*(1), 70–74.

Mazzocco, M. M. M., & Hanich, L. B. (2010, April). Math achievement, numerical processing, and executive functions in girls with Turner syndrome: Do girls with Turner syndrome have math learning disability? *Learning and Individual Differences, 20,* 70–81.

McCallum, R. S., Bell, S. M., Coles, J. T., Miller, K. C., Hopkins, M. B., & Hilton-Prillhart, A. (2013, October). A model for screening twice-exceptional students (gifted with learning disabilities) within a response to intervention paradigm. *Gifted Child Quarterly, 57*(4), 209–222.

McGee, L., & Ukrainetz, T. (2009). Using scaffolding to teach phonemic awareness in preschool and kindergarten. *The Reading Teacher, 62,* 599–603.

McKeague, I. W., Brown, A. S., Bao, Y., Hinkka-Yli-Salomäki, S., Huttunen, J., & Sourander, A. (2015, May). Autism with intellectual disability related to dynamics of head circumference growth during early infancy. *Biological Psychiatry, 77*(9), 833–840.

McNamara, J. K., Scissons, M., & Gutknecht, N. (2011, September/October). A longitudinal study of kindergarten children at risk for reading disabilities: The poor really are getting poorer. *Journal of Learning Disabilities, 44*(5), 421–430.

Meaux, E., & Vuilleumier, P. (2015). Emotion perception and elicitation. *Brain Mapping, 3,* 79–90.

Meersma, B. (2015). *A dyslexic student's perspective: Which tablet features work best for dyslexics?* Retrieved from http://dyslexia.yale.edu/2014TabletComparison.html.

Melin, K. H., Skärsäter, I., Haugland, B. S. M., & Ivarsson, T. (2015, July). Treatment and 12-month outcome of children and adolescents with obsessive–compulsive disorder: A naturalistic study. *Journal of Obsessive-Compulsive and Related Disorders, 6,* 1–6.

Miller-Loncar, C., Lester, B. M., Seifer, R., Lagasse, L. L., Bauer, C. R., Shankaran, S., . . . Liu, J. (2005, March-April). Predictors of motor development in children prenatally exposed to cocaine. *Neurotoxicology and Teratology, 27,* 231–220.

Millichap, J. G. (2008, February). Etiologic classification of attention-deficit/hyperactivity disorder. *Pediatrics, 121*(2), e358–365.

Minjarez, M. B., Mercier, E. M., Williams, S. E., & Hardan, A. Y. (2013, April). Impact of pivotal response training group therapy on stress and empowerment in parents of children with autism. *Journal of Positive Behavior Interventions, 15*(2), 71–78.

Moeller, K., Neuburger, S., Kaufmann, L., Landerl, K., & Nuerk, H.-C. (2009). Basic number processing deficits in developmental dyscalculia: Evidence from eye tracking. *Cognitive Development, 24*(4), 371–386.

Moll, K., Snowling, M. J., Göbel, S. M., & Hulme, C. (2015, August). Early language and executive skills predict variations in number and arithmetic skills in children at family-risk of dyslexia and typically developing controls. *Learning and Instruction, 38,* 53–62.

Montes, L. G. A., Alcántara, H. P., García, R. B. M., De La Torre, L. B., Acosta, D. A., & Duarte, M. G. (2013, November). Brain cortical thickness in ADHD: Age, sex, and clinical correlations. *Journal of Attention Disorders, 17*(8), 641–654.

Monuteaux, M. C., Faraone, S. V., Herzig, K., Navsaria, N., & Biederman, J. (2005, January-February). ADHD and dyscalculia: Evidence for independent familial transmission. *Journal of Learning Disabilities, 38,* 86–93.

Moon, R. Y. (2013). *Sleep: What every parent needs to know.* Elk Grove Village, IL: American Academy of Pediatrics.

Morgan, H. (2015, Spring). Creating a class blog: A strategy that can promote collaboration, motivation, and improvement in literacy. *Reading Improvement, 52*(1), 27–31.

Mossabeb, R., Wade, K. C., Finnegan, K., Sivieri, E., & Abbasi, S. (2012, July). Language development survey provides a useful screening tool for language delay in preterm infants. *Clinical Pediatrics, 51*(7), 638–644.

Mueller, P. A., & Oppenheimer, D. M. (2014, June). The pen is mightier than the keyboard: Advantages of longhand over laptop note taking. *Psychological Science, 25,* 1159–1168.

Mussolin, C., Mejias, S., & Noël, M.-P. (2010, April). Symbolic and nonsymbolic number comparison in children with and without dyscalculia. *Cognition, 115,* 10–25.

National Assessment of Educational Progress (NAEP). (2012). *The nation's report card: Trends in academic progress 2012.* Washington, DC: National Center for Education Statistics.

National Assessment of Educational Progress (NAEP). (2015). *The nation's report card: Trends in academic progress 2015: Mathematics assessments.* Washington, DC: National Center for Education Statistics.

National Association for the Education of Young Children (NAEYC). (2009). *Learning to read and write.* Retrieved from http://www.naeyc.org/files/naeyc/file/positions/WWSSLearningToReadAndWriteEnglish.pdf.

National Association of School Psychologists (NASP). (2015). *Implementing RTI.* Retrieved from http://www.nasponline.org.

National Center for Education Statistics (NCES). (2014). *Digest of Education Statistics, 2014.* Washington, DC: Author.

National Center for Education Statistics. (2015, April). *Charter school enrollment.* Washington, DC: Author.

National Center for Learning Disabilities (NCLD). (2015). *Learn about RTI.* Retrieved from http://www.rtinetwork.org.

National Center on Response to Intervention (NCRTI). (2010, March). *Essential components of RTI—A closer look at response to intervention.* Washington, DC: U.S. Department of Education, Office of Special Education Programs.

National Governors Association Center for Best Practices & Council of Chief State School Officers. (2010). *Common Core State Standards for Mathematics.* Washington, DC: Author. Retrieved from http://www.corestandards.org/math/

National Institute of Mental Health (NIMH). (2015a). *Anxiety disorders.* Bethesda, MD: Author.

National Institute of Mental Health (NIMH). (2015b). *What is obsessive-compulsive disorder?* Bethesda, MD: Author.

National Institute of Mental Health (NIMH). (2015c). *What is post-traumatic stress disorder (PTSD)?* Bethesda, MD: Author.

National Institute of Mental Health (NIMH). (2015d). *Depression.* Bethesda, MD: Author.

National Institute of Mental Health (NIMH). (2015e). *What are eating disorders?* Bethesda, MD: Author.

National Institute of Mental Health (NIMH). (2015f). *Autism spectrum disorder.* Bethesda, MD: Author.

National Institute on Alcohol Abuse and Alcoholism (NIAAA). (2015, April). *Fetal alcohol exposure.* Bethesda, MD: Author.

National Institute on Deafness and Other Communication Disorders (NIDCD). (2010a, September). *Speech and language: Developmental milestones.* Bethesda, MD: Author.

National Institute on Deafness and Other Communication Disorders (NIDCD). (2010b). *Stuttering.* Bethesda, MD: Author.

National Institute on Drug Abuse. (2014). *Drug facts: Stimulant ADHD medications: Methylphenidate and amphetamines.* Retrieved from http://www.drugabuse.gov/publications/drugfacts/stimulant-adhd-medications-methylphenidate-amphetamines.

National Reading Panel (NRP). (2000). *Teaching children to read: An evidence-based assessment of the scientific research literature and its implications for reading instruction.* Washington, DC: National Institute of Child Health and Human Development.

National Sleep Foundation (2014). *2014 Sleep in America poll: Sleep in the modern family.* Arlington, VA: Author.

Nelson, J. M., & Harwood, H. (2011, January/February). Learning disabilities and anxiety: A meta-analysis. *Journal of Learning Disabilities, 44*(1), 3–17.

Nelson, K. E., Welsh, J. A., Trup, E. M. V., & Greenberg, M. T. (2011, May). Language delays of impoverished preschool children in relation to early academic and emotion recognition skills. *First Language, 31*(2), 164–194.

Newbury, D. F., Monaco, A. P. (2010, October). Genetic advances in the study of speech and language disorders. *Neuron, 68*(2), 309–320.

Nicolson, R. I., & Fawcett, A. J. (2008). *Dyslexia, learning, and the brain.* Cambridge: The MIT Press.

Nicolson, R. I., & Fawcett, A. J. (2011, January). Dyslexia, dysgraphia, procedural learning and the cerebellum. *Cortex, 47*(1), 117–127.

Niessen, N. L., Strattman, K., & Scudder, R. (2011, February). The influence of three emergent literacy skills on the invented spellings of 4-year-olds. *Communication Disorders Quarterly, 32*(2), 93–102.

Nigg, J. T., Lewis, K., Edinger, T., & Falk. M. (2012, January). Meta-analysis of attention-deficit/hyperactivity disorder or attention-deficit/hyperactivity disorder symptoms, restriction diet, and synthetic food color additives. *Journal of the American Academy of Child & Adolescent Psychiatry, 51*(1), 86–97.

Noe, S., Spencer, T. D., Kruse, L., & Goldstein, H. (2014, May). Effects of a Tier 3 phonological awareness intervention on preschoolers' emergent literacy. *Topics in Early Childhood Special Education, 34*(1), 27–39.

Noll, B. (2013, March). Seven ways to kill RTI. *Phi Delta Kappan, 94*(6), 55–59.

Nomi, J. S., & Uddin, L. Q. (2015, May). Face processing in autism spectrum disorders: From brain regions to brain networks. *Neuropsychologia, 71*, 201–216.

Nomura, Y., Marks, D. J., & Halperin, J. M. (2010, September). Prenatal exposure to maternal and paternal smoking on attention deficit hyperactivity disorders symptoms and diagnosis in offspring. *Journal of Nervous and Mental Disease, 198*(9), 672–678.

Northwest Regional Educational Laboratory (NWREL). (2006). *6+1 Trait Writing.* Retrieved from http://www.nwrel.org/assessment.

Nosek, B. A., & Smyth, F. L. (2011, October). Implicit social cognitions predict sex differences in math engagement and achievement. *American Educational Research Journal, 48*(5), 1125–1156.

O'Brien, E. K., Zhang, X., Nishimura, C., Tomblin, J. B., & Murray, J. C. (2003, June). Association of specific language impairment (SLI) to the region of 7q31. *American Journal of Human Genetics, 72*, 1536–1543.

O'Connor, R. E., Bocian, K. M., Sanchez, V., & Beach, K. D. (2014, July/August). Access to a responsiveness to intervention model: Does beginning intervention in kindergarten matter? *Journal of Learning Disabilities, 47*(4), 307–328.

Oberman, L. M., Hubbard, E. M., McCleery, J. P., Altschuler, E. L., Ramachandran, V. S., & Pineda, J. A. (2005, July). EEG evidence for mirror neuron dysfunction in autism spectrum disorders. *Cognitive Brain Research, 24*, 190–198.

Olney, J. W. (2014). Focus on apoptosis to decipher how alcohol and many other drugs disrupt brain development. *Frontiers in Pediatrics, 2*(81). doi: 10.3389/fped.2014.00081

Oosterwijk, S., Lindquist, K. A., Anderson, E., Dautoff, R., Moriguchi, Y., & Barrett, L. F. (2012, September). States of mind: Emotions, body feelings, and thoughts share distributed neural networks. *NeuroImage, 62*(3), 2110–2128.

Pagani, L. S. (2014, July). Environmental tobacco smoke exposure and brain development: The case of attention deficit/hyperactivity disorder. *Neuroscience & Biobehavioral Reviews, 44*, 195–205.

Paiva, T., Gaspar, T., & Matos, M. G. (2015, April). Sleep deprivation in adolescents: Correlations with health complaints and health-related quality of life. *Sleep Medicine, 16*(4), 521–527.

Palincsar, A. S., & Brown, A. L. (1984). The reciprocal teaching of comprehension-fostering and comprehension-monitoring activities. *Cognition and Instruction, 1,* 117–175.

Palm, M. (2012, December/2013, January). First, do no harm. *Phi Delta Kappan, 94*(4), 13–15.

Papmeyer, M., Giles, S., Sussmann, J. E., Kielty, S., Stewart, T., Lawrie, S. M., . . . McIntosh, A. M. (2015, July). Cortical thickness in individuals at high familial risk of mood disorders as they develop major depressive disorder. *Biological Psychiatry, 78*(1), 58–66.

Paradis, J. (2010). The interface between bilingual development and specific language impairment. *Applied Psycholinguistics, 31,* 227–252.

Paradis, J., Genesee, F., & Crago, M. (2011). *Dual language development and disorders: A handbook on bilingualism and second language learning.* Baltimore, MD: Paul H. Brookes Publishing.

Parr, J. R., Gray, L., Wigham, S., McConachie, H., & Le Couteur, A. (2015, December). Measuring the relationship between the parental Broader Autism Phenotype, parent-child interaction, and children's progress following parent mediated intervention. *Research in Autism Spectrum Disorders, 20,* 24–30.

Passamonti, L., Fairchild, G., Goodyer, I., Hurford, G., Hagan, C., Rowe, J., & Calder, A. (2010). Neural abnormalities in early-onset and adolescence-onset conduct disorder. *Archives of General Psychiatry 67*(7), 729–738.

Pelligra, V., Isoni, A., Fadda, R., & Doneddu, G. (2015, August). Theory of mind, perceived intentions and reciprocal behaviour: Evidence from individuals with Autism Spectrum Disorder. *Journal of Economic Psychology, 49,* 95–107.

Peng, P., Congying, S., Beilei, L., & Sha, T. (2012, August). Phonological storage and executive function deficits in children with mathematics difficulties. *Journal of Experimental Child Psychology, 112,* 452–466.

Pennington, B. F., (1990). The genetics of dyslexia. *Journal of Child Psychology and Psychiatry, 31,* 193–201.

Perreault, C., & Mathew, S. (2012). Dating the origin of language using phonemic diversity. *PLoS One, 7*(4), e35289.

Petersen, D. B., Allen, M. M., & Spencer, T. D. (2014, June). Predicting reading difficulty in first grade using dynamic assessment of decoding in early kindergarten: A large-scale longitudinal study. *Journal of Learning Disabilities, 26,* 269–280.

Peterson, S. S. (2014, February). Supporting struggling writers. *What Works: Research into Practice, 49,* University of Toronto, 1–4.

Pew Research Center (2015). *Teens relationships survey.* Washington, DC: Author.

Philips, G. T., Kopec, A. M., & Carew, T. J. (2013, October). Pattern and predictability in memory formation: From molecular mechanisms to clinical relevance. *Neurobiology of Learning and Memory, 105,* 117–124.

Pieretti, R. A., Kaul, S. D., Zarchy, R. M., & O'Hanlon, L. M. (2015, May). Using a multimodal approach to facilitate articulation, phonemic awareness, and literacy in young children. *Communication Disorders Quarterly, 36*(3), 131–141.

Pinel, P., & Dehaene, S. (2013, November). Genetic and environmental contributions to brain activation during calculation. *NeuroImage, 81,* 306–316.

Pinker, S. (1994). *The language instinct: How the mind creates language.* New York: William Morrow.

Planton, S., Jucla, M., Roux, F. E., & Démonet, J. F. (2013, November/December). The "handwriting brain": A meta-analysis of neuroimaging studies of motor versus orthographic processes. *Cortex, 49*(10), 2772–2787. doi: 10.1016/j.cortex.2013.05.011

Platt, M. P., Adler, W. T., Mehlhorn, A. J., Johnson, G. C., Wright, K. A., Choi, R. T., . . . Rosen, G. D. (2013, September). Embryonic disruption of the candidate dyslexia susceptibility gene homolog Kiaa0319-like results in neuronal migration disorders. *Neuroscience, 248,* 585–593.

Plomin, R., & Kovas, Y. (2005, July). Generalist genes and learning disabilities. *Psychological Bulletin, 131,* 592–617.

Posner, M. I., Rothbart, M. K., & Rueda, M. R. (2013). Chapter 22—Developing attention and self-regulation in infancy and childhood. *Neural Circuit Development and Function in the Brain,* 395–411.

Price, G. R., & Ansari, D. (2013). Chapter 25—Developmental dyscalculia. *Handbook of Clinical Neurology, 111,* 241–244.

Printy, S. M., & Williams, S. M. (2015). Principals' decisions: Implementing response to intervention. *Educational Policy, 29*(1), 179–205.

Qin, Y., Carter, C. S., Silk, E. M., Stenger, A., Fissell, K., Goode, A., & Anderson, J. R. (2004, April). The change of the brain activation patterns as children learn algebra equation solving. *Proceedings of the National Academy of Sciences USA, 101,* 5686–5691.

Quinn, J. M., & Wagner, R. K. (2013). Gender differences in reading impairment and in the identification of impaired readers: Results from a large-scale study of at-risk readers. *Journal of Learning Disabilities, 48*(4), 433–445.

Rapcsak, S. Z., Beeson, P. M., Henry, M. L., Leyden, A., Kim, E., Rising, K., . . . Cho, H-S. (2009, May). Phonological dyslexia and dysgraphia: Cognitive mechanisms and neural substrates. *Cortex, 45*(5), 575–591.

Renvall, H., & Hari, R. (2002). Auditory cortical responses to speech-like stimuli in dyslexic adults. *Journal of Cognitive Neuroscience, 14,* 757–768.

Rescorla, L. (2009, February). Age 17 language and reading outcomes in late-talking toddlers: Support for a dimensional perspective on language delay. *Journal of Speech, Language, and Hearing Research, 52,* 16–30.

Rescorla, L., & Turner, H. L. (2015, April). Morphology and syntax in late talkers at age 5. *Journal of Speech, Language, and Hearing Research, 58,* 434–444.

Richards, T. L., Grabowski, T. J., Boord, P., Yagle, K., Askren, M., Mestre, Z., . . . Berninger, V. (2015). Contrasting brain patterns of writing-related DTI parameters, fMRI connectivity, and DTI–fMRI connectivity correlations in children with and without dysgraphia or dyslexia. *NeuroImage: Clinical, 8,* 408–421.

Richardson, G. A., Goldschmidt, L., Larkby, C., & Day, N. L. (2015, May–June). Effects of prenatal cocaine exposure on adolescent development. *Neurotoxicology and Teratology, 49,* 41–48.

Richter, J., Henze, R., Vomstein, K., Stieltjes, B., Parzer, P., Haffner, J., Brandeis, D., & Poustka, L. (2015). Reduced cortical thickness and its association with social reactivity in children with autism spectrum disorder. *Psychiatry Research: Neuroimaging, 234*(1), 15–24.

Ricketts, J., Dockrell, J. E., Patel, N., Charman, T., & Lindsay, G. (2015, June). Do children with specific language impairment and autism spectrum disorders benefit from the presence of orthography when learning new spoken words? *Journal of Experimental Child Psychology, 134,* 43–61.

Rimland, B. (2000). The autism epidemic, vaccinations and mercury. *Journal of Nutritional and Environmental Medicine, 10,* 261–266.

Ring, J. J., Barefoot, L. C., Avrit, K. J., Brown, S. A., & Black, J. L., (2013, March/April). Reading fluency instruction for students at risk for reading failure. *Remedial and Special Education, 34*(2), 102–112.

Ritchey, K. D., Silverman, R. D., Schatschneider, C., & Speece, D. L. (2015, May/June). Prediction and stability of reading problems in middle childhood. *Journal of Learning Disabilities, 48*(3), 298–309.

Roitman, J. D., Brannon, E. M., & Platt, M. L. (2012, May). Representation of numerosity in posterior parietal cortex. *Frontiers in Integrative Neuroscience, 6,* 1–9.

Rolland, R. G. (2012, December). Synthesizing the evidence on classroom goal structures in middle and secondary schools: A meta-analysis and narrative review. *Review of Educational Research, 82*(4), 396–435.

Roşca, E. C. (2009, November). Arithmetic procedural knowledge: A cortico-subcortical circuit. *Brain Research, 1302*, 148–156.

Rosen, S., Cohen, M., & Vanniasegaram, I. (2010, June). Auditory and cognitive abilities of children suspected of auditory processing disorder (APD). *International Journal of Pediatric Otorhinolaryngology, 74*(6), 594–600.

Rowe, K., Pollard, J., & Rowe, K. (2005). *Literacy, behavior, and auditory processing.* Paper presented at the Royal Australasian College of Physicians Scientific Meeting, May 8–11, 2005, Wellington, New Zealand.

Rumsey, J., Horwitz, B., Donohue, B. C., Nace, K. L., Maisog, J. M., & Andreason, P. (1999). A functional lesion in developmental dyslexia: Left angular gyral flow predicts severity. *Brain and Language, 70,* 187–204.

Sanders, E. J., Irvin, D. W., Belardi, K., McCune, L., Boyd, B. A., & Odom, S. L. (2015, March). The questions verbal children with autism spectrum disorder encounter in the inclusive preschool classroom. *Autism.* doi: 10.1177

Santos, N. F., & Costa, R. A. (2015, July/August). Parental tobacco consumption and child development. *Jornal de Pediatria, 91*(4), 366–372.

Scammacca, N. K., Roberts, G., Vaughn, S., & Stuebing, K. K. (2015, July/August). A meta-analysis of interventions for struggling readers in grades 4–12: 1980–2011. *Journal of Learning Disabilities, 48*(4), 369–390.

Schack, T., & Mechsner, F. (2006, January). Representation of motor skills in human long-term memory. *Neuroscience Letters, 391,* 77–81.

Schneps, M. H. (2015, January/February). The advantages of dyslexia. *Scientific American Mind, 26*(1), 24–25.

Schulte-Körne, G., & Bruder, J. (2010, November). Clinical neurophysiology of visual and auditory processing in dyslexia: A review. *Clinical Neurophysiology, 121*(110), 1794–1809.

Schultz, T. R., Schmidt, C. T., & Stichter, J. P. (2011, June). A review of parent education programs for parents of children with Autism Spectrum Disorders. *Focus on Autism and Other Developmental Disabilities, 26*(2), 96–104.

Schumacher, J., Anthoni, H., Dahdouh, F., Konig, I. R., Hillmer, A. M., Kluck, N., . . . Kere, J. (2006, January). Strong genetic evidence of DCDC2 as a susceptibility gene for dyslexia. *American Journal of Human Genetics, 78,* 52–62.

Scott, T., Anderson, C. M., & Alter, P. (2011). *Principles of positive behavior support in the classroom: Management of instruction and behavior.* New York: Pearson.

Sealander, K. A., Johnson, G. R., Lockwood, A. B., & Medina, C. M. (2012, December). Concrete–semiconcrete–abstract (CSA) instruction: A decision rule for improving instructional efficacy. *Assessment for Effective Intervention, 38*(1), 53–65.

Seminowicz, D. A., Mayberg, H. S., McIntosh, A. R., Goldapple, K., Kennedy, S., Segal, Z., & Rafi-Tari, S. (2004, May). Limbic-frontal circuitry in major depression: A path modeling meta-analysis. *NeuroImage, 22,* 409–418.

Semrud-Clikeman, M. (2005, November-December). Neuropsychological aspects for evaluating learning disabilities. *Journal of Learning Disabilities, 38,* 563–568.

Sexton, C. C., Gelhorn, H. L., Bell, J. A., & Classi, P. M. (2012, November/December). The co-occurrence of reading disorder and ADHD: Epidemiology, treatment, psychosocial impact, and economic burden. *Journal of Learning Disabilities, 45*(6), 538–564.

Shannon, T. R., & Polloway, E. A. (1993). Promoting error monitoring in middle school students with LD. *Intervention in School and Clinic, 28,* 60–164.

Sharma, M. (2006). *How children learn mathematics.* Framingham, MA: Center for Teaching/Learning Mathematics.

Shaw, P., Eckstrand, K., Sharp, W., Blumenthal, J., Lerch, J. P., Greenstein, D., . . . Rapoport, J. L. (2007, December 4). Attention-deficit/hyperactivity disorder is characterized by a delay in cortical maturation. *Proceedings of the National Academy of Sciences, 104*(49), 19649–19654.

Shaw, P., Malek, M., Watson, B., Sharp, W., Evans, A., & Greenstein, D. (2012, August 1). Development of cortical surface area and gyrification in attention-deficit/hyperactivity disorder. *Biological Psychiatry,72*(3), 191–197.

Shaywitz, S.E. (2003). *Overcoming dyslexia: A new and complete science-based program for reading problems at any level.* New York: Knopf.

Short, M. A., & Louca, M. (2015, August). Sleep deprivation leads to mood deficits in healthy adolescents. *Sleep Medicine, 16*(8), 987–993.

Silver, L. (2008). *How do you know if your child might have a learning disability?* Retrieved from http://www.ldonline.org.

Singh, L. (2008, February). Influences of high and low variability on infant word recognition. *Cognition, 106*(2), 833–870.

Siok, W. T., Spinks, J. A., Jin, Z., & Tan, L. H. (2009). Developmental dyslexia is characterized by the co-existence of visuospatial and phonological disorders in Chinese children. *Current Biology, 19*, 890–892.

Sipe, L. R. (2001). Invention, convention, and intervention: Invented spelling and the teacher's role. *The Reading Teacher, 55,* 264–273.

Slavin, R. E., Lake, C., Chambers, B., Cheung, A., & Davis, S. (2009, December). Effective reading programs for the elementary grades: A best-evidence synthesis. *Review of Educational Research, 79*(4), 1391–1466.

Smith, A. W., Holden, K. R., Dwivedi, A., Dupont, B. R., & Lyons, M. J. (2015, March). Deletion of 16q24.1 supports a role for the atp2c2 gene in specific language impairment. *Journal of Child Neurology. 30*(4), 517–521.

Solis, M., Ciullo, S., Vaughn, S., Pyle, N., Hassaram, B., & Leroux, A. (2012, July/August). Reading comprehension interventions for middle school students with learning disabilities: A synthesis of 30 years of research. *Journal of Learning Disabilities, 45*(4), 327–340.

Solis, M., El Zein, F., Vaughn, S., McCulley, L. V., & Falcomata, T. S. (2015, April). Reading comprehension interventions for students with Autism Spectrum Disorders: An alternating treatments comparison. *Focus on Autism and Other Developmental Disabilities.* doi:10.1177.

Sousa, C., Herrenkohl, T. I., Moylan, C. A., Tajima, E. A., Klika, J. B., Herrenkohl, R. C., & Russo, M. J. (2011, January). Longitudinal study on the effects of child abuse and children's exposure to domestic violence, parent-child attachments, and antisocial behavior in adolescence. *Journal of Interpersonal Violence, 26*(1), 111–136.

Sousa, D. A. (2011). *How the brain learns* (4th ed.). Thousand Oaks, CA: Corwin.

Sousa, D. A. (2014). *How the brain learns to read* (2nd ed.). Thousand Oaks, CA: Corwin.

Sousa, D. A. (2015). *How the brain learns mathematics* (2nd ed.). Thousand Oaks, CA: Corwin.

Spandel, V. (2009). *Creating writers through 6-trait writing* (5th ed.). Boston: Pearson.

Speece, D. L., & Mills, C. (2003). Initial evidence that letter fluency tasks are valid indicators of early reading skill. *Journal of Special Education, 36*, 223–233.

Spencer, T. J., Biederman, J., Faraone, S. V., Madras, B. K., Bonab, A. A., Dougherty, D. D., . . . Fischman. A. J. (2013, July). Functional genomics of attention-deficit/hyperactivity disorder (ADHD) risk alleles on dopamine transporter binding in ADHD and healthy control subjects. *Biological Psychiatry, 74*(2), 84–89.

Stagg, C. J., Jayaram, G., Pastor, D., Kincses, Z. T., Matthews, P. M., & Johansen-Berg, H. (2011, April). Polarity and timing-dependent effects of transcranial direct current stimulation in explicit motor learning. *Neuropsychologia, 49*(5), 800–804.

Stamm, T. J., Stingl, J., Wiethoff, K., Ricken, R., Heinz, A., Bauer, M., . . . Adli, M. (2013, November). Depression with psychotic features is influenced by the polymorphism of the serotonin transporter gene. *Journal of Affective Disorders, 151*(2), 605–610.

Stanberry, K., & Raskind, M. H. (2009). *Assistive technology for kids with learning disabilities: An overview.* Retrieved from www.readingrockets.org/comment/1575#comment-1575.

Steinbrink, C., Klatte, M., & Lachmann, T. (2014, November). Phonological, temporal and spectral processing in vowel length discrimination is impaired in German primary school children with developmental dyslexia. *Research in Developmental Disabilities, 35*(11), 3034–3045.

Steinbrink, C., Vogt, K., Kastrup, A., Müller, H.-P., Jeungling, F. D., Kassubek, J., & Riecker, A. (2008, November). The contribution of white and gray matter differences to developmental dyslexia: Insights from DTI and VBM at 3.0 T. *Neuropsychologia, 46*(13), 3170–3178.

Sterzer, P., Stadler, C., Krebs, A., Kleinschmidt, A., & Poustka, F. (2005, January). Abnormal neural responses to emotional visual stimuli in adolescents with conduct disorder. *Biological Psychiatry, 57*, 7–15.

Stoodley, C. J., Harrison, E. P. D., & Stein, J. F. (2006). Implicit motor learning deficits in dyslexic adults. *Neuropsychologia, 44*, 795–798.

Stoodley, C. J., & Stein, J. F. (2011, January). The cerebellum and dyslexia. *Cortex, 47*(1), 101–116.

Stormshak, E. A., Dishion, T. J., Light, J., & Yasui, M. (2005, December). Implementing family-centered interventions within the public middle school: Linking service delivery to change in student problem behavior. *Journal of Abnormal Child Psychology, 33*, 723–733.

Strain, P. S., & Bovey II, E. H. (2011, November). Randomized, controlled trial of the LEAP model of early intervention for young children with Autism Spectrum Disorders. *Topics in Early Childhood Special Education, 31*(3), 133–154.

Strategic Instruction Model™ (SIM). (2015). *Content enhancement routines.* Retrieved from http://www.sim.kucrl.org.

Strickland, T. K., & Maccini, P. (2013, May/June). The effects of the concrete–representational–abstract integration strategy on the ability of students with learning disabilities to multiply linear expressions within area problems. *Remedial and Special Education, 34*(3), 142–153.

Stricklin, K. (2011, May). Hands-on reciprocal teaching: A comprehension technique. The *Reading Teacher, 64*(8), 620–625.

Suárez-Pellicioni, M., Núñez-Peña, M. I., & Colomé, A., (2014, June). Reactive recruitment of attentional control in math anxiety: An ERP study of numeric conflict monitoring and adaptation. *PLoS ONE, 9*(6). doi: 10.1371/0099579

Suhrheinrich, J. (2015, August). A sustainable model for training teachers to use pivotal response training. *Autism, 19*(6), 713–723.

Sun, H., Chen, W., Wang, D., Jin, Y., Chen, X., Xu, Y., & Huang, L. (2015, June). Inverse association between intelligence quotient and urinary retinol binding protein in Chinese school-age children with low blood lead levels: Results from a cross-sectional investigation. *Chemosphere, 128*, 155–160.

Swanson, J., Greenhill, L., Wigal, T., Kollins, S., Stehli, A., Davies, M., . . . Wigal, S. (2006, November). Stimulant-related reductions of growth rates in the PATS. *Journal of the American Academy of Child and Adolescent Psychiatry, 45*(11), 1304–1313.

Szucs, D., Devine, A., Soltesz, F., Nobes, A., & Gabriel, F. (2013, November/December). Developmental dyscalculia is related to visuo-spatial memory and inhibition impairment. *Cortex, 49*, 2674–2688.

Tallal, P., & Heim, S. (2015). Language learning impairment. *International Encyclopedia of the Social & Behavioral Sciences* (2nd Edition), 344–352.

Taylor, L. E., Swerdfeger, A. L., & Eslick, G. D. (2014, June). Vaccines are not associated with autism: An evidence-based meta-analysis of case-control and cohort studies. *Vaccine, 32*(29), 3623–3629.

Temple, E., Deutsch, G. K., Poldrack, R. A., Miller, S. L., Tallal, P., Merzenich, M. M., & Gabrieli, J. D. E. (2003, March). Neural deficits in children with dyslexia ameliorated by behavioral remediation: Evidence from functional MRI. *Proceedings of the National Academy of Sciences, 100,* 2860–2865.

Terband, H., van Brenk, F., & van Doornik-van der Zee, A. (2014, September–October). Auditory feedback perturbation in children with developmental speech sound disorders. *Journal of Communication Disorders, 51,* 64–77.

Tettamanti, M., Rognoni, E., Cafiero, R., Costa, T., Galati, D., & Perani, D. (2012, January). Distinct pathways of neural coupling for different basic emotions. *NeuroImage, 59*(2), 1804–1817.

Therrien, W. J., Kirk, J. F., & Woods-Groves, S. (2012, September/October). Comparison of a reading fluency intervention with and without passage repetition on reading achievement. *Remedial and Special Education, 33*(5), 309–319.

Tkach, J. A., Chen, X., Freebairn, L. A., Schmithorst, V. J., Holland, S. K., & Lewis, B. A. (2011, October). Neural correlates of phonological processing in speech sound disorder: A functional magnetic resonance imaging study. *Brain and Language, 119*(1), 42–49.

Tosto, M. G., Malykh, S., Voronin, I., Plomin, R., & Kovas, Y. (2013, October). The etiology of individual differences in maths beyond IQ: Insights from 12-year-old twins. *Procedia—Social and Behavioral Sciences, 86,* 429–434.

Tottenham, N., Hertzig, M. E., Gillespie-Lynch, K., Gilhooly, T., Millner, A. J., & Casey, B. J. (2014, January). Elevated amygdala response to faces and gaze aversion in autism spectrum disorder. *Social Cognitive and Affective Neuroscience, 9*(1), 106–117.

Travagin, G., Margola, D., & Revenson, T. A, (2015, March). How effective are expressive writing interventions for adolescents? A meta-analytic review. *Clinical Psychology Review, 36,* 42–55.

Treffert, D. A. (2010). *Islands of genius: The bountiful mind of the autistic, acquired and sudden savant.* London: Jessica Kingsley.

Tzvi, E., Münte, T. F., & Krämer, U. M. (2014, July). Delineating the cortico-striatal-cerebellar network in implicit motor sequence learning. *NeuroImage, 94*(1), 222–230.

Uno, Y., Uchiyama, T., Kurosawa, M., Aleksic, B., & Ozaki, N. (2015, May). Early exposure to the combined measles–mumps–rubella vaccine and thimerosal-containing vaccines and risk of autism spectrum disorder. *Vaccine, 33*(21), 2511–2516.

Van Damme, T., Sabbe, B., van West, D., & Simons, J. (2015, May). Motor abilities of adolescents with a disruptive behavior disorder: The role of comorbidity with ADHD. *Research in Developmental Disabilities, 40,* 1–10.

Vandermosten, M., Boets, B., Luts, H., Poelmans, H., Wouters, J., & Ghesquière, P. (2011, March/April). Impairments in speech and nonspeech sound categorization in children with dyslexia are driven by temporal processing difficulties. *Research in Developmental Disabilities, 32*(2), 593–603.

Van der Paelt, S., Warreyn, P., & Roeyers, H. (2014, May). Social-communicative abilities and language in preschoolers with autism spectrum disorders: Associations differ depending on language age. *Research in Autism Spectrum Disorders, 8*(5), 518–528.

van Ermingen-Marbach, M., Grande, M., Pape-Neumann, J., Sass, K., & Heim, S. (2013). Distinct neural signatures of cognitive subtypes of dyslexia with and without phonological deficits. *NeuroImage: Clinical, 2,* 477–490.

Van Loo, K. J., & Rydell, R. J. (2013). On the experience of feeling powerful: Perceived power moderates the effect of stereotype threat on women's math performance. *Personality and Social Psychology Bulletin, 39*(3), 387–400.

Vannest, K. J., Harrison, J. R., Temple-Harvey, K., Ramsey, L., & Parker, R. I. (2011). Improvement rate differences of academic interventions for students with emotional and behavioral disorders. *Remedial and Special Education, 32*(6), 521–34.

van Rijn, R. R., & Spevak, M. R. (2011, November). Imaging of neonatal child abuse with an emphasis on abusive head trauma. *Magnetic Resonance Imaging Clinics of North America, 19*(4), 791–812.

van Steensel, F. J. A., Bögels, S. M., & Perrin, S. (2011, September). Anxiety disorders in children and adolescents with autistic spectrum disorders: A meta-analysis. *Clinical Child and Family Psychology Review, 14*(3), 302–317.

Vaughn, S., & Fletcher, J. (2012). Response to intervention with secondary school students with reading difficulties. *Journal of Learning Disabilities, 45*, 244–256.

Vaughn, S., Klingner, J. K., Swanson, E. A., Boardman, A. G., Roberts, G., Mohammed, S. S., & Stillman-Spisak, S. J. (2011, August). Efficacy of collaborative strategic reading with middle school students. *American Educational Research Journal, 48*(4), 938–964.

Verhoeven, L., Steenge, J., van Weerdenburg, M., & van Balkom, H. (2011, September–October). Assessment of second language proficiency in bilingual children with specific language impairment: A clinical perspective. *Research in Developmental Disabilities, 32*(5), 1798–1807.

Vlachos, F., & Karapetsas, A. (2003, December). Visual memory deficit in children with dysgraphia. *Perceptual Motor Skills, 97*, 1281–1288.

Vugs, B., Hendriks, M., Cuperus, J., & Verhoeven, L. (2014, January). Working memory performance and executive function behaviors in young children with SLI. *Research in Developmental Disabilities, 35*(1), 62–74.

Vukovic, R. K., & Lesaux, N. K. (2013). The relationship between linguistic skills and arithmetic knowledge. *Learning and Individual Differences, 23*, 87–91.

Walker, H. M., & Gresham, F. M. (Eds.). (2014). *Handbook of evidence-based practices for emotional and behavioral disorders: Applications in schools.* New York: Guilford.

Walkowiak, T. A. (2014, March). Elementary and middle school students' analyses of pictorial growth patterns. *Journal of Mathematical Behavior, 33*, 56–71.

Wang, J.-J., Bi, H.-Y., Gao, L.-Q., & Wydell, T. N. (2010, October). The visual magnocellular pathway in Chinese-speaking children with developmental dyslexia. *Neuropsychologia, 48*(12), 3627–3633.

Wang, S., Allen, R. J., Lee, J. R., & Hsieh, C.-E. (2015, May). Evaluating the developmental trajectory of the episodic buffer component of working memory and its relation to word recognition in children. *Journal of Experimental Child Psychology, 133*, 16–28.

Wang, S., & Gathercole, S. E. (2013, May). Working memory deficits in children with reading difficulties: Memory span and dual task coordination. *Journal of Experimental Child Psychology, 115*(1), 188–197.

Waterhouse, L. (2013). Chapter 6—Savant skills, special skills, and intelligence vary widely in autism. *Rethinking Autism*, 281–344.

Waugh, C. K. (2002, Summer). Raising self-expectations: The key to motivating students with disabilities. *Academic Exchange Quarterly, 6*, 68–72.

Waxmonsky, J. G., Wymbs, F. A., Pariseau, M. E., Belin, P. J., Waschbusch, D. A., Babocsai, L., . . . Pelham, W. E. (2013, August). A novel group therapy for children with ADHD and severe mood dysregulation. *Journal of Attention Disorders, 17*(6), 527–541.

What Works Clearinghouse. (2015). *Effectiveness of reading programs.* Retrieved from www.ies.ed.gov/ncee/wwc/.

Wheeler, R., Cartwright, K. B., & Swords, R. (2012, March). Factoring AAVE into reading assessment and instruction. *The Reading Teacher, 65*(6), 416–425.

Wheldall, K., & Limbrick, L. (2010). Do more boys than girls have reading problems? *Journal of Learning Disabilities, 43*, 418–429.

Willard-Holt, C., Weber, J., Morrison, K. L., & Horgan, J. (2013, October). Twice-exceptional learners' perspectives on effective learning strategies. *Gifted Child Quarterly, 57*(4), 247–262.

Willcutt, E. G., Petrill, S. A., Wu, S., Boada, R., DeFries, J. C., Olson, R. K., & Pennington, B. F. (2013, November/December). Comorbidity between reading disability and math disability: Concurrent psychopathology, functional impairment, and neuropsychological functioning. *Journal of Learning Disabilities, 46,* 500–516.

Williams, J. A. (2010, December). Taking on the role of questioner: Revisiting reciprocal teaching. *The Reading Teacher, 64*(4), 278–281.

Willits, J. A., Seidenberg, M. S., & Saffran, J. R. (2014, September). Distributional structure in language: Contributions to noun–verb difficulty differences in infant word recognition. *Cognition, 132*(3), 429–436.

Wing, A. M. (2000). Mechanisms of motor equivalence in handwriting. *Current Biology, 10,* R245–R248.

Witzel, B. S. (2005). Using CRA to teach algebra to students with math difficulties in inclusive settings. *Learning Disabilities: A Contemporary Journal, 3*(2), 53–64.

Witzel, B. S., Mercer, C. D., & Miller, M. D. (2003, May). Teaching algebra to students with learning difficulties: An investigation of an explicit instruction model. *Learning Disabilities Research and Practice, 18,* 121–131.

Witzel, B. S., Riccomini, P. J., & Schneider, E. (2008). Implementing CRA with secondary students with learning disabilities in mathematics. *Intervention in School and Clinic, 43,* 270–276.

Wolfe, J., Kar, K., Perry, A., Reynolds, C., Gradisar, M., & Short, M. A. (2014, October). Single night video-game use leads to sleep loss and attention deficits in older adolescents. *Journal of Adolescence, 37*(7), 1003–1009.

Wright, B. A., Bowen, R. W., & Zecker, S. G. (2000). Nonlinguistic perceptual deficits associated with reading and language disorders. *Current Opinion in Neurobiology, 10,* 482–486.

Wu, S. S., Willcutt, E. G., Escovar, E., & Menon, V. (2014, November/December). Mathematics achievement and anxiety and their relation to internalizing and externalizing behaviors. *Journal of Learning Disabilities, 47*(6), 503–514.

Xiang, J., Korostenskaja, M., Molloy, C., deGrauw, X., Leiken, K., Gilman, C., . . . Murray, D. S. (2016). Multi-frequency localization of aberrant brain activity in autism spectrum disorder. *Brain and Development, 38*(1), 82–90.

Yakubova, G., & Taber-Doughty, T. (2015, May). Improving problem-solving performance of students with Autism Spectrum Disorders. *Focus on Autism and Other Developmental Disabilities.* doi: 10.1177

Yang, C.-J., Tan, H.-P., Yang, F.-Y., Wang, H.-P., Liu, C.-L., He, H.-Z., . . . Du, Y.-J. (2015, October). The cortisol, serotonin and oxytocin are associated with repetitive behavior in autism spectrum disorder. *Research in Autism Spectrum Disorders, 18,* 12–20.

Yurick, A., Cartledge, G., Kourea, L., & Keyes, S. (2012, March/April). Reducing reading failure for kindergarten urban students: A study of early literacy instruction, treatment quality, and treatment duration. *Remedial and Special Education, 33*(2), 89–102.

Zachry, T., Wulf, G., Mercer, J., & Bezodis, N. (2005, October). Increased movement accuracy and reduced EMG activity as a result of adopting an external focus of attention. *Brain Research Bulletin, 67,* 304–309.

Zamarian, L., Ischebeck, A., & Delazer, M. (2009, June). Neuroscience of learning arithmetic—Evidence from brain imaging studies. *Neuroscience & Biobehavioral Reviews, 33*(6), 909–925.

Zhang, X., & Lin. D. (2015, April). Pathways to arithmetic: The role of visual-spatial and language skills in written arithmetic, arithmetic word problems, and nonsymbolic arithmetic. *Contemporary Educational Psychology, 41,* 188–197.

Zheng, B., Warschauer, W., & Farkas, G. (2013). Digital writing and diversity: The effects of school laptop programs on literacy processes and outcomes. *Journal of Educational Computing Research, 48*(3), 267–299.

Zhou, S., Rosenthal, D. G., Sherman, S., Zelikoff, J., Gordon, T., & Weitzman, M. (2014, September). Physical, behavioral, and cognitive effects of prenatal tobacco and postnatal secondhand smoke exposure. *Current Problems in Pediatric and Adolescent Health Care, 44*(8), 219–241.

Zuffianò, A., Alessandri, G., Gerbino, M., Kanacri, B. P. L., Di Giunta, L., Milioni, M., & Caprara, G. V. (2013, February). Academic achievement: The unique contribution of self-efficacy beliefs in self-regulated learning beyond intelligence, personality traits, and self-esteem. *Learning and Individual Differences, 23*, 158–162.

Index

Page numbers in **boldface** are Strategies to Consider